Winning Strategies

for the

New Latin Markets

ISBN 0-13-061716-4

90000

9 790130 617162

FINANCIAL TIMES
Prentice Hall

In an increasingly competitive world, it is quality
of thinking that gives an edge—an idea that opens new
doors, a technique that solves a problem, or an insight
that simply helps make sense of it all.

We work with leading authors in the various arenas
of business and finance to bring cutting-edge thinking
and best learning practice to a global market.

It is our goal to create world-class print publications
and electronic products that give readers
knowledge and understanding which can then be
applied, whether studying or at work.

To find out more about our business
products, you can visit us at www.ft-ph.com

Pearson
Education

Praise for Winning Strategies for the New Latin Markets

"*Winning Strategies for the New Latin Markets* is a must read for every business person operating in today's global economy. The authors' clear and innovative analysis of the specific business drivers of Latin American markets with the well-documented description of the various strategies adopted by local and international companies across industries will help potential investors shape their business approaches to the region."

—OLIVIER BRANDICOURT, M.D.
Area President, Latin America, Pfizer

"*Winning Strategies for the New Latin Markets* fills a vacuum in development thinking and business strategies. While the Ibero American market has been one of the most powerful creations of technological progress over the past century, this promising economic force had attracted little interest in scholars and business analysts. Robles, Simon, and Haar have not only created an accurate road map to the region, but also developed valuable analytic approaches to successful business strategies in the market that has greatest growth prospects in the Western Hemisphere."

—GUSTAVO A. CISNEROS
Chairman, Cisneros Group

"*Winning Strategies for the New Latin Markets* is a crucial work that every person—be they a businessman, entrepreneur, student, or layman—interested in knowing the Latin American market should have in today's globalized economy. The world of finance and economics cannot be comprehended without taking into account the continental blocs that have been formed in today's global trade game. The Latin American bloc emerges as one of the major potential trade groups, with many initiatives and business ventures yet to be undertaken. Revealing its peculiarities, culture, certain facets of its market, its political-institutional and social-economic conditions, and how companies have been successful in making Latin America a platform for worldwide business is one of the high points of Robles, Simon, and Haar's work."

—LUIZ FERNANDO FURLAN
Chairman, Sadia S.A.-Brazil

"*Winning Strategies for the New Latin Markets* is a first-rate contribution to the growing body of business economic literature concerned with the rich but volatile markets in Latin America. As a hands-on manager of consumer and technology businesses exposed to the dynamic economic and political forces in the region, I can appreciate the value of this useful volume. Professors Robles, Simon, and Haar have an understanding and empathy for Latin America that yield a savvy blend of political and business analysis. This book is a fine work of scholarship. But it is much more; it offers serious, practical, real-world information and insight. I commend it with enthusiasm to those who seek to better understand what makes the Latin American region tick and how to position their business interests in such a way as to grow and prosper in the flow of the region's sometimes surprising development."

—CHARLES HERINGTON
President and CEO, AOL Latin America

"An in-depth, knowledgeable collection of valuable insights for anyone wishing to go to market in Latin America. Not to be underestimated, as this continent and culture are challengingly unique."

—MARCIO MOREIRA
Vice Chairman, McCann-Erickson

"Critics of globalization should read *Winning Strategies for the New Latin Markets*. This impressive volume shows how reforms modernized the Latin American economies, providing new opportunities for companies interested in tapping the 600 million-strong Latin markets. Focusing on technological trends, changes in market structures, and consumption patterns, the authors provide a much-needed analysis of winning strategies for penetrating these dynamic markets. This book should be required reading for current and potential investors in the region, as well as for anyone interested in understanding the perils and promise of emerging markets in general."

—SUSAN KAUFMAN PURCELL
Vice President, Council of the Americas

"*Winning Strategies for the New Latin Markets* is the definitive business book for managing multinational enterprises and reaching customers in the Latin markets' digital decade."

—MAURICIO SANTILLÁN
Vice President Latin America, Microsoft

WINNING STRATEGIES
FOR THE
NEW LATIN MARKETS

FERNANDO ROBLES

FRANÇOISE SIMON

JERRY HAAR

An Imprint of PEARSON EDUCATION

Upper Saddle River, NJ • New York • London • San Francisco • Toronto • Sydney
Tokyo • Singapore • Hong Kong • Cape Town • Madrid
Paris • Milan • Munich • Amsterdam

www.ft-ph.com

Library of Congress Cataloging-in-Publication Data

Robles, Fernando.
    Winning strategies for the new Latin markets / Fernando Robles, Françoise Simon,
Jerry Haar.
        p. cm.— (Financial Times Prentice Hall books)
    Includes bibliographical references and index.
    ISBN 0-13-061716-4
        1. Latin America—Commerce. 2. Consumption (Economics)—Latin America. 3.
Competition—Latin America. 4. Infrastructure (Economics)—Latin America. 5.
Industries—Latin America—Case studies. I. Simon, Françoise. II. Haar, Jerry. III.
Title. IV. Series.

HF3230.5.Z5 R63 2002
330.98—dc21

                                                                      2002026400

Editorial/production supervision: *Jane Bonnell*
Composition: *Pine Tree Composition*
Cover design director: *Jerry Votta*
Cover design: *Talar A. Boorujy*
Interior design: *Gail Cocker-Boguss*

Manufacturing buyer: *Maura Zaldivar*
Editor-in-Chief: *Tim Moore*
Editorial assistant: *Allyson Kloss*
Development editor: *Russ Hall*
Marketing manager: *Bryan Gambrel*

© 2003 Pearson Education, Inc.
Publishing as Financial Times Prentice Hall
Upper Saddle River, New Jersey 07458

Financial Times Prentice Hall books are widely used by corporations and government agencies
for training, marketing, and resale.
For information regarding corporate and government bulk discounts please contact:
Corporate and Government Sales (800) 382-3419 or corpsales@pearsontechgroup.com

Company and product names mentioned herein are the trademarks or registered trademarks of
their respective owners.

Printed in the United States of America
10   9   8   7   6   5   4   3   2   1

ISBN 0-13-061716-4

Pearson Education LTD.
Pearson Education Australia PTY, Limited
Pearson Education Singapore, Pte. Ltd.
Pearson Education North Asia Ltd.
Pearson Education Canada, Ltd.
Pearson Educación de Mexico, S.A. de C.V.
Pearson Education—Japan
Pearson Education Malaysia, Pte. Ltd.

To Carol and Natalie

To Ivonne David

*To Albert Haar, a great executive
and an even greater father*

CONTENTS

PART 3 CONCLUSION

Chapter 8   WINDOWS OF OPPORTUNITY AND WINNING STRATEGIES FOR LATIN MARKETS   299

FOREWORD

Citibank has a long history in the emerging markets of the world. This year we celebrate 100 years in Asia, and Latin America is not far behind. It was not so easy, 100 years ago, for those bankers in Hartford and New York to head halfway around the world and begin a new enterprise in an unfamiliar place. And it's still not easy: emerging markets are not for the faint of heart. If you are doing business in 80 countries, you can pretty much expect that at any given moment, *somewhere* you'll be dealing with a volatile situation, economically if not politically. Without question, operating in the emerging markets entails the vigorous, ongoing assessment and management of risk. Lessons learned from each situation must be applied going forward, and stress test scenarios must continually be evaluated and updated to reflect those lessons.

The fact remains that even with risk ever-present, the rewards can be great. This is certainly the case in Latin America, even now. North American, European, and Asian firms continue to maintain a significant presence in the region, and these firms have learned to live with the volatility that characterizes business in the region.

Success in Latin America, as in all emerging markets, requires genuine commitment. Without a long-term view, firms are likely to flee at the first sign of trouble; and assuredly, this is not a formula for success in these regions. At Citibank, our strategy is to put down roots wherever we do business—to become as local as any indigenous enterprise, with the added advantage of our global perspective and strength. We hire local staff as much as possible, and we play an active part in the communities where we operate. Our goal of becoming an "embedded bank" may entail strategic acquisitions that strengthen our position in the local market. Our recent acquisition of Banamex in Mexico is an example of the seriousness of our commitment.

Our long-term vision for Latin America remains positive. Globalization is transforming Latin America's business landscape, ushering in new trends in corporate organization, technology utilization, consumer demographics, patterns of financing, infrastructure, and government responses to the challenges of economic growth and development.

If multinational firms and their suppliers are to achieve and sustain success in Latin America, they will need to develop and implement sound strategies. *Winning Strategies for the New Latin Markets* contributes to this goal. This text presents a framework for understanding and responding to the dynamic forces shaping the new Latin markets (U.S. Hispanic as well as Latin American). This book will appeal especially to multinational corporate executives, related business and professional associations, and MBA and Executive MBA faculty and students.

Robles, Simon, and Haar pinpoint the fundamental changes in the region, focusing on the strategic platforms of firms that are meeting the challenges and making the most of the many opportunities of the new Latin markets. They provide a unique contribution with their concepts of the valued-added networking of firms operating in Latin America, and the special characteristics that define firms as "national champions," "integrators," and "specialists."

In an article written in December 2001, Jeffrey Garten, dean of the Yale School of Management, warns firms of the folly of beating a global retreat from emerging markets; our experience at Citibank certainly confirms this. Robles, Simon, and Haar convincingly underscore this observation and provide corporations with an indispensable road map for navigating and winning in the new Latin markets.

Victor J. Menezes, Chairman and CEO, Citibank N.A.

PREFACE

THE EMERGING LATIN WORLD

Globalization is transforming profoundly the business landscape of the Latin world. Firms competing in this region are reacting not only to new trends in technology but also to the impact of fundamental changes that have transformed the economic landscape of the Americas. Several international financial crises have affected the fragile Latin American economies with devastating cycles of growth and contraction. This is the first book to analyze the dynamics of the Latin world and to define key success factors for Latin markets. Based on over 100 executive interviews and in-depth case studies, the book offers managers and analysts engaged in global business a fresh perspective on a dynamic but volatile market. It will be a trendsetter for future strategic studies of emerging markets.

Although Latin America is a challenging region in which to do business, it offers rich rewards. Whereas first-movers had time to adjust to the varying conditions and changing regulations, newcomers to the region do not have that luxury. Cycles of economic upturns and downturns have intensified. Multiple drivers affect Latin American markets in many different ways at different times. The essence of strategy in Latin America is to identify the windows of opportunity, timing of entry, resource commitments, and creative response necessary to succeed. Early-movers have built different business architectures based on their geographic and business scope. National champions have emerged to contest the challenge of integrators and specialists. In this struggle, success will be determined in the two largest markets, Brazil and Mexico. These two countries offer different platforms for success, and some firms may have to choose the focus of their Latin American success. For global firms, Brazil and Mexico are essential components of the global value chain. The future of the region may not be decided in the marketplace but in the political arena. The pressure to minimize the region's vulnerability to global shocks and market-driven economies is increasing. This certainly creates an additional source of uncertainty for investors. In the long term, the region's potential should offer many rewards.

Any strategy for Latin markets must recognize the importance of the U.S. Latin market. The 34 million people of Latin American descent in the United States represent the fourth largest Latin American nation and the third largest in buying power. The future of any large multinational firm in Latin America will be decided by its ability to command enough market power in the three largest markets of Brazil, Mexico, and the U.S. Latin market. A strategy that focuses on market dominance in only one or two of these three large Latin markets will not be enough to achieve regional market predominance.

A ROADMAP TO THE READER

LATIN BUSINESS IN THE NEW ECONOMY

In the first chapter we analyze the transformation of Latin American corporate strategy from the old and traditional brick and mortar model to one in which information technology and the Internet play an increasingly important role in planning, production, control, marketing and distribution, and customer service. In the first part of the chapter we provide an overview of the drivers and barriers to corporate development, growth, and expansion in the region. In the second part of the chapter we summarize the emergence of the "new economy," focusing on both business-to-consumer and business-to-business Internet firms, including hardware and software incumbents and startups, vis-à-vis Latin America. In the third part we examine some of the key ways in which Latin American corporations are beginning to integrate the Internet into their business strategies. In the last part of the chapter we present a framework to assess the transformation of multinational firms in Latin America within the larger context of globalization and Internet-driven pressures.

THE LATIN CONSUMER MARKETS:
CONVERGENCE OR FRAGMENTATION?

In a short period of time, the Latin American social fabric has changed. The region has transformed itself into a complex, fluid social structure of rich and poor, old and young, and cosmopolitan and nationalistic attitudes. If we add to these layers of complexity differences in race, ethnicity, language, and climate, the conclusion is that the Americas are a rich mosaic of diversity that produces a variety of consumption behaviors and different ways of adjusting to the vulnerabilities affecting the region.

The nuclear family remains the focus of consumption, but it is changing rapidly. Families are smaller, more urban, and multigenerational. Their members are working more and generating the same or less income. The population is aging rapidly, and by 2015, Latin markets will resemble those of the developed world. Inequality of income distribution remains unchanged; and the incipient middle class has been losing its share of total national income during the last decade. The fragmentation and varying dynamics of Latin markets present a challenge to all firms. The simpler approaches of the past, based on geography and socioeconomic class, no longer reflect the complexity of the region. Regional strategies based on the logic of convergence and similarities of consumer preferences do not work as well.

In Chapter 2, we provide a guide to navigation of the intricacies of Latin consumer markets. We analyze the size of the market and identify major drivers of buying power. We discuss changing consumption patterns and provide different ways to segment Latin American markets. The chapter is concluded with a discussion of implications and recommendations as to how to approach Latin consumer markets.

THE LATIN MARKET COMPETITIVE LANDSCAPE

In Chapter 3, we discuss our view of the dynamics of competition in Latin America. The key players in the theaters of competition are the large American and European multinationals and strong traditional Latin American groups. We identify the various groups based on their origin, historical presence, and intent. Recognizably, the Latin American competitive landscape is not a level playing field. The presence of large national family-owned conglomerates has created high barriers of entry in many sectors. Many of these conglomerates are embracing the Internet revolution and extending their reach to electronic commerce. In this chapter we develop the conceptual framework to analyze how the various players stake their positions for dominance in the region.

BUILDING THE INFRASTRUCTURE NETWORK

Strategic investors new to the region need to understand a plethora of liberalization and privatization frameworks. Reforms and deregulation have been aimed at dismantling state monopolies, privatizing, and deregulating various components of the infrastructure value chain. This unbundling of state monopolies has taken many approaches in the region. Liberalization has also taken a variety of approaches. In some cases, parts of a sector have been opened for competition; in others, the state has retained ownership and monopoly status. As a result, the region is a mosaic of sector structures, regulatory frameworks, and ownership regimes. In some countries and sectors, the rules are transparent and the regulatory bodies well managed. In others countries and sectors, ambiguous rules and weak regulatory bodies are the rule.

In addition, technology is reshaping the nature of competition and providing new opportunities to all firms. Information technology, including the Internet, is revolutionizing the way that infrastructure services are produced, bought, and used. New technologies give rise to new skills and competencies in the once-stodgy infrastructure industry. New technologies, such as using liners in pipelines or remote metering, reduce the costs of transmission and repair of utility networks. Technology is also blurring the distinction between types of utilities. Network value chains can carry different types of services. Energy companies are finding that their pipelines can also carry telecommunication services.

In Chapter 4 we examine fundamental aspects of infrastructure network strategy and discuss a successful case of transforming a government-owned monopoly into a global-class competitive business.

REACHING THE NEW LATIN CONSUMERS

A new Latin world has emerged as an attractive revenue frontier for multinationals. A powerful network linking the Americas, Spain, and Portugal is targeting a population of nearly 600 million Latins. In the United States alone, the Latin market of nearly 34 million is the largest ethnic group, with annual spending projected to reach $1 trillion by 2010. Like Mexico and Brazil, it has a young population, a rapid technology adoption rate, and an influential culture. Pioneering firms such as Spain's Banco Santander, Mexico's Cemex, AOL, and Unilever are targeting Latin markets with winning strategies in branding and manufacturing, supported by information technology.

To reach Latin American consumers in these difficult and pressing times, firms need to deliver the right market value. The challenge is to find a value proposition that fits the diversity of consumption strategies that one finds in Latin America. The best value/price ratio may depend on a firm's target segment. Clearly, the increasing importance of retail chains and discount stores is part of the value delivery strategy. Another strategic issue is the importance of the brand in meeting consumer value in uncertain times. Do Latin American consumers use familiar brands as indicators of superior and consistent value? Do global brands provide greater value than brands of local champions? Are integrator or specialist strategies better prepared to emerge as strong players out of a recessionary period? In Chapter 5, we address these questions.

FUNDING THE LATIN MARKET GROWTH

No sector has been so affected by the sweeping economic, legal, and regulatory reforms of the 1990s as financial services. At the same time, no sector has affected as extensively the economic liberalization process that has been the hallmark of Latin American development from the late 1980s through the present. In Chapter 6 we highlight trends in the financial services sector, discuss the key drivers of change both globally and regionally, illustrate how three of those drivers—mergers and acquisitions, technology, and customer demand—are revolutionizing this sector, and review the organizational and strategic responses by financial firms to the increasingly competitive environment.

IMPROVING HEALTH SERVICES AND PRODUCTS

Addressing the health care and education needs in the Latin world is essential to the region's further development and global competitiveness. Education and health are the twin foundations of a workforce with world-class skills and are also important factors of economic and political stability. Although significant progress in this area has been made in major countries, challenges remain. In addition, broad discrepancies persist between the least and most developed countries within the region, and health systems are quite dissimilar.

The Latin American health care market is the fourth largest in the world and has a three-pronged appeal for multinationals in both services and manufacturing: (1) a large population with attractive demographics (a rapidly aging segment and a young group with a rising income as it enters the workforce), (2) a regional base of physicians and scientists on a par with those of OECD countries, and (3) a group of local producers and institutions eager to enter into research and marketing alliances. However, these positive market and private-sector forces are countered by political and macroeconomic

problems. The most critical of these are still-inadequate patent protection and insufficient health care coverage as well as corruption and
inefficiency at the local and federal levels in most markets. These will
need to be addressed aggressively, possibly through public–private
partnerships, in order for the region to regain its innovative capacity
and competitiveness vis-à-vis other emerging markets, especially
those in Southeast Asia. In Chapter 7 we review the health sector and
reforms in the region and provide an assessment of the pharmaceutical markets in Mexico, Brazil, and Argentina. The chapter concludes
with an analysis of company strategies and competitive positions in
the Latin American pharmaceutical market.

WINDOWS OF OPPORTUNITY AND WINNING STRATEGIES FOR LATIN MARKETS

The last decade of the twentieth century was a time of profound
economic transformation in Latin America. We began this book with
an identification of key drivers of such transformation: global financial
systems, regulatory reforms, regional integration, market transformation, and the role of technology. With different levels of intensity and
at different times, these drivers have, without exception, had a profound impact on Latin American countries. The impact has transformed industry and business strategy. In the first part of this book we
analyzed the impact of these drivers on the infrastructure, consumer
markets, banking, and health sectors. In Chapter 8, we revise our initial framework, assess the strategy of adapters and shapers introduced
in Chapter 1, and provide recommendations as to how firms may continue to adapt to the Latin American market environment and new uncertainties in this region. Here we explore the impact of various
political and economic scenarios, the sustainability of the emerging
regional strategy, and the intensification of globalization forces in the
region. The chapter ends with a summary of winning strategies.

ACKNOWLEDGMENTS

We would like to thank our publishing team for their support of
this project. We are grateful to Tim Moore and to Russ Hall and Jane
Bonnell for their valuable editing assistance and production support.

We appreciate the contribution of a number of people and institutions that provided support, information, shared their views, and
gave us interviews. For their insights on global strategies and Latin
markets, we would like to thank Victor Menezes, Michael Contreras,
Jorge Gutierrez, and Anita Gupta at Citicorp; Dr. Olivier Brandicourt

at Pfizer; Gustavo Cisneros of the Cisneros Group of Companies; Luiz Fernando Furlan at Sadia; Charles Herington at AOL Latin America; Marcio Moreira at McCann-Erickson; Susan Kaufman Purcell at the Council of the Americas; and Mauricio Santillán at Microsoft. We would also like to thank Faquiry Díaz and Jeff Hughes at Merrill Lynch; George Crosby and Brian Kelley at ABN AMRO; Victor Balestra and Ricardo Espírito Santo at Banco Espírito Santo; Stanley Haar at Salomon Smith Barney; Robert Devlin at Inter-American Development Bank; Linda Distlerath and Sidney Mazel at Merck; Rolf Schumacher and Patrice Zagame at Novartis; and John Price and Uffe Galsgaard at InfoAmericas.

In Latin America, our sincere thanks go to a number of corporate executives, consultants, and public leaders who generously gave their time and shared their views on the many aspects that we cover in this book. In Argentina, we thank Francisco Mezzadri and Héctor Sergio Falzone at CMS Energy; Ing. Juan Carlos Masjoan and Jorge Torres at Telecom Argentina; Luis Palacios at BBVA Banco Francés; Carlos Scott at Santa Rosa-Bongrain; Ing. Eduardo Baglieto and Eduardo Franck at Techint; Marcelo Chao at the Exxel Group; Eduardo Luis D' Alessio at D'Alessio/Louis Harris-Argentina; and Sergio Cocú at McCann-Erickson Argentina. We are especially grateful to José María González Eiras at FIEL, who provided critical support to our field research in this country. In Brazil, we express our appreciation to Luiz Fernando Furlan, chairman of Sadia S.A.; Henri Penchas and Silvio Carvalho at Banco Itaú; Mauro Calliari at Editora Abril; Denise Figuereido at Natura; Durval de Noronha Goyos, Jr. at Noronha Advogados; José Carlos de Salles G. Neto at Group M&M; Paulo Sergio Rodriguez at Protran Engenharia; Denise Redoschi and Antonio Perella at Latin Panel; and Solange Montenegro at IBOPE. In Mexico, we thank Lilian Gomez and Francisco Young at Gruma. In Chile, we thank Ricardo Alvial and Susana Rey Muller at Enersis; and Agustín Solari at Falabella.

Very special thanks to the following people for their generous help in providing timely and comprehensive research information: John Barham, editor of *Latin Finance;* Mike Zellner, editor of *Latin Trade;* J. P. Faber, editor of *Latin CEO;* Albert Capozzelli at the Economist Intelligence Unit; Tim Daley at Decision Resources; Bill Machtiger and Carlo Ciapparelli at IMS Health; and Peg Willingham at PhRMA. Many thanks also to Kelly Puig for her valuable technical assistance. We also express our thanks to Allen Adamson of Landor Associates for allowing us to share the Latin American brand maps in Chapter 5.

Additionally, we thank a number of colleagues at academic institutions for their continuous support. We are especially grateful to John

Forrer and Loula Kinna at the Institute for Global Management and Research at George Washington University; Anjali Mahadevan at George Washington for her help in researching the Terra case; the staff of the North-South Center, especially Antonio Garrastazu, Kathleen Hamman, Mary Mapes, and José Grave de Peralta; and Christian Schneider at the Wharton School, University of Pennsylvania.

We are well aware that the dynamics of change in Latin America are constantly evolving. Although we have tried to capture the fundamental and long-term drivers of strategy, we are solely responsible for the ideas, interpretations, and limitations that might be reflected in this book.

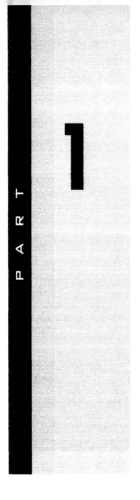

THE NEW ENVIRONMENT

P A R T

1

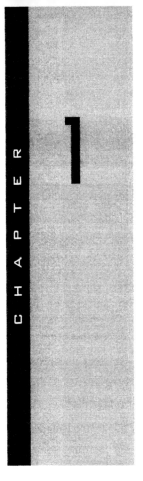

LATIN BUSINESS IN THE NEW ECONOMY

O ver the past decade, the Latin world (Latin America, the U.S. Hispanic population, Spain, and Portugal) has emerged as a dynamic market, driven by a web of transatlantic and pan-American investment after Latin American economies opened in the early 1990s. The banking sector illustrates this change. In the 1990s, "Spanish conquistadors" such as Banco Santander and BBV (Banco Bilbao Vizcaya) made over 30 acquisitions to build extensive networks in Latin America. North American banks ranging from Bank of Nova Scotia and Bank of Montréal to Citibank also bought large stakes; in May 2001, Citigroup acquired Grupo Financiero Banamex–Accival (Banacci), Mexico's second-largest bank, for $12.5 billion. In the 1990s, foreign ownership in the banking sector rose from 0 to 54% in Mexico, 0 to 45% in Venezuela, 35 to 54% in Argentina, and 8 to 27% in Brazil.[1]

The size, growth, and demographic profile of the Latin markets have been the main drawing points for U.S. and European investors. Latin America's population of approximately 508 million is projected to grow to 800 million by 2050, and 60% of people are under 30 years of age. In Europe, Spain and Portugal add another 50 million people. Last but not least, the U.S. Hispanic market now totals nearly 34 million, with annual spending on goods and services of $444 billion in 2000, projected to grow to $1 trillion in 2010 by Standard and Poor's DRI. U.S. Hispanics are expected to grow to almost 75 million in two decades—versus 45 million African-Americans and 22 million Asians. By 2020, one in five Americans will be Hispanic.

The Hispanic market is already influencing mainstream culture and purchasing patterns. Salsa started to outsell ketchup in 1991, and in markets such as New York and Miami, Telemundo and Univisión soap operas often get more viewers than major network shows, and Hispanic compact discs (CDs) and radio stations top charts and ratings.[2] Investors have reacted accordingly. Despite a dismal economic environment, General Electric's NBC announced in October 2001 that it was paying nearly $2 billion in cash and stock for Telemundo, in addition to assuming $700 million of the network's debt, the largest deal in NBC's history. Rival bidders were Viacom (following an earlier unsuccessful bid for Univisión) and the Spanish Broadcasting System. Telemundo built its audience by 48% after a programming overhaul in 1997 and expanded its stations to 24 by 2000.[3]

Major multinationals across industry sectors are also increasing their reach of the Hispanic market. Procter & Gamble established a unit in Puerto Rico to direct its Latin marketing and spent nearly $50 million in 2000 in Hispanic advertising. Other major advertisers to this market range from MCI and AT&T to McDonald's and Toyota.[4] Besides banking and energy, the media sector is the one where Latin networks are emerging most clearly, in both traditional and new media. Major portals are now backed by established U.S. and European players: Telefónica integrated its Lycos acquisition into Terra Networks, Chase Capital Partners and other U.S. venture funds have invested in Starmedia, AOL and Cisneros have formed AOL Latin America as a 50–50 joint venture, and El Sitio has the backing of Cisneros and Dallas-based Hicks, Muse, Tate & Furst. This reflects the region's Internet potential. Twenty million people are now online in Latin America, and Brazil is the second-fastest-growing market in the world, after China. Although 120 million people are affluent enough to own personal computers (PCs), only a fraction use them, leaving room for growth. In addition, the European pattern of m-commerce leapfrogging e-commerce applies to Latin America, as wireless subscribers are projected to reach 143 million by 2004.[5] Although this new Latin world is showing long-term potential, the region also retains significant constraints. Some directly affect the development of new technologies (unreliable power, inadequate infrastructure, scarce capital), others are broader. One of the most worrisome is income disparity; the wealthiest 5% in Latin America hold 25% of total income, whereas the top 20% of the U.S. population control less than 50%.[6]

Industry transformation therefore depends as much on macroeconomic trends as on technology and market drivers (see Figure 1.1). Since Latin America is more dependent than Asia on foreign investment, global financial policy, especially the role of the International Monetary Fund (IMF), is crucial for the region's development. Regional reforms are equally vital: Privatization of state-owned assets in energy, transportation, telecommunications, and banking triggered a massive wave of European and U.S. investment in the 1990s, but it also led to widespread layoffs and labor instability.

Regional integration also spurred foreign investment and business consolidation, but it did so in uneven ways, and its future scenarios are still very much in question. Mexico has now surpassed Brazil as the largest economy in Latin America, with a gross domestic product (GDP) of $615 billion, thanks in large part to NAFTA (the North American Free Trade Agreement), but also to its more recent trade pact with the European Union. Access to both the American and European markets, as well as productivity and quality gains over the past decade, make Mexico the most attractive investment platform in the region. What remains to be seen is the future of the FTAA (Free Trade Area of the Americas) and of Mercosur (the South Cone Common Market). The latter led to impressive gains in Brazil–Argentina trade and investment in the 1990s, but these were recently brought to a standstill by turmoil in Argentina and currency devaluation in Brazil.

The key drivers of development in the Latin world, investment and market growth, are linked to these macroenvironmental factors. A 2001 McKinsey survey of private equity investors showed that institutional reforms were at least as important as company transformation. Key investment drivers in emerging markets were enforceability of legal rights (cited by 94% of respondents), quality of economic management (90%), control of corruption, independence

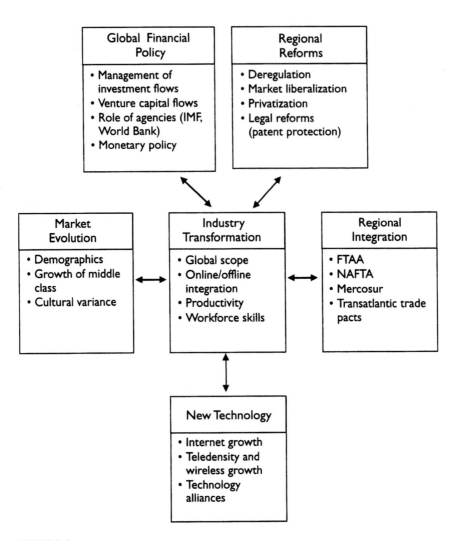

FIGURE 1.1
Industry Transformation

and quality of legal system, and quality of accounting standards (all three cited by 71%).[7] Accordingly, in this chapter we review, first, the macroeconomic and integration outlook, then technology trends and transformation strategies at the company level. Market evolution is addressed in Chapter 2.

MACRO OUTLOOK: ECONOMICS OF UNCERTAINTY

As Latin economies opened up in the past decade, they became more vulnerable to global events. The economic downturn that was already spreading from the United States to Europe became exacerbated by the September 2001 terrorist attacks, and their impact was felt instantly, unlike what happened in previous downturns. One week after September 11, stock markets in Brazil and Mexico fell, respectively, by 5% and 4.2%.[8] On September 14, Telefónica Moviles, Spain's largest mobile phone company, canceled its plan to acquire 54% of Brazil's Celular CT Participaçoes.[9]

The most direct impact was felt by Mexico, which sends 84% of its exports to the United States and depends on U.S. inbound traffic to drive a tourism sector that generates about $9 billion annually. The regional growth outlook, already adjusted down to 1.9%, was projected post-September to remain barely positive.[10] Foreign direct investment (FDI) flows are also under pressure in the region. FDI in Mexico was very strong in 2001, rising to $20 billion from $13 billion in 2000; Brazil, however, received $30 billion in 2000 but forecast only $20 billion in 2001.[11] The fallout is also evident in Europe, where forecasts for euro-zone GDP growth were halved for 2002, to 1.1%. Although growth held up better in France and Spain than in Germany, all European economies were moving in a negative direction.[12]

ECONOMIC VARIANCE IN THE REGION

Latin America has a unique profile that presents a business challenge. It is characterized by an economic, demographic, and cultural asymmetry which stands in the way of pan-regional strategies. As in Europe, the region is dominated by a group of Big Five markets. Unlike in Europe, these are markedly dissimilar. Brazil, Mexico, and Argentina alone account for 60% of the region's population and 77% of its GDP; with the addition of Colombia and Venezuela, the Big Five group reaches fully 73% of the population and 86% of GDP.[13] Even within this top tier, there are significant variances. Real GDP per capita ranges from $7,644 in Argentina to $1,913 in Colombia (see Table 1.1).

Demographic profiles are also heterogeneous, which hinders pan-regional strategies in everything from videogames to pharmaceuticals. Although the region has the market appeal of a younger population, Brazil and Mexico have greater proportions of young

TABLE 1.1 Americas: Key Economic Indicators

	NOMINAL GDP ($ BILLIONS)	REAL GDP PER CAPITA ($)	AVERAGE ANNUAL GDP REAL INCREASE, 1996–2000 (%)	INFLATION (%)	CURRENT ACCOUNT BALANCE ($ BILLIONS)
U.S.	9,937.9	36,100	4.4	3.4	–444.7
Canada	706.8	22,900	3.7	2.7	18
Argentina	28.31	7,644	3	–0.7	–11.5
Brazil	651.1	3,767	2.1	7.1	–23.5
Colombia	80.9	1,913	0.9	9.3	–1.4
Mexico	567.2	5,827	5.5	9.5	–16.9
Venezuela	106.9	4,425	0.4	16.2	13

Source: Economist Intelligence Unit, Latin America at a Glance, 2001, pp. 7, 30; EIU Country Report, United States, April 2002, p. 6; EIU Country Report, Canada, April 2002, p. 3. (Indicators are for 2000.)

TABLE 1.2 Americas: Key Market Indicators

	Passenger Cars (per 1,000 people)	TV Sets (per 1,000 people)	PCs (per 1,000 people)	Telephone Mainlines (per 1,000 people)	Mobile Subscribers (per 100 people)	Internet Users (thousands)	Energy Consumption (kg oil equivalent per head)	Total Length of Roads (km thousands)
U.S.	478	847	459	66	26	60,000	8,076	6,452,484
Canada	441	715	330	63	18	7,500	7,930	901,902
Argentina	137	289	44	20	8	200	1,730	220,348
Brazil	82	316	30	12	4	2,500	1,051	2,096,072
Colombia	24	217	28	17	4	350	761	115,565
Mexico	97	261	47	10	3	1,350	1,501	256,000
Venezuela	71	185	43	12	8	350	2,526	87,510

Source: Economist Intelligence Unit, Latin America at a Glance, 2001, pp. 30–31. (Indicators are for 2000.)

people than do Argentina and Chile, which have a demographic profile closer to that of European countries. The population of 19 years old and younger reaches 43% in Mexico versus 37% in Argentina. Market indicators also show discrepancies. In key categories, passenger cars per 1,000 people vary from 24 in Colombia to 97 in Mexico. Although TV penetration is uniformly high through the region, PCs per 1,000 people range from 28 in Colombia to 47 in Mexico (see Table 1.2). This intercountry variance is compounded by intracountry discrepancies. In Brazil, for instance, the state of São Paulo has reached an economic development level comparable to that of OECD (Organization for Economic Cooperation and Development) countries, while the northern states are at the bottom tier of the regional scale. The same disparities exist in Mexico and Argentina. A more detailed assessment of each of the top three markets will demonstrate their economic heterogeneity.

MEXICO: U.S.-DRIVEN ECONOMY

Mexico's ever-closer links to the United States have the economic impact of a double-edged sword. Although as recently as 1996, its GDP was only half that of Brazil, Mexico overtook Brazil by June 2001. Driven by the huge rise of its exports to the United States (now 89% of the total), the Mexican economy grew at an annual average of 5.6% in 1996–2000, versus 2.2% in Brazil. Currency trends followed the same pattern: The peso devaluation of 1994 was greatly alleviated by the recently signed NAFTA pact and the related U.S. bailout, and the peso rebounded, then remained strong. Although it fell only 18% in 1996–2000, the Real lost 61% of its value against the dollar in the same period.[14]

However, NAFTA works both ways, and Mexico was first to feel the impact of the U.S. recession. Growth may reach, at best, 2.5% in 2002. One of Mexico's strengths is that 90% of its exports are manufactured goods (albeit with relatively low value added from the border assembly plants, the *maquiladoras*). However, most of these are bound for the United States, and may drop to $143 billion from the projected $161 billion in 2002.[15]

Mexico has more free trade agreements than any other country, and its NAFTA links as well as its trade pact with the European Union (EU) give it privileged access to the two blocks. This is appealing for Asian companies, given Mexico's advantages of fairly low labor costs and incentives for assembly-for-export plants. In the longer term, Mexico's appeal lies in its positive performance over the past five years. In 1997–2000, real GDP growth averaged 5.6% and exports rose by 51%; importantly, these are mostly manufactured goods, with oil accounting for only 10% of the total in 2000.

BRAZIL: INVESTMENT CHAMPION

By contrast with Mexico, the other economic powerhouse of the region, Brazil, has experienced more severe economic fluctuations, despite its more diversified trade profile. Less than a quarter of its exports go to the United States, and despite its Mercosur membership, only 11% go to Argentina, with a larger proportion to EU markets such as Germany and the Netherlands.[16] Unlike Mexico, Brazil is still dependent on commodities. By 1998, 70% of South Cone exports were still derived from natural resources and related products.

On the other hand, Brazil has been the region's FDI champion, drawing 45% of total investment flows to Latin America in 2000. This performance has been sustained over time: FDI to Brazil grew more than tenfold, from $2.6 billion in 1994 to $30 billion in 2000. Progress was especially swift in the second half of the 1990s, due to the stabilization initiated by the Real Plan, regional integration, and extensive privatizations. By 1999, nearly 30% of FDI was driven by privatizations, including $7 billion in telecoms and over $2 billion in gas and electricity. Telecom and utilities have remained attractive targets. Telefónica bought minority stakes in Telesp and Tele Sudeste Celular, Portugal Telecom acquired shares in Telesp Celular, and the U.S. firm AES increased its stake in Eletricidade Metropolitana de São Paulo by over $1 billion.[17]

Despite its global trade profile, Brazil has been vulnerable to external events. Its real GDP growth, averaging 3.4% in 1995–1997, turned negative in 1998 as a result of the emerging-markets crisis and did not recover until 2000.[18] Brazil has the largest current account deficit of all emerging markets, reaching $27 billion in 2001. The weakening of the Real, however, should improve the trade balance by spurring exports; trade surplus of $5 billion is forecast by the central bank for 2002.[19]

ARGENTINA: DEEP RECESSION

Argentina's three years of recession and subsequent default and devaluation come in sharp contrast to its radical improvement after the launch of its 1991 convertibility plan, which pegged the peso to the U.S. dollar under a currency board, led to a wave of foreign investment, and eliminated its chronic hyperinflation after 1996.

After Argentina's stellar performance in the early 1990s (annual GDP growth averaged nearly 10% in 1991–1994), its crisis evolved from four main factors: the currency board, the fiscal policy of President Menem's second term, external factors, and overdependence on Brazil. The peso peg to the dollar resulted in an economic straight-jacket and caused exports to become overpriced, especially as Brazil's Real dropped 40% in 1999. This was exacerbated by Argentina's lack of export diversification. Nearly 30% of exports go to Brazil versus only 12% to the United States and 20% to Europe. Trade with the EU also suffered as the peso (following the dollar) appreciated by over 20% against the euro in 1999–2000. Matters got worse in President Menem's second term, during which a loose fiscal policy caused public debt to rise from 40% to 50% of GDP. Finally, external blows contributed to the downfall: weak prices for agricultural commodities, OECD trade barriers against them, and the decrease of capital flows to all emerging markets since 1998; FDI in Argentina fell by 25% from the start of 1999 to the start of 2001.

By December 2001, Argentina had to declare a moratorium on its $155 billion of public foreign currency debt in what amounted to the biggest default in history. Bailouts from the IMF, consisting of a $40 billion package in December 2000 and an additional $8 billion seven months later, were not sufficient to end the crisis.[20] In January 2002, the Duhalde administration followed this with a peso devaluation of nearly 30%. The alternative solution, considered in 2001, was dollarization. This would have eliminated the currency risk for investments in Argentina and should therefore have brought lower interest rates. But it would also have perpetuated the "economic straightjacket" of the currency's former peg to the dollar. A protection against the threat of hyperinflation would be the repegging of the peso to a basket of currencies, including the dollar and the euro as well as the Real, but exchange-rate pegs in emerging economies have had a poor record in past decades. In Argentina itself, when Economy Minister Cavallo switched the peg to one made up equally of dollars and euros (equivalent to an effective 4% devaluation), a run on the banks led to $8 billion leaving the system in July–August 2001.[21] Most big emerging markets, including Brazil and Mexico, have adopted floating exchange rates. After Brazil devalued in 1999, its floating Real made its exports more competitive and raised import costs and was thereby beneficial to its current account gap. After six years of trade deficits, Brazil had a surplus of about $2.6 billion in 2001.[22]

REGIONAL INTEGRATION SCENARIOS

Spurred by privatizations and economic liberalization, trade and investment boomed through the 1990s. Worldwide exports from Latin America almost tripled, from $127 billion in 1991 to $326 billion in 2000. Foreign direct investment in the region also jumped eightfold, from $11 billion in 1991 to over $90 billion in 2000—three-fourths of it concentrated in Brazil, Argentina, and Mexico. The top region of origin in the 1990s was the EU, responsible for nearly half of total investment, followed by the United States at 34% (see Figure 1.2). European inflows were driven by Spanish purchases in banking, telecoms, and energy (including the largest one, the sale of Argentina's YPF to Spain's Repsol), but also by German, French, and Italian acquisitions in the Southern Cone. Trade flows show the same pattern as investment, since Mexican trade is dominated by the United States and Southern Cone trade is led by Europe.

Another consistent trend is that external trade continues to dwarf internal trade. Although intraregional trade grew by 24% in 1999–2000, it has remained relatively unimportant for the two economic powerhouses, Mexico and Brazil. For Mexico, intra–Latin America trade accounts for only 2% of total, while it is less than one-fourth for Brazil, despite its membership in Mercosur. It is clear that these countries are betting, respectively, on North American and global trade. The global model is exemplified by Chile, which despite its small economy has traded worldwide for decades, belongs to the Asia-Pacific Economic Forum, has bilateral trade pacts with Canada and Mexico, and started trade talks with the United States in 2000. By contrast, countries such as Uruguay and Argentina have, respectively, 54% and 39% of their trade within Latin America.[23] (See Table 1.3.)

FTAA: UNCERTAIN FUTURE?

The Free Trade Area of the Americas was proposed in 1990, and reiterated at the 1994 Summit of the Americas, as a bloc encompassing 34 western hemisphere countries (except Cuba) with a total population of 800 million and a combined output of $11 trillion, which would make it the largest trade zone worldwide (see Figure 1.3). Formal negotiations began in 1998 and a draft agreement was prepared in April 2001 projecting an entry into force by 2005. Under the agreement, import tariffs on trade between member countries would be eliminated within a decade, and nontariff barriers such as quotas

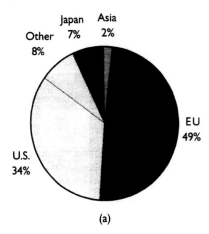

(a)

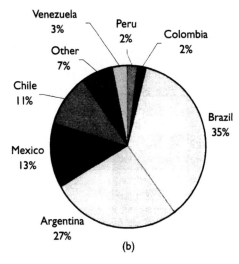

(b)

FIGURE 1.2

(a) FDI into Latin America and the Caribbean, by Source, Cumulative Flows, 1993–1996

(b) Share of FDI Inflows into Latin America and the Caribbean, by Country, 1999

Source: Latin America at a Glance, Economist Intelligence Unit, 2001, pp. 48–49.

TABLE 1.3 Trade Between Latin America and the World (Billions of Dollars)

	1991	1992	1993	1994	1995	1996	1997	1998	1999	2000
Worldwide exports	126.8	134.4	144.7	169.0	205.6	231.5	257.6	251.3	269.6	326.4
Worldwide imports	112.8	139.1	153.1	183.4	205.1	228.8	274.4	286.0	274.2	321.2
Intraregional exports	15.0	19.4	23.6	28.5	35.8	38.3	45.6	43.2	34.7	43.1
Intraregional imports	15.6	20.1	22.9	28.6	35.0	39.3	46.5	44.8	36.7	45.6
LAIA exports to the region as % of total exports	11.8	14.4	16.3	16.9	17.4	16.5	17.7	17.2	12.9	13.3
LAIA imports from the region as % of total imports	13.8	14.5	15.0	15.6	17.1	17.2	16.9	15.7	13.4	14.2

Source: Business Latin America, July 2, 2001, p. 4. Latin American Integration Association (LAIA), 2000 estimates, us reported by the member countries.

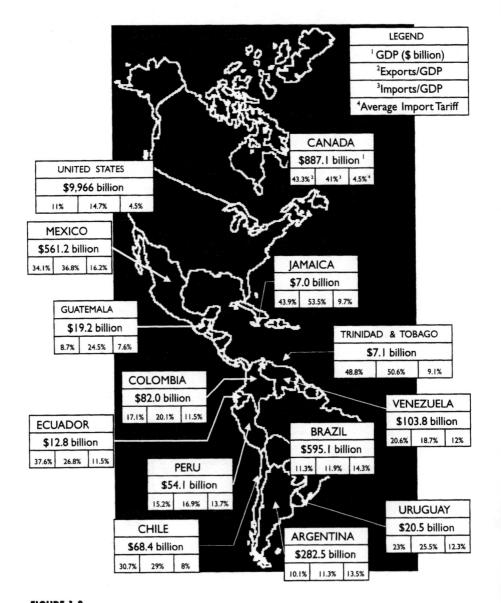

FIGURE 1.3

Free Trade Area of the Americas

Note: All GDP and trade data are estimates for 2000. Tariff figures are all 1999.

Source: Geri Smith, "Betting on Free Trade," *BusinessWeek,* Apr. 23, 2001, p. 61 (data from Economist Intelligence Unit, Inter-American Development Bank). Reprinted by special permission, © 2001 by The McGraw-Hill Companies, Inc.

would gradually be eliminated. Investment rules would also be harmonized.

Implementation of this initiative appears increasingly difficult, as it will be hampered by three factors: the diversity and number of countries involved, the turmoil in the Southern Cone, and the diversion of U.S. resources to the Middle East. Given that it took 50 years for 15 countries with fairly similar economic profiles to form the European Union, it appears wildly optimistic to envision that 34 countries as diverse as the United States, Brazil, and Nicaragua could reach agreement on even a basic trade pact, as it would necessarily touch on sensitive issues such as protected industries, labor, and environmental standards. In Latin America, free trade would be a double-edged sword, spurring exports but also harming inefficient companies, which explains the ambivalence of states with a protectionist legacy. By one estimate, U.S.–Brazilian merchandise trade, about $29 billion in 2000, could double or triple under FTAA, just as Mexico's exports to the United States tripled since NAFTA's start in 1994. Industries where Brazil is competitive include steel, ceramics, agriculture, and textiles; the latter would export much more to the United States if import quotas were lifted, and the Brazilian Textile Industry Association is lobbying for an accelerated time frame for FTAA. Other sectors are mixed, such as the car industry, where free trade would benefit efficient producers but eliminate unproductive ones.[24]

Ambivalence in Brazil is compounded by barriers to FTAA in the United States. For legislators, Argentina's default raises the specter of the Mexican bailout by the United States, which followed less than a year after NAFTA was signed. A positive factor is the stated commitment of the Bush administration to pan-American free trade, but this is offset by the current focus on the Middle East. For these reasons, it is unlikely that the FTAA will be finalized by the 2005 target date. Even if the FTAA eventually happens, it might end up as a lowest-common-denominator agreement or, at best, a shallow economic integration project.[25]

FROM NAFTA TO SUPER-NAFTA?

The North American Free Trade Agreement, which took effect on January 1, 1994, created a bloc of 370 million people producing $6 trillion worth of goods and services annually. The accord's terms included a phase-out of tariffs (some immediately, others in 10 to 15 years), reduction or elimination of nontariff barriers, binding protection for intellectual property rights, and the creation of dispute settlement procedures. NAFTA has been a clear success on its trade promotion objective. Mexican exports to the United States grew 241% in 1993–2000, and U.S. merchandise exports to Mexico rose by 170% (far above the 68% increase in overall exports) in the same period. The trade balance is also better than in other regions; in 2000, the U.S. trade deficit with Mexico was $25 billion, or only 10% of total trade with its NAFTA partner, compared with 14% with the EU, 38% with Japan, and 72% with China.

The negative impact on U.S. jobs and wages, which many feared eight years ago, has largely failed to materialize. The U.S. Labor Department certified 316,000 jobs as weakened or lost since 1994 due to trade with Mexico and Canada, but 20 million jobs were created in the United States in that period. Since U.S. imports from Mexico in 2000 amounted to less than 1.5% of GDP, any negative effect has been limited. In addition, Mexican assembly plants get over 80% of their components from U.S. suppliers, whereas factories in Asia use far fewer U.S. parts.[26] On the Mexican side, the impact has been overwhelmingly positive. The economy has grown 28% in the last seven years and has drawn $85 billion in FDI since 1994, in large part thanks to access to the U.S. market and a solid legal framework.

However, with China's entry in the World Trade Organization, Mexico will face new competition and will need to boost its competitiveness, especially in the crucial area of labor force skills. As in all of Latin America, education and R&D (research and development) spending badly lag behind those in Asia. Whereas South Koreans over 25 average more than 10 years of schooling, Mexicans have fewer than seven, and Brazilians, fewer than five. Spending on R&D in South Korea is over 2.5% of GDP, higher than in the United States, but it is less than 1% in Brazil and Mexico. Companies are filling the gap with intensive training, but this adds to labor costs and is insufficient. GMatrix, a Mexican software design firm, is partnering with the government and 12 universities to train 1,000 software engineers each year, but India produces 37,000 software engineers annually and exports more than $6 billion a year in software.[27]

This competitiveness lag would not be alleviated by a "super-NAFTA" scenario which would add other nations to the bloc. The impact on U.S. jobs would be very limited. In 2000, the value of U.S. trade with the Southern Cone was only $45 billion, or 18% of U.S.–Mexican trade.[28] The major barrier to a formal NAFTA enlargement in the Southern Cone remains the deep financial troubles of Argentina and the uncertainty in Brazil.

THE CHILE MODEL: A GLOBAL TRADE WEB?

A more likely alternative scenario, that of a web of trade agreements following the Chilean model, has already been started by Mexico. In the 1990s alone, Chile signed trade agreements with Canada, Mexico, Venezuela, Bolivia, Colombia, Ecuador, and the Caribbean Community and in 1996 became an associate member of Mercosur. Since it has a significant trade with Asia, it also belongs to APEC (Asia-Pacific Economic Forum). Mexico followed suit, signing agreements with Chile in 1992, Costa Rica in 1995, Nicaragua in 1998, and El Salvador–Guatemala–Honduras in 2001. Beyond the region, it also concluded trade pacts with the EU and Israel in 2000 and with EFTA (European Free Trade Association, including Norway and Switzerland) in 2001.

Mexico now has more free trade agreements than any other country (32 in total). It has also deepened its Group of Three (G-3) pact, signed with Colombia and Venezuela in 1994, which called for zero tariffs by 2004. Exceptions such as telecoms, chemicals, and oil will now be subject to tariff elimination. Since 1994, G-3 internal trade has grown by 87% and the deepening could lead to a further 15% growth.[29] The Mexico–EU pact is the most comprehensive agreement. It will liberalize almost all bilateral trade flows over 10 years and covers both goods and services; it also includes, as NAFTA does, intellectual property rights and dispute settlement mechanisms.[30]

As long as European manufacturers include "local content" (Mexican labor and parts) in their products, they will be able to export to North America as well as to Mexico's Latin American trade partners. European carmakers with subsidiaries in Mexico will be allowed to export cars duty-free back to Europe by 2003, provided that 45 to 60% of vehicle content is local. To save the 7% duty on its New Beetle, produced solely in Mexico, Volkswagen has already brought many of its European suppliers to Mexico.[31]

MERCOSUR: STANDSTILL OR REGRESSION?

Mercosur, the Southern Cone Common Market, came into force in 1995, bringing together Brazil, Argentina, Uruguay, and Paraguay, with a total population of 234 million; Chile and Bolivia now hold associate membership. Its objective was to create a customs union that would eliminate tariffs on 90 to 95% of trade and set a common external tariff of 0 to 20% applied to nonmember exports. Intra-Mercosur trade has quadrupled since its creation, and the region is binding itself with a web of investments and a growing network of cross-border roads, electricity grids, and gas pipelines. However, Mercosur trade is highly asymmetrical: In 2000, Argentina exports to Brazil totaled $8.4 billion, while Brazil's exports to Argentina amounted to only $7.7 billion, a much smaller proportion of its total trade. Uruguay and Paraguay both depend on Mercosur for about half of their exports.[32] Mercosur's leading trade partner is the EU, accounting for 27% of its exports (versus 18% for the United States) in 1999. Despite its strong start, Mercosur is now stalled or even regressing, due to factors such as Brazil's devaluation and Argentina's deep recession. Intra-Mercosur trade has fallen since 1998 and amounts to only about one-fifth of total trade. Most internal trade is now tariff-free, but many nontariff barriers remain. In April 2000, Mercosur presidents "relaunched" the pact by agreeing to harmonize targets for inflation and public debt and to bring the auto sector into the agreement by 2006, although other sensitive items remain excluded.[33]

Argentina's main complaint is that Brazil, whose Real lost over 40% of its value since its forced 1999 devaluation, thus gained an unfair advantage. By early 2000, at least 15 auto-parts companies had moved to Brazil, and GM, Ford, and Fiat had shifted some of their production to Brazil. Goodyear and Tupperware both closed factories in Argentina, deciding to supply the market from Brazil.[34] A possible scenario is that Mercosur would regress to a simple free-trade area, despite official statements to the contrary.

TECHNOLOGY TRENDS

The Latin markets are highly heterogeneous in terms of technology. The United States, along with Scandinavia and some parts of Asia, are some of the most "wired" markets in the world, with an Internet penetration of 45% in 2000; among U.S. Hispanics, penetration was 24% in 2000 but expected to reach almost 50% by 2003. The larger size and younger age of Hispanic households also lead to higher spending in many categories, such as children's clothing and phone services, and the Hispanic e-commerce spending per user ($846 in 2000) is not far behind the national average ($1,162). Hispanic Net users totaled almost 8 million in 2000 and were projected to reach nearly 18 million by 2003, a much higher growth rate than the average U.S. rate (see Table 1.4).[35]

Spain and Portugal, although among the least wired countries in Europe, stand between the U.S. and Latin American markets in terms of technology diffusion. Latin America itself is sharply divided

TABLE 1.4 U.S. Hispanic Market: Demographics and Technographics, 1998–2003

	1998	1999	2000	2001	2002 (E)	2003 (E)
United States						
U.S. population (millions)	270.6	273.1	275.6	278.1	280.6	283.1
U.S. GDP ($ billions)	8,760	9,256	9,901	10,385	10,925	11,517
GDP per capita ($)	32,377	33,889	35,929	37,350	38,938	40,686
U.S. Internet advertising spending ($ millions)	1,260	2,805	5,358	8,680	12,587	17,244
Total U.S. e-commerce spending ($ millions)	44,812	80,543	142,541	240,110	422,824	726,052
Total U.S. Internet users (thousands)	68,900	101,494	122,698	149,036	177,021	197,182
U.S. e-commerce spending per user ($)	650	794	1,162	1,665	2,389	3,682
Internet penetration in U.S. population	25%	37%	45%	54%	63%	70%
U.S. Hispanics						
U.S. Hispanic population (millions)	30.3	31.4	32.5	33.6	34.8	35.9
GDP associated w/ U.S. Hispanics ($ billions)	714	774	850	915	986	1,065
GDP per capita ($)	23,589	24,690	26,176	27,211	28,369	29,642
U.S. Hispanic Internet advertising spending ($ millions)	18	62	178	362	647	1,035
Total U.S. Hispanic e-commerce spending ($ millions)	310	845	1,854	3,177	5,150	8,150
Total U.S. Hispanic Internet users (thousands)	2,420	4,703	7,632	10,757	14,080	17,600
U.S. Hispanic e-commerce spending per user ($)	474	578	846	1,233	1,740	2,683
Internet penetration in U.S. Hispanic population	8%	15%	24%	32%	41%	49%

Source: U.S. Bureau of the Census, CSFB Technology Group, cited in Latin America Technology Industry Update, Credit Suisse First Boston, Jan. 17, 2001, p. 48.

21

between top-tier countries and the rest. The regional PC penetration of 29% is low compared to the global average of 37% and especially lags the 66% rate in developed Asia, 54% in North America, and 66% in Europe—but regional averages are meaningless in this case. In Argentina and Mexico, PC penetration is, respectively, 40% and 37%.[36] Penetration rates based on home ownership also misstate actual use, since there are other access points. Strategy Research estimates that of all households with Internet access, 71% have it at home versus 60% at work and 14% at school.[37] Net access is also projected to grow faster from non-PC devices, following the European pattern of m-commerce but also spurred by the very high television penetration rate in the region (about 300 sets per 1,000 inhabitants in Brazil, Argentina, and Mexico).[38]

The current user population in Latin America and Hispanic United States reaches nearly 24 million, not far behind the 29 million Japanese population. Growth estimates for Internet use are notoriously unreliable, even more so in the current recessionary context. For Latin America, they range from 55 million by 2003 (Jupiter Research) to 41 million (eMarketer);[39] the more conservative estimate from Credit Suisse First Boston of nearly 38 million users by 2003 would reflect a 63% penetration rate of the expected addressable market at that time (see Table 1.5).

A widespread phenomenon that may speed up technology diffusion in Latin America is leapfrogging (i.e., skipping development stages). In telecommunications, in particular, the landline infrastructure is still poor (despite the fact that 70% of countries have partly or fully privatized their telecoms), but wireless is seen as a key growth sector. In 2000, Latin America had 62 million cellular subscribers (versus 112 million in North America), and this was expected to grow to 140 million by 2004.[40]

DRIVERS AND BARRIERS OF TECHNOLOGY

In addition to favorable demographics, wireless growth, and high TV penetration, three major growth drivers will fuel technology diffusion: free Internet service providers (ISPs), lower access prices, and proactive government policies. Free ISPs entered Latin America in 2000 and were the single largest contributor to Internet diffusion. Even though their long-term outlook is questionable, they may have caused the online migration of a large group of users who may soon be ready to convert to premium ISPs. Brazil's iG (Internet Gratis) led the charge, followed by many others—most of which have since shut down.

TABLE 1.5 Latin America: Demographics and Technographics

	1998	1999	2000	2001	2002	2003
Population (millions)	463.2	470.7	478.2	485.7	493.2	600.7
Gross domestic product						
Nominal GDP ($ billions)	1,945	1,752	1,942	2,032	2,109	2,188
GDP per capita ($)	4,199	3,722	4,062	4,185	4,276	4,370
PC installed base (thousands)						
Home	4,820	6,087	7,632	9,393	11,311	13,513
Small business	4,174	5,088	6,212	7,500	9,041	10,709
Medium/large business	5,706	6,611	7,702	8,937	10,444	12,133
Government	1,603	1,799	2,075	2,409	2,820	3,331
Education	1,248	1,456	1,717	2,030	2,423	2,856
Total PC installed base	17,552	21,040	25,338	30,269	36,040	42,543
Internet users (thousands)						
Home	2,672	4,615	7,689	10,856	14,391	18,759
Small business	669	1,328	2,179	3,233	4,512	5,752
Medium/large business	1,217	2,106	3,169	4,516	5,766	7,012
Government	906	960	1,257	1,692	1,811	2,396
Education	829	1,190	1,868	2,291	3,018	3,751
Total Internet users	6,293	10,199	16,162	22,588	29,498	37,670
Penetration	1.38%	2.17%	3.38%	4.65%	5.98%	7.52%
Internet commerce market value ($ millions)						
Home	47	131	276	592	1,164	2,096
Small business	37	125	333	800	1,573	2,674
Medium/large business	75	237	610	1,437	2,764	4,616
Government	19	46	102	230	429	765
Education	25	60	132	273	491	805
Total Internet commerce market value	203	600	1,453	3,331	6,420	10,957

Source: IDC, CSFB Technology Group, cited in Latin America Technology Industry Update, Credit Suisse First Boston, Jan. 17, 2001, p. 76.

This increased competition quickly led to lower access prices. In 1999–2000, total Internet access costs (ISP plus telephone charges) decreased 23%, 20%, and 8% in Argentina, Brazil, and Mexico, respectively, most of this due to lower ISP fees, as phone charges remained stable.[41]

Local governments are also a positive force in technology diffusion. In a first wave of reform, they began large-scale privatizations in the 1990s, driving up teledensity. In 1990, Mexico privatized Teléfonos de Mexico (Telmex), and by 1999, teledensity had increased by 104%. Argentina followed in the early 1990s and saw similar improvements. Brazil delayed the process until 1997 but sold in 1998 a 51% stake of its national company, Telebrás, for $19 billion, and has since shown the sharpest increase in teledensity.

A second wave of reform is now taking place with schools and subsidy programs, often done through public–private partnerships. Brazil's CEF Bank (Caixa Economica Federal) and portal Globo.com agreed to provide financing for PC and Internet access, with the credit risk assumed by CEF. Argentina's Banco Nación also opened a $1 billion line of credit for PC purchases, with an annual goal of 330,000 computers. In addition, the Brazilian Science and Technology Ministry announced an initiative to connect some 73,000 schools to the Internet in a partnership with private firms and nonprofit groups.[42]

Despite these growth drivers, a number of region-specific barriers still exist, the major one being income disparity, which will be infinitely harder to resolve than hardware issues such as low PC penetration. Another barrier is the region's poor infrastructure, which poses a severe logistics problem for both business-to-business (B2B) and business-to-consumer (B2C). A study by McKinsey & Company showed a significant fulfillment lag in Latin America (five days versus two days in North America and Europe) and an accuracy problem (55% of orders filled accurately versus 75 to 85%).[43]

This leads to an amplified "Amazon effect" in the region, since companies have to commit high capital expenditures to their logistics and warehousing operations without ever achieving the Dell-like efficiencies of a just-in-time supply system. This is especially critical in some B2B sectors—in the PC business, for instance, inventory loses about 1% of its value for every week spent in the supply chain. This is compounded by the high cost and scarcity of capital in the region, especially for small and midsize companies. For all these reasons, it is highly likely that the winners in this sector will be bricks-and-clicks companies able to leverage their existing retail chains, supplier relationships, and logistic systems.[44]

Finally, two related barriers to technology diffusion are inadequate regulation and concerns about security. Most online merchants in Latin America do not have the risk-scoring and address-verification services provided by banks in the United States. Similarly, consumers do not have a guarantee of zero liability for credit card fraud, and as a result, most credit card holders are reluctant to buy online. This is compounded by low credit card penetration: 27% in Argentina, 22% in Mexico, and 18% in Brazil versus 80% in the United States and South Korea.[45] This is being partly addressed with alternative forms of payment, ranging from cash on delivery to deposits to merchant bank accounts, smart cards, and personal checks. Private initiatives are also attempting to fill regulatory gaps. In Brazil, Visa launched a "Zero Liability" program in which its member banks were to assume the risk of fraud. In addition, a consortium including AOL, Banco Itaú, Submarino, Terra, and UOL launched a $1 million secure Internet campaign in 2000 to research and resolve consumer concerns.

Governments still lag in terms of regulation. Mexico is the most advanced; its NAFTA membership led to the 1996 law on intellectual property, amended in 1998 and recognizing rights to computer programs and electronic databases. Recent changes in the consumer protection law address confidentiality and transaction security issues, and two other laws recognize the validity of electronic transactions. By contrast, software piracy remains a severe problem in Brazil, even after a 1998 law set penalties for infringement; changes in the consumer protection code address Internet purchases, but consumer protection and security are still inadequate. In 2000 it was estimated that 70% of Latin American Web sites requested credit card numbers in unsecured environments.[46]

E-COMMERCE MARKET POTENTIAL

Total e-commerce revenues in Latin America were estimated by eMarketer at $3.6 billion in 2000, which was still only 1.3% of the total worldwide market of $286 billion. B2B transactions far outweighed B2C sales ($2.9 billion versus $784 million in 2000) and this trend was expected to continue. Projections for 2004 were $58 billion for B2B against $8 billion for B2C; these may be revised downward in the near future. Brazil's share dwarfs that of other countries, with $2.5 billion or almost 70% of the region's revenues in 2000. This is due partly to an advanced, automated industrial sector ready to benefit from online procurement, as well as a fairly cohesive consumer market in large urban areas. By 2004, if current trends continue,

Brazil is projected to reach $40 billion in value versus $13 billion for Mexico.[47]

Total e-commerce revenues in North America reached $207 billion in 2000. In the United States, it is impossible to estimate what portion of those revenues can be attributed to Hispanics for B2B, but B2C e-commerce sales to Hispanics were estimated at $1.9 billion in 2000 versus $42 billion in total U.S. B2C spending. E-commerce sales to Hispanics are projected to reach $8 billion by 2003. Although Hispanic sales are only 4% of the U.S. B2C market, spending per user is quite high ($243 against a U.S. average of $340) and the 1998–2003 growth is projected to be almost twice as high for Hispanics as for the United States in general.[48]

LOCAL VERSUS REGIONAL APPROACHES

E-commerce revenues, like Internet users, are highly concentrated geographically. Brazil and Mexico account for 71% of total e-commerce and 84% of B2B e-commerce in the region. This would imply that a uniform strategy addressing the top markets might be appropriate, but there is mounting evidence to the contrary. B2B supply patterns follow those of trade and investment flows, which are quite distinct for Mexico and Brazil. This may also apply on the consumer side. According to Tim Parsa, CEO of Todito.com, a Mexican portal with a goal to expand among U.S. Hispanics (70% of whom are of Mexican descent): "There are two great fallacies about the Latin American Internet market: pan-regionality and first-mover advantage. Pan-regionality doesn't work. The cultures are so distinct. You end up creating a network of small, country-focused portals that hemorrhage cash in administering the necessary local content, producers and e-commerce." Similarly, first-mover advantage is plausible in "an addressable and ready-made market [of] 30 to 40 million computer users," but it does not apply to Latin America.[49] Accordingly, the dominant e-commerce business model in Latin America mimics the European one of bricks-and-clicks alliances rather than "pure play" startups. Todito.com was founded by the Salinas–Pliego family, controlling TV Azteca, the retail chain Elektra, wireless company Unefon, and computer distributor Dataflux.

In this context, pan-regional companies such as AOL face an uphill battle in competing for ad revenues with established local media groups that are skilled at linking their off-line and online resources. Regional models are also increasingly difficult to finance, as investors now realize the cost of replicating infrastructure in different countries. In addition, currencies, financial systems, and payment methods vary by country; so do Spanish dialects and the Spanish–Portuguese language barrier, which require producing local content. As a result, of 56 major Web sites originating in Latin America, 36 have stayed in their home markets, 6 have added one other country, and only 14 have expanded into three or more countries.[50]

The localized pattern also applies to ISPs, none of which has market dominance in all three top markets. While UOL led in Brazil with over 800,000 subscribers in 2000, Prodigy/Telmex was the top ISP in Mexico with almost 600,000 subscribers, and ArNet/Telecom had the top spot in Argentina with a 200,000-subscriber base. Terra Lycos, a unit of Telefónica, was a distant second in Brazil and Mexico.[51]

CROSS-BORDER INVESTMENTS

While Web sites tend to be localized, their capital needs have required a bricks-and-clicks model that includes a large cross-border component. Among portals, all of the major players are backed by Spanish or American investors, as well as by local brick-and-mortar players. Terra Networks, which acquired U.S.-based Lycos, is a unit of Telefónica de España; UOL is backed by publishing groups Abril and Folha as well as by Morgan Stanley Dean Witter, and Globo.com is backed by parent Globo as well as Telecom Italia. Industry-specific sites show the same pattern: Banco Santander Central Hispano, a leading transregional bank established in 12 countries, paid $529 million for Patagon, a financial supermarket operating in five Latin American countries, the United States, and Spain.[52]

Portuguese companies are also active in the region. Portugal Telecom has significant assets in Brazil, including the largest mobile phone provider, Telesp Celular, and its unit PT Multimedia has invested in Globo.com and also (through its PTM.com division) acquired Zip.net, one of the 10 destinations in Brazil, in March 2000. The company's goal is to become the leading ISP to Portuguese speakers globally (see Table 1.6).

B2C SUCCESS FACTORS

There will only be a few winners in the Latin markets, as the current consolidation accelerates. As in the United States, start-ups are disappearing or being acquired by established players. An emerging business model that is likely to dominate appears to be: bricks-and-clicks structure, pan-regional scope but differentiated by strong local content (preferably exclusively sourced from a parent

TABLE 1.6 Cross-Border Investments in Major Portals and ISPs

COMPANY	STRATEGIC INVESTORS	BUSINESS MODEL	AREA OF OPERATION
AOL Latin America	AOL, Cisneros Group, Banco Itaú	Subscription access, portal with broad content	Brazil, Mexico, Argentina
Ciudad Internet	Clarín Group	Subscription access, portal with broad content	Argentina, Brazil
El Sitio	Hicks, Muse, Tate & Furst, Cisneros Group	Subscription access, portal with broad content	Pan-regional
Globo.com	Globo, Telecom Italia, PT Multimedia	Portal with broad content, broadband access	Brazil
Starmedia Network	Chase Capital Partners, eBay	Portal with broad content	Pan-regional, Spain, U.S.
T1MSN	Telmex, Microsoft	Portal with broad content	Mexico
Terra Networks	Telefónica, Banco Bilbao Vizcaya	Subscription access, portal with broad content	Pan-regional, Spain
Universo OnLine (UOL)	Editora Abril, Grupo Folha, Morgan Stanley Dean Witter	Subscription access, free access through BOL	Brazil
Brasil OnLine (BOL)		Portal with broad content	Pan-regional, Spain
Yupi.com	Sony, News Corp, IFX	Portal with broad content	Argentina, Colombia, Ecuador, Mexico, Spain, U.S.

Source: E-Business in Latin America, Economist Intelligence Unit, Aug, 2000, p. 48.

company), and diversified revenue sources (connectivity, wireless, and e-commerce in addition to advertising).

The bricks-and-clicks structure subdivides into three types, according to the nature of the parent company:

- Latin networks (Globo.com/Globo, UOL/Abril and Folha, El Sitio/Cisneros, Ciudad Internet/Grupo Clarin)
- European networks (Terra Lycos/Telefónica, PT Multimedia/ Portugal Telecom)
- U.S./Latin networks (AOL Latin America/Cisneros, T1MSN/ Telmex and MSN)

UOL and Ciudad Internet, the clear leaders in their respective home markets of Brazil and Argentina, have both emerged from print media groups. UOL's main shareholders are Grupo Folha (owner of Brazil's largest newspaper, Folha de São Paulo) and Grupo Abril (second media group in Brazil, with a 63% share of magazine advertising). The network has an 82% reach of the Brazilian market, and its 810,000 paying subscribers also make it the largest ISP in Latin America. According to Media Matrix, its flagship domain UOL.com.br and search engine BOL are the two most navigated destinations in the country.

UOL has retained a local model for the ISP business but has expanded its print partnership model to evolve into a regional portal. It entered Venezuela through an alliance with *Diario El Universal*, in which the newspaper transferred all of its Internet content to the UOL Venezuela portal against a 40% stake in it. Similar agreements were reached with Perfil in Argentina. However, UOL has since retrenched somewhat, exiting Chile and Spain and downsizing in Colombia and Venezuela. Given the scalability of the Brazilian market, it is likely that UOL will refocus on it.[53]

Terra Networks and PT Multimedia are examples of another bricks-and-clicks model led by a European telecom. Telefónica was first to enter the Internet market in 1999, acquiring the second ISP and portal Zaz.com.br. Telefónica is the largest operator in Latin America and the largest shareholder in Terra Lycos, the $6.5 billion merger of Terra Networks and Lycos. Terra Lycos is also Europe's largest online distributor of books and entertainment, thanks to its links to Bertelsmann, which owns 20% of Lycos Europe.[54]

The prime example of a U.S.-led network is AOL Latin America, an ISP operating in Brazil, Mexico, and Argentina. AOL owns a 40.6% stake, with the Cisneros Group holding 39.1% and Banco Itaú owning 12.2%. The Cisneros Group has transformed itself from a

Venezuelan conglomerate to a multimedia leader, shedding super-market and department store operations as well as its cola franchise and spending over $1.5 billion to acquire a portfolio of broadcast, cable, and Internet holdings, including Univisión in the United States, satellite TV network Galaxy, and part of portal El Sitio.[55]

Despite its deep resources, AOL Latin America still trails leaders such as UOL and Terra Networks. It has been plagued by missteps, such as a slow eight-month rollout in Mexico, the distribution of faulty software CDs in Brazil, and most important, a failed initial public offering in August 2000, salvaged only when AOL and Cis-neros each purchased 30% of all the shares offered. Some local ob-servers felt that it was "too late, too arrogant, and too Yankee," overestimating the appeal of its brand name abroad and under-estimating the importance of local content. Even though it had sourcing alliances with 150 local companies, it could not compete on content richness against players such as UOL, Terra Networks, or Globo.com.[56]

Starmedia illustrates the risk of independence. It had a first-mover advantage in Brazil but never could surpass UOL and its homegrown content. It had a successful 1999 IPO and an added $25 million investment by BellSouth (against an 11% stake) in 2001, but it unraveled by year's end. Amid criticism of improper accounting practices, Starmedia's founder and CEO was replaced, and despite 2000 revenues of $60 million, the stock dropped from a 1999 peak of $70 to 38 cents. The company was expected to restate financial re-sults in the aftermath.[57]

B2B SUCCESS FACTORS

The B2C pattern of dominance by bricks-and-clicks players is even clearer for B2B. Large companies, due to their market power and their desire to streamline their supply chains (which are fairly inefficient in the region), have incentives to shift some of their oper-ations online. Industry sectors at the forefront of B2B activity are automotive, retailing, high technology telecom, and financial serv-ices, including key players such as Ford, Intel, Cisco, insurer Sul América, and Telefónica.

Brazil has a clear geographic lead, as it does in B2C. B2B ven-tures accounted for 1.5% of total intracorporate commerce ($4.75 billion) in the country in 2000, and this share could grow to 10% by 2005. Ford and Volkswagen are both leaders in the automotive sec-tor and launched their B2B initiatives in 1999. Since the end of that year, all of Ford's 400 distributors in Brazil place their orders online, and 90% of Ford's revenue (over R3 billion; $1.7 billion) is received via the Internet; the company has also started to use reverse auctions for procurement of nonstrategic commodity items. In 1999 Volkswagen launched its Net 2000 online purchasing system in Brazil and Argentina. It also operates as a reverse auction, and all 5,000 suppliers in both countries are registered with the system. This is now the only channel for components purchases, and these totaled $1.8 billion in 1999. General Motors has set up a similar online system with its dealership network in Brazil.

Retailers, with their razor-thin margins, can also benefit from a reduction in procurement costs. A pioneer was a local company, Pão de Açúcar, the second largest retailer in Brazil. It began integrating its 6,000-supplier network through the Internet at the end of 1999 and planned a $4.5 million investment in this initiative. Foreign retailers such as Wal-Mart already have their own systems or belong to global buying consortia. The Dutch group Royal Ahold, controlling the third largest Brazilian supermarket chain, Bompreço, belongs to the World Retail Exchange, which includes K-mart, CVS, and Walgreen. Carrefour, Brazil's top retailer for a decade, has invested $25 million in the Global Net Exchange with the U.S. retailer Krieger, the German group Metro, and J. Sainsbury in the UK. The system was to be rolled out in Brazil after market tests in Europe.

Telecom and financial services companies are also uniquely positioned to benefit from B2B operations—telecom companies because they already have the infrastructure, and financial firms because they do not depend on physical shipping of goods, which is the main barrier to e-commerce in Latin America. In January 2000, Telefónica established in Miami a separate unit, Telefónica B2B, and gave it the objective to partner with 15 to 20 companies in Latin America for B2B initiatives. In e-procurement, Telefónica invested about $100 million, in partnership with software provider Ariba, to develop a regionwide horizontal portal. In retail, the company took a majority stake in Mercador.com, a third-party platform with an extensive retailer network in Brazil.

In financial services, most major banks have set up their own B2B operations, and insurers have followed. Sul América, Brazil's largest insurance company, has developed an extranet to link its brokers. By 2001, the company received 60% of its monthly 70,000 car insurance proposals through the Internet; this reduced lead time between receipt of proposals and final processing from 15 days to 8 days.[58]

These established companies clearly dominate B2B e-commerce and they hold an estimated 90% market share in Brazil. The remaining 10% is split between corporate-backed units such as Telefónica B2B, venture-backed groups such as Genexis in health care and Mercado Electrônico, and industry consortia such as Latinexus (linking Votorantim, Cemex, and Alfa in construction) and Agrega (linking British American Tobacco/Souza Cruz and AmBev in the beverage sector). Of the top 10 B2B players in Brazil, ranked by value of transactions in 2000, only two (Genexis and Mercado Electrônico) were independent hubs. All the others were the B2B operations of large companies (see Table 1.7).

As in the United States and Europe, a consolidation is in progress, and company-specific B2B operations may prevail over consortia and third-party hubs.

Among independent B2B exchanges, the majority of both vertical and horizontal hubs will not be able to survive based on their transaction capabilities, and they are likely to be absorbed by bigger players.[59] A few exceptions may follow the horizontal portal model of Mercado Electrônico. It was set up in 1994 as an offline outsourcer for the purchase of indirect goods and moved online in 2000. It is the only liquid independent marketplace in Brazil, due to its first-mover advantage and solid client base of 15,000 suppliers and 300 buyers, ranging from GE and Alcan to Whirlpool and Solvay. These clients have experienced procurement cost reductions of up to 50% and direct savings of up to 20% on large-item purchases.[60]

TABLE 1.7 Key B2B Players in Brazil

COMPANY	TRANSACTIONS IN 2000 (R MILLIONS)	CORE BUSINESS
Ford	3,311	Automotive
Intel	1,848	Computer hardware
Cisco	932	Computer hardware
Hewlett-Packard	768	Computer hardware
Porto Seguro	651	Insurance
Genexis (independent hub)	585	Procurement
Itaú Seguros	388	Insurance
Mercado Electrônico (independent hub)	378	Procurement
Ticket Serviços	307	Services
Tele Centro Oeste	243	Telecommunications

Source: Info Exame, *Balanço Anual 2000, May 2001.*

COMPANY STRATEGIES

In this context of rapid technological change and high economic uncertainty, what are the most potentially profitable options for companies operating in the Latin markets? After their retreat from the region in the "lost decade" of the 1980s, foreign multinationals are now forming pan-American or transatlantic networks. Local companies must decide whether to bet on the region or to globalize, since their national markets are no longer protected and are invaded by foreign competitors. Financials indicate that local companies are in catch-up mode at best; they have two major weaknesses, both due to historical factors: lack of scope and dependence on commodities. The largest Latin American companies tend to belong to primary sectors such as energy and mining. This stands in sharp contrast to developing Asia, dominated by sectors such as consumer electronics and machinery.

The foreign multinationals could be expected to transfer some technology, but few of them are in high technology. Of the top 25 largest transnationals present in Latin America, six were in the primary sector (Exxon, Royal Dutch–Shell, Cargill, etc.), another six were in the medium-technology automotive sector, and only four were in high technology (IBM, GE, Intel, Motorola) (see Table 1.8).

However, this dependence on the low-value-added primary sector is not evenly distributed. While multinationals have tended to invest in Mexico to use it as a pan-American manufacturing hub and improve their global efficiency, they have depended to a greater extent on the South Cone for oil, gas, minerals, and agribusiness.[61]

STRATEGY TYPES: FROM SHAPERS TO INTEGRATORS

In environments characterized by uncertainty and rapid technological change, companies have tended to follow either shaping or adapting strategies.[62] *Shapers* strive to reduce uncertainty by driving change in an entire industry or one of its subsectors. A classic early example of shaping strategy was Microsoft's effort to promote its MS-DOS (and later Windows) operating system as the industry standard. Other shapers redefine the basis of competition with innovations in product, service, or business system. FedEx, for instance, radically changed the package delivery business with its "absolutely, positively there overnight" concept. Although shapers tend to emerge in innovation-driven industries, they can also be low-technology companies. The Body Shop reversed the conventional

TABLE 1.8 25 Largest Transnational Firms in Latin America by Consolidated Sales (Millions of Dollars)

	FIRM	COUNTRY OF ORIGIN	SECTOR	ARGENTINA	BRAZIL	MEXICO	TOTAL (INCL. OTHER)
1	Telefónica de España	Spain	Telecommunications	4,634	5,010	—	12,439
2	General Motors	U.S.	Motor vehicles	600	3,895	7,340	12,425
3	Volkswagen	Germany	Motor vehicles	1,020	3,976	6,906	11,902
4	DaimlerChrysler	Germany	Motor vehicles	784	1,610	7,352	9,746
5	Carrefour Group/Promodès	France	Commerce	5,092	4,469	—	9,561
6	Ford	U.S.	Motor vehicles	1,144	2,406	4,689	8,252
7	Repsol–YPF	Spain	Petroleum	7,980	14	—	8,109
8	Fiat Spa	Italy	Motor vehicles	1,160	6,499	—	7,659
9	Royal Dutch–Shell	UK/Netherlands	Petroleum	1,834	3,658	—	6,449
10	ExxonMobil	U.S.	Petroleum	1,675	2,625	—	6,403
11	IBM	U.S.	Electronics	586	1,500	3,393	5,479
12	Endesa España	Spain	Electricity	814	466	—	5,475
13	AES	U.S.	Electricity	753	2,214	—	5,182
14	Wal-Mart	U.S.	Commerce	500	534	3,782	4,816
15	Nestlé	Switzerland	Foodstuffs	430	1,770	1,811	4,766
16	Renault/Nissan	France	Motor vehicles	1,139	285	2,684	4,179
17	Unilever	UK/Netherlands	Foodstuffs	1,213	1,734	524	4,126
18	Motorola	U.S.	Electronics	208	1,000	2,600	3,817
19	Cargill	U.S.	Foodstuffs	2,059	1,482	—	3,541
20	Intel	U.S.	Electronics	—	840	—	3,540
21	PepsiCo	U.S.	Beverages	630	189	2,673	3,532
22	Royal Ahold	Netherlands	Commerce	2,117	811	—	3,442
23	Coca-Cola	U.S.	Beverages	1,620	395	891	3,336
24	Olivetti Spa./Italia Telecom	Italy	Telecommunications	2,326	308	143	3,162
25	General Electric	U.S.	Machinery	—	—	3,048	3,142

Source: Foreign Investment in Latin America and the Caribbean, *ECLAC, 2000, p. 46. (Figures are for 1999 sales.)*

wisdom in the cosmetics industry (heavily promoted artificial products) and pioneered its "green" line of natural recyclable products, with no initial advertising beyond its point-of-sale brochures. It has now been imitated by all major players with their own lines of organics.

Other shapers restructure their competitive landscape with aggressive mergers and acquisitions. At a time when the normally stable banking sector was fluid in Latin America due to privatizations and market liberalization, major Spanish banks reshaped their industry by merging among themselves as well as making extensive acquisitions in Latin America. Foremost among those were Banco Santander and Banco Bilbao Vizcaya, which became almost overnight the largest foreign bankers in the region and created a "Latin banking world" with their transatlantic holdings.

Adapters, on the other hand, do not attempt to change their industry structure radically, but thrive within its confines by leveraging their resources and differential advantages. This strategy is especially appropriate when a first-mover advantage is not evident, as is the case in the Internet sector. Even in a relatively mature market such as the United States, it is not obvious that early shapers such as Amazon or Yahoo! have created a workable business model. What is already clear is that winners, if any, in the Latin world will be bricks-and-clicks players such as Telefónica or the Abril and Globo groups and their Internet arms.

Depending on the scope and nature of their resources, adapters further subdivide into specialists, integrators, and regionals (see Figure 1.4).[63] *Specialists* may focus on one part of the value chain or on an industry subsector. They have assumed more importance as new technologies have led to disaggregation of the value chain. In the automotive sector, for instance, Delphi was spun off from its parent company and now operates as an autonomous manufacturer of auto parts. An example of a value chain specialist that became a shaper is Cisco, which focused on an early stage of the Internet value chain (i.e., routers that enable the switching of data and voice communications between networks). Cisco gained dominance, first by heavy investment in technology, then by a massive wave of acquisitions. It can be qualified as an industry shaper because it is redefining telecommunications through its dominance of a narrow industry "sliver," the router market.

In Latin America, specialists can also be found in various industry sectors. In aviation, Brazil-based Embraer occupies a niche similar to that of its Canadian competitor Bombardier. By contrast with Boeing and its full product line, Embraer focuses on regional civilian

Geographic Scope

	Narrow	Broad
Narrow **Industry Focus**	**Specialists** • Best-in-class in specialty • Focus on part of value chain [Delphi, Embraer]	**Shapers** • Create and dominate industry "slivers" • Shape a new sector or reshape an industry [Cisco, Banco Santander]
Broad	**Regionals** • Access/scale advantage limited to home region • Dominance in market share, channels, and supplier links [AmBev, Aché]	**Integrators** • Global access/scale superiority • Advantage from cross-border integration [Telefónica, Cemex]

FIGURE 1.4

Strategy Options

Source: Adapted from Lowell Bryan, Jane Fraser, Jeremy Oppenheim, and Wilhelm Rall, *Race for the World,* Harvard Business School Press, 1999, p. 91. Reprinted by permission of the Harvard Business School Press. © 1999 Harvard Business School Publishing Corporation; all rights reserved.

jets and military aircraft. Its basis of specialization is not a part of the value chain, but rather, an industry subsector. Although specialists often start operating on a regional basis due to their initially limited resources, they can globalize successfully. Embraer dominates the Latin America military market, but it has worldwide customers for its regional civilian jets.

Due to their worldwide scope and broad portfolios, most large multinationals have adopted *integrator* strategies, often through cross-border acquisitions which deepen their scale and market access advantages. They often—but not always—own or control the entire value chain in their industry. Agribusiness companies such as Cargill or Archer Daniels Midland, for instance, claim that their operations extend "from dirt to dinner." Integration is especially prevalent in the primary sector, including energy and construction. Oil companies from Exxon to British Petroleum globalized the entire value chain rapidly by controlling every stage, from exploring and production to shipping, refining, and retail distribution. In this sector, Latin America's largest acquisition was that of Argentina's formerly state-owned YPF (Yacimientos Petrolíferos Fiscales) by Spain's Repsol.

The last type of adapter is the *regional* company, which historically dominated the region in the form of family-owned conglomerates such as Bunge in agribusiness. These were the most appropriate structure in closed markets, where an inadequate legal system (especially in regard to the rights of minority shareholders) was a barrier to going public. They remain fairly prevalent in the region. Even in new economy sectors such as media, private groups such as Abril and Cisneros have a dominant position. Their challenge, in the coming decade, will be to retain their home-market advantage in terms of brand strength and customer and supplier relationships, while expanding globally to reduce their vulnerability to regional turbulence.

A brief look at key examples of shapers, specialists, integrators, and regionals will further define the potential of each strategy.

BANCO SANTANDER: A LATIN SHAPER

In a half-decade, Banco Santander built an extensive Latin empire through acquisitions of leading banks in Brazil, Mexico, and several other Caribbean and Latin American countries. The largest of these include Banco Río de la Plata in Argentina for $1 billion in 1997–2001, Banco Noroeste and Banco Geral do Comércio in Brazil for $500 million and $202 million, respectively, in 1997, and in that same year, Grupo Financiero InverMéxico for $502 million.[64] This expansion was remarkable, not only for its scope and rapidity, but also for its strategic objective. Although major banks globalized their commercial and investment operations early, due to the worldwide scope of their key customers, they have rarely aimed to dominate mass-market banking in a foreign region, especially one with countries as disparate as Brazil, Chile, and Puerto Rico. In its home market, Santander had strengthened its position with the acquisition of Banesto (48% in 1994 and the remaining shares four years later). It also shook up the Spanish market by offering new high-yield checking and savings accounts and low-interest mortgages, as well as the first telephone banking service. At the same time, Santander was expanding in Portugal with the acquisition of Banco de Comércio e Indústria in 1990 and in Latin America, although it retreated from the region in the early 80s, as did most foreign multinationals. It quickly regained the lost ground after the mid-1990s, with the ambition of being the "best franchise in Latin America." After its 1999 merger with Banco Central Hispano, BSCH became the largest bank in the euro zone by market capitalization (€37 billion) and also the largest bank in Latin America (9.4% of assets). It expanded its scope in brokerage and insurance with the 1997 acquisition of 60% of InverMéxico, and also bought patagon.com, Latin America's largest financial portal. With these aggressive moves, Santander helped redefine the Latin banking environment from a stagnant sector to a dynamic industry.

CEMEX: A GLOBAL INTEGRATOR

In the past 15 years, Cemex transformed itself from a national player to the third largest cement manufacturer in the world. Although construction is an intensely local business, Cemex was able to build a global network which diversified its asset base and reduced the high volatility of cement prices by transporting cement by sea from low-demand to high-demand sites.[65] While it deliberately focused on its core cement business and divested its tourism, petroleum, and mining operations, it built up its related acquisitions, such as important marine terminals in California and Texas. Its international expansion started in 1992 with two cement companies in Spain, which made it the top producer in the country and formed a base for further growth. It then moved to Venezuela with the 1994 acquisition of top producer Vencemos; that same year, purchases followed in Texas and Panama, as well as in the Dominican Republic and Colombia in the next two years. By 1998, Cemex had become the top cement trader worldwide, and the third largest manufacturer, with assets of $10.5 billion; by then, Mexico accounted for less than 50% of sales. It has had a sustained, higher than industry average profitability, driven by operational expertise, business focus, and a unique position in emerging markets. The company took advantage of the 1998 Asian currency crisis to expand into a market accounting for 60% of the world cement consumption (versus 7% each in North America and Latin America, and 18% in Europe). Cemex then made two acquisitions in the Philippines (including two marine terminals) and took a stake in an Indonesian producer.

The Cemex trading arm is a key strength; it allows the firm to maintain a stable cash flow by shipping cement to high-demand regions. Its focus on cement also differentiates it from its competitors, which tend to be more diversified. The top producer, Holderbank, is a family conglomerate that includes financial and real estate assets. While actively expanding in emerging markets, Holderbank still has over half of its portfolio in mature countries; similarly, the second-largest producer, Lafarge, is strong in Europe, where cement demand is low. By contrast, about 70% of the Cemex cash flow comes from markets such as Colombia and Mexico.

Cemex has also leveraged its global network online as well as offline. Together with Grupo Industrial Alfa and Brazil's Votorantim and Bradespar (Banco Bradesco's nonfinancial arm), Cemex created Latinexus, a cross-border, cross-sector e-marketplace for procurement of indirect goods (i.e., general supplies). Member companies expect that by 2003, over 10% of their sales will be conducted online, which is significant, since their combined purchases of indirect goods amount to about $2 billion. The group also aims to extend the use of this marketplace to other companies and has formed a core of 15 to 20 companies (ranging from banks to telecoms) to invest jointly in expanding Latinexus. Transaction-based fees will be supplemented by value-added services, and expansion is planned in Argentina, Colombia, and Venezuela.[66]

AmBev: A Strong Regional

AmBev (Compania de Bebidas das Américas, the largest Brazilian company) was created by the 1999 merger of Brahma (with $7 billion in sales) and Antarctica (with $3.3 billion). It has a combined 70% share of the Brazilian beer market.[67] The new company became the third-largest beer producer, after Anheuser-Busch and Heineken, and the fifth-largest beverage company in the world. Another Latin American company, Mexico's Modelo, was in the top 10, with $2 billion in 1998 sales—others were based in South Africa, Europe, Japan, the United States, and Australia. Although a regional giant, AmBev is still far from a global player. It acquired in 1994 Venezuela's second-largest producer, Cervecería Nacional, and set up production in Argentina. Its sales in the rest of Latin America are largely in the form of exports, and it still relies on foreign partners for distribution beyond the region. AmBev's alliance with PepsiCo may be critical in this respect. It started in 1984 with an agreement to distribute Pepsi in Rio de Janeiro and to operate three factories in Rio Grande do Sul. AmBev moved from bottler to partner with a 1999 agreement that its Guaraná Antarctica product would be distributed internationally by Pepsi. Guaraná had the potential to gain 1% of the global soft drinks market, valued at $70 billion a year.

In addition to this indirect expansion beyond the region, AmBev has restructured aggressively for a decade and implemented a productivity improvement plan which increased capacity from 1,200 hectoliters per employee in 1989 to 8,700 hectoliters per employee 10 years later. While employees were reduced from 25,000 to 10,700, distribution increased dramatically, from 760,000 retail outlets to over 1 million. At the same time, the distribution network was rationalized with a sharp reduction in the number of distributors, and net income grew from $36 million to $272 million.

On the technology front, AmBev established with Souza Cruz (BAT's Brazilian subsidiary) a B2B marketplace to source indirect goods for them and future consortium members. Savings of $10 million were expected in the first year of operation.[68]

CONCLUSION

The best-case scenario for the region will be that more local companies migrate from the regional to the integrator model and from the specialist to shaper model. In the medium-term, the regional-to-integrator evolution is more likely than the specialist-to-shaper change. The latter is generally driven by technological innovation and is prevalent in sectors such as computing and biotechnology, which are underrepresented or absent from Latin America. A key issue is the inadequacy of patent protection and the prevalence of piracy in the region; another factor is the role of governments, which are far behind Asia in promoting high-value-added industries.

In the following chapters we explore in more depth these strategic approaches in sectors ranging from consumer goods to health care, and in the final chapter we synthesize key findings and conclude with the options presenting the most promise in the uncertain environment of the next decade.

2

THE LATIN CONSUMER MARKETS: CONVERGENCE OR FRAGMENTATION?

 atin consumer markets have gone through a wild ride in the 1990s. Although periods of growth and recession have affected the region in similar ways, their impact does not affect consumers in the same way or at the same time. In a short period of time, the Latin American social fabric has changed. The region has transformed itself into a complex, fluid social structure of rich and poor, old and young, and cosmopolitan and nationalistic attitudes. If we add to these layers of complexity differences in race, ethnicity, language, and climate, the conclusion is that Latin America is a rich mosaic of diversity that produces a variety of consumption behaviors and different ways of adjusting to the vulnerabilities affecting the region.

The nuclear family remains the focus of consumption, but it is changing rapidly. Families are smaller, more urban, and multigenerational. Their members are working more and generating the same income or less. The population is aging fast, and by 2015, Latin

markets will resemble those of the developed world. Inequality of income distribution remains unchanged. The incipient middle class
has been losing its share of total national income during the last
decade. In fact, the mobility of middle- and low-income social
classes has generated a debate on the definition of social classes in
Latin America. Education, professional status, and connectivity are
now better indicators of social classes.

In contrast to the market deprivation of the past, economic
liberalization offers more and better choices, especially in Latin
American urban markets, and consumers are overwhelmed with
information and selection. To cope with increasingly complex
lifestyles, constrained buying power, and increasing choice, consumers constantly seek the best value. Latin American consumers of
the twenty-first century have become proficient value shoppers. The
Latin American market represents 25% of the European and 18% of
the U.S. personal consumption power. Surging economies in the
early 1990s unleashed a wave of consumer optimism in the region
that did not last for long. As a result, Latin American consumer buying power has increased steadily, peaked in 1996, suffered a contraction in 1999, and is now growing again to an estimated $1.5 to $1.7
billion.

Boom and bust cycles in Latin American consumer markets are
not new. Older generations of Latin American consumers can re-
member clearly going through similar economic cycles triggered by
the volatility of commodity prices and world recessions. What is new
is that the booms and busts of the last decade took place in the context of market liberalization and economic reforms that ostensibly
would create a thriving middle class and open most economies to
global markets. As economic reforms diminished the role of the
state, Latin American families had to shoulder a greater share of the
costs for basic social services such as health and education.

The fragmentation and different dynamics of Latin American
markets is a challenge to all firms. The simpler approaches of the
past, based on geography and socioeconomic classes, do not reflect
the complexity of the region. Regional strategies based on the logic
of convergence and similarities of consumer preferences do not
work as well. Firms that unravel the complexities and sort out the
differences and similarities will prevail. A nesting approach to Latin
American markets from more macro segments based on the transformation of the demographic, gender, work, and other macro variables layered with more localized strategies based on micro
segments such as lifestyles will be more effective strategies for
twenty-first century Latin American markets.

In this chapter we provide a map to navigate the intricacies of Latin American consumer markets. First, we address the size of the market and identify major drivers that may affect future buying power. Second, we look at the consumption patterns in Latin America. Third, we analyze various ways to segment Latin American markets. Then we discuss the connectivity of Latin American consumers. In the final section we provide implications and recommendations as to how to approach Latin American consumer markets.

SIZE OF THE LATIN MARKET

How large is the Latin market in relationship to other world markets? The Economist Intelligence Unit (EIU) provides estimates of total private consumption for several world regions and countries that permit comparison. The EIU estimates the Latin American private consumption expenditure (PCE) at $1,222 billion, which represents 25% of the European PCE and 18% of the North American PCE.[1] Thus, the Latin American region should be an important market for any multinational company.

How large is the Latin consumer market? What drives the long-term trends of consumer expenditures? A country's PCE measures the final consumption expenditures of households and private non-profit institutions serving households in a country. The Strategy Research Corporation has developed a buying power model that estimates the national and household buying power based on PCE on the aggregate, by socioeconomic strata, and by rural versus urban.[2] As defined by the Strategy Research Corporation, Latin America excludes all of the non-Spanish-speaking Caribbean and Cuba but includes Puerto Rico and the Dominican Republic. Regional consumer buying power grew to $1,315 billion in 2000 from about $1,033 billion in 1994. Furthermore, from 1994 through 1998, Latin American consumer buying power increased every year, peaking in 1996. In 1999, it suffered a contraction of about 9% and it grew again in 2000.

A better definition of the Latin American market potential should include the Latin population in the United States.[3] The Latin population in the United States, referred to by the Census Bureau as the Hispanic population, is estimated at 34 million or about 12.3% of the U.S. population. By 2010, the Latin population is estimated to reach 40.6 million, 20% of the total population. The U.S. Census of Population reports that there were 8.590 million households of Latino origin in the United States with a median income of $26,628.[4]

Using the U.S. Census information, the Strategy Research Corporation estimates that the number of Latin households in the United States at 9.326 million, with a mean household annual buying power of $34,900.[5] A simple calculation based on the Strategy Research Corporation estimate yields a consumer buying power of $1,315 billion in 2000. The Latin market in the United States adds $325 billion of market power for a total of $1,640 billion. Other reports put the U.S. Latino market power at $300 to $452 billion.[6] Based on these estimates, the extended Latin American buying power may range from $1,543 billion to $1,767 billion, a sizable market for any multinational company.

Consumer buying power is concentrated in the top three markets of Brazil, Mexico, and Argentina. As Table 2.1 shows, these three countries represent 75% of total Latin American consumer buying power and 68% of all the households in the region in 2000. These percentages drop to 63 and 64% respectively, if one includes Latin Americans in the United States in the total. Regardless of definition, it is clear that the three largest economies of Latin America hold about two-thirds of the market power in the region.

Household buying power tells a different story. The relatively more affluent markets are Argentina, Mexico, Venezuela, Uruguay, Puerto Rico, and Latinos in the United States. Household incomes in these more affluent countries range from $15,000 to $26,000. In this group, Mexico, Venezuela, and to a lesser extent, Uruguay, have experienced income gains from 1997 to 2000. The other countries have suffered a reduction in household income. Puerto Rico's households have lost 24% of buying power in the same period.

A second group is represented by high-middle-income countries with household incomes ranging from $7,000 to $15,000. In this bracket, Chile stands alone, with an average annual household buying power of close to $12,000. A second subgroup, composed of Brazil, Colombia, Chile, Peru, Panama, Guatemala, and the Dominican Republic, shows a more moderate middle buying power, ranging from $7,000 to $10,000. Household buying power in Brazil, Colombia, and Peru decreased from 1997 to 2000. Smaller economies in this group, such as Guatemala, Panama, and the Dominican Republic experienced gains in household income. The last group is composed of small and poor household incomes of less than $8,000 per year. This group consists primarily of Central America, Bolivia, and Paraguay.

Most Latin American countries experienced sustained growth in consumer buying power in the early 1990s. The exception was Mexico, which lost almost 40% of its buying power in 1995 after the peso

TABLE 2.1 Household Buying Power in Latin America

Country	Total Buying Power		Number of Households		Household Buying Power	
	$ Billions	% Change 1997–2000	Thousands	% Change 1997–2000	$	% Change 1997–2000
Brazil	386.9	−23	54,188	6.6	7,132	−28
Mexico	383.1	62	18,087	5.9	19,989	53
Argentina	207	−5	10,009	3.1	20,679	−8
Venezuela	73.7	63	4,702	6.6	15,679	53
Colombia	54.9	−8	7,490	7.1	7,333	14.6
Chile	47.2	−2	3,982	5.1	11,851	−7
Peru	41.9	−12	5,132	3.6	8,160	−15
Puerto Rico	24.5	−15	1,271	9.8	19,272	−24
Guatemala	16.3	14.7	1,758	2.5	9,309	9.3
Uruguay	15.8	5	993	1.2	15,949	4
Dominican Republic	13.6	28	1,759	2.0	7,755	22.9
El Salvador	11.0	17	1,591	1.2	6,911	16
Ecuador	8.8	−28	2,731	5.7	3,229	−32.5
Paraguay	6.8	19	1,031	3.7	6,598	−24
Bolivia	6.2	6	1,268	1.2	4,904	3
Costa Rica	6.1	11	849	3.3	5,752	−17.5
Panama	5.7	29	714	2.8	8,042	23.7
Honduras	3.8	1,800	1,210	4.0	3,191	88
Nicaragua	2.2	29	953	3.4	2,289	15
Total Latin America	1,315.5	3	120,794	5.6		
Latin Americans in the U.S.	325		9,326	5.6	34,900	
Extended Latin America	1,640.5		130,120			

Source: Strategic Research Corporation, 2001 Latin American Market Planning Report and 2000 U.S Hispanic Market.

devaluation of December 1994. Latin American consumer buying power started to slow in 1998 after the adjustment of Brazil's currency, entered into deep contraction in 1999, and started to recover in 2000. In the second part of the 1990s, Mexico and Venezuela are the exception to the generalized decline in consumption power. Mexico's integration with the growing U.S. economy and favorable prices for oil may have insulated its economy from the recession that affected the rest of Latin America at the end of the last decade.

Among the U.S. Latin population, Cuban households represent one of the smaller groups of ethnic extraction. Cubans households, however, have achieved the highest levels of household income. The median household income for Cuban households in 2000 was $40,760. The next group in terms of affluence includes Latin households of Central or South American origin with median incomes of $39,000, followed by Mexican households with $32,400, and Puerto Rican with $30,300.[7]

DRIVERS OF BUYING POWER
IN LATIN MARKETS

Among the many factors that influence consumers, economic insecurity, demographic shifts, and income distribution are paramount. In this section we provide a brief account of how these drivers are affecting consumer buying power.

ECONOMIC INSECURITY

Consumption levels in Latin America adjust quickly to external shocks but take a long time to regain past levels. Latin America's history of repeated booms and busts has a strong influence on consumer confidence and consumption patterns. Wage earners, who represent the mass market for many consumer items in Latin America, have been through a roller coaster of volatility. As macro economic and structural reforms worked themselves through the economies of Latin America, labor markets have experienced high volatility in employment, unemployment, and earnings. *Economic insecurity* refers to the uncertain environment faced by households and wage earners due to erratic movements in key economic variables such as prices, employment, income, and real wages.[8] Economic insecurity arises from two sources: (1) external shocks from changes in global financial and goods markets, and (2) rapid changes in a given sector due to the obsolescence of skills, changes in technology, or changing allocations of resources across different sectors in an economy.

The first source is a macro impact that affects all economic actors equally. For instance, the macro devaluation of the Mexican peso in 1994 had a generalized impact on consumption patterns at all levels of Mexican society. Conversely, the taming of high inflation in the region has resulted in an increase in real buying power to all economic actors, particularly the poor. Buying power increases further as lower inflation lures banks to extend more credit to more consumers, allowing consumers to purchase more durable goods.

The second source of economic insecurity affects specific groups. A drop in coffee prices will have an impact only on the economic actors laboring in this sector. Both forces will affect real buying power, consumer confidence, and consumption patterns. Fluctuating incomes create greater economic insecurity and, therefore, poor consumer confidence. A study by the UN's Economic Commission on Latin America (ECLA) found that workers without contracts range from 22% in Chile to 65% in Paraguay.[9]

Annual changes in consumption levels represent the adjustment of consumption to the uncertainty created by these two forces. The variability of these changes over time can be estimated by the extent to which the changes depart from a long-term average or mean value of consumption.[10] A recent World Bank study of long-term patterns of volatility of aggregate private consumption found that such volatility in Latin America is three times higher than in the advanced economies and East Asia, and above the levels of South Asia and the Middle East. Higher consumption volatility was found only in Africa and East Asia and Pacific countries.[11] According to the study, the largest variability in annual consumption growth, defined as variability in excess of 10% was found among smaller economies in the region, such as Panama and Paraguay but also in Chile. It is interesting to note that Chile is by far the most open and liberalized economy in the region and thus is more exposed to external shocks. Chilean sectors such as mining or agriculture which are highly integrated to the world economy are more prone to rapid adjustment of industry wages and employment levels to price and demand fluctuations in world markets.

DEMOGRAPHIC SHIFTS

The Latin American household has become a multigenerational unit, packed in large urban centers, with dual or multiple income-earning members and with less leisure time and money to spend. A shift in population demographics drives this change, which includes smaller nuclear family size, the aging of the population, increased concentration and inequality of buying power in cities and social classes, and the growing role of women as heads of households and wage earners. In this section we provide a stylized account of these major demographic shifts.

At the start of the twenty-first century, a bubble of Latin American baby-boomers are coming of age as a result of high rates of population growth in the 1970s. By the year 2025, the population of Latin America will resemble the age distribution of that of the developed world. As Table 2.2 indicates, certain countries including Argentina, Chile, and Uruguay, are rapidly approaching growth rates of 1% or less. Other Latin American countries still resemble a developing country profile of high population growth, low life expectancy, high infant mortality, and extremely young population. Based on population growth dynamics, countries can be grouped in three stages of transformation.[12] A group of countries, including Argentina, Chile, Uruguay, and Puerto Rico, have achieved an advanced demographic transition, with population growth rates at or below 1%, small households of 3.4 members, and a rapidly aging population. A second group of countries have entered a full demographic transition with population growth rates between 1 and 2% and an average household size of 4.63. Countries in this second group will be approaching a 1% population growth rate in the 2020–2025 period. The shift will be more dramatic in Brazil and Mexico, which currently exhibit large young populations. Countries in this group also include Colombia, Peru, and Ecuador. Finally, a third group of countries show vigorous population growth and an average household size of 5.36 members.

The U.S. Latin population is also young. The median age of the Latin population is 24.8 years, much younger than that of the non-Latin population, which is 38.4 years. About 36% of the Latin population is 20 years old or less.[13] The average household size of the Latin population in the United States is 3.6 members. As mentioned earlier, the majority of the Latino households live in metropolitan areas. With this profile, the U.S. Latin market resembles that of Puerto Rico.

Smaller household units may restrict household buying power, as there are fewer members contributing to household income. Latin American nuclear families tend to pool their household income to share major household purchases such an automobile or a household appliance.[14] The aging population will penalize countries where the nuclear family size is shrinking. This impact is particularly severe among the poor since one of the strategies to cope with declining buying power is to send more family members, in many cases adolescents, to work. In other countries where pension systems are in place, pension funds of senior family members contribute 5 to 7% of household income in Uruguay and Argentina and 2% in Chile and Panama.[15] With the prospects of aging, multigenerational households will have to adapt their consumption patterns in the future. As the dynamics of transition work through the region, the market for services will boom and that of consumer goods will decline.

INCREASED CONCENTRATION OF BUYING POWER IN CITIES

Close to 70% of Latin American buying power is concentrated in 10 metropolitan areas. These markets have reached saturation because of the concentration of incumbent firms and the entry of new competitors as a result of market liberalization and deregulation. The second tier of cities in Latin America will represent the battleground for further growth. Understanding the process of urbanization and transformation of Latin American cities is essential for market planning.

The relentless process of migration to the cities continued unabated in the 1990s. Almost 75% of the population of the region live in cities.[16] There are 52 cities with populations of over 1 million inhabitants; Brazil alone has 13 cities with over 1 million inhabitants. As Table 2.2 indicates, about 80% or more of the population live in cities in Venezuela, Argentina, Chile, and Brazil. Furthermore, trade integration in North America through NAFTA and Mercosur has stimulated labor mobility and concentration of complementary industrial activity. As a result, increased urbanization has occurred along the U.S.–Mexican border and the border of Paraguay with Brazil in the Alto Parana.

Latin America's cities have always been not only magnets for people but also political, economic, and cultural centers in their respective countries. The concentration of buying power is quite apparent in the 10 largest markets in Latin America. The top 10 markets generate 69% of the total urban buying power in Latin America. Average household income in the top urban markets ranged from a low $8,192 in Rio de Janeiro to a very affluent $28,210 in Caracas and $30,959 in Mexico City. If one includes the next 10 largest metro markets in the region, the concentration increases to a whopping 83% of all urban buying power in the region.

The U.S. Latin market is also concentrated in a few geographic markets. California, Texas, and New York account for 62% of the total U.S. population of Latin origin or descent. In fact, 1.2 million Latinos, 36% of the Latin population, live in three large cities: Los

TABLE 2.2 Demographic Transformation in Latin America

POPULATION GROWTH

DEMOGRAPHIC TRANSFORMATION	COUNTRY	ANNUAL RATE POPULATION GROWTH, 1995–2000	AVERAGE HOUSEHOLD SIZE
Advanced transition	Puerto Rico	0.56	3.01
	Uruguay	0.70	3.36
	Argentina	1.26	0.78
	Chile	1.36	3.82
Full transition	Brazil	1.34	3.15
	Mexico	1.63	3.15
	Panama	1.64	4.00

URBANIZATION

LEVEL OF URBANIZATION	COUNTRY	PERCENT URBAN POPULATION, 2000
Highly urbanized	Uruguay	92.6
	Argentina	89.6
	Venezuela	87.4
	Chile	85.7
Somewhat urbanized	Brazil	79.9
	Mexico	75.4
	Puerto Rico	75.2

Dominican Republic	1.64	4.83
Peru	1.73	5.00
Ecuador	1.97	4.63
Colombia	1.87	5.65
Moderate transition		
Venezuela	2.02	???
El Salvador	2.04	3.94
Bolivia	2.33	6.57
Costa Rica	2.48	4.74
Paraguay	2.59	5.33
Guatemala	2.64	6.48
Nicaragua	2.73	5.32
Honduras	2.74	5.36

Peru	72.3
Colombia	74.5
Mostly rural	
Bolivia	64.6
Ecuador	62.7
Dominican Republic	60.2
Panama	57.6
Paraguay	56.1
Nicaragua	55.3
El Salvador	55.2
Costa Rica	50.4
Guatemala	39.4
Honduras	48.2

Source: Strategy Research Corporation, 2001 Latin American Market Planning Report.

Angeles, New York, and Miami. According to the Strategy Research Corporation, these three large metropolitan areas account for 38% of the $325 billion market power.[17]

Marketers noted attention to this concentration of market power and decided to penetrate these large urban markets first. The penetration of certain products is greater than the share of urban population alone would have suggested. One study found that the share of athletic shoes in major Latin American cities was 30%, which was in proportion with the share of the total population of these cities. The share of urban markets of particular brands, however, ranged from 17 to 46% suggesting that certain brands have not made any effort to penetrate secondary cities or rural markets.

Second-tier cities will represent the battlegrounds for further growth in the future. This challenge is quite clear to global and national discount and grocery stores that are now in the process of expansion to secondary cities after having spent the last 10 or 15 years building a market base in first-tier markets. Giant global retailers in Argentina are now expanding to secondary markets in the interior. After entering Argentina in 1982, Carrefour concentrated its effort in building presence in greater Buenos Aires. Without much competition locally or from other global retailers, Carrefour had ample time to plan its expansion. The entry of Wal-Mart in 1994 and emergence of a strong local competitor, Disco, changed the competitive landscape. In 1994, self-service stores accounted for 67% of all the store space in Buenos Aires and only 45% in the interior. Between 1994 and 1999, the rate of growth of self-service stores in the interior, however, surpassed that of Buenos Aires. In 1999, Wal-Mart entered the coveted Mendoza market. In the same year, Argentina's Disco acquired food chain stores in Cordoba, San Juan, and La Plata and concluded its acquisition of a national food chain, Ekono. In the short period of one year, Disco doubled its number of stores in Argentina. In the segment of food chain stores, retail space grew at the rate of 26.8% in the interior and the increase in Buenos Aires was 19.5%. With this rapid increase and given the small population base, food chain stores controlled 79% of all store space in the interior, a penetration that is still below the 86% control in Buenos Aires.[18]

DUAL-INCOME FAMILIES AND WOMEN AT WORK

The proportion of dual-income families in Latin America has been increasing. The massive incorporation of women into the workforce at all levels of the socioeconomic ladder changes the dynamics and provides additional income sources to the Latin American nuclear family. Working women have been a permanent feature among the Latin American poor. In recent times, women from all classes are in the workforce. More women at work will postpone or decrease family creation and thus reduce nuclear family size. Furthermore, working women contribute to household income.

Women make up approximately 30% of the workforce in Latin America.[19] The percentage of women of active age who are employed provides a better metric. A longitudinal study in the 1990–1997 period in urban labor markets of 12 Latin American countries by ECLA shows that women's participation in the labor force has increased steadily in the 1990s.[20] The levels of participation range from 35% in Brazil, 38% in Colombia, 34% in Venezuela, and 32% in Argentina (see Table 2.3). What is remarkable is that in all countries the percentage of working women has increased at all levels of household income. As expected, the percentage of the lowest income bracket in all countries is greater than that of other income brackets. In Colombia, for instance, 56% of women able to work are employed.[21] Although in many cases, the wages of these women are low, whatever they earn contributes to the household income.

Another impact of the changing role of women in Latin America is the rise of female-headed households. Factors affecting this trend include an increased divorce rate, the widespread use of consensual unions, and an increased level of widowhood due to political violence and crime. A survey of seven Latin American countries (Argentina, Brazil, Chile, Colombia, Mexico, Peru, and Venezuela) found that 24.6% of households were headed by a female.[22] The percentage reaches 31% in Colombia, which may be the result of this country's civil warfare. As expected, in lower socioeconomic brackets female-headed households reach 30% whereas in the most affluent bracket it is 14%. By age, the percentage is higher in the 45–54 age bracket and lowest in the youngest bracket, 19 years or younger.

PERSISTENT POOR INCOME DISTRIBUTION

The Latin American middle class has been losing its share of national income systematically in the last decade. Income distribution has been historically skewed in Latin America and remains unchanged over time. A study of long-term trends in inequality by the World Bank shows that inequality grew across the region from 1986 through 1989 and tapered off from 1989 to 1996.[23] Although earlier thinking indicated that policies designed to stimulate economic growth, such as market openness and macroeconomic stability would reduce inequality, this has not been the case. It has been

TABLE 2.3 Women in the Workforce and Income Inequality in Latin America

Women in the Workforce

Level and Growth of Women Participation	Country	Women in Labor Force (%)	Change in Participation, 1980–1998
High participation and growth	Uruguay	41	10
	Colombia	38	8
	El Salvador	36	9
	Brazil	35	7
	Nicaragua	35	7
	Venezuela	34	7
High participation, low growth	Bolivia	38	5
	Panama	35	5
	Chile	33	5
	Mexico	33	5
	Peru	31	7
Low participation, high growth	Costa Rica	31	10
	Argentina	32	4
	Honduras	31	6
Low participation, low growth	Paraguay	30	3
	Dominican Republic	30	5
	Guatemala	28	6

Income Inequality

Inequality Level	Country	Gini Index Level Inequality	Annual Change (%)
Bad, getting worse	Nicaragua	0.60	1.25
	Brazil	0.59	3.11
	El Salvador	0.56	3.55
Bad and stable	Bolivia	0.59	0.23
	Honduras	0.58	0.50
	Panama	0.57	0.38
	Ecuador	0.56	0.01
	Colombia	0.56	0.02
	Chile	0.56	0.44
Bad and improving	Paraguay	0.57	-2.74
Not as bad, deteriorating	Peru	0.50	1.47
	Venezuela	0.49	2.761
Not as bad and stable	Costa Rica	0.45	-0.05
	Uruguay	0.40	0.96

Source: World Bank, World Development Indicators 1999–2000; Miguel Szekely and M. Hilgert, The 1990s in Latin America: Another Decade of Persistent Inequality, Inter-American Development Bank, Dec. 1999.

documented that economic growth has reduced poverty, but inequality remains the same. Poverty levels in Latin America have dropped to 36% in 1997 from a high of 41% in 1990.[24] Furthermore, the drastic reduction of inflation in the region appears to have benefited the poor the most. Employment in the region grew faster among the poor and more affluent segments and less in the middle-income brackets between 1990 and 1996. In the same period, income grew faster only in the more affluent segment.[25]

Levels of inequality vary within the region. Inequality is worse in Brazil (see Table 2.3) and Bolivia and relatively less in Costa Rica and Uruguay.[26] In the 1990s, inequality increased sharply in El Salvador, Honduras, Nicaragua, Peru, and Venezuela, and slightly in Brazil, Panama, and Uruguay. In Mexico, Bolivia, Chile, Colombia, and Ecuador, inequality remained the same during the 1990s.[27] One clear result from trends in income distribution is the shrinking middle class. The middle class has been losing its share of total national income systematically throughout the 1990s. In Argentina, the share has declined to 21% in 1996 from 27.3% in 1992. A similar reduction is found in Venezuela, Peru, and Chile, where the shares declined to 21, 24.1, and 18% respectively, in 1996 from 27.3, 24.8, and 22.6% in 1992.[28]

An impoverished middle class and an increasingly affluent elite class challenge companies to develop differentiated marketing strategies for two- or three-tiered income-based market segments or to use a mass market approach. The level of differentiation depends on the income elasticity of a category of consumption. A study of share of consumption categories and income inequality in Mexico revealed important differences. The impact of price or tax increases on consumption categories could increase or decrease income inequality of the entire group. In this case, increased consumption of leisure activities, private transportation, communications, housing, and education were found to increase inequality of income distribution. Expenditures for clothing, cars, energy, tobacco, alcohol, water, and pasteurized milk beverages were inequality neutral, whereas expenditures for other food items, such as cereals, fruits, public transportation, oils, sugar, and flour, tend to decrease inequality. Here the implication is pervasive: The greater the consumption expenditures in the communications, culture, and education categories by certain groups of consumers, the greater the inequality. An unintended consequence of marketing strategies that target more affluent segments exclusively is the likelihood that they will increase income inequality.

SUMMING UP BUYING POWER

In Figure 2.1 we summarize the discussion so far. As the figure shows, the drivers will make certain countries more or less attractive. This is indicated by the area of the circle for each country that is proportional to its buying power. Another feature of this figure is the clustering of countries in terms of their similarities as drivers of consumer buying power. Using a diagonal that starts in the origin and ends in the uppermost right corner of Figure 2.1, three clusters can be determined. Argentina, Chile, Uruguay, and Puerto Rico form

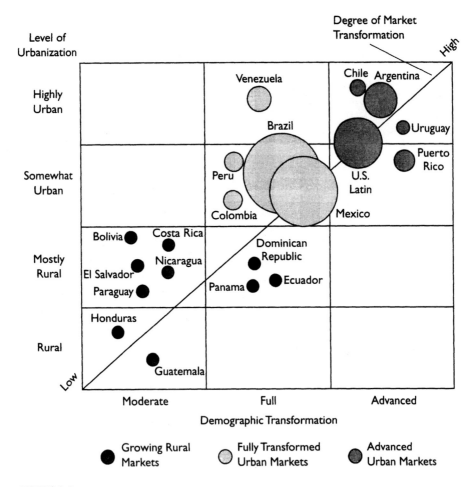

FIGURE 2.1
Latin Markets Clusters

the first cluster. The continental U.S. Latin market can also be grouped in this first cluster. This group of highly urbanized countries also exhibits a high level of demographic transformation. In terms of market size, this group is the second-largest market in the region. A second group that clusters in the center of the matrix consists of a large number of medium-sized countries and giant Brazil. This group has the greatest buying power in the region. Their populations are in full transition, and the levels of urbanization range from highly urban to somewhat rural. The last cluster is composed of small countries, mostly from Central America, and Paraguay. The populations are growing fast and are largely rural.

The clustering of countries in terms of main drivers of buying power may serve as a basis to develop country strategies along the lines of the three-cluster definitions described above. Clearly, consumer needs and expectations are different in each cluster. It is unlikely that one strategy will appeal to consumers in all clusters.

LATIN MARKET CONSUMPTION PATTERNS

HOUSEHOLD CONSUMPTION PATTERNS[29]

With about one-third of household budgets going to food consumption, the key to reaching Latin American consumers is through their stomachs. Food consumption styles reflect the rich mix of native and European, African, and Asian roots of Latin American societies. Although there are substantial differences among adult consumers, Latin American children exhibit remarkably similar consumer preferences. This group of younger consumers is being raised during a period of market liberalization and globalization. Their aspirations and consumption patterns are in sharp contrast with older generations.

Latin American household consumption patterns are typical of countries in the process of economic development. Table 2.4 shows that more than one-third of household budgets go to food consumption. Households in Peru, Argentina, and Mexico are the top three in allocation expenditures. In fact, if we combined food and clothing expenditures, households in these countries spend more than half of their budgets to cover these two basic needs.

The next two most important categories of consumption are housing and the combined transportation and telecommunications category. In the housing category, Chilean families allocated a larger percent of their household budget than any of the other Latin

TABLE 2.4 Urban Household Expenditures in Latin America (Percent)

CONSUMPTION CATEGORY	BRAZIL	MEXICO	ARGENTINA	VENEZUELA	CHILE	PERU	PUERTO RICO	URUGUAY	AVERAGE
Food	30	35	41	40	38	43	21	32	35.4
Clothing	9	7	9	7	8	9	8	7	7.7
Housing	11	12	11	11	14	7	12	12	11.1
Household furnishing	7	10	7	4	9	11	12	6	8
Health	6	4	6	3	4	7	14	6	6.2
Transportation	11	14	10	7	16	7	13	10	11.7
Education and leisure	5	8	5	5	8	8	3	4	5.3
Other	11	11	11	23	3	8	17	23	14.3
Total urban buying power	313.9	313.9	186.3	68.73	41.4	37.1	18.9	14.9	

Source: Strategy Research Corporation, Latin American Planning 2000–2001.

American countries featured in Table 2.4. With respect to transportation and telecommunications, households in Colombia, Chile, and Mexico top the rest of the countries. Since the category combines transportation and telecommunications, it is difficult to disaggregate them. In the case of telecommunications, it is more likely that an earlier and more profound liberalization of telecommunications markets in Chile and Mexico may have stimulated greater consumption of telecommunications services in these countries.

Household furnishings represent the next-largest category of household expenditures. Households in Peru, Mexico, and Puerto Rico spent more in these categories than do other countries in the region. Greater investments in household décor and appearance may result from cultural differences or higher prices. Health care represents about 6.2% of household allocation. Although vital for survival, this low percentage may suggest the lack of health insurance coverage in the region. Since basic health needs may go untreated in many cases, they will not have an impact on the household budget. Sadly, household expenditures in education receive the lowest budget allocation in Latin America. It is well known that education is a key factor in improving a person's ability to obtain employment and progress in society. Apparently, this message has not permeated the majority of households in the region. In sum, the analysis of budget allocation of Latin American families clearly shows a pattern typical of developing countries. Puerto Rico, and to a lesser extent Brazil, depart from this profile. The influence of the U.S. consumer culture and prices has developed a consumption pattern in Puerto Rico similar to that of the United States.

Consumption within a category reveals similarities or differences within a regional market. Some factors, such as income and relative prices, will have a generalized impact. Households in more affluent countries can afford more luxurious and pricier products purely because of greater buying power. Other factors, such as culture, climate, local food supplies, and degree of urbanization, also determine preferences for certain types of products. Given that food represents the bulk of household expenditures in Latin America, we decided to analyze in greater detail the particular preferences for diverse types of foods in a group of large and medium-sized countries. Another reason to focus on this consumption category is that food consumption is also an expression of a country's cultural heritage.

In Latin America, a rich stem of native and European traditions mixed with the diverse conditions of climate and geography produce a mosaic of food consumption styles. Modernization and globalization have introduced a variety of other factors that affect food consumption, such as less time for traditional home cooking. The blend of all these factors determines what is being consumed in Latin American markets. Our examination of food consumption levels per capita of several food categories in a set of large and medium-sized markets in Latin America reveals some interesting contrasts.

Argentina stands alone as a prime example of large dairy and meat intake. Given the rich and flat land that supports cattle raising, it is not a surprise to find that the level of dairy intake and meat consumption is higher than that of the United States. Argentina, together with Chile and Venezuela, are also part of the pasta culture, with levels of consumption that are 2.6 greater than other countries, such as Mexico, Colombia, and the United States. When it comes to the use of ready-to-eat breakfast cereals, Mexico is the only country in the region that stands out as a breakfast culture, with levels of consumption similar to that of the United States.[30] Working hours introduced by a flurry of U.S. industrial complexes may require a large intake at breakfast time and may be altering the traditional mealtimes during the day that are still prevalent in other Latin American countries. The impact of modernization is also apparent in the relatively higher levels of consumption of frozen foods in Brazil, Mexico, and Venezuela. Although the level of frozen food consumption is two-fifths of U.S. consumption, this food category is growing very fast, 206% in Brazil and 265% in Colombia between 1993 and 1996.[31]

In contrast to the differences explained above, Latin Americans are very similar when it comes to nonalcoholic beverage consumption. Mexicans have the largest beverage consumption per capita in Latin America, with an intake of 144 liters. Brazilians, Argentineans, and Colombians follow and to a lesser extent, but also high are Venezuelans and Chileans. Despite these high levels of consumption, Latin Americans reach only about one-third of the U.S. consumption per capita. Another similarity among Latin American consumers can be detected through an analysis of what they do not consume. Latin Americans are not consumers of snacks, whether salty or sweet, nor are they tea drinkers.

A low consumption level is not necessarily an indicator of an unattractive market. It may be that societal changes may also drive changes in a given category. This is the case of snack foods in Latin America. As mentioned before, greater urbanization, two-income households, increased commuting time, and legendary poor urban transportation systems in most large Latin American cities are fueling an increased growth in snack consumption. A recent study showed that Latin American snack markets are growing at three to four times the U.S. growth. The increasing importance of discount retailers, convenience stores, and supermarkets are also driving sales of snacks. Firms such as Frito-Lay and Nabisco are reporting record sales growth in Latin America.[32]

Some of the differences in food consumption may be blurred when one looks at food consumption preferences by age or income levels. A study of food consumption by Latin American children between the ages of 7 and 11 showed similar patterns of consumption across countries. This study revealed that the top five food categories in this group were rice, chicken, bread, potatoes, and eggs. The smallest food categories in Latin American children's diet were vegetables, beans, and corn.[33]

In sum, when it comes to food, Latin America is hardly homogeneous. A variety of food consumption styles have emerged for a variety of reasons. Food marketers have learned to make adaptations.

COPING WITH ECONOMIC CYCLES

As was mentioned earlier, lower inflation and economic growth in the early 1990s brought to the market first-time buyers of a range of household goods and durables. Many Latin American consumers bought their first car, refrigerator, or washing machine. Business journal headlines were quick to point out this trend with titles such as "Latin America: the big move to free markets."[34] For some countries, such as Mexico, the boom did not last long. The *Wall Street Journal* carried the story with the title "Peso crisis threatens the Mexican Dream."[35] Other Latin American markets weathered the Mexican crisis and continued or began their own cycles of market growth. In 1998, *BusinessWeek* reported that millions of young, hip consumers in Latin America were on a shopping spree and the multinationals started a race to grab their attention.[36]

If during times of growth, everyone wins, when economies contract, not everyone loses, and no one country adjusts to economic cycles in the same way. Although economic crises are not new to Latin America, previous crises had longer cycles and adjustments, and consumers lost buying power gradually over a long period. The decade of the 1980s is a good example of long-term deterioration of standards of living throughout the region. The crisis of the 1990s was different. One major difference is that market recessions occurred in the context of market economies. Interest rates for consumer credit doubled to 43% in Brazil in 1999.[37] Older generations of Latin Americans were unable to apply their past experience to the new context. For younger generations of Latin Americans, these crises were their first.

In coping with recession, Latin American consumers used some strategies that were similar throughout the region and others that were unique to their situation. The common strategies were as follows:

1. *Avoid or postpone long-term obligations.* Many Latin American households canceled plans to buy cars, household appliances, and frills such as family vacations.

2. *Renegotiate or cancel consumer credit.* Latin American consumers unable to service high payments for household goods or cars bought on credit returned the goods or declared themselves insolvent. Whether initiated by the credit holder or the lender, credit card penetration also declined in 1999.

3. *Change the consumption basket.* Latin American consumers made reallocations of the consumption mix. In most cases, expenditures of basic commodities increased. Changes in other consumption categories, however, changed with the country and the culture. An analysis of changes of volume of sales between 1998 and 1999 in Argentina, Brazil, and Chile shows remarkable similarities in the top main categories of adjustment and large differences in others. Health concerns account for categories with the largest increases: infant formulas in Argentina, mineral water in Brazil, and natural juices in Chile. Another category where volume of sales increased consistently in all countries is hair colorants. Local market observers suggest that in the midst of bad times, Argentineans want to look good and invest in themselves.[38] For the remaining categories, each country is unique. The largest declines were different in each country. In Brazil, the largest decline was in shaving kits. In Argentina, cookies had the largest decline, whereas in Chile liquid insecticides were the top category of decline.

4. *Change shopping habits.* Latin American consumers increased their patronage of self-service, discount stores, and large hypermarkets. The increased use coincided with the entry of discount retailers to the region and the entry of local retailers to the discount format. Discount retailers introduced to Latin markets the concept of private brands and promoted secondary brands and generic products. All of a sudden, Latin American consumers had more product

choice and were able to compare a range of product–quality options. It was inevitable that this segment of the market would grab a substantial share.[39]

5. *Search for a better quality-to-price ratio.* Whereas in the past, Latin American consumers flocked to low-priced products, our analysis of consumption patterns in the region during the crises suggests that Latin American consumers did not want to sacrifice quality. Price alone was not a determinant factor influencing product choice. A study of attitudes toward shopping styles in Colombia revealed generalized disagreement with the statement of buying unknown brands just to save money. According to the study, loyal brand shoppers were found in only one of four shopping styles identified. The other segments were made up of consumers actively seeking alternative brands, looking for promotions and offers or with no specific style at all.[40] A similar study in Argentina found that 25% of consumers were not interested in buying unknown brands to save money.[41] Another study in Argentina showed that the percent of consumers who preferred only branded products declined to 22% in 2000 from 46% in 1998. Self-service grocery stores and discount retailers seized this opportunity and filled their shelves with their private and store brands with attractive packaging and prices 30 to 40% lower than premium brands. As a result, discount stores such as France's Carrefour and Argentina's Disco grew rapidly. Good-quality local brands, not positioned as premium, also increased sales. An additional attraction of shopping in discount stores is access to store credit. In fact, store credit cards seem to be replacing bank credit cards.

Overall, Latin American consumers have drastically adjusted their consumption and shopping habits in a very short period. The more remarkable trend in adjustment to the ups and downs of the economy is the Latin American consumer's search for value. Latin American consumers are becoming more rational and constantly explore price–quality options. Greater product and shopping alternatives have provided more options than those available to other generations in the past.

Companies that position their offerings in terms of value will be the winners. A holistic approach to consumer value, such as one-stop, reasonable credit access, reasonable prices, and good-enough quality, seems to be the right mix for Latin America. The challenge for premium brands is to justify their premium position in Latin America. If not, the only strategy is to reduce the premium difference relative to private and B-brands. The following examples illustrate how some companies have adapted to this new market environment.

Coca-Cola has felt the brunt of an increase in alternative colas and soft drinks in the region. For example, more than 200 soft-drink brands dispute the $3.1 billion Argentinean market, with B-brands accounting for almost one-fourth of the market. In a price lineup, where premium brands such as Coke sell for $1 for 1½ liters, medium-priced brands operate in the range $0.64 to 0.75. Low-priced brands that are based primarily on artificial colorants and sugar sell for less than $0.60 for 2-liter bottles. Coca-Cola introduced Tai, a fruit-based clear cola, in Brazil and Argentina primarily to challenge the low-priced brands. In Argentina, Coca-Cola set up an introductory price of $0.75 and quickly had to lower it to $0.48 to remain competitive. Tai has been able to secure 0.4% of the market. France's Carrefour has also decided to protect its house brand with the introduction of a low-priced product line, Sí, that covers about 500 different categories. This brand is 30% lower in price than Carrefour's own private brands and 40% less than the premium brands. The introduction of the low-priced brand strategy is Carrefour's response to pressure from low-priced brands not only in Latin America but also in other parts of the world. On the other hand Unilever has been successful in defending its brands' position in Argentina against low-priced detergents through a strategy of innovation and multiple brands with distinct but different positions. Argentinean consumers are said to be worried about the performance of low-priced detergents. They fear that cheap brands may ruin their garments. As mentioned before, Argentineans do not compromise their personal appearance.[42]

SEGMENTING THE LATIN MARKET

Consumer markets are a reflection of society. Latin American society is complex and fragmented. One way to reduce complexity is market segmentation. For many years, marketers have relied on the socioeconomic segmentation of Latin American markets to formulate differentiated marketing strategies and targeted their products for affluent and lower-class segments. With a fickle middle class and blurring distinctions of income-based segments, this conventional strategy is no longer effective. New definitions and different market segmentation are becoming the norm.

THE CONVENTIONAL APPROACH: SOCIOECONOMIC SEGMENTATION

In more advanced countries where reliable household or personal income data exist, segments based on income are highly robust. In emerging markets such as those in Latin America, a classification based purely on income is suspect.[43] National organizations and marketing institutions in Latin American use additional variables that measure other indicators of social class, such as education of the head of the household, occupation, possession of household goods, and housing characteristics. Using a scoring system where points are allocated by possession of those characteristics, households are classified typically into social-class categories. The Gallup organization, for instance, uses five categories: (1) upper class, (2) emerging elite, (3) middle class, (4) working class, and (5) extreme poverty.[44] The Strategy Research Corporation uses other terms for social-class segments: (A) upper class, (B) middle-to-upper class, (C) middle class, and (D) subsistence or poverty levels. National organizations in Latin America use different scoring systems and weights to define basically the same segments, making comparison of information across countries rather difficult. Other organizations, such as Gallup or Roper Starch, have used common definitions when conducting pan-regional surveys.

The upper class represents on average about 2.3% of all Latin American households, ranging from a low of 0.9% in Nicaragua to a high of 7.2% in Uruguay. Given the small percentage of upper-class households in Latin America, it makes sense to treat the A and B classes as the high-end market, C as the true middle class, and D and E as the lower-income class. Given Latin America's unequal distribution as discussed previously, buying power is concentrated in the upper classes, making these segments very attractive for high-end marketers. As Table 2.5 indicates, the highest concentration of buying power in urban markets is found in Venezuela. In this country, 5.3% of the urban households are in the upper-upper-middle class and they account for 40% of the total urban buying power in that country. Other countries exhibit similar degrees of buying power concentration in the upper-class segment. For instance, in Brazil, 18.6% of urban families in the A and B class account for 63% of the urban buying power in that country.

TABLE 2.5 Total Buying Power by Socioeconomic Class in Latin American Urban Markets

Country		Urban Households (millions)	Urban Buying Power ($ billions)	Socioeconomic Class				
				Upper Class	Upper– Middle Class	Middle Class	Low– Poor Class
Argentina		8.9	186.3				
	% households			1.6	8.3	35.4	54.7
	% buying power			13	22	29	36
Brazil		43.3	354.7				
	% households			2.6	16.0	28.9	52.5
	% buying power			29	34	26	11
Chile		3.4	41.5				
	% households			2.1	6.2	41.8	49.9
	% buying power			19	23	46	12
Colombia		5.6	47.7				
	% households			2.2	7.7	37.1	53.0
	% buying power			24	32	34	10

Mexico	% households	14.4	1.5	10.9	22.4	65.2
	% buying power	313.9	19	33	29	19
Peru	% households	3.7	2.5	8.2	32.9	56.4
	% buying power	37.1	23	35	34	8
Venezuela	% households	4.1	1.1	4.2	20.1	74.6
	% buying power	68.7	15	25	43	17
Latin America	% households	93.2	2.2	12.4	29.6	55.8
	% buying power	730	19.6	26.0	37.8	16.5

Source: Strategy Research Corporation, 2001 Latin American Market Research Report.

The middle class is attractive because it represents the base for mass markets in many countries. This class includes small-business owners, skilled workers, and clerical professionals with at least a primary school education. Mobility in this segment is high, as people can move up or down as a result of the booms and busts in the economy. In Latin America, Chile is the only country with a relatively large number of households in the middle-class segment, which also accounts for a large percentage of buying power. However, the share of buying power of the middle class has been declining or stagnant in recent years as a result of economic crisis and other factors discussed before. Analysis by the Strategy Research Corporation of the impact of Mexican peso devaluation showed that the percentage of households classified as middle class changed to 36.9% in 1996 from levels of 58% in 1994. In 2000, the percentage of middle class in Mexico stands at only 22.4%. Clearly, many middle-class families have moved lower on the income ladder.

The average buying power of households in different socioeconomic segments is naturally an indication of the ability to consume. Upper-class Mexican households have the highest income level in Latin America, followed closely by the Venezuelans. Households in these two countries have incomes more than 2.5 times the average income of Latin American households in this class. There are perils in classifying households in class segments based on income alone. If income were the only indicator, Argentinean poor households could be classified as middle class in most other Latin American countries except Mexico and Venezuela.

An analysis of household buying power in the top 10 metro markets provides a closer look.[45] Upper-class households in three Mexican cities—Mexico D.F., Guadalajara, and Monterrey—and in Caracas, Venezuela are the most affluent in Latin America. Their average annual buying power, not income, give these households a buying power equal to upper-class households in most cities worldwide. Affluence is relative, as exhibited by upper-class households in Rio de Janeiro with only about one-fourth of the buying power of their counterparts in Mexico City. Upper-middle-class households in Caracas have a very reasonable average annual buying power of $134,000. At the other extreme, poor households in Rio de Janeiro, Lima–Callao, and Brasília are the poorest of the top 10 metro markets.

Our analysis of socioeconomic segments in Latin America shows the market divide of affluent and poor mass markets in the region. The conventional approach in dealing with this market dichotomy is to differentiate the marketing offering in terms of high end, high price or basic product, low price. There is, however, an alternative approach to positioning the offering right in the middle with a price-to-value ratio that is right for all socioeconomic classes. This strategy is based on attracting enough consumers from both ends of the middle class. For the affluent classes, the product quality should be good enough to be acceptable and at the same time enjoy the benefit of price savings. For the lower middle class, the price gap relative to the premium product would be narrow enough to justify trading to a better-quality product. Our discussion of private brands and good-quality B-brands before showed that this strategy is very appealing in Latin American markets.

OTHER SEGMENTATION APPROACHES

Definitions of social classes based on possession alone are not enough to understand or highlight consumer differences among classes. Greater penetration of household goods, such as color television or telephone, across socioeconomic segments is blurring the distinction among classes despite income differences. Thus, other segmentation approaches are being used to address these differences. The J. Walter Thompson group advocates the use of two simple indicators, education and profession, to define social classes. Under this classification, the upper class includes owners and top executives of large firms with college degrees. The upper middle class is composed of executives and owners of firms with some college education but without a college degree. In the middle class, J. Walter Thompson places middle-level professionals, employees, public servants, skilled labor, and small business owners. Members of this group would have either a high school education or hold some vocational certification, but not a college degree. The lower group is made up of unskilled workers and entry-level employees with up to a high school education. The lowest level consists of people without permanent employment, with some level of primary education or none. Based on this classification, the J. Walter Thompson analysis of Chile found that 4% of the Chilean society could be grouped as upper class, 10% as upper-middle class, 38% as middle class, 38% as lower class, and 10% as poor.[46] The new definitions of social classes for Chile offer an interesting contrast to the conventional classification. The upper-class segment under the new definition is twice as large as the old one. The upper class and upper-middle class combined under the new definition is greater and more in line with the average for the region. Also, the new classification puts the middle class in Chile in line with that of other Latin American countries. In other words, the middle class in Chile was overestimated. The implication of the definition of socioeconomic classes as presented by J. Walter Thompson may be a better indicator of differences in consumption habits and styles. This classification may be more useful for marketers in formulating their marketing strategies in Latin America.

Another market segmentation approach is based on grouping consumers by their activities, interests, and opinions to come up with lifestyle segments. Audits & Surveys Worldwide performed such a study of Latin American consumers and found five distinct groups. A first group, labeled image seekers, was composed of teenagers living at home, who are current with styles and fashions and willing to try something new. A second group consisted of curious cosmopolitans, who are college students, with a variety of interests, wishing to visit new places and learn about other cultures. A third group, labeled global professionals, included males 18–34, college educated, affluent, from the A or B socioeconomic class, willing to pay for good-quality brand names. The fourth group consisted of concerned traditionalists, age 35–54, married with family, concerned about the cost of products, worried about job loss, concerned with the environment, preferring national products, and not up-to-date on technology. The last group included people age 50 or over, married with family, of lower socioeconomic class, preferring to watch television and not interested in new things.[47]

The groups based on lifestyles as described by Audits & Surveys Worldwide seem to follow the life-cycle stages of people over time. The market needs of households shift with age-based changes. Brazil's opinion firm IBOPE uses this approach to segment the Brazilian market. Seven different life-stage segments span youth to empty nest. Table 2.6 shows the % of Brazilian households in each stage as well as the changes in their shares from 1994 to 2000. IBOPE's study shows significant differences in consumption levels across a range of consumer categories. Using an index of use relative to the average national consumption, IBOPE's analysis found differences in relative consumption of beverages, milk, snacks, and types of toothpaste.[48]

Another study of lifestyle segments in Peru illustrates the use of this approach. In this case, nine lifestyle segments were proposed. The segments and their relative share of the Peruvian population were as follows: economizers (20.5%), traditional (18.1%), progressive (17.6%), survivors (16%), adapters (8.2%), workers (10.5%), fortunate (4.2%), entrepreneurs (2.8%), and hedonists (2.1%). According to the study, Peruvian society is highly fragmented into

TABLE 2.6 Life-Cycle Segments in Brazil (Percent of Households)

LIFE-CYCLE SEGMENT	1994	1997	2000
Single (up to 39 years old)	5	5	5
Married with children 6 years or younger	22	20	19
Married with children 7–12 years	23	22	19
Married with children 13–17 years	10	12	13
Married with children 17 years or older living at home	12	12	15
Empty nest	15	16	17
Single seniors	13	13	13

Source: IBOPE, Brazil's Latin Panel 2001.

many groups, each with their particular strategy to cope with the volatility and hardships that Peruvian society has experienced during several decades. These lifestyle groups exhibit significant differences in buying power and media habits and cut across socioeconomic levels. For instance, people that fit the progressive style, characterized by a high-achievement motivation, work ethic, and emphasis on education, come from upper class (4.9%), middle class (11.8%), lower class (40.7%), and poor (42.6%).[49]

Segmentation of the U.S. Latin population is based on basic descriptors such as generation level, levels of acculturation, and country of origin. The generation level breaks the population into two large groups, which include those not born in the United States and U.S.-born. Among the second group, a further refinement classifies the population in number of generations. According to the Strategy Research Corporation (SRC), 72% of Latinos in the United States were not born in the United States, 14% were first generation, 5% second generation, and 9% third generation. SRC's study reports different patterns of household product penetrations between U.S.-born Latins and those who emigrated to the United States. The main differences were in the possession of connectivity devices such as cellular phones, Internet access, or PCs. The U.S.-born Latins exhibit levels no different from those of the larger non-Latin population, whereas those that emigrated had much lower levels.[50]

Levels of acculturation define the extent to which Latins view themselves as being part of the mainstream U.S. culture. Acculturation can be measured by a number of indicators, such as language preference in daily activities and the extent of education achieved in the United States. The SRC study found that 11% of U.S. Latins were highly acculturated, 64% were partly acculturated, and 25% were unacculturated. Moreover, SRC analysis of household product use by level of acculturation revealed significant differences in standard of living, measured by the type of possession between the unacculturated group and the other two. The acculturated groups have achieved levels of penetration of products such as automobiles, cable, cellular phone, or credit card penetration close to the average U.S. household. There was clearly a product, digital (connectivity), and financial (credit card) divide between the group of unacculturated Latins and the more acculturated ones.

Finally, U.S. Latin markets can be segmented by the country of origin of their population. By country of origin, Latinos of Mexican background account for 63.3%, Central and South Americans for 15%, Puerto Ricans for 10.5%, and Cubans about 5%.

SUMMING UP SEGMENTATION

Our discussion above suggests that there are many ways to identify market segments. One conclusion is clear—the use of socioeconomic class as a basis for segmentation does not provide a full picture of the Latin American market reality. A better solution is to layer several approaches and find one or a combination of ways that correspond best to the type of business or consumer category that one is analyzing. The prism or view of the market could be a combination of life-cycle segments and socioeconomic classes or any other combination. Market success may depend on seeing opportunities for positioning and segmentation where others see only threats.

Another complication in making sense of Latin American market segments is whether the segments are pan-regional or national. Segments based on universal bases such as life-cycle segments can be found in any country. The proportion and characteristics may vary, but the definition of the segments is invariable. On the other hand, lifestyle segments may be nation-specific; the context that supports lifestyles is unique to each country and market culture. As the Peruvian example shows, the particular lifestyles may be a reflection of coping with a harsh environment. Peruvians have learned particular styles to cope with their volatile economy and difficult macroenvironment, but Peruvian lifestyles may not transfer well into other environments.

One strategy to simplify the complexity of segments and market contexts in Latin America is to use a nesting approach. The nesting approach should move from the general to the specific. For instance, in a first level of analysis, a socioeconomic approach is used to determine a high level strategy for socioeconomic classes. At a second level, strategies can be based on life-cycle segments. At a third level, lifestyles are investigated to determine the positioning and offering for one or several segments within a given country.

CONNECTIVITY IN LATIN AMERICA

To reach Latin American markets it is necessary to analyze their patterns of media use and connectivity platforms. New technologies and deregulation have invigorated and attracted new players to the media and telecommunications sectors. In most cases, the telecommunications infrastructure has been expanded and modernized, providing more and better connectivity. As a result, firms have many more channels to reach Latin American consumers. For many, the creation of a regional village is in the making. In this section we explore the level of penetration of telecommunications and media, both new and traditional.

THE TRADITIONAL CHANNELS

Telephone Connectivity. Telecommunications has been one of the first sectors to become privatized and deregulated. The privatization process, however, has not been the same or contemporaneous. The approach has been different in every country and thus resulted in a variety of industry compositions. In some countries, such as Mexico, the plan created a private monopoly for a set period of time. In others, such as Argentina, the plan created a duopoly of nonoverlapping territories. During the early part of the privatization process, the telecommunication provider focused on building and modernization of the network. This process that in most cases started in the early 1990s resulted in increased access. By 1998, early and aggressive reformers, Argentina, Chile, Venezuela, and Colombia, achieved household penetration levels of more than half of households.

In several cases, the monopoly status of the first stage of privatization has ended and the sector has been open to free competition, such as in Argentina, Brazil, Chile, Mexico, and Peru. Price competition and the introduction of new services characterized this second phase. New markets, such as wireless telephony and Internet access, became the focus of a renewed round of market dynamics. License auctions for wireless telephony attracted a number of operators willing to invest in building the networks. In contrast to the experience of advanced countries, where wireless is a complement or a second line to many households, wireless became the only option for Latin American households that could not afford the wired service installation fee or were outside the main network reach (rural or marginal metropolitan areas). The surge in demand propelled wireless services to reach compound annual growth rate levels of 45% whereas the wired alternative increased at only 11% during the late 1990s. With a lower investment per line in infrastructure, the wireless network grew quickly to meet the growing demand. Furthermore, in an open and competitive market with several operators, the cost of subscribing and use decline, making wireless more affordable. The adoption of calling-party-pays resulted in an increased use of the service.

Another reason for the popularity of wireless services can be traced to the changes in lifestyles and family structure in Latin America. As mentioned earlier, Latin American families are working more and leading more hurried and complex lives to cope with economic crisis and uncertainty. Cellular telephones suit these modern lifestyles well and provide the needed connectivity to other family members. At the end of 2001, there were 58 million cellular telephone subscribers in Latin America. In countries with competition and more modernized lifestyles, such as Chile, the number of cellular subscribers have surpassed that of fixed-line phones. By the end of 2001, Chile's cellular subscribers were projected to be 4.37 million, in contrast to 3.65 fixed-line subscribers. The process will repeat itself in several Latin American countries. Wireless subscribers will equal or surpass line subscribers in Mexico and Brazil in 2001 and in Argentina by 2006.[51]

Television. Television is the principal source of information and entertainment in Latin America. The average Latin American household watches 4.87 hours of television per day. The size and passion of this captive audience has given birth to powerful media groups such as Brazil's Globo, Mexico's Televisa, and Venezuela's Cisneros Group TV Broadcasting Venevision. These groups have been very successful in capturing TV audiences with local programming. The telenovela is perhaps the most important program genre, which on the average attracts one-third of the audience on any given day in Latin America.[52] The popularity of these programs sometimes reaches the entire region and a few cross-cultural boundaries, and they have become export icons of Latin American culture.

With almost universal television penetration, Latin American families are becoming two-or-more-TV-set households. In Chile and Brazil, more than half of the households have two or more television sets. A household of multiple sets is an indication not only of increased affluence but of a variety of viewing preferences within the household. Latin Americans watch TV mostly for entertainment and movies. On the average, Latin Americans devoted 41% of their viewing time to these programming genres. At one extreme, more than half of Mexicans viewing time is given to entertainment and movie watching; at the other, Colombians allocate 31%. Programs for children, news, and international programs followed in terms of viewing preferences. Surprisingly, sports, music, and family programming received the least amount of viewing time.

Although the average profile provides an initial picture of TV viewing habits in Latin America, we note that there are substantial differences across countries. Chilean audiences, for instance, prefer movies to any other program, Mexicans prefer comedy programs, Colombians are more interested in international programs, and Venezuelans prefer programs for children. In addition to differences in viewing preferences, other cultural factors impede the creation of regional Latin American content. The differences appear not only at the national level but also at the city level within a country. At the national level we would imagine it is not possible to create content that would appeal to the entire region. For instance, as to sports programs, Argentineans, Mexicans, and Brazilians have a passion for soccer, but Venezuelans, Panamanians, and Puerto Ricans prefer baseball. Even within given sport categories, some versions of a sport attract regional viewing, whereas others do not. Brazilian soccer tends to travel well, but Mexican soccer is difficult to promote. A mix of local accents and the use of local slang prevent the regionalization of certain programs, such as comedy and music. Within a country, regional differences are also marked and important. For instance, viewing habits and preferences are different in São Paulo and Rio de Janeiro in Brazil, Bogotá and Cali in Colombia, and Mexico City and Monterrey in Mexico. Thus, the only potential for some regional content remains in areas of common interest and where some of the national and local differences can be standardized. One can thus explain the regional acceptance of relatively standardized programs such as CNN or MTV Latina. These genres, however, do not attract most Latin American audiences. On the average, the two combined account for 16% of viewing time.[53]

Multichannel television has been gaining ground in Latin America. Multichannel includes such alternatives to traditional broadcast TV as wired cable TV, direct-to-home TV (satellite), small master antenna TV (SMATV), and multipoint distribution services (MMDS). The large potential regional audience and the opening of the market through licenses have attracted investors and operators to the region. In the period of 1994–1998, multichannel TV grew at the rate of 34%. By far the most popular platform has been wired cable. Some of the reasons for the popularity of cable TV include the mature technology, more predictable network expansion to wired households, and in some cases a very transparent regulatory framework.[54] With greater flexibility as to where to build the network, cable TV has focused mostly in urban and affluent neighborhoods. In countries with more favorable conditions regarding these factors, multichannel and, specifically, cable TV exhibit higher levels of penetration. Multichannel penetration reaches 67% of households in Argentina and 50% in Mexico. Levels of penetration in these countries are comparable to those in more industrialized countries. With technological developments, cable TV becomes an important conduit to other forms of telecommunications, such as telephony and Internet access. Obviously, cable TV companies may eventually become powerful rivals to traditional telecommunication operators that provide the same services.

CONNECTIVITY BY SOCIAL ECONOMIC CLASS

The improvement in connectivity has been felt more dramatically in the middle and lower classes. Between the period of 1994–1998, wired telephones and multichannel subscriptions increased by a factor of 1.5 in the middle class. In contrast, by 1994 almost all of the upper class and the majority of the high middle class had already reached universal access to wired telephones, and multichannel subscriptions increased by a factor of 1.18 in 1998.[55] As a result, by 1998, wired telephone penetration was high in upper and upper-middle classes across the region, had reached more than half of the middle class, and remained low in the lower classes. Despite these figures for the lower class, it is interesting to note that more than one-fourth had telephones in Colombia and Venezuela.

Being a relatively new service, wireless penetration has not reached the same levels as wired telephony. By 1998, only Venezuela and Argentina exhibited greater levels of penetration in the middle- to upper-class segments. In the remainder of the countries, wireless seemed to be an upper-class platform for connectivity (see Table 2.7).

Internet access is perhaps in its infancy in Latin America but is growing faster than any other platform.[56] At this early stage of adoption in Latin America, Internet access is mostly through computer dial-up services. To a large extent, access to Internet depends on access to computers at home, work, or school. Computer ownership is relatively high in Argentina, Brazil, and Venezuela. As connectivity and other platforms increase in the region, we would expect that Internet household penetration would accelerate at a faster rate. Our analysis of Internet penetration by social classes confirms the same digital divide that has been found in other regions. Given the important role that this medium will have in the future, we turn our attention next to the evolution of the Internet in Latin America.

INTERNET CONNECTIVITY IN LATIN MARKETS[57]

Relative to the average U.S. level of Internet access of about 42%, Latin households in the United States are quite far behind, at only 24%.[58] The Latin Internet user prefers to navigate on English language sites and does not frequent Spanish-only Internet sites. Firms targeting the U.S. Latin market, however, believe that it is important to offer bilingual options. Chase Bank, for instance, has created a separate BancoChase.com site for this segment, with bilingual information, applications, and customer service for their financial products and services. Bilingual language capabilities also extend to other platforms, such as automated teller machines (ATMs), call centers, and direct marketing programs.[59]

Internet use in Latin America is still the domain of the affluent social classes. Internet penetration in this region is expected to grow significantly during the next several years, at a compound annual growth rate of 47%. Factors driving this growth are a young, techno-savvy population, high television penetration, increasing telephony capacity, especially in the wireless area, reduced or free Internet access charges, and reduced cost of personal computers.[60] Estimates of total Internet users vary widely. IDC puts the number at 15 million in 2000 and forecasts that more than 75 million will have access by 2005.[61] Credit Suisse estimates the population of online users in Latin America at 16 million and growing at a compound annual growth rate of 39%.[62] According to Jupiter Research, Latin American Internet users will increase from 21 million in 2000 to 77 million in 2005.[63] Morgan Stanley Dean Witter estimates that home users cur-

TABLE 2.7 Latin American Connectivity by Social Class (Percent of Households)

COUNTRY	WIRED TELEPHONES				WIRELESS TELEPHONES				MULTICHANNEL				INTERNET ACCESS			
	A	B	C	D	A	B	C	D	A	B	C	D	A	B	C	D
Argentina	97	87	46	4	23	18	13	0	89	80	66	37	14	1	0	0
Brazil	99	90	47	4	22	12	6	1.7	32	10	7	3	13	2	0.2	0.1
Chile	94	91	62	9	19	3	1	0.6	71	48	33	15	7	3.2	0	0.1
Colombia	92	90	87	37	25	8	3	0	78	71	53	35	18	3.5	1.4	0
Mexico	96	80	51	6	8	4	3	0	52	25	17	3	12	3.4	0.2	0
Venezuela	90	92	69	19	54	26	14	1.5	51	30	11	2	14	1	0.1	0
Total Latin America	97	89	55	9	22	11	7	0.9	51	32	23	7	13	2.2	0.3	0

Source: Audits & Surveys, Telecommunications in Latin America, 1999.

rently account for 37% of total Internet use in Latin America.[64] The Internet will not be able to develop any faster in other segments because of limited disposable income and purchasing power, as well as low telephone, personal computer, and cable television penetration.

Internet users in Latin America fall into four clusters: infrequent users who access the Internet for informational purposes, heavy business users who access for business-related information, home users who visit for information and entertainment purposes, and affluent teenage students, who visit chat rooms to converse with their friends.[65] The fourth cluster, affluent teens, use the Internet primarily to chat and is more evenly split between males and females: 56% to 44%, suggesting that Internet use by men and women will even out in the near future. The two primary groups are young professional males in their 20s and 30s, "cosmopolitans," who use the Internet primarily to read online publications, and students in their teens and 20s who use the Internet to chat.

When they go online, the majority of Internet users in Latin America read online newspapers or magazines (44%), visit government or educational institution Web sites (37%), or visit news or sports sites (32%).[66] The typical Latin American Internet shopper is a male in his late 20s (74%). The majority of shoppers state that saving time is their principal reason for shopping over the Internet, followed by the ability to buy a product not available in stores, better prices and brands, and increased product information. The top five items purchased via the Internet are software, books, music, magazine subscriptions, and accessories for personal computers.[67]

Latin American Internet users are increasing their time spent on the Internet, up to 10.4 hours each week in 2000 up from 8.2 hours per week in 1998. They are also trying to keep up with the latest technology. 50% of home Internet users have connections at speeds of 56 kbps or faster, which is the standard in the United States, an increase of 33% from 1998. Although the majority of Internet users in Latin America connect via dial-up access, 13% have access via a mobile device, and 65% would like to be able to connect to the Internet via cellular telephone or pager. Only 10% access the Internet by Web television, although 67% would like to do so if it were an option.[68]

E-commerce transactions are expected to increase at a compound annual growth rate of 117%, according to IDC estimates. Business-to-consumer (B2C) estimates for Latin America in 2000 put projected spending at $226 million and business-to-business (B2B) spending at $645 million.[69] According to another source, Forrester Research, the Latin American Internet economy will be powered by business-to-business transactions. By 2004, B2B will account for 93% of the total, or $76 billion.[70] E-commerce in Latin America is limited by low credit card penetration, inefficient postal systems which require the use of expensive third-party delivery services, lack of a customer service culture, high taxes and customs duties, and privacy and security concerns.

Competition among Internet service providers (ISPs) is fierce. Average monthly rates have plummeted and free Internet access is common. Banco Bradesco, Brazil's leading retail bank, began offering its customers up to 20 hours of free access in December 1999, signing up to 2,000 Internet accounts per day and jolting major retail banks in the region to do the same or at least to offer online banking services.[71] Several ISPs quickly followed suit, including Internet-Gratis, BRFree, Super11, Netgratuita, and Catolico (sponsored by the Catholic Church). Universo Online began a free service in addition to its pay service in Brazil; and Terra Networks began to offer free services regionally. The crash of the tech boom has ended the free service option, and most ISPs are now shifting to subscription bases.

Given the high telecommunications costs in the region, free Internet access in Latin America is important to growth of the Latin American Internet. With metered calls, Latin American Internet users pay for the local telephone call as well as per minute Internet access. In Mexico, users pay per local call, whereas in Argentina and Mexico, users pay by the minute. This adds up to $3 in Mexico, $9 in Brazil, and $17 in Argentina of monthly use costs, to the $26, $21, and $36 Internet access costs, respectively.[72] The three largest online markets, Argentina, Brazil, and Mexico, account for close to 80% of all users in Latin America.

LATIN MARKETS IN THE TWENTY-FIRST CENTURY

Latin markets at present are complex, fragmented, and fluid. In this chapter we have described how global financial shocks, demographic shifts, and technology are altering the social fabric and consumer markets in Latin America. Although the Latin nuclear family is becoming smaller, urban, multigenerational, and older, it still represents the center of social and consumption activity. All members of the nuclear family are working more hours and not necessarily making more income. In many cases, buying power has been stagnant or has decreased. To preserve living standards, consumers are becoming goal-oriented, and their overriding goal is to find the best value-to-price solution. Given the intense market liberalization process of recent years, consumers have plenty of choices. This is especially the case in large urban markets, where most companies have focused their investment effort. In searching for the best value, affordable price is paramount but not the only the factor that influences consumer choice. The challenge for firms is to find the right value-to-price ratio. Given the vulnerability of Latin American economies, the right ratio could be difficult to find as external conditions change—it becomes a moving target. Online firms have to monitor relative prices constantly across categories and against those of close competitors.

Another conclusion that emerges from our analysis is that when the drivers are unfavorable, markets adjust rapidly. Once adjustment takes place, it takes several years to regain confidence and previous levels of consumption. Consumers are developing coping consumption styles for harsh times that seem to prevail when conditions improve. These coping styles depend on the country and type of shock. These adjustments show the danger of using linear extrapolations based on periods of rapid growth. Firms that have based their investment decisions on such predictions are particularly vulnerable to overcapacity in the future.

Our analysis of market segments in Latin America shows that the market is fluid and fragmented. A conventional approach of using socioeconomic classes is not enough to build a sustainable strategy in Latin markets unless a firm's intent is to be a niche marketer. Consumption patterns and styles are not differentiated by income classes alone. Other indicators, such as education, professional status, and connectivity seem to be better indicators of social class affiliation. The fact that education and connectivity determine social class suggests some degree of mobility in society as education and professional competence leads to success. Thus, the implication for firms is that positioning should be based on enabling success through the ability to empower such mobility. This approach should also be consistent with our observation that consumers are becoming more goal-oriented.

The shrinking middle class poses a challenge to firms that have based their strategy on the expectation of growth of this market segment. As pointed out in this chapter, the middle-class segment is the most fluid. If niche marketers are targeting the upper class and some share of the upper middle class, firms that aim at volume business have the difficult task of building a market base on a mobile and shrinking middle class. As we have argued before, the key is to aim at attracting enough customers from all segments with a value proposition that is right for all.

Is the Latin market ready for a regional strategy approach? Given the diversity of market demographics, consumer preferences, and consumption styles, this question cannot be resolved with a simple answer. To a great extent, the answer depends on the consumer category. On the other hand, we argue that independent of the category, some universal consumer styles are regional, such as the goal- and value-seeking behaviors observed in this chapter. Apparent differences can be simplified through some nesting or layering of market conditions. Firms should group or cluster markets and develop differentiated strategies for each cluster. The conventional approach to use geography may not be effective. In recent years, multinational firms have used trade blocs and geography as a base to organize and coordinate their strategies. Using a Mercosur or NAFTA base, firms have coordinated their operations within these groups. As pointed out in our analysis of demographic transformation, the countries within a given trade bloc may not share the same level of demographic transformation. For example, from a demographic perspective, Brazil has more in common with Mexico, Colombia, and Peru than it has with its partners in Mercosur. A market strategy that treats Brazil, Uruguay, and Argentina as one group may not be very effective. Rather, we propose that a combination of a grouping of countries based on their level of demographic transformation (see Figure 2.1), layered with segmentation based on the life cycle of the nuclear family, may be a more effective way to approach Latin markets. Depending on the product category, other combinations may be more effective. The main point is that Latin markets are complex and multidimensional. Firms that are able to unravel their complexity will prevail.

3

THE LATIN MARKET COMPETITIVE LANDSCAPE

The fluid and fragmented consumer markets in Latin America pose strategic, organizational, and operational challenges for multinational companies. Adding to the complexity of the Latin American business landscape are macro forces and factors that have emerged as shapers of competition in the region. The most important are the international financial system, fiscal and financial reforms, and legal and institutional reforms. Multilateral lending organizations such as the World Bank and the International Monetary Fund have shaped the context for business in the hemisphere. These reforms, as well as those of governments that have adopted neoliberal reform measures (privatization, trade liberalization, financial modernization, macroeconomic stabilization), have had mixed results. These reforms have not been a panacea for long-standing structural and institutional problems—social and legal as well as economic. Moreover, in many countries, such as Argentina and Venezuela, implementation has been executed partially, poorly, or not at all.

The prime focus of this chapter, however, is the structure of competition among key players: large domestic firms, state-owned enterprises, small and medium-sized businesses, and multinational companies.

THE STRUCTURE OF COMPETITION IN LATIN AMERICA

The Latin American competitive landscape encompasses four categories of players: large domestic firms, state-owned enterprises, small and medium-sized businesses, and multinational firms. The economic prowess of large domestic and foreign firms, whether public or private, is formidable (see Table 3.1). In this section we provide an overview of the nature, characteristics, scope, and operational features of four different groups of businesses, enterprises that have been affected by (and have affected) the macroenvironmental forces cited earlier in the chapter: the international financial system, fiscal and financial reforms, and legal and institutional reforms.

THE EVOLUTION OF LARGE DOMESTIC FIRMS: FAMILY CONGLOMERATES

The jewels in the crown of private-sector development in Latin America have been large domestic firms;[1] most are family businesses. Although liberalization of trade and investment has threatened or destroyed many, others have linked up with multinationals or been acquired by them and, in turn, have developed new businesses. Many powerful CEOs of these enterprises have embraced the need for transparency and modern business practices, whereas others cling to their privacy and traditional ways of conducting business.[2]

In his definitive work on the subject, Wilson Peres refers to these large domestic conglomerates, family owned for the most part, as *grandes grupos económicos* (GGEs);[3] for the sake of brevity, we use the Spanish acronym here. GGEs presently occupy a leading role in the Latin American business world. Most were formed during the import substitution industrialization (ISI) period following World War II, although some date to the beginning of the twentieth century, when the industrialization process began in the more advanced countries of the region (Bunge and Born in Argentina, Alpargatas in Argentina and Brazil, the nucleus of the Grupo Monterrey in Mexico, Bavaria in Colombia, and Compañía de Cervecerías Unidas in Chile, among others).

The origin of the main GGEs centered on three strategic pillars:

1. Expansion based on the development of natural resources.
2. Growth based on diversification, for the purpose of generating synergies through a core industrial base. An example is the Grupo Monterrey, whose extensive business holdings range from breweries to manufacturing of glass containers, sheet metal, and corrugated boxes.
3. The acquisition by financial, construction, and service firms of businesses in their respective industries.[4]

Along with the GGEs originating before and after the ISI period, there are presently new and often very powerful economic groups that came into being and began to flourish during the course of neoliberal reform and economic restructuring in the 1980s. These new organizations resulted from the privatization of traditional activities (Enersis in Chile) as well as the dynamic growth of conglomerates with their portfolio approach to governance and management (Grupo Carso en Mexico).[5] In the second half of the 1990s new GGES arose just as traditional ones were disappearing. This suggests the existence of different capabilities in strategic response to political and economic changes as well as competition between large investor groups and traditional oligopolies that had been thriving in protected markets.

The new GGES, as well as traditional ones, have generally remained under the ownership of personal or family groups. They have structured themselves around formal or informal business groups through which they determine ownership, control, financing, and resource allocation.[6] The principal reasons for this preference are greater flexibility and decision making during volatile times, the ability (and agility) to settle inheritance disputes upon the death of the founder, and the existence of a legal framework that limits the rights of minority shareholders and the uncertainty that could be raised over contracts.[7]

Before Latin America's opening of their economies to foreign competition, the GGEs had started to export nontraditional products to boost their sales overseas.[8] Other groups, the largest ones, internationalized more widely and deeply, exporting not only merchandise but also capital. GGEs for the most part have pursued three types of strategies:

1. *Withdrawal.* This is the tendency to concentrate on the complete sale or sales of majority control of the enterprise

TABLE 3.1 Latin America's 50 Largest Firms

BUSINESS NAME	2000 REVENUE ($ MILLIONS)	2000 INCOME ($ MILLIONS)	COUNTRY	INDUSTRY
Petrobrás	26,955	5,342	Brazil	Energy, oil, gas
Carso Global Telecom	12,919	662	Mexico	Holding company, telecom
Telmex—Teléfonos de México	10,645	2,598	Mexico	Telecommunications
Itausa-Investimentos Itaú, S.A.	8,891	964	Brazil	Conglomerate
Petrobras Distribuidora	7,924	143	Brazil	Petroleum distribution
Walmex-Wal-Mart de México	7,685	371	Mexico	Retail, department stores
Banco Bradesco	6,200	890	Brazil	Financial services/banking
Eletrobrás-Centrais Elétricas Brasileiras	5,758	1,151	Brazil	Utilities, electricity
Grupo Sanborns Hermanos	5,707	113	Mexico	Retail, department store
Cemex S.A.	5,620	999	Mexico	Concrete, cement
Unibanco	5,412	379	Brazil	Financial services/banking
Companhia Vale do Rio Doce	5,034	1,093	Brazil	Diversified mining
Femsa Ubd—Fomento Económico Mexicano	4,724	263	Mexico	Beverage, retail
Banco Itaú	4,626	944	Brazil	Financial services/banking
Alfa	4,620	178	Mexico	Manufacturing, steel, auto parts
Enersis	4,513	157	Chile	Utilities, electricity
Telesp—Telecomunicacoes de Sao Paulo	4,466	754	Brazil	Telecommunications
Telemar—Tele Norte Leste	4,168	369	Brazil	Telecommunications
Companhia Brasileira de Distribuicao Grupo Pao de Açucar	3,913	170	Brazil	Retail, grocery
Companhia Brasileira de Petroleo Ipiranga	3,645	24	Brazil	Energy, oil, gas
Nueva Grupo Mexico	3,621	256	Mexico	Mining: copper, silver, zinc
Telefónica de Argentina	3,565	395	Argentina	Telecommunications
Embratel	3,443	251	Brazil	Telecom, long distance
Controladora Comercial Mexicana	3,285	115	Mexico	Retail, grocery

Company	Country	Value	Industry
Grupo Bimbo, S.A.	Mexico	3,271	Food: grains, breads, cereal
Nortel Inversora, S.A.	Argentina	3,227	Telecommunications
Telecom Argentina	Argentina	3,226	Telecommunications
Cintra	Mexico	3,212	Holding company, Airlines
Savia	Mexico	3,211	Agriculture, insurance
Banacci—Grupo Financiero Banamex-Accival, S.A.	Mexico	3,067	Financial services/banking
Grupo Modelo	Mexico	3,048	Beer, tobacco
América Móvil ADS	Mexico	3,008	Telecom, wireless
Vitro, S.A.	Mexico	2,870	Manufacturing: glass, clay
Grupo Gigante	Mexico	2,842	Retail, grocery
CANTV—Compañia Anónima Nacional Teléfonos de Venezuela	Venezuela	2,781	Telecommunications
Varig	Brazil	2,728	Airlines
AmBev	Brazil	2,692	Beer, tobacco
Organización Soriana, S.A.	Mexico	2,636	Retail, grocery
Panamco	Mexico	2,599	Bottler, distributor
Embraer	Brazil	2,538	Manufacturing: aerospace, defense
Grupo Financiero BBVA—Bancomer	Mexico	2,511	Financial services/banking
Desc	Mexico	2,406	Holding co., auto parts, real estate
EletroPaulo Metropolitana	Brazil	2,377	Utilities, electricity
Gerdau	Brazil	2,246	Steel production
IMSA	Mexico	2,206	Steel production
Grupo Televisa	Mexico	2,162	Media: broadcasting, print, Internet
Brasil Telecom Participacoes	Brazil	1,948	Telecommunications
Copec-Compañia de Petróleos de Chile	Chile	1,935	Conglomerate
Gruma	Mexico	1,891	Food: grains, breads, cereal
Ultrapar Participacoes, S.A.	Brazil	1,878	Oil, energy

Source: Latin CEO, May 2001.

to foreign investors rather than closing the business (e.g., the oil company Astra in Argentina, the auto-parts manufacturer Cofap in Brazil, or the two largest cigarette manufacturers in Mexico).

2. *Defensive.* Defending the domestic market has required GGEs to adopt different survival modes. The most relevant are: those linked to "preventive" investments (a preemptive purchase of an acquisition target or purchase of a large, existing domestic competitor); the importation of finished goods for their sale in-country, thereby taking advantage of local distribution networks; a greater and more intensive orientation toward the customer (particularly in the food industry); the formation of industrial and financial groups; and the search for profitability via access to fiscal or business incentives or sectoral promotion policies. One modality of defensive strategy has been the growth of industrial and service activities by GGEs, motivated by market deregulation or their privileged access in competing for business opportunities, particularly the privatization of communications, electricity distribution, and infrastructure in general.

3. *Offensive.* There are several options that GGEs can employ to enhance growth.[9] One is to strengthen and expand the firm's core business activities, such as those of companies dedicated to processing natural resources (Perez Companc in Argentina, Klabin in Brazil, or Alfa in Mexico). Also included in this grouping of GGEs are firms that have traditionally pursued this option, such as Mexico's Cemex.[10] Another option is moderate growth through the pursuit of diversification. This course of action entails both major supply chain disaggregation and an increase in vertical or horizontal integration.[11] This typically applies to GGEs that benefit from privatizations or the acquisition of other private firms. The achievement of potential synergies is the basic aim of these types of business operations. Examples include Techint and Pescahermosa in Argentina, Angelini in Chile, Suzano and Votorantim in Brazil, Santo Domingo in Colombia, and Pulsar in Mexico.

Finally, there is growth with extensive diversification, for the most part the result of participation in a number of privatizations. In these cases, one witnesses the emergence of true conglomerates, businesses that are profitable but lack synergies in production manufacturing, commercial operations, and financial management.[12] For the most part, these GGEs are run as individual holdings in a portfolio. Examples are: La Sociedad Comercial del Plata (energy, construction, services) in Argentina, Vicuña (textiles, steel, mining) in Brazil, and Carso (telephony, commerce, banking, manufacturing, mining, and auto parts) in Mexico.

In the following section we profile four of the most important GGEs in Latin America to illustrate the evolution, growth, operations, and organizational dynamics of these conglomerates, enterprises whose importance has not waned in poor economic times and whose presence, power, and influence are destined to increase in the years ahead.[13]

Grupo Carso (Mexico).   Carlos Slim Helú, the richest man in Latin America, whose wealth has been estimated at $12.5 billion, was for 10 years a trader in Mexico's stock market, where he began to write one of the country's biggest success stories of all time. Grupo Carso is Latin America's largest industrial conglomerate. It is not an exaggeration to say that "every time Mexicans eat a croissant or visit their bank, every time they use the telephone or light a cigarette, the chances are that Carlos Slim is making money. He probably even sold them the clothes on their back."[14] Perhaps he is known best as the billionaire acquirer of Telmex, the former government-owned telephone monopoly. Along with Carso Global Telecom, the two companies represent 40% of the Mexican stock exchange, a fact that seems to have made the government authorities reluctant to curb Telmex's power. (Its high long-distance interconnection charges prompted AT&T and MCI WorldCom to bring charges against Telmex before the WTO). It is interesting to note that when Telmex was still in public ownership, it barely made any money. Now it is among the most profitable telecom companies in the world, with net profits in 2000 of over $3 billion on sales of $11 billion and margins double those of most European carriers.

Grupo Carso has forged a $3.5 billion alliance with Bell Canada and SBC Communications. The venture brings together the largest telecom company in Canada, a leading U.S. operator, and Mexico's dominant carrier, to target broadband, wireless, and Internet markets in South America. This powerful North American pact is in competition with Spain's Telefónica and Telecom Italia for a share of the fast-growing market. Slim manages his companies according to a traditional, top-down, family-run structure. His three sons run Grupo Carso and his financial subsidiary, Grupo Inbursa, since he handed over the reins in 1998. His two sons-in-law are charged with the cellular and Internet divisions of Telmex. Slim remains at the head of Telmex and still reserves the final word on most things.

The chronology of Slim's empire building is awe-inspiring. He founded Carso on October 22, 1980, under the name Grupo Galas. In 1981, he changed the name to Grupo Inbursa, which became the present-day Grupo Carso (Carso Group) in May 1990. Between 1980 and 1990, the company bought the majority of shares of Cigatam, Artes Gráficas Unidas (Agusa), Fábricas de Papel Loreto y Peña Pobre, and Galas de México. In 1990, he merged with the Corporación Industrial Carso (Carso Industrial Corporation) and acquired a large part of the shares of the firms Sanborns, Frisco, and Nacobre. That same year, together with Southwestern Bell, France Telecom, and a group of Mexican investors, he won the bid to gain control of Teléfonos de México (Telmex), the top company on the Mexican stock market. In 1991, he acquired more shares in Frisco, Nacobre, and Sanborns. Also that year, Carso bought out 35% of the shares of Compañía Hulera Euzkadi and bought stock in Real Turismo "Calindra" (an independent company of the Carso Group).

In 1992, Slim acquired 30.4% of Condumex's shares in Pirelli S.P.A. Also in 1992, Nacobre took over 77.8% of the shares in Grupo Aluminio S.A. In 1993 he bought 99% of General Tire de México S.A. Three years later he gained nearly total control of Porcelanite and Conductores Laticansa S.A. Moreover, Carso also acquired 60% of Sears–México that same year. In 1998, he sold his stocks in the Compañía Hulera Euzkadi to Continental General Tire, a firm in which he acquired nearly 20% of the total capital. In the summer of 1999, he purchased 25% of the stock of Televisa through the Grupo Financiero Inbursa, which began to reengineer the television company, right after the death of Emilio Azcárraga Milmo, the famous "Tigre." In 2000, Slim joined Microsoft and launched with Bill Gates the online T1MSN network, a news service that will eventually offer financial and telecommunication services as well as a host server through Prodigy Turbo, a subsidiary of Telmex.

In March 2000, as part of its internationalization strategy, the group acquired CompUSA. They also signed an agreement with the U.S. company SBC Communications to buy 50% of the Brazilian firm Algar Telecom Leste, a cellular phone company with 900,000 customers in São Paulo and Rio de Janeiro. The group also acquired Guatemala Telgua, that country's telephone company, and they joined SBC to purchase the biggest cellular phone company in Puerto Rico. Slim's Latin American expansion targeted two distinct areas: telecommunications and the Internet. Through Telmex, Slim's strategy has been to target areas of low competition or to join a local, well-established company.

Perez Companc (Argentina). The small shipping company Perez Companc, founded in 1946, is the largest holding company in Argentina today. However, the company's guiding light, Gregorio ("Goyo") Perez Companc, is no ordinary person either—being Argentina's wealthiest man is not easy.

Thanks to the company's good international record and to the owner's low profile, both fared very well as a result of Argentina's state privatizations under the Carlos Menem administrations (1989–1999). Companies such as the Enron Corporation, Entergy Corp., and the British Gas GLP joined Perez Companc and helped him become a giant in the energy market. Today, the group has the Perez Companc family and the Fundación Perez Companc as its major stockholders, with 53.5% ownership in the company stock; Maipú Inversora holds 7.5 percent; and the rest is traded on the Buenos Aires stock exchange.

In 1997, Perez Companc sold Banco Río, a firm bought by the family in 1964. Under the group's management, the banking institution became Argentina's most important private bank as well as a pivotal force behind the growth of the group itself. During President Raúl Alfonsín's administration (1983–1989), the bank was a leader in financing the country's foreign debt. However, according to Perez Companc insiders, the holding company's most brilliant idea was the creation, in the middle of Argentina's hyperinflationary period, of the Argentine Private Development Trust (APDT), an investment fund formed by 21 international banks that allowed it to play a prominent role in the privatization process, as bookkeeper for all Argentine companies.

However, "Goyo" Perez Companc now faces another challenge as he considers expanding into two other sectors: the energy and food industries. He is planning to make large investments in the Latin American gas and oil industries, and in 2000 his holding company acquired Molinos and the La Paulina milk company. Molinos is Argentina's largest and oldest food producer. It has operations in 18 food categories, such as frozen foods, meat, oilseeds, and wheat. It sells its products in 40 countries and acts as a distributor for Monsanto products in South America. La Paulina, founded over 75 years ago, is a major producer of dairy products throughout the country.

Grupo Polar (Venezuela). The Grupo Polar dates back to 1938, when Lorenzo Alejandro Mendoza Fleury, majority owner of the family firm, Mendoza & Compañía, which had been making soap since 1855, decided to expand the business and become a pioneer in the beer industry. The group imported all its equipment to set up a brewery from Europe. They installed a bottling plant in a small neighborhood of Caracas, the Cervecería Polar C.A., hiring 50 employees and producing 30,000 liters of two different beers per month, Polar Beer and Bock Beer. Using a "tropicalized recipe" developed by master brewer Carlos Roubicek in 1942, Polar Beer soon began to control the Venezuelan market.

However, the brewery's success story needed a good distribution strategy, and this led to the creation in 1948 of the Distribuidora Polar S.A. (Diposa), which was in charge of selling the beer in Caracas. Actually, Diposa was the model for similar companies set up in the interior of Venezuela, and these companies eventually became Venezuela's most prominent network of distributors. However, Polar was not content only to brew beer. In 1954, Polar entered the food industry with the creation of Remaveca, a company that produced precooked corn flour. The launching of Harina P.A.N. in 1960 was an absolute success. In the first year alone, total sales of corn flour reached more than 1 million kilograms per month. In fact, this product is still going strong and has remained an important part of the Venezuelans' daily diet. The Polar Group gradually expanded into other business areas as well. In 1960, the group ventured into the production and distribution of processed food for animals with the creation of the Procría company. In 1986 they began to produce rice and pastas. In 1990 they also produced young wines together with the Bodegas Pomar winery, another of the group's companies, and in 1993, they entered the soda beverage market with the purchase of Golden Cup.

In 1996, in the middle of the "cola wars," when the Cisneros Group left PepsiCo to become associated with Coca-Cola, Polar went into business with PepsiCo to produce and distribute Pepsi in Venezuela. By 1988, the Venezuelan market was too small for the Polar Group and they began to go international by buying what is today Savoy Brands International and marketing snack foods in Colombia, Guatemala, Honduras, and Panama. In 1995, the Polar Group created its affiliate beer industry, Cervecería Polar Colombiana, taking advantage of the Colombian–Venezuelan integration process going on at that time, with the idea of distributing its best products in this neighboring country.

In addition to its Colombian expansion, Polar has successfully ventured into other markets of the Americas: the United States, Guatemala, Chile, Ecuador, Peru, Panama, Honduras, and Argentina. As capital-only investors, the Polar Group has increased its involvement in petrochemical projects for the past 10 years through the Zuliano Group as well as in other businesses related to petrochemicals. The group also took part in the third round of oil exploration as a capital investor, together with Inelectra as operator and with Arco as foreign company, acquiring two oil fields in the process.

The Globo Group (Brazil).   The Marinho family controls Globo Organizations, the leader in the media and entertainment businesses in Latin America and an important producer of a wide range of high-quality information and entertainment content. Among the Globo companies are the leading Brazilian broadcast television network, cable television service, leading newspapers and magazines, and a network of radio stations and telecommunications companies. Founded in 1925, *O Globo* newspaper grew to become a media conglomerate under the prowess of the founder Irineu Marinho's 21-year-old son Roberto. Building *O Globo* into Rio de Janeiro's largest daily newspaper, he expanded into radio stations in the 1940s and 1950s along with real estate, and added television (TV Globo) in 1965. It is now the largest television network in South America and the leader in the Brazilian market since the very beginning.

During the 1960s and 1970s, Roberto Marinho's three sons entered the family business, and at the beginning of the 1990s, they began a careful scrutiny of the group's operations. In consultation with their father, they came to the conclusion that that they could no longer rely on traditional ways of doing business. With the support of consultants (including one specializing in family businesses), they identified some weaknesses in the conglomerate structure, which included lack of focus and synergy in the group's operations, no succession plan, and the need for more modern management strategies. The family decided that the three brothers would together succeed their father. In addition, they decided that the group should focus its operations in media, communication, and distribution areas. They began the process of selling noncore holdings, including an investment bank and a hotel. They also hired new professionals to help them with day-to-day management.

Recognizing that the media industry is a capital- and technology-intensive sector, the family began its search to form alliances with strong international partners. In the mid-1990s the patriarch Roberto Marinho officially handed control of Globo Organizations to his three sons. At that time he had created the world's fourth-largest television network (after NBC, CBS, and ABC), Brazil's major radio network, a leading Rio de Janeiro newspaper (*O Globo*), and the country's second-biggest publishing house (Editora Globo). During the last two years the company has attracted new investors, restructured its debt, cut operating costs, launched low-cost programming packages, and added new sources of income by launching Internet access services. The Marinho family's strategy has so far proved to be successful. They are aware that they must maintain a dominant market share in an increasingly technologically based sector, one in which cross-border data flows via Internet surpass traditional foreign-investment restrictions.

As GGEs face increasing competition due to globalization, one may expect to see their numbers reduced dramatically, with the remaining players responding in a variety of ways to competition and making a strong push to internationalize their business activities.[15]

STATE-OWNED ENTERPRISES: DOWN BUT NOT OUT

The Keynesian influence on public policy prior to and following World War II fueled the expansion of the state's role not only in the provision of public goods but in the acquisition, control, production, and distribution of goods and services normally provided by the private sector (e.g., steel, financial services, mining, chemicals, transport services). Latin America was no exception. In fact, the adoption of the ISI (import substitution industrialization) model, and neomercantilist, protectionist tendencies which were part of the economic fabric of the region since colonial and post-independence times, catalyzed an even larger, more activist, and interventionist state presence in basic industries, one that was nourished by massive amounts of multilateral funding from development banks, bilateral aid, and sovereign lending by global financial institutions. A strong trajectory of worldwide economic growth during the first three decades following the war broadened and deepened the trend toward large state-owned companies as a key engine of development.

State-owned enterprises (SOEs) have shrunk dramatically, due to the privatization wave from the early 1990s; nevertheless, many remain (especially in public utilities) and compete with or prevent competition with large private firms. SOEs that have not been sold off—because they are not financially attractive candidates for privatization, are cash cows for the government (e.g., Pemex), or for reasons of nationalism (e.g., Petrobrás, CFE in Mexico)—are now turning to private management and contracting out services to boost efficiency and effectiveness. Nearly two decades have passed since Latin America began to sell off its SOEs, and the benefits from this process have been well documented. Privatizations have reduced public deficits, created new productive employment, increased government revenues, and created competition and improvement in the quality of public services.[16]

There are a number of motives for government intervention in production, the principal one being market failure, including economies of scale, public goods, externalities, and information asymmetries. What this means is that "when the size of the market precludes competition, when private producers will not enter a market because of the free-rider nature of the good, when others rather than the producing firms bear the costs or appropriate the benefits of production, or when the information needed to make rational decisions is itself scarce," the market will not provide efficient results.[17] Other motives for government ownership include ideology, economic sovereignty, income, finance, and employment. Ideology and economic sovereignty would include nationalism and populism, as in the case of Venezuela. Income reasons would include profit generation through the control of money-producing ventures normally left to the private sector (e.g., energy production and distribution). Finance implies seeking loans from foreign financial institutions, invariably more willing to lend to governments than to privately owned businesses. (In cases of government default, the lender more easily gets a court ruling to attach the assets of the state than if the borrower were a private company.) As for employment, governments often use SOEs as employers of least resort, sopping up excessively high levels of unemployment and underemployment, and as vessels of political patronage.

Their generally poor performance has been the principal criticism of SOEs. Reasons for poor performance are well documented and bear a uniform pattern globally.[18] State ownership is abstract and leaves no visible residual claimant to profits; SOE managers are shielded from stock market effects and stockholder accountability; SOE managers have to satisfy multiple objectives set by politicians; government subsidies protect internal inefficiencies; and the risk–reward structure for SOE employees is performance neutral.[19] Clearly, political preferences and pressures govern key project parameters such as plant location, capacity planning, implementation time frame, employment, and product/service pricing. In essence, a set of three interrelated factors affect the performance of SOEs: (1) objective factors such as input prices and level of available infrastructure; (2) decisions made externally regarding labor policies, investment, and pricing; and (3) the internal organization of the firm.[20] Additionally, poorly performing SOEs are awarded subsidies, and better-performing SOEs are penalized through restricted access to capital compared to other competitive enterprises.

Measuring SOE performance is particularly challenging. Accounting systems are rarely designed to report on economic viability. When the government fixes input and output prices (irrespective of economic scarcities), the true economic picture of a firm cannot be discerned. The financial picture often gets distorted, as well. Not all costs, (e.g., indirect taxes) are recorded. The employment of redundant labor makes the calculation of true wage costs difficult to measure. Obviously, when prices are held down to subsidize users (e.g., public utilities) it is impossible to measure true economic costs. Public-sector firms can be managed more efficiently, to be sure, even to approximate the performance of privately owned firms. However, prerequisites are "clarity of corporate objectives, clear lines of responsibility, independent agencies for monitoring and the greater use of competitive pressures and financial incentives."[21] All these factors can play an important role in improving public-sector performance, even in the absence of privatization.[22]

In an increasing effort to improve performance, transparency, and accountability, governments have turned to outsourcing to the private sector. Recognizably, the provision of services need not be the same as government production. Contracting out an entire operation (e.g., management of government-owned airlines or hotels) or only part of it (building cleaning, cafeteria, office security services) can accomplish multiple objectives. These include cost reduction (through an incentive structure), less political interference, more adaptable labor force practices, management flexibility, improved chances to innovate, and improved effectiveness of service provision through performance-based contracts themselves.[23]

In an increasingly globalized world, the organization, operation, and strategic goals of SOEs have competitive implications, as well, in the international business arena. Although governments officially claim adherence to trade liberalization and nondiscrimination, they continue to assist their domestic firms to promote exports and reduce imports. One important vehicle for this purpose has been SOEs.[24] Although SOEs have been diminished markedly during the last decade, they still play a role in international commerce as large purchasers of raw materials and inputs and as exporters of commodities, manufactured goods, and services. Subsidization (despite multilateral trade rules barring this practice), preferential access to financing, and administrative pricing of inputs and outputs give SOEs unfair advantages in many instances vis-à-vis private companies. Moreover, SOEs are more likely than private firms to be charged with predatory behavior such as dumping.[25] Although it is clear that SOEs compete with local and multinational enterprises in many instances, in many others they serve as a rich source business for private-sector suppliers of everything from energy products (Enron, Elf-Aquitaine) to engineering, construction, and procurement services (Techint, Bechtel) and information technology and telecommunications (Microsoft, Nortel).

Despite the massive Latin American privatizations in the late 1990s, SOEs are down but not out. There have been exceptions to the selling spree; and the exceptions are large. Among the 500 biggest companies in Latin America, the three biggest are SOEs; and these three have held the top spots for the last 10 years: Pemex (Mexico), PDVSA (Venezuela), and Petrobrás (Brazil), all oil companies. These are globally competitive firms, to whose ranks should be added Codelco (Chile), the world's largest copper producer. These four firms produce $90 billion in revenue annually. As mentioned above, they have not been privatized for various reasons: nationalist sentiment, political opposition, and especially, their enormous importance as revenue producers for the government.[26] Presented below are profiles of these four SOE powerhouses, illuminating some of the more salient characteristics and operations of these firms.

Codelco. The world's largest producer of copper, Codelco (Corporación Nacional del Cobre) produces 40% of the world's total output and annually reports revenue of $1 billion. This figure represents an amount larger than corporate income tax collections from Chilean businesses. According to Juan Villarzú, Codelco's president: "I am strongly in favor of privatizations; in fact, I was responsible for managing the sale of water and waste water plants. However, Codelco is an exception—not only because of the extremely large revenue stream it produces, but because the Chilean economy would not be able to absorb all the money produced from the sale."[27]

Codelco's strategy is to boost efficiency and avoid being caught up in the ongoing consolidation process within the mining industry. To date, Codelco has been quite successful in this regard. Copper production has increased 42% in the last five years, during which the number of employees has decreased from 24,000 to 17,000. Net costs of production per pound have fallen 26%, making Codelco one of the lowest-cost producers of copper worldwide.[28] Codelco's performance is all the more impressive given the fact that legal restrictions prevent the firm from being more flexible and competitive. It has to negotiate its budget year after year, it is restricted from issuing shares in the company, and its executives do not receive comparable salaries or benefits (including bonuses) to those of their counterparts in the private sector. Additionally, Codelco is subjected to the Ley Reservada, a law from the Pinochet era that sets aside 10% of sales revenue to finance weapons sales for the armed forces. Nevertheless, Codelco has been able to overcome these restrictions. It has been able to negotiate an investment plan ($3.6 billion over the next six years) with a great deal of operational flexibility. Also, thanks to a 1994 law, Codelco has authority to joint venture with private investors in new projects and acquisitions and it can issue shares in these new public–private ventures.

Pemex. Petróleos Mexicanos (Pemex) not only fuels Mexico's automobile engines, the state-owned oil company also fuels the nation's economy, accounting for one-third of the Mexican government's revenues and 7% of its export earnings. The integrated company's operations, spread throughout Mexico, range from exploration and production to refining and petrochemicals. Pemex's P.M.I. Comercio Internacional subsidiary manages the company's trading operations outside the country. Mexico's vast oil and gas resources include proved oil reserves of 28.4 billion barrels of oil equivalent.[29] With sales of $36.5 billion, Pemex was the largest firm in Latin America last year.

In 1990 the Salinas administration removed 15 products from its list of 34 basic petrochemicals reserved for state development, and under the terms of NAFTA, it agreed to reduce the number of "exclusive" basic petrochemicals to only six, thus facilitating the eventual privatization of the subsidiary for secondary petrochemicals. Under his successor, Ernesto Zedillo, Pemex began to adopt modern business practices (such as trimming its bloated payroll), look for more reserves, and improve its refining capability. The government tried to sell some petrochemical assets in 1995, but had to modify the scheme the next year after massive public protests by the country's nationalists. Still, Pemex began selling off natural gas production, distribution, and storage networks to private companies.

President Vicente Fox, the country's first non–Institutional Revolutionary Party (PRI) leader in seven decades, has replaced Pemex's politician-staffed board with professionals and is modernizing the company, in an effort to make it more businesslike. He named Raul Muñoz Leos, a former executive of Dupont, as Pemex's chief. Since nationalization of the oil industry in 1938, it had been led by bureaucrats. Fox intends to solicit private-sector advice in shaping policy and management guidelines for the "new" Pemex. Muñoz said his aim was to create "just one Pemex" and indicated he would rethink part of the decentralization the company underwent during previous governments. It is divided into four separate units: exploration and production, gas, petrochemicals, and refining. He stated that a more centralized focus would better enable Pemex to compete against the world's largest oil companies, which have grown in a wave of mergers. In a drive for efficiency, Muñoz said that he would develop a set of benchmarks to measure Pemex against private-sector rivals such as Royal Dutch–Shell Group and ExxonMobil Corp. (Pemex has modernized less than have many of the other large SOEs in Latin America; additionally, its geographic scope is confined to the Gulf of Mexico.)[30]

Unquestionably, Pemex is saddled with serious problems. It urgently needs to sink some $4.5 billion a year over the next decade into exploration. Mexico's congress is debating fiscal reform designed in part to ease Pemex's tax burden, thereby freeing cash for such investments: 61% of its gross revenues go to the national treasury, which in 1999 left the company with a $2 billion net loss. Despite protests by the Oil Workers Union, Pemex's bloated payroll will have to be trimmed. At 129,159, its workforce is nearly 2½ times that of Venezuela's PDVSA, a state-run oil company with comparable revenues. (Pemex gets about 75 barrels of oil per worker, compared with 90 or 95 in the best private firms.)[31]

As a cash cow for the state, Pemex was never charged with maximizing its value. Its exploration budget has been limited in order to transfer larger quantities of money to the national treasury; on the other hand, its monopoly on extraction, production, and commercialization of selected products, from natural gas to basic petrochemicals, has put the brakes on the competitiveness of the economy and Mexican businesses. Additionally, regulations placed on Pemex including the inability to access cheap capital and restrictions on issuing stock, have been severe impediments to the firm's growth, stability, efficiency, and competitiveness.[32]

In March 2001, the Mexican energy minister Ernesto Martens said that the Fox administration was considering the possibility of opening up gas and oil exploration in Mexico to private foreign companies in the medium term, but not immediately. President Fox has adamantly refused to consider privatizing Pemex, deeming it politically unfeasible. Admittedly, Pemex is too important as a government revenue producer; and even if the government wanted to privatize tomorrow, it would need a sweeping overhaul of tax policy and collections to compensate for the severe revenue shortfall.

PDVSA. PDVSA, a government-owned company, boasts proved reserves of 76.9 billion barrels of oil, the most outside the Middle East, and 146.8 trillion cubic feet of natural gas. Although PDVSA's exploration and production take place in Venezuela, the company has refining and marketing operations in the Caribbean, Europe, and the United States as well as at home. Subsidiary Citgo Petroleum operates 14,000 gas stations in the United States. PDVSA also makes Orimulsion, a patented fuel made from bitumen, and markets it to electricity generators as an alternative to coal. With nearly 40 affiliate, branch, and support offices globally, PDVSA is active in upstream production of retail products, including fuels, lubricants, automotive specialty products, asphalts, solvents, and industrial specialty products, covering the needs of national and international clients in the automotive, industrial, marine, and aviation sectors.[33]

With the increase in oil prices, Venezuela was forecast to have some $25 billion in reserves by year end 2000, but the final figure came to only $21 billion. Venezuela has always ranked near the bottom of Latin America's data transparency league. Some suspect there is a heavy component of money being kept offshore. Exports, the bulk of which is oil pumped by PDVSA, totaled $24.5 billion in the first nine months of 2000, according to the central bank. After imports, a capital account deficit, and $3 billion in "errors and omissions"—a proxy for capital flight—reserves should have increased by $4.7 billion. In reality, they rose by only $4 billion. At the same time, Venezuela's foreign debt was forecast to rise from $20.8 billion at the end of 2000 to $22.1 billion by the end of 2001. President Hugo Chávez, however, who once called PDVSA a "state within a state," named General Guaicaipuro Lameda, formerly in charge of the budget office, as its new head in late 2000, and ordered him to examine PDVSA's accounts with a "magnifying glass."

Despite populist rhetoric, anti-American pronouncements, ratification of OPEC production quotas, and an unswerving belief in a large state role in the economy, President Chávez has taken measures to attract foreign direct investment in the energy and natural resources sectors. International energy consortium Sincor inaugurated a massive new facility to refine superheavy crude from Venezuela's oil-rich Orinoco basin as part of a $4 billion energy development project. The new facility was constructed by the consortium, whose partners are French oil giant TotalFinaElf, with a 47% stake; state-owned PDVSA, with a 38% stake; and Norway's Statoil, which has a 15% stake in the project. On February 13, 2001, President Chávez dedicated major manufacturing facilities that will transform heavy crude oil into synthetic crude to be refined into usable products. The upgrading unit is part of the $2.5 billion Petrozuata project, a joint venture of Conoco Inc.[34]

One of the distinguishing features of PDVSA as a SOE is the priority it gives to management improvement, through systems infrastructure upgrading and human resource development. For example, to support its complex environment, reduce cost, and maintain a competitive edge, it formed Intesa, in partnership with SAIC (Science Applications International Corporation), a Fortune 500 research and engineering company. As an IT entity, Intesa serves all PDVSA information technology needs worldwide. After the successful transition of 1,500 technical personnel to the new company, SAIC led the effort to consolidate and upgrade the IT management infrastructure.

As an example of investment in professional development of managers, engineers, and technical staff, PDVSA and Babson College formed an alliance in 1996 to help implement the company's strategy for future growth. (PDVSA's mission is to double oil production by the year 2005 without increasing its present employee base of 48,000.) Human resource development is critical to PDVSA's three-pronged strategy: (1) improving technology management; (2) creating multiple channels for private investment; and (3) investing in education. The Babson–PDVSA alliance addresses PDVSA managers' entrepreneurial and global management skills through a series of educational programs held in various cities in Venezuela and on Babson's campus in Wellesley, Massachusetts.[35]

For the next 10 years, PDVSA seeks to aggressively expand and broaden its presence as an SOE in international markets. Its 2000–2009 business plan calls for investments of over $53 billion in its oil, natural gas, chemicals, and manufacturing and marketing operations. The plan is structured to almost double PDVSA's crude oil production and increase PDVSA's exports to the United States over the next 10 years. The goal of the overall plan is to strengthen and enhance PDVSA's role both in the world energy market and in the economic development of Venezuela.

Private-sector participation will account for $31 billion or more than 50% of the total anticipated investments under the plan. In accordance with the guidelines set by the shareholder and the dynamics of the market, under the plan PDVSA, will increase its crude oil production capacity substantially, from 3.56 million barrels per day by the end of 1999 to 5.8 million barrels per day by 2009, focusing on high-value light- and medium-gravity crude oils. The plan also calls for crude oil exploration activity, funded solely by PDVSA, which is expected to add 10 billion barrels of crude oil to Venezuela's official proven reserves of 76.8 billion barrels.

Throughout the next 10 years, significant attention will be given to expanding PDVSA's natural gas operations, whose development will be funded primarily by private capital. Venezuela has one of the world's largest natural gas reserves, with 142.5 trillion cubic feet. By

2009, exports of methane gas are anticipated to reach 1 billion cubic feet per day, production of natural gas liquids will almost double to 370,000 barrels per day, and export projects for liquefied natural gas (LNG) will be developed.[36]

Petrobrás. Petróleo Brasileiro (Petrobrás) is Brazil's largest industrial company. It engages in exploration for oil and gas and in production, refining, purchasing, and transportation of oil, gas, and petrochemical products. The firm is also the third-largest industrial corporation in Latin America and the world's seventh-largest publicly traded oil and gas company based on estimated proved reserves, 9.6 billion barrels of oil equivalent. Petrobrás is a leader in retail distribution of oil products in Brazil, with 32% of market share based on volume of sales. It owns one of the most important refining complexes in South America, with total refining capacity representing approximately 27% of the current total crude oil refining capacity in South American and the Caribbean.

Additionally, Petrobrás has attained notable milestones, including world records for deepest offshore producing well (6,157 feet water depth) and deepest exploration well drilled (9,111 feet water depth). Its subsidiary Petrobrás Distribuidora is Brazil's leading retailer of oil products and fuel alcohol. Petrobrás Internacional operates the company's worldwide exploration, production, and marketing services. With foreign offices in New York and London, Petrobrás coordinates its worldwide activities through a subsidiary network of three companies: Braspetro, Gaspetro, and BR. Its upstream and downstream operations take place in Angola, Argentina, Bolivia, Colombia, Cuba, Ecuador, the United States, Equatorial Guinea, Libya, Nigeria, Peru, the UK, and Trinidad and Tobago. The Brazilian government owns a controlling stake in the firm.[37] Petrobrás president Philippe Reichstul, an ex-banker appointed by President Fernando Henrique Cardoso in March 1999, has a mandate to transform the SOE into a more efficient and aggressive competitor in the global energy market.

Petrobrás achieved a $4.97 billion profit on sales of $15.8 billion in 2000, compared with a $356 million loss in 1999. Soaring oil prices are a leading factor behind the turnaround. However, the company president also deserves credit. Petrobrás's finances are now more transparent, and relations with investors have improved. Borrowing costs have fallen as a result. Formerly, the company was paying 9.5% interest on short-term debt; it now pays less than 7%.[38]

The fourteenth-largest oil company in the world, Petrobrás has significant strengths, not least of which are difficult technologies that other oil majors have not achieved. Like PDVSA, the firm believes in continuous improvement of its personnel and technological systems. The company produces nearly 1.5 million barrels per day with 34,000 employees, compared with Repsol–YPF in Argentina, which produces half that output with the same number of workers. In early 2001, PetroCosm Corporation, a business-to-business e-commerce marketplace for the oil and gas industry, and Petrobrás, announced that they would enter into a joint venture to create a Brazilian digital marketplace for procurement in the oil and gas industry. The venture would be jointly funded and own the Brazilian-based marketplace.[39]

The company's main weakness is downstream. Its refineries are outdated, and its pipelines and ships are accident-prone. In 2000 it had a series of oil spills, resulting in fines of at least $93 million. On March 15, 2001, a Petrobrás oil rig, the world's largest (40 stories), exploded, killing 10 members of its 175-person crew. Petrobrás lost 6% of its daily output with the rig and is expected to take a loss of up to $450 million in its 2001 earnings.[40] Nevertheless, with annual revenue of more than $16 billion, Petrobrás will be able to withstand that hit, although 2002's output target has been reduced from 1.58 million barrels per day to 1.52.[41] The company is presently engaged in a three-year $1 billion spending program to upgrade refineries and create special teams to deal with environmental emergencies.

In terms of business operations, Brazil is close to realizing its goal of becoming self-sufficient in oil; it now imports 30% of what it consumes. Petrobrás has embarked on a $33 billion investment plan over five years to virtually double oil and gas production, clean up the company's financial affairs, and expand abroad. There are 50 joint ventures now operating in Brazil: Chevron, Texaco, Royal Dutch–Shell, and Repsol–YPF, among others. Close to $4 billion has been committed to these projects, all of which are in the exploration stage.

Petrobrás's goals are to become a transnational corporation and an important regional player, and to evolve from an oil company into an energy company. The firm's growth, development, and direction will be based on consolidating and maintaining leadership in the oil and derivatives market; establishing a natural gas market in Brazil; and expanding international activities. The firm intends to raise $33 billion to achieve the goals in its strategic plan. Initially, two-thirds of the money will come from the cash flow of the company; the rest will come from project finance and loans. More than two-thirds of the amount will go to exploration and production, with substantial investment in gas and some marginal investments in refining.[42] Other financial mechanisms have also been mobilized. In early 2001, Petrobrás selected Citibank as depositary for its American Depositary Receipt (ADR) program, representing preferred shares listed on the New York Stock Exchange (NYSE). ADRs representing preferred shares previously traded on the over-the-counter (OTC) market.[43] In early April 2001, Repsol–YPF and Petrobrás agreed to a $1 billion asset swap, which allows Repsol–YPF to reach two objectives. It fulfills its divestment commitments to Argentina following the purchase of YPF. The company has also taken an important step with regard to strengthening its presence and integrating its upstream and downstream businesses in Brazil. In turn, Petrobrás takes control of the fourth-largest refining and marketing company in Argentina, holding a market share of almost 12%, thus achieving an important step in its internationalization strategy, particularly in Latin America.[44]

Although there are no plans to privatize Petrobrás completely, for many of the same reasons cited above in the profiles of the three other SOEs, there is every intention to boost Petrobrás's productivity, efficiency, financial soundness, and strategic presence in global energy markets. One must bear in mind that the four SOEs cited above are exceptional cases. SOEs in general tend to reduce economic growth. They are usually less efficient than private firms and are often financed in ways that undermine macroeconomic stability. In addition, they divert resources from other public spending arenas, such as education, health care, social services, and housing. Nevertheless, SOEs have been and will continue to be a source business for multinational vendors of product and services.

SMALL BUSINESS: FORMAL AND INFORMAL

The small-business sector in Latin America, both formal and informal, accounts for nearly 90% of private-sector activity (including private-sector employment) in the region. Small and medium-sized enterprises (SMEs), along with microenterprises, are engaged in a broad range of economic activities in agriculture, manufacturing, retailing, services, and transportation. Definitions of enterprises based on size vary widely.[45] The principal market for both industrial and consumer goods and services of the SME sector is the domestic market; however, macro- and microeconomic reforms and trade liberalization have energized a number of enterprises, from handicrafts and apparel to food products and industrial materials, to seek markets beyond their borders. The increased economic activity due to trade, finance, and investment integration in NAFTA, Mercosur, and the Andean Community has also fostered the growth of SME suppliers to multinational firms and to large local enterprises.

The competitive challenges to SMEs have increased and intensified given the market-opening measures (unilateral, bilateral, and multilateral) that have accompanied regional economic reform.[46] Mercosur provides an excellent example. Here the integration process is having structural repercussions on the conduct of firms in terms of production, on the definition of their future business strategies, and on their investment decisions. For many SMEs, especially those who produce tradable manufactures subjected to the influence of international technological and consumption patterns, or for producers of intermediate goods, parts, or components for use by assembly or terminal industries, the present challenge is to redesign their businesses, rethinking both production activity and business strategies. The reason is that the conditions under which these enterprises were set up and managed by their owners in the past have undergone substantial changes. According to available partial information, a reasonable estimate for the mid-1990s would indicate that the total universe of industrial SMEs in Mercosur comprised between 120,000 and 130,000 manufacturing enterprises, generating some 2,700,000 direct jobs. Approximately, it may be assumed that about 80% of these enterprises were located in Brazil and 15 to 17% in Argentina.

Small and medium-sized enterprises in Mercosur are concentrated in labor-intensive manufacturing activities, especially natural resources-based (wood and furniture), agroindustries, agrofood industries, and mature manufacturing activities (clothing and footwear, plastics, and metal products and machinery). SMEs in the food sector account for a larger share of the total in Uruguay than in the rest of the countries. In contrast, those engaged in manufacturing activities with a high technological content (defined as a function of the type of good produced rather than of the processes used) have a low share in the composition of production, since they account for less than 5 to 7% of the total value of production of the SMEs. A significant part of the activities of SMEs is connected with the manufacture of intermediate products, parts, components, processes, or subassemblies incorporated in other manufactured goods.

Throughout the hemisphere, not just within Mercosur, SME entrepreneurs are faced with a number of serious business challenges. These include restructuring a firm's business operations to respond to regional economic integration and its impacts on local markets, repositioning the firm and developing competitive strategies to ward off threats and seize opportunities brought about by internationalization, and improving technological capability.[47] As SMEs strive to meet these challenges, they are faced with internal constraints characteristic of such firms. These include a high degree of centralization of decision making, a closed structure of ownership, a lack of formal operating procedures, intuition-based strategic management, and the absence of long-term planning. Additionally, these firms manifest a high degree of intrafirm vertical integration, few forms of collective action (networks and consortia), and low levels of subcontracting. They tend to produce a wide variety of products and low volumes of production, their sources of finance are erratic and costly, and they normally market to a restricted geographical area.

As economic reform intensifies, the role of SMEs will not diminish but increase. Data analysis of SME presence in the industrial structure of Latin America demonstrates that these firms are not marginal players.[48] Although their productivity is significantly lower that that of large enterprises, the gap has narrowed or closed in some countries. Since SMEs export very little, domestic macroeconomic conditions have been the principal determinants of how these enterprises have faired. The impacts of trade liberalization have not escaped the SME sector, but the effects have not been generalized: Some SME sectors have been winners, others have been losers (see Table 3.2).

In the large-market countries of Latin America, foodstuffs, textiles and apparel, chemicals and plastics, and machinery and equipment weigh heavily in total SME production. In all countries in the region, foodstuffs occupy an important place in SME production, due to the industry's labor intensiveness and natural comparative advantages with low economies of scale. Given the fact that these two industries are aimed almost exclusively at the local market (where the industries have well-defined and efficient channels of distribution and long-standing relationships with buyers), domestic demand is far more important than trade liberalization (i.e., inflows of imports) in affecting the competitiveness of these SMEs.[49]

As for microenterprises, their profile is distinct but not unrelated to that of SMEs. Among the principal features of these businesses—informal as well as formal—are that they are owner-operated, employ 10 or fewer people (80% in the region are so staffed), are financed out of personal savings, and have fixed assets of less than $20,000. These small firms have a high percentage of female owners (30 to 60%), depend on members on their family as workers, and have limited access to financing. Additionally, microenterprise workers are not able to avail themselves of technical or

TABLE 3.2 Winner and Loser Sectors in the Production of SMEs

COUNTRIES	WINNER SECTORS	LOSER SECTORS
Argentina	Nonalcoholic beverages, medicines, paints, iron and steel, machinery of general use	Textiles, garments, sawmills, pottery
Brazil	Footwear, furniture, printing, plastic products	Food, garments, chemical products
Chile		
1981–1990	Chemical products	Food, sawmills, medicines, metal products
1990–1996	Sawmills, medicines, building materials, metal products	Textiles, chemical products, refining of copper, iron, and steel
Colombia	Food, plastic products, metal products	Beverages, medicines, electrical machinery
Costa Rica	Food, beverages, medicines, building materials	Sawmills, chemical products, metal products
Ecuador	Paper, chemical products, medicines, electrical machinery and apparatus	Food, garments, iron and steel, metal products
Mexico	Beverages, garments, furniture, printing, building materials	Food, textiles, chemical products, nonelectrical machinery
Peru	Printing, medicines, plastic products, iron and steel	Food, textiles
Uruguay	Food, beverages, printing, iron and steel	Textiles, footwear, leather, auto parts
Venezuela	Foods, printing, building materials, iron and steel	Beverages, medicines, metal products

Source: Data based on industrial SMEs, Industrial and Technological Development Unit, Division of Production, Productivity and Management, ECLAC; winner (loser) sectors are sectors that increase (decrease) their share in total production of SMEs.

management or business assistance services.[50] For microenterprises in the region, the many serious business challenges seem undaunting—from complex tax and registration procedures to the lack of services (financial and nonfinancial). The four basic areas in which such obstacles are found are: the policy and regulatory environment, access to financing, access to business development services, and access of resources to the sector as a whole.[51]

For every country in the region, access to capital ranks as the most serious barrier to business survival, let alone expansion, among SMEs as well as microenterprises.[52] Multilateral lending institutions and governments have been involved in SME and microenterprise lending for the past two decades. Commercial lenders (to a lesser extent) are dedicating resources to this sector as well.[53] To illustrate, Banco Bilbao Vizcaya Argentaria's subsidiaries in Chile and Mexico launched major SME support programs in 2001. The Chilean loan program will help SMEs train hundreds of thousands of employees (750,000 is the target number for 2001). In Mexico, companies and entrepreneurs can receive $10,000 to $200,000 in loans to purchase raw materials, machinery, and other capital equipment.[54] In Brazil, Banco do Brazil, the nation's largest bank, offers its services through local post offices and supermarkets to target low-income customers, SMEs and microenterprise entrepreneurs. Other banks, such as Bradesco, are considering pursuing similar strategies.[55]

THE INFORMAL ECONOMY

It is not possible to discuss the small business landscape in Latin America without including the informal economy. These businesses include, most prominently, street vendors and home workers, but run the gamut from building trades (electricians, carpenters, plumbers) to beauticians, mechanics, maids, and caregivers. One may say that underground activities are those that have legal ends but employ illicit means. That is, they are activities that do not intrinsically have a criminal content but must be carried out illicitly, even though they are licit and desirable activities for the country. The most important characteristic of informal activities is that those involved in them directly as well as society in general benefit more if the law is violated than if it is not.[56]

In his seminal work on Latin America's informal sector, using the case example of Peru, Hernando de Soto asserts that when legality is a privilege, available only to those with political and economic power, there is no alternative but illegality.[57] Since the legal and administrative costs to incorporate and maintain a legitimate business are so high, small business entrepreneurs opt to work outside the formal economy. Although they do not pay taxes or fees for permits, their costs of doing business are high nonetheless. They cannot go to a court of justice to enforce their contracts, they cannot ensure themselves against risk; and they cannot acquire or secure property rights. Consequently, their long-term productivity suffers.[58]

The size of the informal sector is often considered to be a measure of the failure of the economy to generate enough decent-paying jobs. It may also be taken as a measure of the inefficiency of the labor market due to its imperfections, some of them policy-induced.[59]

Clearly, government- or union-imposed regulations can push labor costs above market-clearing levels, leading to inefficiencies in the allocation and use of labor. One of the benefits of flexibilizing reforms is the reduction in these costs.[60] From the 1980s through the present time, the informal sector's expansion continues unabated. In addition to inequality, there is significant movement of people between the formal sector and several segments of the informal sector. Urban Mexico provides a good example. When blue-collar workers hit advancement ceilings (with sufficient time in service), many tend to go out on their own. But most important, paid informal-sector work (often viewed as the bottom of the informal-sector scale) seems to serve as the main entry vehicle for young, poorly educated workers into paid employment.

To fully grasp the composition and dynamics of Latin America's informal sector, it is worthwhile to examine some key statistical indicators. The informal economy has generated as many as 85% of the new jobs in Latin America during the 1990s.[61] Nearly 60% of Latin American workers are employed in the informal sector, and the number of informal jobs has increased at an average annual rate of 4.6%. Latin American small enterprises have accounted for an estimated 40% of the new informal jobs. Between 65 and 95% of those employed in the informal economy have no employment contract and 65 to 80% lack basic health care or pension arrangements.

Some Latin American economies performed better than others during the 1990s. In Chile, Bolivia, Costa Rica, and Colombia, unemployment fell, pay improved, and the informal economy hardly increased. But in Argentina, Brazil, Mexico, Uruguay, and Venezuela, unemployment and job insecurity grew; and in Argentina and Venezuela, the situation has worsened significantly. In Latin America as a whole, the expansion in the number of jobs in the informal sector during the 1990s was equivalent to 80% of the net increase in employment. In Argentina and Mexico, this coefficient was greater than 100%, since those countries experienced a net elimination of formal jobs.[62]

Looking at Argentina, during the late 1980s some observers estimated that the Argentine underground economy was as large as 40% of the formal economy. At that time, the sector of the population generally classified as poor—that is, persons who operated on the fringes of the formal economy—was increasing as more and more of the lower-middle-class blue-collar industrial and white-collar office workers were displaced by cutbacks in inefficient operations (mainly in state-owned enterprises, but also in many private businesses).[63] It has been estimated that by the end of 1999, more than one-third of the Argentine workforce consisted of informal workers: illegal, often immigrant or underage workers who are paid off the books, who themselves pay little or no tax, and for whom employers make no payments for social security, benefits, or taxes.

In the case of Mexico, the workforce is estimated at around 39.5 million, of which nearly 15 million are registered with the Mexican Social Security Institute (IMSS). The number of workers in the informal economy is widely believed to represent between 25 and 40% of the workforce.[64] The informal economy in Mexico represents 13% of gross domestic product (GDP), according to a study done by the Instituto Nacional de Estadística.[65] Approximately 37% of workers in the informal sector are women and 63% are men; 36% work to increase family income, 33% because they earn more money in the informal sector than in a formal job, 13.6% because they could not find a formal job, and 5.5% because of family tradition. The study found that 93% of informal companies do not utilize credit; and for those that do, the primary source is friends and family.

Owners spend only 19% of their income on overhead and 9.2% on wages, whereas the formal sector business pays on average 44.2% for overhead and 18.7% for wages. The principal activity of informal industry is trade and services, with 47.2% of the total; manufacturing, 23.7%; other services, 22.8%; transport, 4.2%; and construction, 2.1%. (Informal business generates 12.7% of the GDP.) Profits from informal businesses total 17% of earnings generated by the total economy.

Small business, both formal and informal, has been affected by the changing economic and political landscape in the Americas. Many firms have benefited from market liberalization policies, trade opening, deregulation, and administrative reform; many others have been affected negatively, unwilling to change (due to the parochial orientation of the owners/management) or unable (lack of resources, particularly access to credit) to meet the challenges of increased competition from both within and outside their markets. Evidence to date indicates that there will be winners and losers from the ongoing process of globalization and that SMEs will continue to play an important role in the economic growth and development of Latin America.[66]

MULTINATIONAL FIRMS AND CORPORATE STRATEGIES

The 1990s will long be remembered as the decade during which Latin America experienced a *gran viraje*, or major turnaround, in its economic orientation and undertook a major transformation to come into its own. Following several decades of stagnation, countries throughout the region took decisive action to begin realizing their immense economic potential. The reform programs initially adopted by Mexico and Chile and, subsequently, by Argentina, Brazil, and several Andean countries, have enhanced the area's investment appeal in the eyes of international investors (see Table 3.3). Consequently, Latin America has become a major destination for direct investment by many of the world's leading multinationals. Of the world's five largest emerging countries (Russia, India, China, Indonesia, and Brazil), Brazil has covered the most ground in economic reform and is by far the most attractive business destination. Brazil's role as the locomotive of Mercosur only reinforces its attractiveness.

Multinational corporations (MNCs) are uniquely well equipped to seize opportunities in the new, liberalized economic environment. Their global reach, capabilities (particularly technology, financial prowess, and product design/quality/function), and scale provide them with distinct competitive advantages vis-à-vis local firms. Nevertheless, some multinationals are encountering internal obstacles in translating their global advantages into superior local performance—difficulties not uncommon to business entry in many emerging markets. As the new economic model of neoliberal reform dramatically altered the business landscape in Latin America, MNCs mobilized to commit to and actively pursue new ventures. Accordingly, these firms have designed and implemented strategies appropriate to achieving their objectives in the region.

Statistics validate the impact of the new economic model on MNCs. Whereas average annual foreign direct investment (FDI) inflows reached about $23 billion during the first half of the 1990s, they skyrocketed to $70 billion in the 1997–1998 period. In broad economic terms, inflows jumped from the equivalent of 1% to over 4% of GDP between the 1980s and 1997.[67] Globalization, national and subregional policies, and new developments in virtually all industries and sectors have precipitated changes in the operating environment in the Americas. Existing competitive positions are shifting rapidly, and one clearly notes a long-term tendency toward a single universal market.[68] The quest for international markets requires, first, an analysis of the structure of specific product markets, competitor analysis within those markets, the basis and form of technological change, and the impact of new international norms, such as World Trade Organization (WTO) rules on trade, investment, intellectual property, services, and agriculture.

During the 1970s in Latin America, government policies and positions toward foreign investment were generally restrictive.[69] Two decades later, Latin American leaders and policymakers had done a

TABLE 3.3 100 Largest Transnational Firms Present in Latin America, by Consolidated Sales, 1999 (Millions of Dollars)

	FIRM	COUNTRY OF ORIGIN	SECTOR	TOTAL
1	Telefónica de España	Spain	Telecom.	12,439
2	General Motors	U.S.	Motor vehicles	12,425
3	Volkswagen	Germany	Motor vehicles	11,902
4	DaimlerChrysler	Germany	Motor vehicles	9,746
5	Carrefour Group/Promodès[a]	France	Commerce	9,561
6	Ford	U.S.	Motor vehicles	8,252
7	Repsol-YPF	Spain	Petroleum	8,109
8	Fiat Spa	Italy	Motor vehicles	7,659
9	Royal Dutch–Shell Group	UK/Netherlands	Petroleum	6,449
10	ExxonMobil	U.S.	Petroleum	6,403
11	IBM	U.S.	Electronics	5,479
12	Endesa España	Spain	Electricity	5,475
13	AES	U.S.	Electricity	5,182
14	Wal-Mart	U.S.	Commerce	4,816
15	Nestlé	Switzerland	Foodstuffs	4,766
16	Renault/Nissan[a]	France	Motor vehicles	4,179
17	Unilever	UK/Netherlands	Foodstuffs	4,126
18	Motorola	U.S.	Electronics	3,817
19	Cargill	U.S.	Foodstuffs	3,541
20	Intel	U.S.	Electronics	3,540
21	PepsiCo	U.S.	Beverages	3,532
22	Royal Ahold	Netherlands	Commerce	3,442
23	Coca-Cola	U.S.	Beverages	3,336
24	Olivetti Spa./Italia Telecom[a]	Italy	Telecom.	3,162
25	General Electric	U.S.	Machinery	3,142
26	Siemens	Germany	Machinery	2,771

27	BASF	Germany	Chemicals	2,498
28	Hewlett-Packard	U.S.	Electronics	2,469
29	Aventis/Hoechst/Rhône-Poulenc	Germany	Chemicals	2,422
30	Exxel Group	U.S.	Various	2,263
31	L.M. Ericsson	Sweden	Machinery	2,262
32	Philip Morris[b]	U.S.	Tobacco	2,128
33	Procter & Gamble	U.S.	Hygiene/cleaning	2,080
34	BellSouth	U.S.	Telecom.	1,981
35	Nippin Electric (NEC)	Japan	Electronics	1,895
36	Casino Guichard-Perrachon	France	Commerce	1,882
37	E.I. du Pont de Nemours	U.S.	Chemicals	1,877
38	Xerox	U.S.	Electronics	1,744
39	Cisco Systems	U.S.	Electronics	1,723
40	Pirelli	Italy	Tires	1,723
41	Royal Philips Electronics	Netherlands	Electronics	1,693
42	Bayer AG	Germany	Chemicals	1,544
43	Novartis	Switzerland	Chemicals	1,499
44	British American Tobacco (BAT)	UK	Tobacco	1,490
45	Anheuser-Busch	U.S.	Beverages	1,410
46	Électricité De France (EDF)	France	Electricity	1,396
47	Holderbank	Switzerland	Cements	1,383
48	Eastman Kodak	U.S.	Photography	1,378
49	Lucent Technologies	U.S.	Electronics	1,363
50	Compaq Computer	U.S.	Electronics	1,345
51	Sony	Japan	Electronics	1,327
52	Groupe Danone	France	Foodstuffs	1,306
53	Glencore	Switzerland	Commerce	1,294

(continued)

TABLE 3.3 100 Largest Transnational Firms Present in Latin America, by Consolidated Sales, 1999 (Millions of Dollars) (Continued)

	FIRM	COUNTRY OF ORIGIN	SECTOR	TOTAL
54	Colgate-Palmolive	U.S.	Hygiene/cleaning	1,187
55	France Télécom (FTE)	France	Telecom.	1,186
56	Iberdrola	Spain	Electricity	1,138
57	GTE	U.S.	Telecom.	1,081
58	Nabisco Group Holdings[b]	U.S.	Foodstuffs	1,046
59	Monsanto	U.S.	Chemicals	1,020
60	Okram South America Holding	Switzerland	Various	978
61	Whirlpool	U.S.	Household appliances	973
62	Louis Dreyfus	France	Commerce	952
63	McDonald's	U.S.	Commerce	937
64	Avon	U.S.	Hygiene/cleaning	937
65	Kimberly Clark	U.S.	Cellulose/paper	933
66	Broken Hill Proprietary (BHP)	Australia	Mining	848
67	Sonae de Distribuição	Portugal	Commerce	843
68	Parmalat Finanziaria	Italy	Foodstuffs	836
69	Praxair Technologies	U.S.	Various	825
70	Iberia Lineas Aéreas de España	Spain	Transport	808
71	Kraft Foods[b]	U.S.	Foodstuffs	797
72	Electricidade de Portugal	Portugal	Electricity	797
73	BP Amoco (British Petroleum)	UK	Petroleum	770
74	Johnson & Johnson	U.S.	Hygiene/cleaning	767
75	Robert Bosch	Germany	Motor vehicle parts	755
76	Alcoa	U.S.	Metals	745
77	Deere	U.S.	Machinery	708
78	Scania	Sweden	Motor vehicles	692
79	Grupo André	Switzerland	Chemicals	687

80	Gillette	U.S.	Hygiene/cleaning	656
81	PSA Peugeot Citroen	France	Motor vehicles	645
82	Goodyear	U.S.	Tires	634
83	3M	U.S.	Chemicals	613
84	Roche Holding	Switzerland	Chemicals	610
85	ENI	Italy	Petroleum	566
86	WorldCom	U.S.	Telecom.	558
87	Phelps Dodge	U.S.	Mining	551
88	Kenworth Motor Truck	U.S.	Motor vehicles	547
89	Caterpillar	U.S.	Machinery	535
90	Southern Energy	U.S.	Electricity	528
91	Lear	U.S.	Motor vehicle parts	527
92	Anglo American	UK	Mining	518
93	Portugal Telecom	Portugal	Telecom.	509
94	John Labatt	Canada	Beverages	506
95	Navistar	U.S.	Motor vehicles	502
96	Total Fina Elf	France	Petroleum	498
97	Asea Brown Boveri (ABB)	Switzerland	Various	490
98	Bridgestone	Japan	Tires	489
99	Sempra Energy	U.S.	Electricity	483
100	MIM Holding	Australia	Electricity	481

Source: Information derived from ECLAC, Information Centre of the Unit on Investment and Corporate Strategies, Division of Production, Productivity and Management.

[a] *Generated by mergers and acquisitions in the period 1999–2000.*

[b] *Kraft and Nabisco (June 2000) are owned by Philip Morris.*

180-degree turnaround, recasting their view of MNCs to one of "engines of growth" and implementing measures to promote and provide guarantees to FDI and MNC operations. Consequently, there has been a flurry of bilateral investment promotion and guarantee agreements, interest in gaining access to the OECD's (Organization for Economic Cooperation and Development) multilateral agreement on investment, and active participation in the FTAA (Free Trade Area of the Americas) process, particularly in those negotiating groups responsible for investment and market access.

The responses of MNCs have been varied, across industries, sectors, and countries. For existing affiliates, opening up national economies pits them against increased competition from imports and FDI inflows from competitors. The deregulation and liberalization of government policy at a sectoral or company level changes their basic operating conditions. In essence, they are compelled to adapt their corporate strategies to the new environment.[70] For new entrants, new operating conditions combined with the sale of state-owned enterprises unleashed opportunities to grow and consolidate their international systems of integrated production.

The strategic motivations of MNCs have been to increase their access to natural resources and markets for manufactures, gain new access to markets for services, and improve the efficiency of their international systems of integrated production (see Table 3.4). In the case of new entrants, access to natural resources, through the liberalization and deregulation of the mining and energy sectors (often facilitated via the sale of state assets and the granting of concessions), have been key drivers. In Venezuela and Colombia the concession of petroleum rights was central to FDI inflows. In 1995 the state petroleum company of Venezuela PDVSA established a 10-year investment program on the order of $65 billion. Concessions were sold to Mobil, Dupont–Conoco, Enron, Amoco, Elf, Aquitaine, and British Petroleum, and joint ventures were established with Arco, Phillips Petroleum, and Texaco. In Argentina, Repsol of Spain spent $1 billion to buy up local firms such as Pluspetrol, Mexopetrol Argentina, and Algas; and in 1999, Repsol purchased YPF for $15 billion.

For firms striving for greater market access in manufactures, their strategies aimed to adapt to the new competitive situation that derived from the opening of the national markets to increased import competition. These companies generally were ones that had existing operations in the Mercosur countries, mainly Brazil and Argentina. Rather than seek to boost their business via exports, these firms were interested principally in defending their market po-

TABLE 3.4 Focal Points of FDI in Latin America and the Caribbean During the 1990s

SECTOR/OBJECTIVE	PRIMARY	MANUFACTURING	SERVICES
Natural resource seeking	*Petroleum and gas:* Venezuela, Colombia, Argentina *Minerals*: Chile, Argentina, Peru		
Market access seeking			
Manufactures		*Automotive*: Mercosur *Chemicals*: Brazil *Agroindustry*: Argentina, Brazil, Mexico	
Services			*Financial services*: Brazil, Mexico, Chile, Argentina *Telecommunications*: Brazil, Argentina, Chile, Peru *Electrical energy*: Colombia, Brazil, Argentina, Central America *Gas distribution*: Argentina, Brazil, Chile, Colombia
Efficiency seeking		*Automotive*: Mexico *Electronics*: Mexico and Caribbean Basin *Apparel*: Caribbean Basin and Mexico	

Source: ECLAC, *Foreign Investment in Latin America and the Caribbean,* Santiago. ECLAC, 2001; *Information Centre of the Unit on Investment and Corporate Strategies, Division of Production, Productivity and Management.*

sitions, mainly by merging or acquiring prominent local firms in mature industries such as chemicals, food products, beverages, and tobacco. ICI bought Tintas Coral (Brazil) and Alba (Argentina). Parmalat acquired Indústria Alimentícia Batavia (Brazil).

The services sector is another area where FDI has been vigorous, especially since the sector had been off-limits prior to market-opening reforms. New entrants predominated in this sector, taking advantage of opportunities in telecommunications and energy distribution, mergers and acquisitions, and financial services, especially banks, and particularly in Brazil. Other services that took off at this time included consulting, construction and engineering, law and accounting, logistics, and franchising. The vigorous expansion of MNCs in the region in the early 1990s centered on FDI aimed at boosting the efficiency of globally integrated production and distribution systems. An important component of this strategy was the restructuring of existing operations to convert them into an export platform. The automobile industry in Mexico provides a good example, as well as newly created asset bases in auto parts, electronics, and apparel.

Strategic asset seeking by MNCs in Latin America, especially in terms of research and investment to develop world-class technologies, did not weigh heavily as a factor in FDI strategies. However, in the future R&D (in selected countries) could become a driver, albeit a second-tier driver. R&D spending in six countries (Argentina, Brazil, Mexico, Chile, Costa Rica, and Venezuela) jumped 40% between 1990 and 1996 ($8.7 billion to $12.3 billion). The public sector was the principal financial source and performer of R&D activities. Chile is a dominant competitor in Latin American R&D. The nation maintains three national funds that support basic research, applied research, and innovation in production.[71]

Unquestionably, the two most important objectives of FDI in recent years have been improving the efficiency of their globally integrated systems of production and distribution (particularly through FDI in Mexico and the Caribbean Basin) and gaining market access for services by way of FDI (Brazil). The importance of these objectives is attributed to the proportion of the total FDI inflows that they represent and the very significant trade flows produced as a consequence.

The automobile sector provides a vivid example of how FDI (through firms setting up new operations or restructuring existing ones) can improve the efficiency of globally integrated production and distribution systems.[72] It is this sector where the biggest foreign firms by sales are found in the region, accounting for seven of the 10 largest foreign corporations by consolidated sales: GM–Mexico,

VW–Brazil, GM–Brazil, Chrysler–Mexico, VW–Mexico, Fiat–Brazil, and Ford–Mexico. The case of Mexico is the best example of a country that has undergone a very significant structural transformation in the context of the globalization process, especially in the automotive sector.[73]

The globalization of Mexico's automobile industry had its roots in the 1970s when Japanese automobile producers began challenging the U.S. and European auto MNCs. By investing in lean production technologies, flexible organization, defect prevention, and just-in-time delivery of inputs—not to mention fuel efficiency at a time of two global oil shocks—the Japanese auto MNCs came to pose a serious threat to U.S. and European competitors. The Big Three U.S. auto companies (GM, Ford, and Chrysler) assumed a defensive position through an offensive move: improving their competition in the U.S. market by establishing more efficient production facilities in neighboring Mexico.

The repositioning, in fact the transforming, of the U.S. auto companies was abetted by national policies in the United States and Mexico; new corporate strategies were developed to boost efficiency, sales, market share, and financial performance.[74] Two principal elements were involved in corporate strategic responses: auto parts and vehicle assembly. By using production-sharing arrangements, U.S. firms could export components for assembly while the imported final product was charged tax only on the value-added (mainly wages). At the same time, Mexico vigorously promoted its *maquiladora* program, offering tax-free operations similar to export-processing zones. Taken together, this produced great cost reductions.

Mexico clearly saw the advantages in abandoning its previously restrictive national automobile policy and developing one aimed at facilitating the implementation of new export-oriented plants. This policy was complemented with NAFTA provisions that gave preferences to U.S. auto producers in integration of the continental automobile industry. The regional (U.S., Canadian, and Mexican) norms of origin (62.5% of production costs) in particular were influential in this respect. As a consequence of the synergistic policies of the U.S. and Mexican governments, FDI in the Mexican automobile industry by auto MNCs as well as their parts suppliers skyrocketed. This response, a reaction of the Big Three U.S. auto companies, led to the creation of world-class vehicle assembly plants in Mexico. During 1990–1996 the Big Three invested over $5.5 billion in new plants in Mexico on top of considerable FDI during the 1980s.

By 1998, Mexico's automobile industry was producing 1 to 1.5 million vehicles, and the Big Three were responsible not only for two-thirds of the production but more important, for about 70% of the exports. Chrysler and Ford exported over 84% of the vehicles that they produced in Mexico. The linkage between FDI and trade in auto MNCs operating in Mexico became one of Mexico's principal means of integration into the international economy.

If one compares corporate strategies in Mexico's automobile industry with Mercosur's, sharp differences emerge. The challenges of international markets and new national and subregional policy packages forced firms to react by way of new corporate strategies—some phased out, selling their assets, licensing local firms, or shutting down all together. Others rationalized their operations; that is, without making major new investments, they tried to maintain their market shares by reducing operational costs through downsizing, streamlining, and so on. Some chose restructuring, undertaking major new investments to recast the role of the existing plants within the new global strategy of corporate headquarters, usually in terms of its international system of integrated production.

Affiliates of U.S. auto firms in Mexico chose the latter strategy; the response by Mercosur auto MNCs was quite different. The principal auto MNCs in the Mercosur market (Fiat, VW, Ford, GM, Renault, and PSA) are mainly European. Interestingly, U.S. assemblers' (Ford and GM) links are mainly to the European operations of their particular headquarter's corporation. In the 1980s, in Brazil and Argentina most of these companies reacted by pulling back/pulling out (Renault and Fiat began to operate through local licensees in Argentina) or rationalizing productions (Ford and VW merged their operations in Autolatina until 1995).[75]

When less competitive European (and U.S.) auto firms announced substantial FDI to improve the competitiveness of their operations in Mercosur, the reasons were "defensive"; they did not do so to establish export platforms. They were attempting to defend their existing Mercosur market shares. Recognizably, the Mercosur market possessed neither the geographical proximity to a major market, the capacity to produce labor-intensive auto parts in export-processing zones, nor the same degree of liberalization or deregulation. Additionally, they had relatively high levels of import protection for vehicles and high levels of obligatory subregional content. In essence, the impact on the local economy of the defensive FDI in Mercosur has not been as positive or far-reaching as the efficiency-seeking FDI in the Mexican automobile industry in terms of exports, balance of payments, and especially, the quality of the vehicle produced. A strategy that opted for the efficiency-seeking option in Mexico appeared to produce much better results than the market defense-based strategy in Mercosur.

As mentioned earlier, another objective of FDI is to gain market access for services, for example through the privatization of electricity (generation and distribution) and telecommunications. Over half the FDI inflows to Latin America during 1995–1998 came about due to the liberalization and deregulations of services. Although these inflows do not usually produce significant trade flows, the increased competition permitted by the new national regulations can have a significant impact on the overall structural competitiveness of an economy.

Although Brazil was not a major recipient of FDI inflows during the first half of the 1990s, by 1998 it had replaced Mexico as the primary destination of foreign investment. At the same time, manufacturing was edged out by services as the principal stock of FDI (56%). Those MNCs seeking market access did so primarily by purchasing existing assets, via the privatization programs in the electricity and telecommunications sectors or the private acquisition of banks and other financial institutions.

Admittedly, international market factors were not the principal motivation behind the FDI in services in Brazil; however, they were very important secondary factors. Market openings in Brazil provided opportunities for major players in other markets and new entrants within the region, as well as outside, to position themselves in Latin America. Multilateral agreements, such as the General Agreement on Trade in Services (GATSs) relating to telecommunications and financial services enhanced the attractiveness of establishing a presence in the region. Although globally integrated operations are not a crowning feature of MNC competitiveness in the services sector, they can, in fact, provide advantages, especially in limiting the possibilities for expansion of competitors in two key sectors: telecommunications and electricity. Again, Brazil serves as a prime example. Laws were changed to permit foreign investment in previously reserved sectors. The liberalization and deregulation of services in telecommunications, electricity and financial services, and retail commerce attracted huge inflows of FDI.[76]

As Latin American nations and the companies operating there— local, multinational, and state-owned—strive to compete in the rapidly changing global environment, productivity will be paramount. During the 1990s, the region made progress in improving productivity; nevertheless, its performance, in the aggregate, vis-à-vis industrialized nations remains subpar. In a Latin American labor productivity study by McKinsey, examining steel, food processing, telecommunications, and retail banking in the five largest economies (Argentina, Brazil, Colombia, Mexico, and Venezuela), researchers found productivity levels to be only around 30% of world-class levels in three of the four cases. (Only telecommunications boosted a much higher level.) Disappointingly, the World Economic Forum's most recent global competitiveness report reveals that with the exception of Mexico, these nations have actually experienced declines in productivity during the past five years.[77]

Although economic liberalization has had a hugely positive impact and productivity-inhibiting factors such as protectionism and overregulation are disappearing, bureaucratic inertia, nontariff barriers, and rigid labor rules are mitigating against greater gains in productivity.[78] Recognizably, the productivity gap widened between industrialized nations and developing ones after World War II, with the former group's widespread and faster-paced adoption of new methods of work organization, technology, and production methods. Still, the productivity gap is not uniform but varies across industries and within sectors. For example, in petroleum refining and oil derivatives, Latin American performance approximates that of the United States and Europe. Moreover, given the fast cycle life of information and production technologies, a number of Latin American sectors and industries can make quantum leaps from systems that were obsolete decades ago to state-of-the-art systems.[79]

While the transfer of technology and know-how to Latin America and significant financing and investment are essential for nations and firms to improve their productivity and competitiveness continuously, they are by no means the most determining factors. In fact, in a study of Brazilian productivity, researchers found that underinvestment in technology did not account for a large part of the gap: ". . . a large portion of the gap, about 35 percent, could be closed by improving the way work is organized, and another 30 percent by making modest capital improvements with payback periods of less than two years. Simply to optimize existing processes without investing any new capital would increase GDP growth by almost 2 percentage points."[80] Countries and firms that heed these lessons are sure to experience marked gains in productivity. As globalization spreads and intensifies, they will need to do so merely to hold their own, let alone achieve a sustainable competitive advantage vis-à-vis their competitors, domestic as well as foreign.

This, then, is the current business landscape in Latin America, one fraught with both challenges and opportunities for multinational firms, their suppliers and financiers, and for governments in the region and the vast majority of consumers. The globalization process is accelerating neoliberal economic reforms, including trade, investment, and financial liberalization and the deepening of regional and subregional integration. Multinational firms in key sectors of the economy are positioning themselves to maintain and expand their competitive advantages through the development of networks, technology, and management savvy. They will also need to concentrate simultaneously on three key, interrelated disciplines: the design of the organizational structure; management processes for allocating resources and measuring/rewarding performance; and the culture, values, and behavior espoused.[81]

In Part 2 of this book, beginning with Chapter 4, we present and analyze the status of four key sectors—infrastructure (including telecom and energy), consumer goods, financial services, and health care—and the associated strategic concerns, plans, and responses of multinational firms in Latin America's big emerging markets.

PART

2

SECTOR-SPECIFIC STRATEGIES

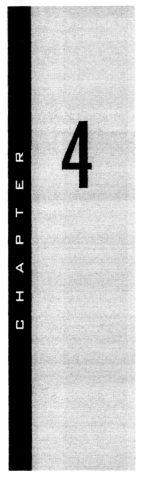

4 BUILDING THE INFRASTRUCTURE NETWORK

Any observer of Latin America today will see a region where poor infrastructure is apparent everywhere. In the background, however, many firms and governments are participating in building a modern network of telecommunications, power grids, and undersea fiber-optic cables that will move the region to the twenty-first century. Telefónica of Spain is building an undersea fiber-optic cable around South America that will connect with the firm's own national networks in several countries and allow broadband city-to-city connections. Telecom Italia, Global Crossing, and Alcatel are all building their own undersea and land fiber-optic network. The race is on to capture the new demand for data, Internet traffic, and other value-added services in the region. The demand for these services is growing at a much faster rate than for local or even national voice traffic. Other firms, including U.S. Tenneco, Chile's Enersis, British Gas, Argentina's YPF, and CMS, have built several trans-Andean gas pipelines to provide Chile with Argentinean gas. Similar gas pipelines built by a consortium of Argentinean, Brazilian, and Canadian firms, including YPF, Techint, Total Fina, and the Ipiranga group, connect Argentina's northwestern gas basins with southern Brazil. Bolivia gas basins are also providing needed natural gas to Brazil through a pipeline built and managed by Enron. Similarly, a consortium of firms led by PG&E, Sempra, and Mexico's Proxima Gas is building a pipeline that will connect U.S. and Mexican natural gas grids. Northern Mexico's power grid is already connected with the U.S. grid.[1] Just how did the private sector become an active player in building infrastructure networks in the Americas?

Latin America is one of the first regions to adopt wholesale infrastructure reforms. As early as the late 1980s, Latin American governments have privatized, deregulated, and restructured their energy, telecommunications, railroads, water, and sewage. In response to these investment opportunities, private capital flows during 1982–1998 have reached $257 billion, with most of the investment taking place in the 1990s.[2] Despite the massive capital investment in this sector, expert studies indicate that as much as $50 billion will be needed in the future, and strategic investors will be looking for additional opportunities in the expansion of Latin American infrastructure. In addition, there are still large amounts of assets to be privatized in the region. Infrastructure networks are the equivalent of the blood system in any economy. Whether the content is people, information, energy, money, goods, or services, the key function of a network is to facilitate the exchange and delivery of vital elements to economic agents efficiently and reliably.

In the past, the conventional thinking was to control the entire value chain in a network. Thus ownership of a vertically integrated system was essential to provide adequate service. The economic drivers of this strategy were economies of scale, network externalities, interconnectivity, and protected access to markets. All of these factors favor vertical integration and monopoly conditions. The building of such a network requires sizable investments in long-lived assets, and the expansion and maintenance of such assets require substantial investments during the period.

The radical reforms of infrastructure networks in Latin America have challenged the conventional thinking in two fundamental ways: (1) that the government should be the pure owner of infrastructure assets, and (2) that vertical integration is necessary to provide high-quality, efficient services. As mentioned above, Latin American governments have initiated substantial privatization of their railroads, ports, telecommunications, energy, roads, and water infrastructures. Second, the economic activities have been disaggregated in several independent activities or businesses where independent providers compete for markets.

Strategic investors new to the region need to understand a plethora of liberalization and privatization frameworks. Reforms and deregulation in Latin America have been aimed at dismantling the state monopoly, privatizing, and deregulating different components of the infrastructure value chain. This unbundling of the state monopoly has taken many approaches in the region. Liberalization of the sectors has also taken different approaches. In some cases, parts of the sector have been open for competition, whereas in others the state has retained ownership and monopoly status. As a result, the region is a mosaic of different sector structures, regulatory frameworks, and ownership regimes. In some countries and sectors, the rules are transparent and the regulatory bodies well managed. In others countries and sectors, ambiguous rules and weak regulatory bodies are the rule.

In addition, technology is reshaping the nature of competition and providing new opportunities to all firms. Information technology including the Internet, is revolutionizing the way that infrastructure services are produced, bought, and used. New technologies give rise to new skills and competencies in the once stodgy infrastructure industry. New technologies such as using liners in pipelines or remote metering reduce the costs of transmission and repair of utility networks. Technology is also blurring the distinction between types of utilities. Network value chains can carry different types of services. Energy companies are finding that their pipelines can also carry telecommunication services.

How does a company sort out differences in the reformed infrastructure markets in Latin America? What strategy works better in the region? Should companies develop regional strategies or focus on a few selected opportunities in the region? Should new investment projects capitalize on new technologies to exploit convergence in infrastructure business in Latin America? What strategies will protect the firm against increasing competitive, regulatory, and technology uncertainties? Do large integrated firms with regional scope fare better than specialists controlling narrow slivers of the infrastructure value chain in Latin America? Should a firm pursue acquisitions or organic growth? In this chapter we analyze the regulatory reforms in Latin America and assess the infrastructure investment needs to support future economic growth. We examine fundamental aspects of infrastructure network strategy and discuss a successful case of transforming a government-owned monopoly into a global-class competitive business.

MASSIVE INFRASTRUCTURE INVESTMENT NEEDS

According to a World Bank study, Latin America needs to invest $57 billion per year for the next five years to increase infrastructure capacity necessary to meet demand. Additional $35 billion in investments are necessary to maintain and rehabilitate the present infrastructure stock. These estimates are in line with what other developing regions invest in infrastructure: 4% of gross domestic product (GDP). Since governments have been pulling out of the infrastructure sector, policymakers and development agencies such as the World Bank expect the private sector to address infrastructure in this region. With recent foreign direct investment flows in infrastructure to the region reaching close to $35 billion, there is a gap of 41% of unmet needs. Why is the private sector not investing more? In what infrastructure sectors and which countries is the gap the worst?

Clearly, the gap of infrastructure levels between Latin America and the rest of the world is large. Table 4.1 shows the per capita levels in telecommunications, electricity, roads, railroads, water, and sanitation for lower-income countries and higher-income countries in Latin America and the world. Within Latin America, the gap between higher- and lower-income countries is notable. In comparison with other regions, Latin American lower-income-level countries are at par with similar countries in the world. Latin American middle-income-level countries, however, are only at par in connectivity and lag behind similar countries in electricity, roads, water, and sanitation. The contrast of the region's infrastructure with that of higher income levels shows a dramatic disparity across all infrastructure sectors.

Infrastructure density depends not only on income level but on other factors of economic activity, levels of urbanization, and international trade. A World Bank study developed a model that projects infrastructure density assuming projected growth of population and economic activity that have a direct impact on infrastructure.[3] The projected increases in the stock of infrastructure are then translated in investment needs using best-practice unit costs of infrastructure. Table 4.2 shows the investment needs by sector. Clearly, energy and transportation require massive annual flow of new investments just to supply estimated levels of future economic activity and population growth in the region.

Past infrastructure investments show the sectors and countries most attractive to investors. Private investment flows in the period

TABLE 4.1 Per Capita Stocks of Infrastructure in Latin America, 1995–2005

World Region and Income Level	Year	Wired Phones (Lines/1000 People)	Electricity (KW of Generation Capacity/Person)	Paved Roads (KM/1000 People)	Rail (KM/1000 People)	Water (% of Population with Access)	Sanitation (% of Population with Access)
Lower-middle-income countries in Latin America	1995	80	0.38	0.70	0.34	62	69.8
	2000	105	0.42	0.67	0.38	63	68.1
	2005	152	0.45	0.65	0.32	54	67.3
World lower-middle-income countries	1995	81	0.37	1.08	0.23	70	69.98
Latin American gap with LMIC	1995	1.01	1.02	0.64	1.47	0.88	0.96
Upper-middle income in Latin America	1995	136	0.56	1.12	0.48	78.5	72.7
	2000	183	0.66	1.12	0.41	67.8	78.6
	2005	254	0.82	1.18	0.37	65.5	82.6
World upper-middle-income countries	1995	124	0.62	2.32	0.48	79.9	78.9
Latin American gap with UMIC	1995	1.09	0.61	0.48	0.72	0.81	0.73
World higher-income countries	1995	496	2.12	9.74	0.66	96.6	98.6
Latin American gap with HIC	1995	0.27	0.26	0.11	0.72	0.81	0.73

Source: "Financing the Future: Infrastructure Needs in Latin America, 2000–2005," World Bank Policy Research Working Paper Series No. 2412, available at http://econ.worldbank.org/.

TABLE 4.2 Projected Latin American Infrastructure Needs by Sector, 2000–2005

| | ESTIMATED INVESTMENT NEED | | PRIVATE INVESTMENT | |
SECTOR	$ MILLIONS	AS % OF GDP	$ MILLIONS IN 1998	AS % OF ESTIMATED NEED
Electricity	6,089	0.27	4,536	21
Telecommunications	22,042	0.99	14,546	240
Paved roads	17,836	0.87	12,366	54
Railroads	4,887	0.23		
Water	2,604	0.15	339	5
Sanitation	4,035	0.18		
Total	57,466	2.69	34,997	61

Source: "Financing the Future: Infrastructure Needs in Latin America, 2000–2005," World Bank Policy Research Working Paper Series No. 2412, available at http://econ.worldbank.org/.

of 1982–1998 have overwhelmingly favored the telecommunications sector. The telecommunications sector was the first to be reformed through privatizations and deregulations. After more than 10 years of continuous investing, this sector is reaching maturity and saturation. If future investments continue the pattern of investment flows in 1998, we can conclude that investments in the telecommunications sector have been oversubscribed.

The future wave of big investment needs and opportunities may come from the energy and water utility sectors, where reforms are still incipient and where demand is strong. The most promising sectors are electricity and roads in Brazil, Mexico, and Argentina. The large gaps of potential unmet needs in these sectors suggest large business opportunities. Given these future opportunities, the lack of investment enthusiasm in the transportation, energy, and water sectors appears to be due to greater uncertainty in their reform programs and regulations. In terms of modes of investment participation in infrastructure, investment flows in 1998 revealed that firms used mostly greenfield investments, acquisitions, and concessions (O & Ms). Investors used acquisitions mostly to acquire telecommunications assets being privatized. Greenfield investments were used in about equal proportion in the telecommunications and energy sectors.[4]

What incentives and investment conditions will be necessary to induce more investment in future infrastructure opportunities in Latin America? What options does a firm have to participate in these opportunities while the reforms are introduced and fine-tuned? What can firms learn from reforms in the telecommunications sector? We address these questions next, starting with our analysis of infrastructure reforms.

INFRASTRUCTURE REFORMS

Over the last 15 years, substantial reforms were introduced in Latin America. In countries such as Argentina and Chile, wholesale reforms were introduced and implemented across several infrastructure sectors. In others, reforms were sector-specific and initiated at different times. Tables 4.3 and 4.4 show the status of reforms in the telecommunications and energy (electricity and gas) sectors in Latin America. As these tables show, there is no single model or pattern that is prevalent in the region. In some cases, the legal and regulatory institutions were in place before a wholesale privatization program was undertaken. In other cases, privatization took place within the context of obsolete infrastructure legislation and regulations. In the latter cases, policymakers adjusted the regulatory framework, as issues such as pricing and information sharing arose during early periods of reforms. Winners of early privatization rounds took very large risks when rules and regulations were ambiguous or nonexistent in early rounds. Late reformers benefited from experiences of earlier reformers and incorporated models and features that seemed to work toward the accomplishment of governmental objectives for the privatization.

In most cases, government objectives were to attract private investment, improve the quality and efficiency of service, provide universal access, and develop a self-financed and internationally competitive sector. The main tools for achieving these objectives were privatization programs and the promotion of competition. Firms considering participation in reformed sectors expected that these reforms would give them access to markets, provide well-designed and clear rules of operation, and achieve reasonable rates of return. Issues such as tariff setting, regulation of market power, network access, integrity of the system, and interconnectivity became paramount to both investors and policymakers. The three aspects that capture the various Latin American reforms are industry structure, regulatory conditions for the operation, and forms of private sector participation. We review these three areas next.

UNBUNDLING THE STATE MONOPOLIES

The unbundling of the vertically integrated state monopoly is a daunting task. Two levels of market structure have been the focus of reformers. *Vertical restructuring* refers to the decomposition of the

TABLE 4.3 Telecommunications Privatizations in Latin America

		COUNTRIES ALREADY PRIVATIZED		
COUNTRY	COMPANY	YEAR PRIVATIZED	FULL LIBERALIZATION	PRINCIPAL INVESTORS[a]
Argentina	Telecom Argentina, Telefónica Argentina	1990	1999–2000	STET, France Telecom, Telefónica Spain
Bolivia	Entel	1995	Nov. 27, 2001	n.a.
Brazil	Telesp, Tele Sudeste, Brazil Telecom, Nordeste Celular, Tele Celular Sul, Telebrás, among others	1998	2002–2003	Telecom Italia, TISA, Portugal Telecom, RBS, BBV, Iberdrola, Andrade Gutiérrez, Lafonte e Inepar
Chile	CTC, Entel, Telex Chile (ChileSat)	1987	1992–1994	Telefónica Spain, Bond Corporation (Australia)
Panama	Intel	1997	2002	n.a.
Peru	Telefónica de Peru	1994	1998	Telefónica Spain
Venezuela	CANTV	1991	1997–1998	GTE, Telefónica Spain, AT&T
Guatemala	Telgua	1998	1999	Telmex
Mexico	Telmex	1990	1997–1998	France Telecom

COUNTRIES IN PROCESS OF PRIVATIZATION

COUNTRY	COMPANY	PRIVATIZATION	FULL LIBERALIZATION
El Salvador	CTE, Intel	1998	France Telecom, Telefónica Spain
Honduras	Hondutel	51% in 2001	Unsuccessful
Nicaragua	Enitel	40% in 2001	In progress
Paraguay	Antelco	November 2001	In progress
Ecuador	Andinatel, Pacifitel	2002	Unknown

COUNTRIES RESISTING PRIVATIZATION

COUNTRY	COMPANY
Uruguay	Antel
Costa Rica	ICE
Colombia	Telecom (state owned); ETB, EPM, and smaller local carriers privatized in 1994 (local), 1998 (long distance and international)

Source: Juan A. Díaz (Harris Corporation), "Infrastructure Projects in Latin America," Supercomm Emerging Markets Conference, International Telecommunication Union, June 6, 2001; CIT, Datafile of Latin American Telecommunications, 2001.

[a]n.a., not available.

135

TABLE 4.4 Latin American Energy Reforms

REFORMS	ARGENTINA[a]		CHILE	
	ELECTRICITY[a]	GAS	ELECTRICITY	GAS
Legislation	State reform act, 1989; Electricity law, 1992	State reform act, 1989 Gas law, 1992	Electricity law, 1992	Interconnection protocol with Argentina, 1995
Restructuring period	1992–1994	1992–1993	1986–1990	
State monopoly (year privatized)	SEGBA Aguas y Energia Electrica Hydronor	Gas del Estado, 1992; YPF	Compañía Chilena de Electricidad Endesa (generation, 1987)	

INDUSTRY STRUCTURE, 2000				
Exploitation (natural resource)	n.a.	YPF (80% of gas supply)	Concessions (Hydropower)	Imported from Argentina
Generation	40 IPPs	30 IGPs		Several vertical integrated groups: Enersis, Gener, Edelnor
Wholesale supply	Trading market (open to large users)	Trading market (open to large users)		
Transmission	Private concession, open access	Concessions (35 years) north (TGN), south (TGS), open access	North (SING), South (SIC), negotiated tariffs	
Distribution	14 distributors (95 years concessions)	8 regional distributors (35 years concessions)	Vertical integrated groups	
Regulation	ENRE Tariffs, access, competition	ENARGAS Transmission and retail tariffs, competition	CNE—Policy Mining and energy Ministry—tariffs SEC—compliance CDEC— dispatching	
Interconnection tariffs				
Service tariffs		Transmission: full-cost recovery; distribution: nodal price + transp. + distribution with price caps	Nodal price + trans. + distrib. + rate of return (revised every 4 years)	

[a] n.a., not available

	BRAZIL		MEXICO		PERU	BOLIVIA
	ELECTRICITY	GAS	ELECTRICITY	GAS	ELECTRICITY	GAS
	Concession law, 1995	Petroleum law, 1997	Electricity reforms, 1992	Natural gas law, 1995	Electricity concessions law, 1992	Hydrocarbon law, 1996
		1999–today	1998–date	1996–date	1992–date	1996–1997
	Electrobrás state monopolies		CFE, LFC	Pemex	ElectroPeru municipal plants	YPFB

INDUSTRY STRUCTURE, 2000						
	State-owned	Petrobrás (state owned), mostly imported from Argentina, Bolivia, Venezuela		Pemex	Hydropower	YPFB
	Privatization in progress (15% of capacity as of 2001)	Gaspetro (subsidiary of Petrobrás)	IPP allowed		51% capacity privatized	Two major players: Chacosam (Amoco), Andinasam 17 IGPs
	Subregional trading centers	Gaspetro				
	Concessions	State run (open to large users)	State monopoly	Pemex Transport permits granted (16), open access	Two regional systems: government-managed ETECEN (north); ETESUR (south)	Private concession, Transredes (Exxon/Shell), open access
	14 regional concessions	12 government distributors, 4 private concessions	State monopoly	Regional private concessions (18), exclusivity for 12 years	53% privatized, 7 regional distributors	Concessions (very weak domestic market development as gas is exported)
	ANEEL— overall AME—trading ONS—dispatching	ANP Concessions, distribution, exploration, importation Determined by Gaspetro	CFE— overall	CRE Tariffs, licenses, competition	OSINERG— Overall tariff commission	SIRESE (multisectoral regulation)

monopoly value chain. *Horizontal restructuring* refers to the introduction of competition at a given level of vertical restructuring. The choice of structure, to both levels, depends on economic, technical, and political grounds.[5] The efficiencies derived from economies of scale and scope are two fundamental drivers for favoring privatizing the entire network to a single operator. On the other hand, technological advances in certain aspects of production, especially in generation and distribution of power, show that small-scale operators can be as efficient as large operators, and competition can be introduced. Thus, market structure varies with the time of the reforms (early, late), the sector (energy, telecom, and water), and the stage of the value chain (generation, distribution).

TELECOMMUNICATION REFORMS

The privatization program embarked in the 1980s and 1990s has been relatively successful; it is competitive and encompasses high private-sector participation, as well as boasting the highest proportion of separate and independent regulatory agencies in the world.[6] For example, out of a population of almost 515 million, the region has 67.5 million main telephone lines, and in 1999 its cellular mobile subscribers skyrocketed to 42.2 million from a mere 3.9 million in 1995.[7] Moreover, in terms of foreign direct investment in the telecom sector, about $17.3 billion went to Latin America.

Telecommunications, long regarded as a national asset, began the long and arduous process of privatization throughout the late 1980s and 1990s as governments began to feel the economic and financial burden that the sector placed upon them. Telecommunications upkeep and maintenance, its use as a political and patronage support system, and the continuous needs for advances via research and development were simply too expensive and overwhelming for many countries. As such, privatization became the salvation for governments to "let go" of their costly behemoths, providing both challenges and opportunities. Economic liberalization has torn down protectionist barriers and allowed the penetration of foreign investment in the region.

Indeed, the sale of public telephone operators (PTOs) proved to be quite enticing as the region has amassed over $40 billion in revenues.[8] The impetus toward privatization and deregulation has provided governments with much needed capital. These funds have been used for the stabilization of local currency, debt payments, the bolstering of public saving accounts, societal/social functions, as well as the enhancement of service to the customer. By 1999, more than two-thirds of the 33 Latin American countries had either partially or wholly privatized their telecommunication's industry, while 81% have publicly committed to liberalize basic services.

According to the ITU, Latin America contains the highest percentage of countries that have privatized their national telecommunication systems at an astonishing 70%, as compared to 55% for Europe, 46% for the Asia-Pacific, 33% for the Arab states, and 28% for Africa.[9] These figures adequately depict the region's privatization success in telecommunication market reforms. Latin American governments have pursued privatization in this sector quite aggressively given the link between telecommunications and development. The better equipped and more progressive a country's telecommunication system, the more it is expected to progress. Those at the forefront of telecommunications privatization, the early reformers (1987–1991), were Chile, Argentina, Mexico, and Venezuela, respectively. These countries were followed by the second wave (1994–1997), which included Peru, Bolivia, and Panama, followed by the late reformers (1998): Brazil, Ecuador, El Salvador, Guatemala, and Nicaragua. The region is also made up of several countries that have resisted reforms such as Colombia, Costa Rica, Honduras, Paraguay, and Uruguay.

In the telecommunications sectors, early reformers have favored keeping vertical integration and provided monopoly rights to investors for periods ranging from 7 to 10 years. Since 1985, Chile has transferred control of the local (CTC) and long-distance (Entel) operators reaching full divestiture in 1990. The local exchange has been open to competition since 1992, and the revised telecommunications law of 1994 allowed multicarrier system and vertical integration at all levels. Market entry to other telecommunications sectors, such as the mobile and business networks, have been open at all times. Chile enjoys one of the most open and competitive telecommunications markets in the world. Argentinean policymakers broke down the state-owned monopoly (Entel) into two regional networks (north and south). The privatization of Entel took place in 1990. The winning firms, Telefónica of Spain (South) and Italian STET/France Telecom (North), obtained an exclusive monopoly status for the local, long-distance, and international services in their territories for a period of seven years (guaranteed) plus three years more if service targets were met. In 1999, the fixed-line market was fully liberalized and both operators were free to enter into each other's territories. In addition, a spate of new companies entered the local and long-distance segments using different technologies. In the same year, Argentine regulators issued nationwide mobile operating licenses to incumbents and new entrants. Despite the different approaches to market structure, the Argentinean and Chilean telecommunication sectors are truly competitive and there is free market entry.

Brazil, a late reformer, used a different reform approach. Brazilian policymakers broke down Telebrás monopoly into regional concessions in 1998. Three major regional operations cover the fixed-line and intraregional services of Northeast (Telemar), Central-South (Brazil Telecom), and the São Paulo (Telesp) regions. Four other operators hold licenses for regions not covered by those mentioned previously. The mobile telephony market was divided into 10 regions. Finally, the long-distance and international monopoly, Embratel, was sold to MCI Worldcom. Brazilian reforms introduced a novel approach to market structure by allowing the entry of a small competitor in each market segment. For instance, Intelig (owned by Sprint, France Telcom, and UK National Grid) competed with privatized Embratel. Vesper, a Brazilian-owned operator, entered to compete with Telemar and Telesp. In the mobile market, B-band licenses for the 10 territories were granted in 1998 to compete with the A-band licenses. According to the reform plan, fixed-line telephony will be fully liberalized by 2003. The mobile market segment will be consolidated in three expanded regions, and more concessions will be issued.[10]

As Table 4.3 shows, early reformers were more generous in granting long monopoly rights to investors. The advantage of lack of competition gave the incumbents time to implement long-term network improvements and expansion plans and to obtain a guaranteed return. The case study later in the chapter shows how Telecom Italia and France Telecom were able to plan such a long-term strategy in Argentina. In late reformer countries such as Brazil, investors face competition, albeit limited, from the outset. Furthermore, in a very short term, three years, the markets will open to full competition. In the absence of a long-term planning period, private telecom operators have to do everything at once, from improvement to expansion.

Our analysis of the telecommunications reforms in other countries (see Table 4.3) shows that privatizations and regulatory frameworks peaked in the mid-1990s. The presence of state-owned monopolies in wired telephony indicates the difficulty that these governments faced in initiating reforms or getting their reforms approved. The difficulties seem to arise from political opposition to introduced reforms (Colombia, Nicaragua) or failure to attract investor interest due to the depressed and too-leveraged conditions of the telecommunications sector worldwide (Ecuador).

ENERGY REFORMS

Similar to telecommunications, Latin American governments introduced reforms in the energy sector for the same reasons of lack of investment needs. Three major activities that characterize the energy sector are the generation, transmission, and distribution of energy. The reasons for the structural reforms in this sector were very similar to those mentioned for telecommunications. Powerful state monopolies controlled all aspects of the energy value chain. For most countries, the energy-based monopolies were these countries' flagship enterprises, large enough to be ranked among the world's largest firms. Mexico's Pemex, Brazil's Petrobrás and Electrobrás, and Argentina's YPF commanded large economic and political power.

We use the experience of Chile and Argentina to illustrate the nature of reforms that have shaped the industry structure in both countries. Chile's energy reforms can be characterized by privatization first and regulation later. This approach has generated a concentration of market power and vertical integration of the privatized companies. The dominant firm, Enersis, controls 52% of generation capacity, 29% of distribution market share, and up until recently, control of the country's principal transmission company.[11] Chile's natural gas infrastructure consists mostly of distribution of Argentina's gas. Chile's gas sector is market driven and open to new entrants.

Argentina has been more successful in achieving its goals and creating a more competitive energy market. In terms of energy resources, Argentina counts on a diverse mix of hydroelectric, oil, and gas resources. Thus, this country has fully developed electricity and gas infrastructures. Argentina designed and implemented a strong and clear regulatory framework first and then proceeded with privatization. One feature of Argentina's regulatory framework was to limit any one company control of more than 10% of total generating power.[12] As a result, Argentina has 40 independent electricity generators and 30 independent gas producers. Transmission concessions for 35 years to private companies guarantee open access to users and distributors. Regional distributors also have 35-year concessions in gas and 95 years in electricity. Large users are free to source energy from wholesalers or negotiate contracts in the energy trading markets, or secure long-term contracts with independent energy producers. Fourteen electricity distributors and eight gas distributors have captive small users in their territories but are required to provide access to providers of large end users. Despite the well-designed framework, the privatized oil behemoth, YPF, accounts for

80% of the natural gas contract market. Nevertheless, the Argentinean energy reform has been praised widely.[13]

The Brazilian energy crisis of 2001 revealed the problems and challenges of transforming a state-controlled industry into a market-driven one. The power shortage of 2001 reflects a combination of factors, including (1) a lack of rainfall that has curtailed hydropower generation to one-third of capacity, (2) an energy reform program that has failed to attract investors in generation, and (3) strong political opposition to continuing the privatization of electricity generators. As a result, the Brazilian government has switched focus to the expansion of generating capacity and to improve interconnectivity of the energy grid and away from further privatization sales.

The privatization program went into full force in 1996 after creation of the National Energy Agency (ANEEL) in that year, followed by institution of the energy trading market (MAE), and creation of the interconnected systems operator (ONS). Since 1996, a total of $5.7 billion worth of electricity assets have been sold to private investors.[14] To date, the private sector accounts for 22% of energy generation and close to 63% of distribution. Clearly, the privatization program has been successful in energy distribution but not in generation. At the federal level, government-owned Eletrobras accounts for most of the ration capacity in Brazil. Although some small generation plants have been auctioned off, the privatization of its major units (Chesf, Eletronorte, and Furnas) has encountered major problems, ranging from water rights to political opposition. The privatization effort of these units is more likely to take place after elections in 2002.

Brazilian states have also proceeded with energy reforms. Eletropaulo, the vertically integrated energy monopoly owned by the state of São Paulo, was split into two distribution companies, one transmission company, and a generation unit. The distributor for the city of São Paulo, later named Metropolitana, went to Light, the Rio de Janeiro distributor for the U.S. energy consolidator AES for $1.77 billion. The other distributor, which covers the rest of the state, went to Enron for $1.49 billion. The generation for the city of São Paulo went to AES and for the rest of the state to Duke Energy.[15]

Brazil's gas infrastructure is incipient but growing very rapidly. Natural gas is expected to supply 12% of energy demand in 2010, a large increase from a mere 2% in 2000. The infrastructure is being built through a variety of joint public–private initiatives at all levels. In the short term, the major effort is to import natural gas from Argentina and Bolivia. Government-owned Gaspetro, a subsidiary of Petrobrás, has participated in two major pipeline joint ventures that link Bolivian and Argentinean gas-producing sites with the south and central regions of Brazil. A consortium of companies built the Bolivia–Brazil pipeline in 1999 at the cost of $1.3 billion to bring Bolivian gas to the São Paulo region.[16] Gaspetro also participates in a similar pipeline to connect the Brazilian southern systems and Argentinean northern gas systems with a consortium of Argentinean companies.[17] Natural gas distribution is operated primarily by states. Of the 12 major gas distributors, only two have been transferred to private investors.

Energy reforms in Mexico generate hotly disputed debates. According to the Mexican constitution, the federal government owns and controls oil, gas, and electricity infrastructure. In the electricity sector, government-owned Federal Electricity Commission (CFE) and Luz y Fuerza Centro (LFC) account for 92% of all electricity generation, transmission, and distribution. Both government-owned companies retained their monopoly in transmission and distribution.[18] Since 1998, the private sector participates in power generation, but they must sell their output to CFE.[19] Independent power producers, however, can build and sell energy to single industrial users through long-term contracts.

The 1995 natural gas law opened this growing market for private participation in transportation and distribution through 30-year licenses. The law also redefined the role of Pemex in this sector to become strictly a gas producer.[20] Transportation concessions with no exclusivity were issued to private companies that have been involved in building gas pipelines from production sites in the south or the border with the United States to the demand regions in the northeast (Monterrey) or Baja California. Most of the gas is to supply independent electricity generation producers. Eighteen distribution concessions have been given exclusive rights for 12 years. According to the law, private companies are prohibited from participating in other activities of gas distribution. A proposed electricity bill will again engender a great deal of debate in Mexico.

INVESTORS' EXPECTATIONS FOR REFORMED INFRASTRUCTURE MARKETS

Strategic investors considering participating in Latin American infrastructure reforms will consider the fundamental aspects of any investment decision: returns, degree of control, and risks. Despite the substantial deregulation of the infrastructure networks, regulatory agencies play an important role in determining factors that affect these business fundamentals. We elaborate on two of these elements: tariffs and risk allocation.

RETURNS DEPEND ON TARIFFS

In setting tariffs, regulators try to achieve the lowest possible price for the service, compensate the investor adequately, and provide incentives to improve efficiency either through higher profits to the investor or competition. There is no one formula or pricing strategy that is satisfactory to consumers, regulators, and investors. The most common approaches used are price-cap regulations where the rate of costs that can be passed through is determined by the regulator. Cost-based regulation (including rate of return) allows the operator to pass all costs of providing the service to the end user. When the rate of return is included, investor's risk is removed. The problem with this approach is that there is no incentive to reduce costs. In fact, there is an investment to increase the asset base to increase returns. Profit sharing introduces the incentive to reduce costs. The regulator sets a target of costs based either on ideal best efficient operator, or the most efficient operator if there is competition in the sector.

Tariffs are reviewed in periods as short as less than a year, or longer periods of three to four years. In between periods, automatic adjustments are allowed for inflation. The process of review could be contentious, as information and its interpretation can lead to different conclusions. In some cases, this process could lead to collusion between regulator and operator.

Tariff-setting strategies in Latin American reforms vary not only by countries but also by sector within the same country. In Chile, service tariffs are set based on the efficient company model in telecommunications and the cost-plus model in the energy sector. The use of tariffs also depends on the stage of the value chain. In the case of Chile, the tariff refers only to the distribution part, which includes a rate of return. The assumption is that the price of energy is determined by the market. The transmission cost, although not regulated, has been a contentious issue between the dominant transmission company and the users. Although there is open access in transmission, the dominant company has been free to set transmission fees to other users. A similar situation exists in Mexico's telecommunications market, where new entrants have accused Telmex, the incumbent, of setting high fees for interconnection.

Clearly, in situations where the principles and the process of tariff setting are clearly delineated before privatization, investors have reacted very positively. In situations where the principles are ambiguous and regulators can arbitrarily set tariffs, investors have avoided participation. Brazil is an example that illustrates this situation. The success of the privatization and deregulation of the Brazilian telecommunications sector can be attributed to the clear process in selection and operation after privatization. The opposite can be said about the energy sector. The failure to attract investors in two rounds of attempts to sell federally owned generators, Furnas, Eletronorte, and the state-owned Cemig, can be attributed on a cost-based tariff system that is not reviewed often enough to adjust to highly fluctuating energy prices to meet investors' return expectations. The situation is aggravated in the thermal plant generation sector, which uses imported natural gas. In this sector, the tariffs need to adjust to reflect exchange rate fluctuations of the Brazilian currency. Investor paralysis aggravates Brazil's energy crisis.

UNCLEAR RULES INCREASE THE RISKS

Assessing the risks of participation can be a daunting task for strategic investors. As mentioned above, tariff setting and exchange risks are just two examples of the variety of risks involved in an infrastructure operation. These risks emerge at different times of the project life cycle. Some of these risks are minimized by the nature of the privatization structure proposed by governments, such as a set term of monopoly status or guaranteed returns during the term of the contract. Other risks have to be shared or absorbed by the investor. As illustrated by the Brazilian energy sector above, there are certain types of risks that the private investor will not accept at any price.

There are three types of risks to be considered in privatized and deregulated sectors. The first categories are social and political risks. These include undue political influence or favoritism. Influence can be exercised during competitive bidding, which results in an unfair selection process. Other risks in this category are corruption, bribery, and a lack of sound legal basis for the process and expropriation. Another political risk is the divergent objectives of different levels of government involved in concessions or privatizations. In Brazil, for instance, the opposition of the governor of Minas Gerais, former President Itamar Franco, to proceed with the privatization of the energy generator Cemig was one of the factors influencing the decision to postpone further privation of energy assets until after the 2002 elections. As mentioned before, an evaluation of the legal and regulatory framework should identify the potential risks and weak aspects of investment context.

A second category of risks relate to the potential negative outcomes that may affect the expected economic results. These risks emanate from unpredictable changes in inflation, foreign exchange, currency inconvertibility, interest risks, and liability. Sound business practices and prudent investments would help minimize the potential negative consequences of these risks. One example of this type of risk is the change from a flexible- to a fixed (anchor)-rate currency policy in Argentina after the 1990 privatization of the telecommunications networks. The initial agreement required the indexation of service tariffs to inflation. The Convertibility Act of 1991 made indexation a mute issue, and the government reneged in allowing the adjustment.[21] Argentina's recent financial crisis, however, changed the peso-to-U.S. dollar parity. At the brink of insolvency, the government devalued the peso. Infrastructure sector firms had problems serving hard currency short-term obligations.

A third category of risks emanate from the regulatory process itself. As mentioned before, the process of tariff determination in regulated sectors of the industry is subject to interpretation, and the outcome of the review is uncertain. The risk is highest when rules are ambiguous and at the full discretion of government regulators. A Peruvian case in the electricity sector serves to illustrate the complications of regulating returns. Energy tariffs in Peru are determined by the Electricity Tariff Commission (CTE in Spanish). The energy distribution system used is a three-part cost-plus system. The first element is a nodal price for energy generation, transmission costs, and the distribution value added. The latter component includes distribution costs, energy losses, and the profit to cover investment returns, management, and maintenance. The value-added distribution (VAD) is reviewed every four years. The first determination of the VAD was after the privatization and energy reforms in Peru in 1993. The second revision of the VAD in 1997 resulted in several years of litigation where the privatized distributors argued that CTE was using an asset valuation based on an ideal best efficient distributor. The distributors argue that contractual agreements called for the replacement value of assets or at least the actual value of assets in the rate-of-return determination.[22] This case illustrates that dispute resolution provisions and assessment of a country's contract laws are extremely important in due diligence before deciding to commit resources.

HOW MUCH CONTROL?

In the case of privatized infrastructure, degree of control is determined by the privatization process. Governments determine the amount of shares to be offered to private investors. Typically, the amount of shares is enough to obtain management control, but governments prefer to keep some ownership to have some influence in operations. In some cases, part of the government shares have been transferred to employees of the privatized assets before the auction of the shares to outside investors. Investors decide whether the level of ownership offered would provide enough management control of the privatized enterprise. They also must assess whether they can increase equity share in the future.

The level of control in privatized operations is important in many respects. Control refers to the authority over operational and strategic decisions. Control provides firms with influence over systems, methods, and decisions in the privatized infrastructure operation. Firms prefer higher levels of control to obtain a larger share of the profit generated by the operations and to safeguard their firm-specific advantages.

In the early period of reforms, outright sale of state assets was the preferred way to reduce the fiscal burden of public enterprises. Political opposition and increasing public sentiment that ownership of natural resources should not be transferred to private owners have changed this belief. In more recent privatizations, Latin American governments have used other instruments, such as concessions, licenses, or long-term management contracts maintaining ownership of the assets requiring the transfer of the assets to the state at the end of the concession contract.

Finally, equity participation in companies in the same level of operation (horizontal) or different stage of the process (vertical) has been explicitly prohibited in several countries, including Argentina, Brazil, and Mexico. As was observed, the lack of this restriction in Chile allowed a single company to control a large percentage of the energy sector. In this case, antitrust regulations forced the company to divest certain strategic transmission assets.[23]

REGIONAL NETWORK STRATEGIES IN REFORMED LATIN AMERICAN INFRASTRUCTURE

Network strategies share some business fundamentals common to infrastructure businesses. In network businesses, firms have to count on or provide the ability of right of way, pool of content (energy, voice, data), and efficient distribution and dispatching. Infrastructure businesses also require core competencies in the building, managing, and maintenance of networks, and efficient processes for network traffic distribution and customer management. As infrastructure networks are capital intensive, firms must also have access to financing. Technology and regulatory uncertainty requires good risk management capabilities and processes. Network strategies combine these core elements in some fashion.[24]

No single network strategy may fit the different reformed infrastructure sectors of Latin America. The diverse market structures, regulatory regimes, market-entry conditions, and market challenges require different strategic approaches. Based on the level of business scope, two strategies are those of integrators and specialists.[25] Based on the level of geographic market aggregation, two other strategies are defined as broad regional aggregation and narrow regional integration. The combination of scope and geographic aggregation results in four distinct regional network strategies. In addition, state-owned infrastructure networks or concessions won by private national groups in a given country are defined as national champions. The characteristics of these network strategies are shown in Table 4.5 and discussed further below.

The first strategy is that of the regional integrator. The goal of this strategy is to aggregate several infrastructure businesses within or across sectors. For instance, telecommunications networks aggregate wired, wireless, data, and voice transmissions. Integrators benefit from economies of scale and scope. Synergy effects of sharing resources across different businesses (bill collection) can be leveraged to provide support to several business units. The bundling of services is central to this strategy. Full control of the network allows for interconnectivity of different businesses. The preferred market entry for an integrator is to acquire controlling interest in privatized infrastructure opportunities. Since aggregation requires economies of scale, integrators pursue infrastructure investment opportunities throughout the region. Two levels of geographic market aggregation are broad regional integrator (BRI) and narrow regional integrator (NRI). The *broad regional integrator* (BRI) invests in all markets in the region regardless of size or geography. The BRI strategy requires substantial financial investment, resource commitments, and managerial capacity to coordinate and integrate several national network operations.

Telefónica Spain is an example of a BRI strategy. Telefónica is the largest telecommunications provider in the Spanish- and Portuguese-speaking world with operations in 48 countries. It offers a wide array of services, ranging from fixed-line and mobile telephony, Internet access, broadcast media, content production, and the publication of telephone directories. A global player, whose value exceeds $1 billion, 71 million customers, 148,707 employees, and ranks sixth in world telephony, the company is in a league of its own. In the western hemisphere, Telefónica's most important markets in-

TABLE 4.5 Regional Network Strategies

NETWORK STRATEGY	INTEGRATOR		SPECIALIST	
Degree of management control	Equity control: ownership		Shared control: contractual	
Entry strategy	Acquisitions of privatized assets; long-term exclusive concessions		Service contracts, BOTs, short term concessions	
LEVEL OF MARKET AGGREGATION				
Geographic	Broad regional	Narrow regional	Broad regional	Narrow regional
Business scope	All business segments		Single business focus	
Customer base	Very large	Large	Narrow (3 or more countries)	Very narrow (1 or 2 countries)
Business model	Scale economies Multiple revenue streams Bundling services Cross business and cross-border synergies Resource sharing		Premium services Fee based Fast payback Global class efficiency Global class Technology	
Examples	Telefónica Endesa Duke Energy	Telecom Italia Aguas de Barcelona	BellSouth AES	CMS Energy

clude Argentina, Brazil, Chile, and Peru. The company also maintains a strong presence in Colombia, Costa Rica, El Salvador, Guatemala, Honduras, Mexico, Nicaragua, Panamá, Puerto Rico, Uruguay, and Venezuela, as well as Canada and the United States. In Brazil, Telefónica has controlling interest in the wired network of the city of São Paulo and the state of Bahia. Telefónica is the holding company for Telefónica Moviles (wireless), Telefónica Data (business communications), Terra Networks (Internet), Telemensagem (paging), Telefónica Cable (cable TV), Telefónica Multimedia, Telefónica Sistemas (private network systems). Each one of these independent businesses operates in several Latin American countries. Two of Telefónica's shareholders, Banco Bilbao Viscaya (BBVA) and La Caixa, provide financial leverage for Telefónica's regional integrator strategy in Latin America.

The *narrow regional integrator* (NRI) pursues investments in a few countries, one of which is a large market such as Argentina, Brazil, or Mexico. The large-country market serves as a platform to serve neighboring countries. Within the narrow regional scope, the firm builds a network strategy to support several business units. The key factor of this strategy is whether there is enough scale and if other nonregulated market segments can be entered from a network base. The feasibility of this strategy depends on the regulatory approach used by the Latin American country. For instance, Mexico and Venezuela privatized their national telephone networks in their entirety. Argentina split the national network in two. Brazil's privatization of its telecommunications sector divided the country in four but kept the large long-distance and international business as one entity. Brazil's telecommunications privatization regulations discourage vertical integration within a single geography. Regulatory conditions, however, did not allow for one operator to enter or participate in other business segments. The privatization of fixed telecommunications networks divided the country in two but allowed the operator to enter into mobile, data, and other sectors of telecommunications with no or limited competition.

An example of narrow NRI strategy is Telecom Italia. By carefully selecting some but not all privatization opportunities, Telecom Italia, in partnership with France Telecom, obtained the concession for northern Argentina, the southern region of Brazil (partnering with local investors) which borders their northern Argentinean concession, Chile, and Bolivia. By having two contiguous cross-border territories, the company was well positioned to benefit from increasing Brazil–Argentina commerce. The firm strategy was based on the aggregation of several businesses within the boundaries of their binational concession.

The other regional network strategy is that of the network specialist. Network specialists operate in a single business process or stage of the value chain of a regulated business such as meter reading or energy transmission. Other specialists bundle services for a single customer or market segment in an unregulated infrastructure sector. Network specialists include firms that offer voice and data telecommunications services to corporate clients or meter-reading services in the energy sector. Specialists do not place the same importance on control as the broad regional integrator. What is important is the ability to collaborate and obtain high margins for the rendering of very specialized services to a single client or small market segment. The mode of entry of specialist strategies is typically through contractual relations. The regulatory framework may not allow ownership rights. In this case, firms enter markets through concessions, service contracts, or enter into build–operate–transfer (BOT) contracts.

Broad regional specialists (BRS) operate throughout the region. An example of a BRS strategy is Bell South. The company operates mobile networks in Argentina, Brazil, Peru, Ecuador, Uruguay, Nicaragua, Guatemala, and Panama. The company also has controlling interest in the long-distance Chilean telephony market. Another example of a BRS strategy is Global One. Global One targets the corporate segment in Latin America. In Brazil alone, Global One has built an Internet backbone network connecting 11 cities. The company has contracts with 160 large companies. Another regional specialist company is Argentinean-based IMPSAT. Launched in 1990, it provides private network services to more the 1,500 customers in 17 countries in the Americas via satellite transmission.[26]

Narrow regional specialists (NRSs) operate in a large country such as Brazil, Mexico, or Argentina, or in a few countries. Narrow specialists thrive in privatization programs that are too small to attract large investors or require specialized skills. Specialists also thrive from outsourcing programs of large privatized networks. One example is the energy transmission concessions in Argentina. Two companies, TNG and TSG, manage the north and south natural gas pipelines in this country. The firms are backed by global energy companies, national industry groups, and international investors.

EVOLUTION OF NETWORK STRATEGY

Network strategy evolves over time to adapt to changing market and regulatory conditions.[27] Concession contracts are typically long term, 25 to 30 years. Exclusive or monopoly conditions in acquisitions of privatized programs range from three- to seven-year spans. Typical stages of evolution of the network and regulated environment are the takeover, early stage of privatization, preparing transition to full market liberalization, and competing in unrestricted competitive markets.[28] At each stage, the regulatory, competitive environment, and nature and level of risks changes. Consequently, strategy and resource commitments should match the changing environment.

At the startup stage, the main task is to take over the network or privatized asset. Here the main tasks are those of rebuilding and updating the underinvested network. The strategic focus is to improve operating efficiency and quality of service. The key processes to achieve these objectives are the introduction of sound network management practices, process reengineering, and total quality programs. Resource commitments at this stage are mostly for capital improvement programs and maintenance. The firm's key competencies at this stage are access to capital resources and network management practices. The regulatory challenge at this stage is to update and implement tariff regimes to reflect real costs. If tariffs are lagging and the new operators force rapid tariff increases, the social and political risk will be high. The risk will be lower if the regulator agency has updated those tariffs before privatization. Revenue sources at this stage are mostly from service to the existent customer base. Expansion may be limited to targets set by the regulator, given the challenge to raise funds for both modernization and expansion. Profits will depend on the contractual tariff formula proposed by the regulator. Operators would expect that increased profits will be derived from cost savings, downsizing of the labor force or liquidation of noncore businesses, and lower network losses due to improved technologies and process in meter reading and collections. With increased resource commitments and transition to cost efficiency, returns on increasing assets may be low but gradually increasing at this stage. The takeoff period is critical in setting the business platform for the core business. Firms have the advantage of operating under market exclusivity, which removes the competitive pressure.

The strategic focus of the second stage after privatization shifts to market penetration and quality improvement. An aggressive expansion program at this stage allows firms to expand the customer base and universal access targets imposed by the contract. In addition, network expansion with the most recent technology, fiber-optic cable for energy transmission, improves service and allows for the introduction of value-added services that will increase the revenue mix in the future. This stage is also marked by the first revisions of tariff reviews and negotiations, and full participation or integration with other upstream or downstream operations. The regulator's priorities have also shifted to looking at issues of interconnectivity or passing efficiency gains to customers in terms of tariff reductions. The core competencies at this stage are risk management, regulatory relationships, and large-scale project management. Access to capital for expansion needs continues to be a major competency as well. Revenue sources at this stage improve from increases in the customer base, profit-sharing incentives in tariff reviews, and introduction of new services. In some countries, small competitors enter the market and start building their network. The mirror-competitor approach used in the Brazilian telecommunications reform is an example. In other countries, the firm continues to benefit from lack of competitive pressure. Financial returns should improve and reach maximum levels at the end of this stage.

At the third stage, the firm prepares for the transition to full market liberalization. The assumption here is that efficiency and quality programs are all in place and working continuously. On the technology side, the network transformation to new technologies is completed or close to it. In anticipation of market entry, the focus of the firm is the customer and reaching global class competitiveness in efficiency and perhaps quality. Achieving global class competitiveness forces the firm to look at global markets to benchmark against potential competitors. Reaching those levels may require the introduction of new practices, new information technologies, greater integration, and outsourcing noncore processes to specialists. A customer focus forces the firm to innovate, improve customer service programs, and introduce customer relationship programs. More refined market segmentation may identify different opportunities and strategies to differentiate services and market other value-added services. The regulator's emphasis at this stage is open access, tariff reductions, and determination that contractual targets have been met. Regulators may decide to advance the opening of the sector to other competitors or to extend it further. Also, regulators will press the firm to reach contractually imposed universal access targets. Extending services to rural or disadvantaged sectors of society not only has an impact on the firm's investment plans and profits but creates challenges of connecting remote areas or providing services to the poor. These challenges put the incumbent firm at a disadvantage against new competitors that are not required to do so. The revenue sources increase at this stage from introduction of valued-added sources and participation in new ventures, including new privatizations if permitted. Given the likelihood that new sources of revenue may not compensate for lower tariffs for basic services, the likelihood of decreasing returns of the core businesses may force the firm to diversify. These opportunities and those created by new technologies may require a reorganization of the business. The creation of a holding company with interests in regulated and unregulated businesses could provide clear signals to the market about the different value of different businesses. Integrations invest in further privatizations within a single country or throughout the region.

The last stage of strategy after privatization is competition in fully liberalized markets. The local and long-distance telecommunications sectors in Chile, Argentina, and Mexico have reached this stage. The energy generation and distribution in Argentina, Brazil, and Chile are also fully competitive. The degree of market saturation and the entrance of new competitors drive the service to commodity status, where price is a determinant factor for the customer. In the absence of regulatory restrictions, the focus of the strategy is to bundle services that permit some level of differentiation and leverage the particular technologies or competencies of the firm in full market competition. Brand image and identification become paramount, as they permit effective customer communications and a strong bond with the firm's bundled services. The brand equity that the incumbent firm accumulates depends on its performance during earlier stages of privatization or concessions. In some cases, disputes with regulators, complaints of poor service, and charges of high tariffs increases result in negative brand equity. On the other hand, real improvements in service quality, sharing efficiency gains with customers, and harmonious relations with regulators create strong incumbent brand equity.

At the last stage, information technologies play a key role. IT investments allow the firm to bundle and customize services and manage customer relations effectively. In earlier stages, bundling was not allowed, as tariffs were set for unbundled services and market segments (residential, industrial). In an unrestricted market, both incumbents and new entrants have to compete for customers based not on price but on other customer value features. Further market liberalization provides further market opportunities to enter sectors protected by exclusivity. After liberalization in Argentina, regulators focus on market power, open access of transmission lines, and determination of interconnection tariffs. The independent status and strength of the regulator will determine the market conduct of the players. Clearly, the strategy at this stage is to concentrate on areas where there is maximum leverage of the firm's competencies. Noncore activities and processes should be outsourced. Collaborative strategies allow the firm to explore new businesses. Further investments in information technology (IT) will help the firm bundling services and integrate the diverse relationships and interfaces with customers, suppliers, subcontractors, and regulators. Investment in ERP processes and Internet-based technologies is imperative for success in fully competitive markets. The financial return at this stage will be lower, due to the potential loss of market share and the increasing investments in IT technology.

TELECOM ARGENTINA: A NARROW REGIONAL INTEGRATOR

FROM TAKEOVER TO FULL MARKET LIBERALIZATION

Telecom Argentina was established in 1989 to participate in the Argentinean telecommunication privatization. The principal investor in Telecom Argentina at the time was Nortel Inversora, a holding company owned by Telecom Italia, France Telecom, Argentina's Perez Companc, and JP Morgan. Telecom Argentina won the exclusive concession to provide local, long-distance, and value-added services in the northern territory. The country, and in particular the Buenos Aires market, was split in two. Telefónica Spain won the concession for the southern territory. As required by the reform program, both companies formed three joint ventures for wired international call, data, and cellular services. The exclusive concession was granted for seven years with the expectation of renewing exclusivity for another two or three years, depending on whether the concessionaires met several targets in the contract.[29]

In November 1990, Telecom Argentina took control of the northern region of the network. The network based at the time of takeover included 1.5 million lines, 1.4 million customers, and 12,000 cellular phones (see Table 4.6). The teledensity of the country was 11 lines per hundred people. The 11.5% network digitalization at the time was indicative that the network technology was analog. The size of the labor force at the time was 19,000 employees. Installation fees ranged from $1,500 for residential use to $2,500 for commercial sites with a four-year wait for installation.

The first year of operation was of modest investments and planning the long-term strategy. By the end of 1991, the firm had made modest investment of $149 million, reduced the labor force to about 17,000, and added 360,000 new clients. That year the concessionaires signed an agreement with the regulator whereby tariffs were set in dollar terms. This agreement was made possible when Argentina instituted the convertibility law that pegged the peso to the U.S. dollar at parity. Thus, the dollarization of tariffs removed the exchange risk.[30]

The major network buildup began in 1992–1994 with a significant increase in investments, on the order of $4.17 billion. The focus of the strategy was clearly to improve efficiency and quality. The large investment allowed Telecom Argentina to reconstruct the

TABLE 4.6 Telecom Argentina: Strategy After Privatization

STRATEGIC COMPONENT	TAKEOVER, 1990[a]	BUILDING THE NETWORK, 1991–1995	PREPARING FOR COMPETITION, 1996–1999	FULL COMPETITION AND COUNTRY'S ECONOMIC CRISIS, 2000–PRESENT
Strategic focus	Efficiency, quality	Market growth, quality	Customer service, value-added services	Leverage networks (fixed, mobile), bundling services, new revenue sources
Strategic imperatives	Takeover and rebuild network, clarify regulated framework rules	Network expansion, customer service	Achieve global class efficiency, price competitiveness, full network digitalization, meet regulatory targets	Compete nationally, competitive prices, service innovation, selective diversification, increased international involvement
Core competencies	Access to financial sources, network management	Access to financial sources, regulatory relationship	Service activation responsiveness, customer service skills	Brand image, customer base, service innovation, risk management, outsourcing
Key processes	Transfer of network, technology, reengineering, capital efficiency, maintenance/repair	Productivity improvement, total quality improvement, business process reengineering, tariff renegotiation	Customer service processes, relationship management processes, service innovation	IT transformation, open architecture, leverage technology to bundling and pricing services
Regulatory framework				
1. Tariff setting	Initial tariff setting	First tariff revision	Meeting privatization targets, decision to extend monopoly period	Market based
2. Local service	Exclusivity	Exclusivity	Exclusivity extended to 1999	Full competition
3. Long distance	JV with Telefónica	JV with Telefónica	New limited competition allowed	Full competition
4. Mobile	Exclusivity	Cellular license for Buenos Aires, JV with Telefónica	National licenses allowed; PCS licenses issued	Full competition
5. Value-added services	Liberalized market	Fully liberalized	Full competition	Full competition

Investments over the period ($ millions)	n.a.	4,174	3,582	n.a.
Competition		First cellular license to third competitor issued to Verizon (CTI)	Cellular: two new national competitors (Verizon, BellSouth); four competitors in Buenos Aires (Telecom, Telefónica, BellSouth, and Verizon); international and value-added services: Global One, Mercury, Sedeco	Local services: Telefónica plus 300 other small operators plus 10 new licenses not in operation; six long-distance carriers: AT&T, BellSouth, Verizon, Techtel (Telmex), Comsat, Impsat
Employment	19,002	1991 = 17,712 1995 = 13,728	1996 = 12,985 1999 = 9,270	2000 = 9,645
Lines (millions)	1.5	1991 = 1.428 1995 = 2.594	1996 = 2.824 1999 = 3.422	2000 = 3.713
Network digitization	11.5 %	1991 = 12% 1995 = 86%	1996 = 97% 1997 = 100%	100%
Productivity metrics				
1. Lines in service per employee	73	1992 99	1999 369	2000 385
2. Revenue per employee	n.a.	76	249	230
3. Revenue per line	n.a.	770	675	601
4. Profit per line	n.a.	100	100	70
Key financial metrics (consolidated)	n.a.	1992	1999	2000
1. Change in revenues over last period	n.a.	36.18%	0.3 %	1.4 %
2. ROS	n.a.	12.8%	11.2 %	8.4 %
3. ROA	n.a.	6.0%	5.0 %	3.6 %
4. ROE	n.a.	8.2%	12.9 %	9.8 %

Sources: Telecom Argentina, annual reports and interviews.
n.a., not available.

network and accelerate digitalization. The company also reengineered processes to improve productivity and continued to downsize. At the end of this stage, key indicators showed a dramatic improvement overall. Total fixed lines increased to 2.8 million, and network digitalization reached 86%. The labor force reached a level of 14,400 employees. Lines per employee increased to 134 in 1996 from 73 at the end of 1990.

The Argentinean government introduced competition in the protected regions outside the Buenos Aires mobile markets by granting a license to GTE in 1993. In turn, the joint venture with Telefónica received a second license for the Buenos Aires market to compete with the holder of the first licensee, BellSouth. Telecom's financial indicators improved at this stage. Net margin in the period reached a high of 306 million. The return of sales also peaked in 1995 at 15.9%. Return on assets and net worth remained stable given that the sizable investments in this period increased the asset base. The period of 1991–1995 was marked by constant improvements. At the end of this period, a slowdown in major indicators can be attributed to a shift of emphasis from building to consolidation and also as a result of the aftereffects of the Mexican peso devaluation on the region's economies.

The year of 1997 marked a critical year of revision of the exclusivity contract with the government. The privatization targets were met satisfactorily, and the Argentinean regulator decided to extend the exclusivity concession for two more years instead of three. The plan was to introduce more competition incrementally, in 1998 with public pay phones and data transmission, followed by additional competitors in long distance (domestic and international) by the end of 1999. Partial liberalization would precede full competition in 2000.[31]

The preparations for the transition to full liberalization took place between 1996 and 1999. Having achieved most of the efficiency and productivity targets in the previous stage, Telecom shifted focus to preparation for full competition. Three areas were particularly targeted: customer orientation, technology innovation, and business diversification. In terms of new technologies, Telecom introduced Internet service provider (ISP) and Internet services. Also, in preparation for open competition, Telecom introduced new information system technologies that would facilitate the processing of more information internally and externally. The second was especially important, as open competition would force operators to integrate information systems with other competitors.

In 1998, Telecom's product-based independent subsidiaries became more autonomous, investing in technology and expanding their operations as regulations permitted. For instance, Telecom cellular operator Telecom Personal set up a joint venture in Paraguay to provide personal communication services (PCSs) in 1998. The ISP business became an independent subsidiary, Arnet, with Telecom Argentina holding 99.99% equity share. The data transmission business became a growing source of revenues and income to Telecom. The period of preparation for full liberalization was marked by a second turnaround of major indicators. Consolidated revenues increased by almost 23% in 1998 and net profits reached their highest level. The level of employment stabilized at 13,500, and productivity indicators increased markedly to 369 lines per employee, almost fivefold above the takeover level. The network reached 100% digitalization in 1997. The cost of a new installation was $90, and it took only 10 days to install.

ADAPTING THE ORGANIZATION

Telecom Argentina's organizational structure has also evolved over time. One of the main objectives of the company was to foster an entrepreneurial culture. In October 1995, the company began its first major reorganization since taking over by redefining its corporate structure. There was a shift from a strongly centralized matrix focusing on functions and geographies, in which customers were defined by location, to one centered on customer type. As such, Telecom Argentina switched its operations from geographic to business units. Between 1996 and 1998, Telecom saw the need to create a challenging working environment in order to obtain productivity levels similar to those of the principal world operators. In October 1998, Telecom underwent its second major reorganization in which the position of chief operating officer (COO) was created in an effort to manage the operations of the business units.

In February 2001, as the result of the newly competitive climate, Telecom underwent its third major reorganization since privatization by creating a new management team composed of a chief executive officer (CEO) and an executive committee. The reason for the transformation was to improve decision making via a centralized model where the company's combined operations could be administered and enforced, given the new competitive nature of the telecommunications business. As a result of its expansion, in March 2001 the company set out to expand its corporate purpose to include consultancy and security related to telecommunications and telecomputing.

Telecom Argentina is now part of a wider organization called Grupo Telecom (Telecom Group). Grupo Telecom has ventured out regionally as well as globally. The group consists of nine companies with Telecom Argentina (fixed-line services) at the top. Grupo Telecom controls three data and Internet transmission systems: Telecom Internet, Microsistemas, and Telecom Argentina USA; two cellular companies: Telecom Personal and Núcleo (a cellular service in Paraguay); a telephone directory: Publicom; and other telecom services: Multibrand, Latin American Nautilus, and Nahuelsat, a satellite communications company of which Telecom Argentina owns 5.75%.

INTERNATIONAL BUSINESS VENTURES

Telecom Italia, one of the parent corporations, is a global integrator itself. In Latin America, Telecom Italia's main competitor is another global integrator, Telefónica Spain. In contrast to the regional footprint of Telefónica Spain, Telecom Italia has concentrated in the Southern Cone. In addition to Argentina, the company has a presence in Brazil, Chile, Bolivia, and Peru. In Brazil, Telecom has 38% participation in the fixed-line concession for the southern region, and Brazil Telecom has won licenses to provide wireless services in the northern region (Maxitel), south (Tele Celular Sul), and northeast (Nordeste Celular). The fixed-line concession in southern Brazil is particularly important, as it borders with Telecom Argentina's strong network in northern Argentina. Telecom Italia has 50% or more equity participation in the long-distance and international fixed line network in Bolivia, Cuba (national and international), and Entel Chile (long-distance and business networks). The company also owns a B-license for wireless services in Peru (TIM Peru) and Venezuela. The multimedia and Internet business unit also has strong participation in Latin America. This unit owns 30% of media giant O'Globo.[32]

Historically, Telecom Argentina has been a local player. In recent times, the company has increased its international investments. Via its 10% share of Latin American Nautilus, Telecom Argentina participates with Telecom Italia in the building of an underwater and land fiber-optic network stretching 30,000 kilometers, providing broadband city-to-city connectivity across the region connecting the capitals of South America with Central and North America. Moreover, Nautilus offers housing and Web hosting services to telecommunication operators, including ISPs, content, and applications providers.

In June 1998, Telecom Personal and its subsidiary, Núcleo, launched cellular and PCS services in Paraguay. In early 2001, Grupo Telecom set up a U.S. subsidiary in Delaware, Telecom Argentina USA, and on February 22, 2001, obtained a license to operate telecommunications services in this country. Telecom Argentina USA is the first step that Telecom Argentina has taken outside the Southern Cone. Telecom Argentina USA seeks to provide international telecom services, via its own lines, as a facilities- and/or resale-based international common carrier. Telecom Argentina USA will also extend Internet and data voice transmissions to its clients. The company has headquarters in Miami and strategic installations in New York and Los Angeles forming a dual underwater cable network connecting Argentina to the rest of the world. The first, Atlantis2, connects Argentina with Brazil and Europe; the second, Americas2, with North America and the Caribbean. Telecom Argentina USA intends to provide affordable prices and high-quality services between Argentina and the United States and from there to the rest of the world.[33]

FULL MARKET COMPETITION

After 10 years of managed competition, Argentina has developed one of the most sophisticated telecommunications networks in Latin America. In 1999, the end of the period of partial liberalization, Movicom–BellSouth and CTI Movil and the two regional monopolies competed for the long-distance market nationwide. Telecom as well as rival Telefónica and two other competitors were awarded nationwide PCS licenses. Furthermore, the government regulator (Secom) ordered local tariff reductions of 5.5% for residential users and 19.5% for commercial and government users based on anticipated efficiencies by the operators.[34]

The introduction of a multicarrier system in 2000 sparked the entry of new competitors. A total of 25 companies holding long-distance licenses were ready to roll out services. The new competitors included AT&T and Mexico's Telmex. Other licensed operators planned to target corporate clients with broadband and voice over IP. These specialists included Impsat, Diveo, Metrored Argentina, and Comsat. Electric companies also geared up to provide telecommunications services. UK's National Grid is building a nationwide fiber backbone which will be owned and used by a consortium of 1,500 electric companies to provide voice and Internet services to the communities they serve. The backbone will connect with

Chilean and Brazilian grids. Full implementation was extended to the second quarter of 2001 at the request of the two incumbents.

Full and intense market competition presents Telecom Argentina with many challenges and very few opportunities. The first challenge is to dissolve the joint ventures with Telefónica Spain formed under the monopoly regime. This process started in 1998, when both companies moved to dissolve Miniphone, which provided cellular services in Buenos Aires. In January 2000, the companies dissolved the international telecommunications joint venture. The process of implementing these decisions is long and complicated. For strategic and regulatory reasons, the two companies took several months to reach an agreement on what to do with the wireless physical network after splitting the customer base. Another challenge for Telefónica is to build presence and cellular networks in the southern region of Argentina. Raising funds is hampered by the premium that investors demand for the deteriorating country ratings for Argentina.[35]

Thus far, Telecom Argentina's strategy focuses on unbundling the vestiges of monopoly and expanding to provide nationwide coverage. Other strategies that the company is introducing include introduction of new services such as ADSL, further consolidation of business units, and a divesting of low-growth business such as satellite services and pursuing strategic alliances with other companies. The contrast of the market conditions after privatization and the start of full market liberalization cannot be more different. In hindsight, Telecom's Argentina long-term strategy was sound and well executed. After $9 billion investments in fixed assets, Telecom Argentina not only achieved but surpassed the targets set by the privatization contract. A total of 2.3 new wired lines were installed, less than 0.1% of the phones are out of service at a given time, and the cost of a new installation has declined from $1,500 to about $50 in early 2001. The lines per employee have increased to 385 in 2001 from 73 in 1990. The company has produced consistent returns to investors during the last 10 years.

THE RISKS OF OPERATING IN ARGENTINA

The main risk facing Telecom Argentina is political. Argentina's debt default and devaluation has made access to external financing very difficult. The country's staggering unemployment, stubborn public deficit, and rising social uprising has created a crisis situation which many in the region fear could exacerbate a financial downturn throughout the hemisphere. The crisis has affected the Argentine banking sector as savings deposits have dropped due to the harboring of money in dollar-safe havens.

Perhaps more critical are the depressed market conditions of the Argentine economy. After three years of recession triggered by the Brazilian currency devaluation in 1999, the Argentine economy has not been able to recuperate. The Argentinean economy contracted by 3.8% in 2001 and is projected to contract by 3.5% in 2002.[36] Telecom Argentina's revenues moved in the same direction as the Argentinean economy. After a banner year in 1998, Telecom's revenues dropped 0.3% in 1999, grew 1.1% in year 2000, and contracted 4% in the first nine months of 2001. The difficult market situation in Argentina in early 2001 translated into a sharp reduction in EBITDA and net earnings of 62.5 and 63% respectively.[37]

The Argentinean government's decision to abandon the decade-old convertibility law that pegged the peso to the U.S. dollar at parity made the situation even worse for many firms. As if the large devaluation of the peso were not enough, the government also abandoned the pegging of the utility tariff rates to dollars and limited rate increases to the minimum to alleviate the impact of the devaluation on Argentinean society. It was "déjà vu again," back to the potential inflationary periods that marked the Argentinean economy at the end of the 1980s.[38]

INTEGRATOR OR SPECIALIST?

We conclude this chapter with a discussion of this important question. Our analysis of the largest Latin American infrastructure firms reveals that the narrow regional integrator and that of specialists are the top-performing strategies in this sector in 2000. Today, Latin American infrastructure is a mosaic of different regulatory frameworks, competitive structures, and players with different strategies. After an early start in shaping reforms and competition, the telecommunication sector mosaic established itself for the long term. The sector has reached maturity and is entering full competition with high intensity.

There are very few new opportunities to acquire privatized assets or gain from a first-mover advantage. The large acquisitions have already taken place, and the strategies of broad and narrow regional integrators challenge a few national champions. Small opportunities remain in small countries or late reformers such as Ecuador, Costa Rica, Uruguay, or Colombia. The future rests on the ability of

TABLE 4.7 Largest Telecommunications and Energy Firms in Latin America by Type of Strategy, 2000

FIRM	SECTOR	COUNTRY	OWNERSHIP	STRATEGY[a]	TOTAL ASSETS ($ MILLIONS)	EMPLOYEES	MARKET CAP ($ MILLIONS 12/31/00)	NET WORTH ($ MILLIONS)	REVENUES ($ MILLIONS)	CHANGE REV. (%)	NET PROFITS ($ MILLIONS)	ROS[b] (%)	RONW[c] (%)
Enersis	Energy	Chile	Private	BRI	19,269	10,968	3,316	1,918	4,513	5.2	157	3.5	8.2
Light	Energy	Brazil	Private	BRI	7,735	5,109	1,601	1,118	3,856	11.4	-139	-1.8	-12.4
Telesp	Teleco	Brazil	Private	BRI	10,217	13,414	7,191	7,397	3,738	26.3	752	7.4	10.2
TelefAg	Telecom.	Argentina	Private	BRI	7,808	9,984	1,600	3,383	3,613	6.3	343	9.5	10.1
Embratel	Telecom.	Brazil	Private	BRI	6,015	7,798	5,702	3,110	3,434	18.5	295	4.9	9.5
Telcel	Telecom.	Mexico	Private	BRI	10,743	13,022		7,116	3,056	123	.		
CNTV	Telecom.	Venezuela	Private	BRI	6,631	2,760		4,535	2,607	-1.3	-129	-4.9	-2.8
Elepaulo	Energy	Brazil	Private	BRI	4,406	5,851	2,064	1,308	2,371	9.8	122	5.2	9.3
Endesa	Energy	Chile	Private	BRI	9,880	1,776	3,043	2,259	1,538	-5.4	189	1.9	8.3
CTC	Telecom.	Chile	Private	BRI	5,702	9,250	3,194	2,134	1,475	-8.1	-198	-13.5	-9.3
TelespC	Telecom.	Brazil	Private	BRI	3,173	1,849	5,390	1,972	1,415	14.5	77.8	5.5	3.9
TelefP	Telecom.	Peru	Private	BRI	3,243	6,330		1,378	1,312	5.6	116.7	8.9	8.5
Edesur	Energy	Argentina	Private	BRI	1,507	2,379		987	899	-0.8	93	10.4	9.5
Edenor	Energy	Argentina	Private	BRI	1,664	2,558		881	897	1.5	90	10.1	10.2
Coelba	Energy	Brazil	Private	BRI	2,011	2,956		764	784	14.9	76.5	9.8	10
TelSECel	Telecom.	Brazil	Private	BRI	1,379		1,558	830	782	-6.2	62.3	8	7.5
EDC	Energy	Venezuela	Private	BRI			1,456		772	5.9	-11.2	-14.5	
Gener	Energy	Chile	Private	BRI	3,836	1,103		1,454	769	-7.8	3.8	0.5	0.3
Unifon	Telecom.	Argentina	Private	BRI	1,576	7,665		545	714	146.7	-34	-4.8	-6.2
Telerj	Telecom.	Brazil	Private	BRI	1,156	1,161	2,157	442	698	-4.7	40.7	5.8	9.2
Cerj	Energy	Brazil	Private	BRI	1,373	1,402		195	636	11.1	1.7	0.3	0.9
Avantel	Telecom.	Mexico	Private	BRI	1,200				616	12			
Iusacell	Telecom.	Mexico	Private	BRI	1,648	1,983	1,328	661	573	29.8	-112.3	-19.6	-17
Gerasul	Energy	Brazil	Private	BRI	2,649	830	923	1,244	554	36.4	83.3	15	6.7
Chilectra	Energy	Chile	Private	BRI	1,899	867	1,310	747	519	3.1	109.9	21.2	14.7
CTImovil	Telecom.	Argentina	Private	BRI	1,863	1,577		441	505	5	-112	-22.2	-25.4
Alestra	Telecom.	Mexico	Private	BRI	914	2,698		195	474	13.9	54.1	11.4	27.7
Celpe	Energy	Brazil	Private	BRI	606	2,158		296	420	13.2	-25.8	-6.1	-8.7
AESsul	Energy	Brazil	Private	BRI	1,083	792		53	400	12.2	-15.7	-18.9	-29.6
CRTeel	Telecom.	Brazil	Private	BRI	684	807	1,022	329	388	5.7	30.7	7.9	9.3
Average BRI					4,202.414	4,409.148	2,678.438	1,703.286	1,477.6	16.59	68.625	1.460714	2.318519
Telmex	Telecom.	Mexico	Private	NC	16,416	74,911	40,619	5,184	10,701	19.5	2,765	25.8	53.3
Telemar	Telecom.	Brazil	Private	NC	9,950		8,881	5,283	4,156	19.5	363	3.6	6.9

Company	Sector	Country	Ownership	Type									
CPFL	Energy	Brazil	Private	NC	3,757	2,927	1,452	2,181	1,426	13.8	40	2.8	1.8
EBE	Energy	Brazil	Private	NC	1,346	2,799		336	1,205	15.2	25.7	2.1	7.7
cge	Energy	Chile	Private	NC	2,115	2,708	1,483	630	715	36	88.7	12.4	14.1
Telecom	Telecom.	Colombia	Government	NC	2,550	6,960		315	677	-14.4	-42.5	-6.3	-13.5
Eletrosul	Energy	Brazil	Private	NC	1,005			780	511	-6.3	37.8	7.4	4.8
Chilquinta	Energy	Chile	Private	NC	926			101	443	4.9	-15.9	-3.6	-15.8
Average NC					4,758.125	18,061	13,108.75	1,851.25	2,479.25	11.025	407.725	5.525	7.4125
Telecom Argentina (consolidated)	Telecom.	Argentina	Private	NRI	7,579	14,894	3,475	2,772	3,226	1.4	271	3.6	9.8
Brtelcom	Telecom.	Brazil	Private	NRI	7,226	2,702		3,126	2,306	34.9	209	9.1	6.7
Telemarrj	Telecom.	Brazil	Private	NRI	2,956	8,544		1,993	1,176	22.5	-11.8	-1	-0.6
Telemig	Telecom.	Brazil	Private	NRI	1,827	1,116		1,149	975	15	258	26.5	22.5
Entel	Telecom.	Chile	Private	NRI	1,825	4,701	1,945	802	908	27.6	47.7	5.2	5.9
TelemarBA	Telecom.	Brazil	Private	NRI	943	1,758		679	472	18.1	63.6	13.5	9.4
TeleCBCel	Telecom.	Brazil	Private	NRI	979		1,339	458	462	42.7	66.1	14.3	14.4
TeleNE	Telecom.	Brazil	Private	NRI	634			294	432	14.7	13.6	3.1	4.6
Average NRI					2,996.125	5,619.167	2,253	1,409.125	1,244.625	22.1125	114.65	9.2875	9.0875
TGS	Energy	Argentina	Private	NRS	2,112	676	1,247	1,088	480	11.6	126.3	11.6	26.3
Average NRS					2,112	676	1,247	1,088	480	11.6	126.3	11.6	26.3
Eletrobras	Telecom.	Brazil	Government	SOE	46,629	9,693		31,777	6,250	2.2	1,256	20.1	4
Furnas	Energy	Brazil	Government	SOE	7,575	3,835		5,042	3,123	-2.6	276	3.6	5.5
Cemig	Energy	Brazil	Government	SOE	6,079	11,648	2,530	3,998	1,734	13.8	212	12.2	5.3
Copel	Energy	Brazil	Government	SOE	4,069	6,148	2,390	2,505	1,033	14.7	220	21.3	8.8
Antel	Telecom.	Uruguay	Government	SOE	1,280	5,200		952	749	1	176	19	13.8
Cesp	Energy	Brazil	Government	SOE	10,002	1,522	1,009	5,468	679	-44.6	-212	-31.2	-3.9
Eletronorte	Energy	Brazil	Government	SOE	8,481	2,413		5,875	618	6.8	-266	-43	-4.5
Celesc	Energy	Brazil	Government	SOE	1,300	4,432		586	611	12.5	2.1	0.3	0.4
CODENSA	Energy	Colombia	Government	SOE	1,772			1,576	465	-1.9	53.5	11.5	3.4
ETB	Energy	Colombia	Government	SOE	1,545	4,914		711	470	18.1	83.1	18	11.7
Celg	Energy	Brazil	Government	SOE	905			177	386	8.6	-33.5	-8.7	-18.9
Average SOE					8,148.818	5,014	6,828.895	5,333.364	1,465.273	2.6	160.6545	2.1	2.327273

Source: Compiled by the authors from América Economía, 500 Largest Latin American Firms, July 2001; Financial Times, The World's Largest Companies.
[a]BRI, broad regional integrator; NRI, narrow regional integrator; NRS, narrow regional specialist; NC, national champion; SOE, state-owned enterprise.
[b]ROS, return on revenues.
[c]RONW, return on net worth.

TABLE 4.8 Performance Profile of Different Strategies of Energy and Telecommunications Firms in Latin America

PROFILE	ALL COMPANIES	NARROW REGIONAL SPECIALIST	NARROW REGIONAL INTEGRATOR	BROAD REGIONAL INTEGRATOR	NATIONAL CHAMPION	STATE-OWNED ENTERPRISE
Total assets ($ millions)	4,836	2,112	2,996	4,202	4,758	8,149
Employees	6,039	676	5,919	4,409	18,061	5,014
Market capitalization ($ millions at 12/31/00)	4,247	1,247	2,253	2,678	13,109	6,829
Net worth ($ millions)	2,384	1,088	1,409	1,703	1,851	5,333
Revenues ($ millions)	1,564	480	1,244	1,477	2,480	1,465
Revenues change over last year (%)	13.8	11.6	22.1	16.6	11.0	2.6
Net profit ($ millions)	142.7	126.3	114.6	68	408	160.6
Net profit/revenue (%)	3.4	11.6	9.3	1.5	5.5	2.1
Net profit/net worth (%)	4.5	26.3	9.1	2.3	7.4	2.3

166

firms to protect their market share under the challenge of full competition or to diversify. [39]Additional competitive pressure is emerging from network convergence. Multiutility strategies may unfold in Latin America. In one case, U.S. energy integrator AES has launched an unsolicited bid to acquire controlling interest of Venezuela's CANTV, the privatized public Telecom network. The controlling interest rests with Verizon.[40]

There are plenty of opportunities in the Latin American energy sector, as reviewed in the first part of this chapter. The example of reforms in pioneering countries such as Argentina and Chile has not been very convincing to policymakers, investors, and the public in general. Recent energy crises have led the public to question the wisdom of further privatizations. Reforms and liberalization programs that started recently, such as in Brazil, have been scaled back or put on the back burner for the moment. The lack of clarity in the regulatory framework has also made investors nervous or eager to recoup their investment fast.

Given the different market conditions in the telecommunications and energy sectors, which strategies work best? To address this question, we look at the major players in the Latin American energy and telecommunications markets. Table 4.7 lists the largest firms in these two sectors based on revenues, employees, total assets, and market capitalization when available. In this table we identify the strategies of firms in terms of their business and geographic scope (see Table 4.5). We also identify firms owned by a national group or the state. Firms were classified as integrators if they were national subsidiaries of a larger global firm such as Telecom Italia or Endesa. Based on our understanding of the global strategy of the parent firm and the scope of countries in which the global firm operates in Latin America, these integrators were defined as broad or narrow. Specialist firms operate in a very narrow business activity in either telecommunications or energy. Only one firm in our sample, TGS in Argentina, is a specialist. This firm operates the gas transportation network in the southern Argentinean region under a 30-year concession and is large enough to be included in the list. There are other specialist firms that are not included in the list mostly because of their small size or lack of information. For instance, Bell South has cellular properties throughout the region, but none of them, individually or collectively, is large enough for inclusion.

Table 4.8 provides a profile of performance and size of firms under each type of strategy. We look at two indicators of performance, net profit over revenues and net profit over net worth.[41] Argentinean TGS, the specialist firm, outscores firms using other strategies. TGS had an outstanding return of net worth of 26% in 2000. By focusing on one business aspect, gas transportation, TGS delivered this high level of performance with one-tenth the employment and half of the assets of the average firm in the sample.

The next best strategy is that of the narrow regional integrator (NRI). The profit margin and return on net worth of this group of firms is twice as high as the average firm. Telecom Italia and its national subsidiaries in Latin America are examples of an NRI strategy. As the case description illustrates, NRI firms select strategically the location where they operate. In the case of Telecom Italia, a strategy of concentration at the heart of Mercosur has allowed this firm to coordinate better operations and to develop a successful cross-border platform (northern Argentina, southern Brazil, Paraguay, and Chile).

National champions are meeting the challenge of specialists and NRI firms. Their returns are slightly above the group average. These firms are large in size. Telmex, for instance, is the largest firm in Latin America based on market capitalization.[42] Their strategy is based not only on size but also on competing in their home base. They understand the customer better and may be better able to manage the regulatory challenges.

Broad regional integrators are not performing as well as the others. These firms are the true builders of regional networks. They have assets in small and large countries throughout the region. With operations in a variety of market and regulatory situations, it is difficult to be consistent. As a result, some of their subsidiaries perform well and others don't. BRI firms are also quite large in all respects. The advantage of size of assets of employment, however, does not translate into larger market capitalization.

State-owned firms do not perform well. These firms are sluggish on revenue increases, and their profit margins are thin. Their large size is a disadvantage. These firms are good candidates to be privatized.

In conclusion, our snapshot of performance in the Latin American infrastructure sector identified the best strategies as those of the specialists and narrow regional integrators.

REACHING
THE NEW LATIN
CONSUMERS

irms in Latin American consumer markets are being challenged to rethink strategies crafted for expansion and the liberalizing market conditions of the 1990s. The first challenge is to deliver a more compelling value proposition that meets the present economic realities. The second challenge is to build new growth platforms in the midst of much decreased consumption. In the short term, the goal for any firm in Latin America is to sustain revenues and protect market share and to be among the market leaders that will survive the shakeout. In this chapter we identify the key strategic areas that firms should focus on in developing a robust strategy for Latin American consumer markets in the future.

Enduring recession and economic volatility have changed Latin American consumption and shopping patterns. Increasingly, Latin American consumers are seeking better values that meet realistic expectations. Price has become an increasing determinant of choice only to the extent that value is not compromised. Strategies based on price differentiation alone no longer respond to Latin American consumer value priorities. Latin American consumers' shopping strategies today blur the socioeconomic distinctions of the past: Increasingly, consumers of all socioeconomic classes shop at hard-discount and self-service stores for the best value-to-price offerings, just as high-scale shopping environments attract consumers from all segments seeking self-gratification. Shopping centers and convenience stores have become the town centers of the twenty-first century. With increased choice of products and brands and access to the Internet, Latin American consumers are becoming more informed and smarter in their choices.

The challenge for firms is to find a value proposition that fits the rapidly changing consumption strategies in Latin America. Once the firm succeeds in finding the right value proposition, the next challenge is to develop a marketing platform that delivers such value at reasonable costs. Building strong brands is at the core of the marketing platform. In searching for the right value, Latin American consumers are experimenting with new options, and finding that price is not necessarily an indicator of superior and consistent value. Local brands have closed the gap of quality and efficiency with global brands. In some consumer categories, local brands have become the epitome of admiration and expression of local culture. Integrators and specialists in consumer markets are vying to conquer the new Latin American consumer. With a highly focused strategy, specialists claim to have superior value and a more intimate relationship with consumers. Integrators base their strategies on the ability to provide a range of products and services under one brand. What do Latin American consumers value most? Will integrators or specialists emerge as strong players in the shakeout? We address these questions in the following sections.

CONSUMER VALUE IN UNCERTAIN TIMES

In changing times, consumer value in Latin America is a moving target because consumers are constantly learning effective strategies to cope with money and time limitations. To grasp the emergence of a new consumer value in Latin America, we explore its key components next.

REALISM AND CYNICISM

Latin American consumers are increasingly translating their sensitivity to social issues such as globalization, financial crisis, and corruption into consumption decisions. The novelty of globalization vanished with the commoditization of the consumption experience, as global brands became more accessible. Increased visibility of corruption as a social issue has also influenced consumer cynicism, especially in younger segments. In this process, there is increasing interest in the past (nostalgia) and in local identity. In general, consumers are more skeptical of marketing claims, global brands have a harder time connecting with more disenfranchised market segments, and consumers rely more on retailers for information.

THE PRICE IMPERATIVE

Low prices are essential to remain competitive, but price alone is no longer an overriding factor to win consumer patronage. Consumer prices have been falling across the region for several years since the peaks of 1998.[1] In most countries, single-digit inflation has been the norm for several years.[2] As prices of all competing brands come down, price ceases to be a differentiating factor. Firms have to decide whether it is better to discount a premium brand or introduce reformulated or new products at lower prices.

SELECTIVITY

As mentioned in Chapter 2, Latin American consumers are reallocating their shrinking consumer budgets. Nonessential purchases are postponed and essentials goods are prioritized. Two examples illustrate the drastic changes of consumption strategies in recent times. The market for cars has shrunk 40% in Argentina, but refrigerator sales are up. Consumption of basic personal care categories such as toothpaste and deodorants is down, but consumption of all-purpose cleaning products is up. The implication for firms is that consumer selectivity will create windows of opportunity for some and disappearing markets for others.[3]

STRETCHING THE BUDGET

An important goal for Latin American consumers' value in uncertain times is getting the most from the limited resources of time and effort. For example, the increased use of multiple-purpose products such as cleaning liquids for multiple uses in the house, in the large family economy size, is one way of stretching the budget. Time is also scarce because of increased work commitments and their impact on family lifestyles. The increased popularity of food mart stores in gas stations is one example of how consumers respond to these pressures. Convenience stores offer basic necessities and a range of services, such as prepared foods, automated teller machines (ATMs), mail, and Internet kiosks. Latin American consumers are also increasingly favoring hard-discount stores as part of this strategy of stretching the budget.

INCREASED AWARENESS OF HEALTH AND THE ENVIRONMENT

A shift to more healthy diets and a concern for the environment is part of a global trend but has intensified in Latin America with the crisis. As discussed in Chapter 2, the main drivers for health awareness are increased health costs resulting from less public service benefits. A shift to healthier consumption can offset higher health cost. This shift is not a prerogative of more affluent classes alone; diet and health concerns are shared by all socioeconomic classes. The demand for health products is on the increase. Consumption of bottled water is up and that of carbonated soft beverages is down.[4] As large consumer companies are slow to react to this trend, the opportunity provides small national and regional specialists a quick entry and expansion opportunities in this market niche.

SMALL SELF-GRATIFICATION

Self-gratification is part of the Latin American consumer need to feel good in the midst of economic malaise: A ray of hope is found in small acts of self-gratification. As economic crisis deepens, the type and value of consumer investment in self-gratification vary. Self-gratification also varies with income. In the early part of the economic recession in Argentina, demand for beauty products remained strong. As the crisis deepened, demand for beauty products and even personal care products such as toothpaste and deodorants shrank, whereas the demand for candies and chocolates increased. Beer consumption in this country also remained strong.[5]

WHAT IS LATIN CONSUMER VALUE?

We see the emerging Latin American consumer value in terms of four dimensions. The first is *economic value*. In this dimension, consumers are searching for all-in-one solutions, convenience, and functionality that meet their budgets. The second dimension is *self-gratification* and feeling well in the midst of pessimism. Latin American consumers are looking for a light of hope and welfare. They are concerned increasingly with their personal health and turning to simple, immediate, and more realistic gratifications. The third dimension of consumer value is *belongingness*. Today, Latin American consumers are turning to local values and icons. They look to the past for nostalgic inspiration, as the future seems so uncertain. The final dimension is *honesty and transparency*. As part of a social shift toward more transparency in society, Latin American consumers are demanding honesty and more transparency in commercial transactions. Any claim or practice that seems exaggerated will only erode consumer trust.

Strategies for Latin American consumer markets need to integrate several dimensions of consumer value. Firms that focus on only one dimension, such as price, are doomed to fail. The proper mix of these dimensions depends on the culture and degree of demographic transformation of different countries in Latin America. Some of the dimensions of Latin American consumer value may be more important in some countries and less in others. The right consumer value in Brazil, for instance, should stress the belonging value, an intrinsic part of the Brazilian culture. Thus, a key element of market strategies in Brazil should be based on intense use of customer service and personalization strategies. Given that the deep economic recession makes economic value an overriding factor in Argentina, effective strategies may economize on customer service and pass the savings to the customer. Mexican consumers placed a high value on shopping time given Mexico's robust economy until recently. Consumer market strategies in Mexico should stress the value of one-stop shopping, whether for financial services or groceries.

POSITIONING TO MEET CONSUMER VALUE IN LATIN MARKETS

THE CONVENTIONAL APPROACH

A dramatic realignment of consumer expectations challenges conventional strategy approaches based on socioeconomic segmentation. The traditional view was based on the assumption that markets first develop in affluent segments and trickle down to the masses over time (see Figure 5.1). Under this approach, market offerings that integrate product, service, promotion, and channel strategies were differentiated for affluent and popular segments. Take, for instance, Whirlpool's approach to market refrigerators and washing machines in Argentina: In this market, the firm targets the more affluent families in the ABC1 socioeconomic classes under the Whirlpool brand name.[6] The firm uses the Eslabón de Lujo brand, a basic and affordable appliance, to target the C2 and C3 socioeconomic segments. Both brands are manufactured in Argentina. The company has plans to segment the market even further and introduce a low-priced kerosene-powered refrigerator for rural families not connected to power lines.[7]

The conventional approach worked well for some time, when socioeconomic segments were stable and differentiated and when the competitive challenge came mostly from local firms. As discussed in Chapter 2, however, economic hardship and volatility have blurred socioeconomic class distinctions in many consumer categories. Another factor that challenges the conventional approach is the pressure on premium brand products. As consumers become more realistic in their expectations, they are constantly reevaluating the price–value ratio of alternative product choices. Recent studies of younger consumers in Latin America show a more pragmatic, elusive, less committed, and distrustful consumer.[8] In addition, local competitors are closing the performance gap in quality with global

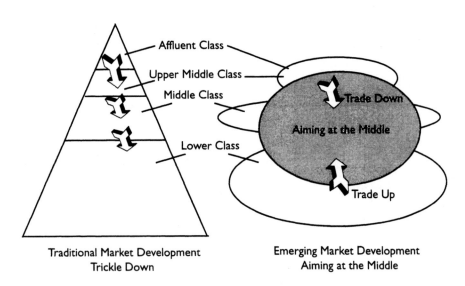

FIGURE 5.1
Market Development in Latin America

brands. Furthermore, discount stores and supermarkets have been very successful in positioning their private brands at substantial discounts from premium brands.

AN EMERGING APPROACH: CONVERGENCE TO THE CENTER

Two strategies appear to be promising in delivering the best consumer value in today's environment. The first strategy is to aim at the middle mass market with the best consumer value in the marketplace. The goal of this strategy is to attract consumers from affluent markets (ABC1) pressured by economic factors, consumers from the embattled middle class (C2 and C3), and upgraded consumers from the popular segment (D) with the best value-to-price offering. Offering the best market value to consumers in a diverse market is a challenge. A key factor of this strategy is to integrate all the dimensions of consumer value discussed above under a single brand offering. In essence, the firm becomes an integrator of services and aggregator of market segments. Another factor of the strategy is not to compromise on quality. The firms should aspire to offer world-class quality in the local market.[9]

Mexico's Telmex is an example of the integrator strategy. Only a fraction of Mexican families have access to the Internet, due to the low level of computer penetration in Mexico. After acquiring the Prodigy Internet service provider (ISP) in 1998, Telmex decided to target the low end of the market to increase computer penetration to build a market base for Prodigy in Mexico.[10] With the prospect of other ISP providers entering the Mexican market, Telmex had to leverage its incumbent advantage to quickly build a customer base for Prodigy. Instead of subscribing to the traditional approach of a trickle-down of computer penetration from affluent to more popular classes, Telmex used a quick market aggregation approach. Telmex offered a consumer credit program to help Mexican consumers buy computers manufactured by Acer, Compaq, IBM, or Hewlett-Packard with the embedded Prodigy ISP. Under this program, Mexican buyers paid $40 per month toward the computer, with unlimited access to the Internet through Prodigy. A key factor of this strategy was to offer a range of options that incorporated the most advanced computer technology available at the time. By offering the best technology, the offer was attractive not only to low-end users but also to high-end users. In the first year of the program, Prodigy acquired 220,000 new subscribers, mostly from the low end. The offer attracted customers who could not afford to buy a computer. Prodigy customers who were Telmex customers of wired and wireless services were able to integrate all services in a single Internet interface. For low-income Mexican families, Telmex delivered the best of the twenty-first century in one package. Telmex training programs nationwide helped educate these families on the use of new powerful technologies. The Telmex example shows the market power of integrating product and services to offer a compelling value to customers from all socioeconomic segments. In 2000, Prodigy boasted 635,000 customers in Mexico, claiming 50% of the market.[11]

The second strategy is that of the specialist. At the high end, premium specialists base their strategies on redefining the notion of premium. After a decade of open market competition, the concept of premium has been commoditized. Competitors' offerings are easily imitated, and consumers expect that companies will provide the same level of quality and service as anyone else. In response to this pressure, many companies have introduced boutique-type strategies that deliver value-added services and personalization. These operations are in many cases spin-offs from mainstream operations and delivered under another brand name. Banco Itau's Personnalité business combines personalized service, financial advice, specialized investment products, and a network of exclusive branches in Brazil. Since its introduction in 1999, Itau has attracted 12,000 new customers.[12] New market competitors are also changing the definition of premium products and services. France's Louis Vuitton Moët Hennessy (LVMH) is redefining what is upscale in accessory, clothing, and cosmetics in Latin America. LVMH opened its first Latin American global retail store in São Paulo in 1999. In a single location, LVMH offers an assortment of leather goods, champagne and cognac, perfumes, cosmetics, watches, and jewelry with luxury brand names that include Dom Perignon, Hennessy, Louis Vuitton, and Christian Dior. With the initial success of the first store, LVMH opened a second store in São Paulo and others in Rio de Janeiro and Brasilia. The next stop for LVMH is Mexico City. Other upscale retailers have also followed LVMH's retail approach. Tiffany opened its first store in São Paulo in 2001.[13] Clearly, Tiffany and LVMH have redefined the retail experience for luxury goods in key Latin American markets.

Specialists can also be found in the low end of the market. Low-income consumers represent an excellent opportunity to develop mass market strategies. Here the strategy is the opposite of the trickle-down approach. The strategy is based on building volume quickly in the short term with low-priced basic products that contribute to high fixed capital costs of building the network. Specialists use a combination of technological advances and low prices to build demand quickly. For example, retail chains of small self-service convenience pharmacy stores aimed at the mass market are competing with large discount and supermarket chains using a strategy of low prices, location, and convenience. We provide particular examples of specialist strategies in the retail section of this chapter.

BRAZIL'S NATURA: A VALUE PROPOSITION FOR ALL

A Brazilian company, Natura, provides an excellent example of aiming at the midmarket with the best customer value that technology and nature can provide. Natura competes in the cosmetics and health market. The $6 billion Brazilian cosmetic market has attracted many global players, such as L'Oreal, Revlon, Nivea, Avon, and Mary Kay.[14] The premium or prestige segment accounts for about 23% of the Brazilian market, measured in revenues. The popular market represents 76%. Mary Kay targets the prestige and popular market segments with different brands and prices, whereas L'Oreal and Nivea focus on the prestige market with high-priced imported products. At the other extreme and based on a low-cost direct sales approach, Avon targets the low end of the market by discounting prices and products.

Natura's vision is simple and universal. The company credo is to help people feel good about themselves and help them integrate physically, emotionally, intellectually, and spiritually with family, work, community, and nature. Such simple guiding principles resonate with Brazilians of all classes and market segments. From its roots in homeopathy, Natura has focused on tapping the indigenous knowledge of the therapeutic properties of Brazil's immense plant biodiversity, combined with advanced scientific knowledge. Based on these intangible resources, Natura has produced a range of cosmetics and health products that meet the characteristics and lifestyles of Brazilians of all types and locations. For instance, Natura distinguishes the large differences in climate, racial, and work conditions in Brazil. The tropical and harsh conditions of northern Brazil require formulations different from those found in the more temperate south. Natura has cleverly positioned its products in the middle to offer the best economic value. Natura offers Brazilians an affordable local solution between high-priced imported prestige brands and discount brands. With a product customized for Brazilian skin or health conditions, Natura offers a local identity that appeals to the strong national identity of Brazilians.

Natura has also worked on the value dimensions of belongingness and value. Natura's 270,000 direct marketing consultants are trained to develop a strong relationship with Brazilian customers.[15] Its customer service center handles about 450,000 telephone calls per month; consultants can tap Natura's product, customer, and distribution information systems either through a telephone call or the company intranet.[16] Natura has an experimental customer online operation where customers can place orders with their designated consultant or learn more about health and new products.

Natura integrates two other dimensions of customer value: honesty and transparency. Natura has demonstrated a commitment to preserve natural assets that are important to all Brazilians and society in general. Natura has also invested in educational programs that foster children's education. These programs encourage Brazilian children to become more self-confident and stress family and community trust.

Since competition for the Brazilian market is intense, Natura focuses on innovation to maintain leadership. The company introduces a new product every three days. To support this effort, Natura invests about 4% of net revenues in R&D and has extensive collaboration agreements with universities and pharmaceutical research institutes in Brazil and abroad. The company also focuses on operating with the most advanced technologies. Its state-of-art facility outside São Paulo is a showcase of how Brazilian companies are building world-class manufacturing facilities.

The Natura example shows how this Brazilian company has used a brand strategy based on fundamental principles of harmony, conservation, transparency, and honesty. Natura has found that the same principles and consumer value proposition are exportable to other Latin American countries. The company has entered Argentina, Chile, Peru, and Bolivia. Natura has full control of all the operations, except in Bolivia, where they have a joint venture. In each country, the population base, biodiversity, climate, and indigenous knowledge are different. Natura's international strategy is to tap on the local indigenous knowledge and biodiversity and their experience with advanced technology to offer customized products that fit the local conditions. Their aim is to expand to replicate their success at a regional level from Argentina to Mexico.[17]

BUILDING BRANDS IN VOLATILE AND UNCERTAIN MARKETS

Building a strong brand, whether global or local, is the principal goal of any business strategy for Latin America. The challenge is to build one that resonates with the new market reality.

THE POWER OF GLOBAL AND LOCAL BRANDS

Global brands entering Latin American markets leverage their world-class status and technological superiority. Global brands appeal to local consumer aspirations of cosmopolitan and sophisticated lifestyles. Furthermore, global brands have access to the world's best creative talent to shape images that support their global appeal. Multinational companies invest substantial amounts in promoting their global brands in local markets. Despite some degree of localization, global brands tend to have consistent market positioning.

Familiarity strikes a chord with consumers who are reluctant to experiment with new products or ideas and are not interested in the allure of the global culture. Local brands derive market power from their identification with local community value, heritage, folklore, and tradition. Since local brands were conceived and produced for the local market, consumers perceive them as more appropriate to their context and consumer situation. Local brands have also improved their market power in terms of exceptional product or service performance. A few national champions, such as Brazil's Sadia, have closed the quality gap in recent years and have reengineered processes to become cost-efficient.

Past brand-building efforts and investments are paying off nicely for both global and local brands. The most successful global and local brands have reached a level of admiration and respect among Latin American consumers.

Using the BrandAsset® Valuator, a Landor/Young & Rubicam proprietary tool for building and managing brands, Landor Associates analyzed top brands in Argentina and Brazil. The BAV model measures several brand dimensions. *Differentiation* is the strength of the brand's meaning. Consumer choice, brand essence, and potential margin are all driven by Differentiation. *Relevance* measures the personal appropriateness of a brand to consumers and is strongly tied to household penetration. Relevance alone is not the key to brand success. Rather, Relevance together with Differentiation form brand *Strength,* an important indicator of future performance and potential. Relevant differentiation is the major challenge for all brands and a leading indicator of brand health. The combination of *Esteem* and *Knowledge* forms *Brand Stature,* a more traditional measure that the BAV has determined to be a lagging indicator of brand health. As part of the diagnostic process for managing brands, Y&R plots brands on a "Power Grid" reflecting a brand's Strength and Stature. The power grid plots for top brands in Argentina and Brazil are shown in Figures 5.2 and 5.3.

The top 20 brands in Brazil are a mix of corporate and product brands. Top corporate global brands include Coca-Cola, Johnson &

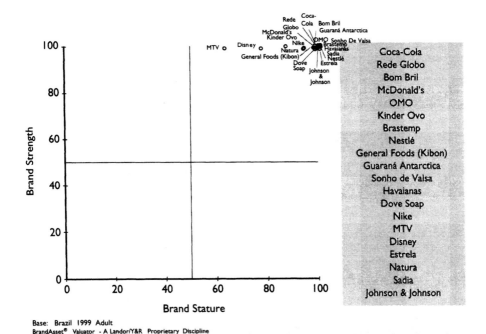

FIGURE 5.2
Top Brands by Strength in Brazil
Reprinted with permission from Landor Associates.

Johnson, Nestlé, Disney, General Foods, McDonald's, and to a lesser extent, MTV. Brazilian corporate brands include Sadia, Guaraná Antarctica, Brastemp, Bom-Bril, Rede Globo, and Natura. Top product brands include Omo and Dove soap, both Unilever brands.

Landor's study in Argentina shows a similar result for global and local brands, although the spread widens in terms of stature. In the case of Argentina, premium global brands are more representative in this group. Prestige and niche brands that did not show in the Brazil study have achieved substantial market power in Argentina. In this country, Rolex, Calvin Klein, Rolls-Royce, Yves Saint Laurent, Ferrari, and Harley-Davidson join mass market global brands such as Seven-Up, Coca-Cola, and Dove. Fewer Argentinean brands—namely, Quilmes, Merengadas, and La Serenísima—shared the top brand power. Surprisingly, Unicef Argentina has achieved top brand power in Argentina.[18]

Another way to determine the impact of brand building is through assessment of brand equity. Under this approach, the finan-

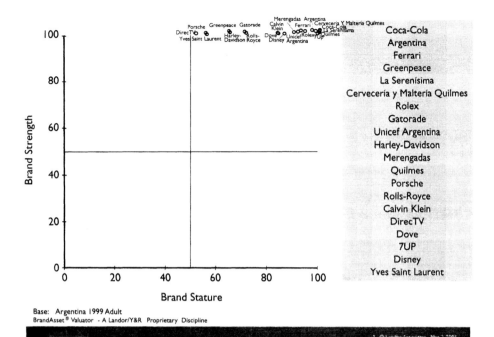

FIGURE 5.3

Top Brands by Strength in Argentina

Reprinted with permission from Landor Associates.

cial valuation of the brand provides an assessment of how the brand contributes to future revenues and profitability of the firm. Although global brands have, periodically, been valued for investments and other purposes, until recently local Latin American brands have not been subject to this exercise. Interbrand, a brand consultancy, has analyzed Brazilian brands for the first time. In their study, the Brazilian brands with the highest brand equity (financial valuation) were Banco Itaú, Bradesco, AmBev (Brahma–Antarctica), Banco do Brasil, Unibanco, Embraer (commuter aircraft manufacturer), Multibrás, Embratel, Gradiente (electronics), Sadia, and Tigre. With a brand equity valuation of $970 million, Banco Itaú would rank 75 among the top 100 global brands.[19]

BRAND EROSION AND MIGRATION TO THE CENTER

Brand equity is difficult to sustain under changing customer preferences during economic hardship. As mentioned earlier, Latin American consumers seek better economic values, self-gratification, transparency, and a sense of community. Brands out of touch with this reality become irrelevant. Private and discount brands seem to have struck a chord with Latin American consumers. In a study of private use in Argentina, Nielsen found that the percentage of consumers buying retail brands increased to 60% in 2000 from 44% in 1998. In 2000, the sales volume of nonbranded products increased by 2% whereas the volume for branded products declined by 6.6%.[20]

To explain how brand erosion drivers affect brands in Latin America, we describe the process of brand building and erosion. Although this process is not unique to Latin America, it will help explain how changing economic conditions have altered the fundamental brand strategy logic in the region. Global brands enter international markets with premium positioning, in the right-hand quadrant in Figure 5.4. Global brands appeal primarily to consumers in AB segments with globalizing lifestyles and aspirations. More often than not, local brands have been positioned at the lower end of price and quality. Efforts to close the quality and innovation gap move local brands to the right along the curve of increased differentiation and targeting the same sophisticated AB consumer. Private and discount brands positioned initially at the lower end of the price–quality relationship improve their quality over time, and increase price. Finally, sales promotions and price adjustments have moved leading brands to the left. Based on sales promotion alone, branded products are not able to sustain category leadership, and customer value quickly erodes, threatening further premium brand discounts. As the price gap for premium brands erodes, the market becomes commoditized, marked by a rapid descent toward the lower-left quadrant. Brand revitalization efforts are typically introduced through innovation. New brand formulations and brand extension strategies move the brand again on the path of differentiation and brand value creation. In most cases, innovation is incremental in nature and easily imitated by local companies and retailers. The cycle of commoditization starts anew.

The new economic reality in Latin America has altered this traditional process of creative destruction in two ways. The first challenge is the irreversibility of the erosion of premium price–quality advantage. Under economic distress, Latin American consumers may stop buying a commodity altogether if high prices force them to reduce expenditures in essential categories. Some recent studies have found that Latin American consumers are reducing consumption categories to maintain telecommunication services. This shift may be especially marked in the middle- and lower-income segments. The shift, as indicated by the decrements in economic value

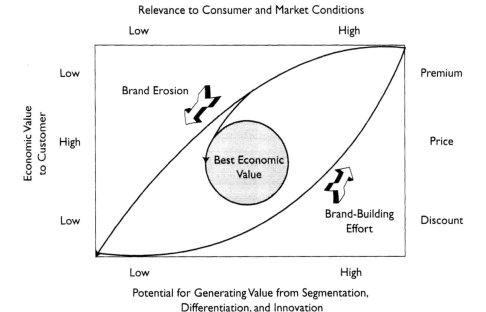

FIGURE 5.4
Brand Erosion and Migration to the Center in Latin American Consumer Markets

(right-hand vertical axes) is difficult to reverse. The other major challenge is brand relevance. Again, if the brand is out of touch with the present reality, any innovation effort to improve product or service performance will be lost. To break the brand erosion cycle in Latin America, firms should focus on a systematic brand-building strategy that achieves market relevance, delivers consumer value, and eliminates consumer confusion.

BUILDING BRAND EQUITY IN UNCERTAIN TIMES

A systematic brand strategy is a carefully orchestrated effort to develop a brand architecture that supports the goal of establishing consumer economic value, relevance, and resonance. This architecture is deconstructed into several brand-building-block efforts, as shown in Figure 5.5.[21] The first building block is *brand salience*. It is not surprising to find that the top advertisers in Latin America are large multinational companies with a broad portfolio of such consumer brands as Nestlé, Unilever, Procter & Gamble, Colgate Pal-

FIGURE 5.5

Latin American Brand Building Pyramid

Source: Adapted from K. Keller, *Strategic Brand Management: Building, Measuring, and Managing Brand Equity,* 2nd ed., Prentice Hall, Upper Saddle River, NJ, 2003.

molive, and Coca-Cola (see Table 5.1). A few local brands are also heavy investors in advertising: Banco Itaú in Brazil, Quilmes in Argentina, Telmex in Mexico, Polar beer in Venezuela, and Cristal beer in Peru. In some cases, strong brands do not rely on advertising. One of the top Brazilian brands in Landor's study, Natura, does not advertise at all. Natura's brand-building effort focuses on meaning.

The second building block is *brand meaning*. The effort here is to establish credibility. We have referred to the importance of a proper value-to-price relationship in uncertain times. Brand performance, however, is only one aspect of brand meaning; the other component is brand personality. Here the effort is to bring out the history, heritage, and experiences that may make the brand relevant to Latin American consumers. In times of economic crisis, Latin

TABLE 5.1 Top Advertisers in Key Latin American Markets

RANK	BRAZIL (2001)	MEXICO (1999)	ARGENTINA (2000)	CHILE (2000)	COLOMBIA (JAN.-JUNE 2001)	VENEZUELA (1999)	PERU (JAN.-JUNE 2001)
1	Intelig (telecom.)	Aurrera (retail)	Unilever	Telefónica	Postobon (beverages/local)	P&G	TIM (Telefónica Cellular)
2	Gessy Lever	Comercial Mexicana (retail)	Telefónica	Unilever	Coca-Cola	Polar (beer/local)	P&G
3	Embratel (telecom./MCI)	Telcel (wireless)	P&G	Nestlé	Tecnoquimicas (pharma./local)	Colgate-Palmolive	Cristal (beer/local)
4	Liderança	P&G	Telecom Argentina	P&G	Orbitel	Banco Provincial (bank/local)	Cuzqueña (beer/local)
5	Volkswagen	Colgate-Palmolive	Coca-Cola	Coca-Cola	Nacional de Chocolates (snacks/local)	Movilnet	SagaFalabella (retail/Chile)
6	Itaú (bank/local)	Telmex	CR Moviles	Falabella (retail/local)	ETB (telecom./local)	Banco Mercantil (bank/local)	Ariel (P&G)
7	Ford	Coca-Cola	Johnson & Johnson	Almacenes Paris (retail/local)	Colgate-Palmolive	Banco de Venezuela	Pilsen (beer/local)
8	General Motors	General Motors	Quilmes	Comercial ECCSA	Conavi (banking/local)	Telcel	Movistar (telecom.)
9	Procter & Gamble (P&G)	Nestlé	Cencosud	Laboratorios Marvel (pharma.)	BanColombia (bank/local)	Loteria de Oriente	Telefónica
10	Nestlé	Domecq	Garbarino	Entel	Bavaria	Corp. Banca	Coca-Cola

Source: www.adlatina.com, *Ibope.*

American consumers tend to favor familiar icons and local heritage, hence giving an advantage to local brands.

The third building block is *emotional response*. Here, the firm seeks positive evaluative responses and judgments toward the brand and the corporation that go beyond product or service performance. The effort here is to assure consumers of the brand's achievements over time and commitment to the future. The strategy seeks to link the brand to corporate competence, innovativeness, and trustworthiness. Take, for instance, the case of Telefónica Spain. When the firm took over the privatized public telephone networks of many Latin American countries, the strategy was based on providing basic service to as many people as possible. During the network and improvement phases, Telefónica's brand stood for fulfilling the promise of installing telephones. When the monopoly period ended in most of Telefónica's concessions, competitors entered the market and offered consumers a choice. Telefónica's effort to sustain brand power shifted to choice. Telefónica's appeal changed to working hard to be your preferred option. As competition intensified and new specialist brands penetrated particular market segments, Telefónica changed to a two-pronged strategy. Telefónica's institutional communications appealed to the irrelevance of choice when the brand is superior. Telefónica followed Coca-Cola's approach in using the slogan "Your best option—Always Telefónica." In addition, Telefónica invested in individual brand-building efforts for its various businesses, such as data transmission or cellular telephony linked to a strong corporate brand image.[22]

Local brands have achieved credibility and reputation in recent times. The challenge for local brands is to build emotional evaluations and brand feelings. With plant closures and economic uncertainty, Latin American consumers question whether their most popular local brand may remain or disappear from the market. In volatile times, firms should constantly reassure Latin American consumers about their long-term viability. Future success depends on the ability of local brands to deliver a sense of security, warmth, self-respect, and social approval.

The final building block is *brand resonance*. Here, firms should strive for customer loyalty and enduring relationships. Achieving this goal is a challenging feat in Latin America. One limitation is a lower incidence of points of contact with consumers. Economic uncertainty may drive Latin American consumers to shop more infrequently, decrease product use, or stop purchasing within the category. Another impact is brand switching. Consumers may switch to other brands in their search for better value. Thus, firms should attempt to be extremely effective at every opportunity of point of contact. Firms that have integrated automated customer relationship technologies in their operations can monitor and leverage every point of consumer contact. Another important implication for building brand resonance is to establish and reinforce the brand identification with larger consumer beliefs and aspirations. As discussed before, Latin American consumers are increasingly demanding transparency and honesty in their relationship with firms. Very few firms have invested in establishing this level of resonance with Latin American consumers. Given the level of cynicism and loyalty, firms will have to pay more attention to this factor. In our assessment, specialists have a better chance to establish better brand resonance because of their focused vision and single-brand image.

Brand strategy must be adjusted to the country and target segment. The need to adjust the strategy is more marked at higher levels of brand building, such as resonance and meaning, than at lower levels. At lower levels, brand-building strategies to achieve brand salience should leverage high levels of mass media penetration and exposure in Latin America. Broadcast TV penetration is the source of information and entertainment for most Latin American households. Close to 95% of households have a television set and watch TV four hours a day on average.[23] Adjustments should be made to different preferences for programming and content by country and socioeconomic classes. For instance, the preferred choice for content are movies in Chile, entertainment in Mexico, programs for children in Brazil and Venezuela, sports in Argentina, and international news in Colombia.[24]

Emotional brand efforts should be highly localized to the customer culture. For instance, only Brazilians may know how to build effective brand images in Brazil. An example of such an effort is Bombril, a manufacturer and marketer of household products. The company has used the "Bombril kid" character for 23 years. In this case, the brand personality is the Bombril kid. The firm keeps the brand personality fresh and relevant by using the character to address controversial current social or political issues in Brazil and the world. The brand image remains realistic by admitting in the message that as human beings, we are all bound to make mistakes.[25]

LEVEL OF MARKET AGGREGATION

A related strategic decision to reach Latin American consumers is to decide on the level of market aggregation. Aggregation in this chapter refers to the broad and narrow geographic scope mentioned in Chapter 1 (see Figure 1.1). The best strategy is to aggregate markets with minimum adjustments to the fundamental consumer value discussed earlier. An example of such strategy was Brazil's Natura. With a highly focused strategy, specialists have less of a problem in aggregation. The level of market aggregation depends on the size of the target segment across the region that fits the strategy. The strategies of global specialists are highly predictable and based on buying power demographics in the region. The market aggregation strategy of Louis Vuitton and Tiffany in Latin America could be limited to a handful of large urban centers with substantial affluent households. Given the diversity of market conditions and consumer cultures in Latin America, integrators should consider the market-nesting strategy suggested in Chapter 2.

In a market-nesting strategy, the first decision is to pick one of the groups of countries identified in Chapter 2. The first group includes markets in advanced stages of demographic transformation, which include the highly urbanized urban markets of Argentina, Chile, Uruguay, and Puerto Rico. The second group includes markets in full demographic transformation with a mix of urban and rural markets, such as Brazil and Mexico, along with Peru, Venezuela, and Colombia. The third group consists of countries with moderate levels of demographic transformation and substantial rural populations in Central America. This group is a difficult market platform, due to its small market size.

Given the choices, firms may choose to select a market platform in either the Southern Cone countries or the mass markets of Brazil and Mexico. These two options lead to two different consumer value propositions. The value proposition for markets at an advanced state of demographic change and level of urbanization is different from that of markets that are at the full stage of transformation. Another difference is market size; Brazilian and Mexican markets are gigantic compared to Argentinean or Chilean markets. For these reasons, firms should focus on developing an effective strategy for one group or the other. We elaborate on the broad elements of these two strategic options below.

Consumers in the highly urbanized, demographically mature, and affluent markets of Argentina, Chile, Uruguay, and Puerto Rico—and those in the U.S. Latin market—have achieved high levels of education and connectivity. The adjustment of consumption styles has been gradual. The economies in these countries have already reached advanced level of structural reforms, privatizations, and integration with the global economy. After a period of expansion, their economies have slowed. Consumers in these countries have been reassessing their expectations and shopping patterns for quite some time. Argentinean consumers have been adjusting consumption styles since the prolonged recession started in 1998. The collapse of the Argentinean economy in 2002, however, has accelerated the adjustment to dramatic levels, and consumer confidence may have reached its lowest levels in the history of this country, which was once at the top of the Latin America's affluence pyramid.

With the two largest economies in the region, a market platform that includes Brazil, Mexico, or both markets is part of any Latin American strategy for major multinationals. Here, the firm has to determine whether the core market platform is Brazil or Mexico. In the early 1990s, Mexico was the preferred market. In the period 1990–1996, Mexico received $24 billion of foreign direct investment, whereas Brazil attracted only $17.7 billion. In the latter part of the 1990s, Brazil was the preferred choice of many multinationals. In the period 1997–2000, Brazil received $134 billion of foreign direct investment, whereas Mexico had $59.8 billion.[26] In the future, however, the choice is not as clear.[27] Building a platform in one of these two countries is no guarantee of success in the other. The different consumer cultures in these two countries limit the transfer of marketing practices and strategies.

Once a decision is made in terms of using Brazil or Mexico as a platform, firms must evaluate expansion strategies. The two options for expansion are markets within the same or different clusters. An example of the first approach is a firm that uses Mexico as the platform and decides to expand to Colombia, Venezuela, or Peru. An example of the second option is a firm using a Brazilian market platform entering the Argentinean market. The second option requires major adjustments to the marketing approach. The logic that consumer values may be similar for bordering countries may lead to major mistakes. For instance, Brazilian and Argentinean firms which assumed that proximity and the Mercosur trade agreement would ensure quick market penetration in each other's markets had to make major adjustments to their marketing strategies because of major differences in consumer culture and demographic patterns.

In addition to regional expansion, Latin American firms may opt to go global. Under this strategy, Latin American firms transform their companies to become globally competitive. Using this approach, Latin American firms that achieve global status may market their products in the most attractive markets in the region across clusters. The consumer value in this case, although geared to international acceptance, has its roots in the Latin American home base of the firm. The Latin American firm may leverage this advantage to create consumer value that is more relevant or more familiar in other Latin American markets.

The higher level of market integration is the pan-regional strategy. This strategy calls for presence in all markets without distinction as to geography or size. Pan-regional strategy requires large-scale use of financial resources and managerial skills to coordinate regionwide operations. Large multinationals have acquired these capabilities and access to international capital markets to fund expansion either organically or through acquisitions. Pan-regional strategies also demand quick implementation to obtain first-mover advantages and to capitalize on one-time opportunities arising from favorable international financial market conditions and regionwide reforms. The effectiveness of this strategy depends on the ability of the firm to replicate core competencies and processes that support the consumer value proposition in many different economies. Once the business architecture supporting is in place, the firm can adapt the consumer value proposition to the market situation.

Several market aggregation strategies have been identified above. We provide examples of using different market platforms below.

A NORTH AMERICAN MARKET PLATFORM

As mentioned in Chapter 2, the Mexican market has 18.1 million Mexican households with an average household buying power of $19,989. A Mexican market platform should include the 3.9 million households of Mexican origin in the United States with an average buying power of $41,500.[28] The total market potential for this region is an impressive $522.8 billion. The case of Mexico's Gruma illustrates the use of a Mexican market platform to reach the extended North American market corridor. Gruma is the leading corn flour and tortilla producer in North America. Since corn flour and tortillas are principal food staples in the Mexican diet, Gruma has grown with Mexico's population growth. Gruma's success is attributed to transformation of this market from traditional artisan-based production to industrial-based production of tortillas. With a proprietary dry corn tortilla production process, Gruma introduced a low-cost, more uniform, longer-shelf-life tortilla that could be distributed in the rapidly modernizing self-service grocery stores nationwide. Gruma's cost advantage is based on its superior process, which yields 1,200 tortillas per minute compared to 50 per minute with traditional machines.

In the 1990s, the Mexican market grew at an annual rate of 5%, driven by the rate of population increase and low prices for tortillas under a Mexican government subsidy program. In 1999, the Mexican government ended the subsidized program and prices went up, depressing domestic demand. Per capita tortilla consumption declined in Mexico for two years in a row. As the market for tortillas decreased by 3%, the market for wheat flour increased by 51%. Another factor that decreased demand for flour tortillas was an increase in the consumption of wheat products among Mexican families due to modernization. In response to changing market conditions in the local markets, Gruma moved to acquire 60% of Archer-Daniels-Midland's wheat flour operations in Mexico. This acquisition allowed Gruma to expand wheat processing capacity quickly and shift to wheat-based products to meet new consumption patterns.[29]

In contrast to flat tortilla sales in the Mexican market, the U.S. market for tortillas grew at 10% per year in the late 1990s. The U.S. market was very fragmented, and tortillas were produced with traditional machines. Through acquisitions of local tortilla factories in border states, Gruma was able to penetrate the U.S. market and achieve national distribution. In 1996, Gruma and Archer-Daniels-Midland (ADM) consolidated their corn flour operations in the United States and captured 82% of the market in value terms.[30] Gruma's market share of the tortilla market is estimated to be 25%. The company owns 13 tortilla plants in the United States, which markets under the Mission tortilla brand. Gruma is also the leading supplier of tortillas to Taco Bell.[31]

In the mid-1990s, Gruma opened corn flour processing mills in Central America. These countries represent a growing opportunity with their emerging demographic characteristics. Gruma focused on corn flour production, due to differences in diets in these countries. To increase the revenue base and leverage its distribution system, Gruma entered into related businesses, such as chips and packaged bread.[32] Gruma also entered Venezuela with a corn-processing plant. Diet and food consumption styles change from northern to southern hemisphere countries. In Venezuela, other grain-based products, such as wheat, rice, and oats, are in demand. To obtain a market position in Venezuela, Gruma acquired the second-largest wheat and corn flour producer in 1999. With both corn and flour production businesses, Gruma has quickly become the third-largest food producer in Venezuela.

Gruma's subregional expansion is paying off. The U.S. market has become the most important in terms of total revenues and growth prospects, contributing 43% of consolidated revenues and growing 5%. In contrast, the mature Mexican market accounts for 36% of revenues and continues to stagnate. Although small, the

Venezuelan and Central American markets contribute 15 and 6% to total corporate revenues but are growing at 10 and 2%, respectively.[33]

In the short term, Gruma's ambition is to make its Mission tortilla brand the market leader and standard for quality in the United States. To accomplish this goal, Gruma will have to shift the focus from production to marketing. We anticipate that Gruma's future effort in the United States will rely on investing more resources in advertising, packaging, in-store promotions, and other brand-building efforts. If this strategy succeeds, the Mission brand may be the first to achieve such a distinction in this commoditized food category.

Gruma is also investing in other capabilities. The deepening of its association with ADM will provide Gruma with access to the U.S. firm's capabilities in procurement, transportation, warehousing, and distribution technologies. In the food value chain, logistics is the area that offers the best opportunity to reduce inefficiencies. In addition, Gruma has invested in information technology as a way to improve operating efficiency. Its operations in Mexico, the United States, and Venezuela have SAP/R3 information systems and received ISO certification.

Gruma's future expansion can take the company farther south, into the Andean region, or to other world regions. In 2000, Gruma opted to cross the Atlantic to tap the increasing appetite for Mexican food products in Europe, a market estimated at $400 million. Following the footsteps of other Mexican products, such as Corona, the company opened its first plant in the UK and is ready to serve this new market opportunity.

A GLOBAL STRATEGY WITH A BRAZILIAN PLATFORM

Many Brazilian companies look at global markets as the next level of market expansion. The case of Sadia illustrates this strategy. Sadia is the market leader in frozen and refrigerated processed foods in Brazil. With roots in the production of poultry and pork processed meats, Sadia has diversified to higher value-added products such as frozen meals, frozen desserts, frozen pastas, pizza, vegetables, and fish. The rapid growth of the Brazilian economy in the second half of the 1990s and nationwide penetration of supermarkets and convenience stores fueled the demand for functional and convenience foods. Sadia was ready to supply Brazilian consumers with more than 600 different products, the majority of them frozen and ready to eat or cook at a reasonable price (economic value). In addition, some of Sadia's product lines met Brazilians' obsession with physical fitness and aesthetics with light-calorie formulations and bright-colored packaging. To make their products affordable to consumers of diverse socioeconomic classes, Sadia introduced total quality and cost reducing programs. To special segments such as single consumers and small families, Sadia introduced personalized and individual packaging. Some frozen pastas and meats were available in personal sizes or fragmented pieces.[34] With changing consumer lifestyles and economic conditions, Sadia is innovating constantly. The company introduces one new product per week and has diversified from meats to fish.

As early as 1991, the company's vision was to become a global leader in the frozen-food business. With formidable global competitors such as Tyson, Cargill, and Archer-Daniels-Midland, the company embarked on a comprehensive quality and cost improvement process. By the end of the 1990s, the company had accomplished most of its goals, obtained ISO quality and environmental standards, and introduced enterprise integration systems (SAP-3) internally. According to Sadia's chairman, Luiz Fernando Furlan, the process of constant improvement was inevitable given the early indicators of Brazil's market liberalization. According to Chairman Furlan, achieving world-class standards would help the firm not only meet global competitors in Brazil but also tap international financial markets.[35]

According to Chairman Furlan, Sadia's goal is to derive 50% of its revenues from international markets. The company has targeted several global markets to achieve this goal. Global quality standards and low costs allowed Sadia to penetrate the European market at a time when the European Union (EU) was relaxing market access for agricultural products. A recent strategic distribution alliance with UK-based Sun, Cargill's European subsidiary, created a new company, Concordia Foods. This new venture allowed Sadia to further penetrate the European market. Sadia has also been successful in penetrating the Russian market. Early entry into the Russian market in collaboration with domestic rival Perdigão[36] gave Sadia an early advantage to tap an estimated $1 billion market for frozen-food imports. Sadia and Perdigão formed an international trading company named BRF International Foods to strengthen their position for exports to emerging markets, among them Russia.[37] The company will also seek to sell poultry and pork in the Ukraine, Byelorussia, South Africa, Egypt, and Cuba, among other countries. Sadia has also been able to customize its process to develop a market for frozen food in the Middle-East, where frozen food is not part of the food consumption culture. With exports of frozen chicken since 1975, Sadia's brand is the market leader in Saudi Arabia and other Middle-Eastern markets.

A favorable international market has helped Sadia weather declining sales in Brazil, as price competition and the cooling of the Brazilian economy have resulted in a 19% contraction in revenues in 2000, despite an increase of 8% in volume sales. Cost reductions and improved margins of export revenues have allowed Sadia to achieve a return of 11.5% in 2000.[38]

THE SOUTHERN CONE MARKET PLATFORM

The Southern Cone market platform includes Argentina, Chile, and Uruguay. This market is home to 10 million households in Argentina with an average buying power of $20,600, 3.9 Chilean households with $11,800, and 0.9 million Uruguayan households with an average income of $15,900. The market potential of this platform is $270 billion.

This subregion is the home base of several Latin American multinationals. This is the territorial base of Argentina's candy manufacturer Arcor and food-processing giant Bunge and Born. A few companies have used this corridor to establish a strong home market position and expand into neighboring countries.

An example of a firm using this platform is Chile's Falabella, a retail company that markets fashion and home products using the department store format. Chilean retail companies dominate the domestic market despite this country's open, free market economy. Falabella's market share of the large department store market is an impressive 40% and its revenue growth in 2001 is expected to be 10%. Despite the slowdown of the Chilean economy, this impressive market performance is based on a strategy of anticipating of trends in the economy, market, and technology. Falabella management has been a leader in incorporating backroom retail technology to integrate the store with suppliers and to use customer databases to drive other services. The retail business accounts for 50%, and other services offered through their stores account for the rest. The company uses a decentralized management style where store managers are empowered to make the best decision for their particular locations. Falabella has also been very conservative and has financed growth and expansion primarily from internal funds.[39]

Falabella entered the Argentinean market in 1993 with a store in Mendoza. Quickly after the first store opening, Falabella entered Rosario, Cordoba, and San Juan before launching its attack on Buenos Aires. It is interesting to note that the firm targeted second-tier Argentinean cities for its first international expansion strategy. The main goals behind this strategy were to learn more about the Argentinean consumer and to build relationships with local suppliers. Falabella made its first investment outside its cluster when the firm acquired a Peruvian department store in 1995.[40] In 1998, Falabella participated in a joint venture to launch the first Home Depot store in Latin America.[41] After disappointing revenues in the first two years of business in Chile, Home Depot has decided to sell its share to Falabella.

Falabella's success is based on its ability to adapt to local markets and replicate its format and technology-based retail competencies in neighboring countries. Expansion beyond the present stronghold, to Colombia or Brazil, for instance, may require either greater adaptation of Falabella's technology-driven strategy or meeting strong local retailers using the same approach.

PAN-REGIONAL LATIN MARKET STRATEGY

Terra Networks in Latin America is an example of a pan-regional strategy in markets where regional aggregation provides a strategic advantage.[42] Of all the pan-regional Internet companies, which include Starmedia Networks, AOL, and MSN, Terra remains the most geographically diversified company in the region. Unlike other global competitors that entered Latin America's biggest markets progressively, Terra entered several country markets simultaneously. Terra was able to ride on the coattail of its parent, Telefónica's, pan-regional presence. With no ties with telecommunication companies, AOL Latin America and MSN rely on alliances or joint ventures with telecommunication operators to provide reliable Internet access. For instance, Starmedia has a joint venture with AT&T.

Terra launched its services by incorporating a Terra subsidiary in each country and acquiring local portals and ISPs. In addition, Terra pursued strategic alliances with media content providers and technological partners. Acquisitions of local portals and the strategic alliances have helped build pan-regional presence. Terra Networks Brazil, incorporated in June 1999, acquired the second-place portal zaz.com.br. Zaz, the second largest portal, had a weak financial position and faced strong competition from Brazil's largest portal, UOL. In October 1999, Terra bought Mexico's Infosel portal for $280 million. Infosel's large subscription base was being challenged by an influx of new ISPs in the Mexican market. The Infosel acquisition allowed Terra to increase its subscription base from 40,000 users to 220,000 users. Terra also gained access to Infosel's financial information service, Infosel-Financiero. Terra incorporated Terra Networks Argentina S.A. in July 1999. In September 1999, Terra acquired Argentina's search engine Donde for $4.5 million and Netgocios for $5.4 million. The Argentinean acquisitions allowed Terra to compete with Arnet, the portal subsidiary of Telecom Argentina. In September 1999, Terra Networks incorporated Telefónica Interactiva Chile S.A., and a month later the company acquired CTC Mundo for $40 million and changed its name to Terra Networks Chile. Terra's regional expansion continued in 2000 with its $4 million acquisition of Venezuela's main search engine and leading portal, Chevere, and acquired a 65% equity participation in Colombia' s La Ciudad for $20 million. In 2000, Terra gained access to the U.S. market through its acquisition of the U.S.-based portal Lycos.

The region's cultural diversity makes it imperative to localize content for each country. Local media portals are major investors in local portals and provide them with rich and deep local content. Several successful local ISPs, such as Mexico's Todito.com, have shunned the pan-regional approach to avoid the high costs associated with developing and customizing content to diverse national markets in Latin America.[43]

For companies such as Terra, content localization requires investment in media development, acquisitions, and/or strategic alliances with local media firms. Terra's pan-regional strategy uses all of these options. Terra acquisition of Mexico's Infosel secured exclusive rights to newspapers of the Reforma Group (former owners of Infosel). In Brazil, Terra secured exclusive rights to leading publishers Dinheiro and IstoÉ. In Venezuela, Terra formed strategic alliances with Caracas's newspaper *El Nacional* and the private television network Globovision. In Chile, Terra established a strategic alliance with Copesa, which gave Terra exclusive rights to newspapers *La Tercera*, *La Hora*, and *La Cuarta* as well as to *Qué Pasa*, Chile's popular magazine.

To overcome the hurdle of integrating diverse technologies used by its acquired portals, Terra uses Cisco Systems and Sun Microsystems technologies for efficient server and application management applications. For instance, Terra was able to integrate the Infosel local server into its system in nine months. Terra also formed alliances with other companies to offer new portal services to its customers. In collaboration with Lotus in the United States, Terra created a global instant messaging service in Brazil and Spain named IstanTerra. This service allows private chats between connected users anywhere in the world.

Despite the heterogeneity of consumers in this region, the examples above illustrate the use of different levels of aggregation and market platforms for a given business in Latin America. In the next section we illustrate the challenge of building a Latin American consumer market strategy for several businesses.

UNILEVER: BLENDING GLOBAL, REGIONAL, AND LOCAL STRATEGIES IN LATIN CONSUMER FOOD MARKETS

The Unilever group is a global company that markets a portfolio of more than 1,000 brands in the foods, home, and personal care categories, through some 300 subsidiaries in more than 130 countries. In 2000, the group generated $43.8 billion in revenues and $3 billion in profits.[44] Unilever's Latin American business accounts for the group's 11.8% of revenues and 10.6% of operating profits. The Latin American group generated $5.2 billion in revenues and $564 million in operating profits. In the same year, the revenues of its largest subsidiaries in Latin America were $2.6 billion in Brazil and $767 million in Argentina.[45] In the first three quarters of 2001 and despite the economic slowdown in the region, Unilever's Latin American group revenues increased by 39% over the previous year and profits by 89%. The region's share of total corporate results increased a notch, reaching 13% of revenues and 12% of profits. The group's operating margin of only 9.5% in Latin America was lower than margins of 13.8% in Europe or 11.7% in the United States, an indication of the pressure of increased price pressure on Unilever's consumer products competition as the Latin American economy deteriorates.

To examine Unilever's regional strategy in Latin America, we focus on the group's food business, representing about 50% of revenues and profits. Within the food business, we focus on three categories that are at different stages of market development in Latin America. Unilever's yellow fats (butter and margarine) business is a mature market. The ice cream business, once a dormant local market, has been energized by the entry of global companies. Finally, the iced-tea-beverage market is a new market in Latin America.[46]

STRATEGY IN MARGARINE AND YELLOW FATS

Latin American margarine and butter consumption patterns differ in terms of the level and types of use of these products. Average consumption of oils and fats ranges from low levels of 2 to 3 kilograms (kg) in Peru and Ecuador to 22 kg in Argentina and 17 kg in

Brazil.[47] In terms of mix of products, Argentinean consumers prefer butter to margarine as a spread. Despite the higher fat content of butter, this form is preferred by Argentinean consumers because of its natural ingredients. Except for Chile, which has a similar profile to Argentina, the rest of Latin America prefers margarine. A price ratio of 2:1 is an important factor in explaining a greater preference for margarine in poorer Latin American countries. Another difference among Latin American countries is the use and forms of these products. In Mexico and Central America, margarine is used mostly for cooking, not as a spread. In Andean countries, consumers buy margarine in sticks for cooking and in tubs for spreading. In the rest of the region, consumers buy only one form.

Unilever's yellow fats business has operated in Latin America for some time and has achieved market leadership in the region's estimated $1.5 billion market. Unilever holds a commanding 30% market share. Unilever has yellow fats production facilities in almost every Latin American country except Bolivia and the Guyanas. Unilever's strengths in yellow fats and the region's capacity for growth make a perfect combination.

Margarine, the main product line for the company, generates more profits for the company (on a global scale) than any other categories combined. In mature markets such as the United States and Europe, margarine consumption has declined an average of 3% per year. In contrast to these regions, the Latin American margarine market offers potential growth. The average annual per capita consumption of margarine in Latin America is 2 kg, whereas in the United States the average is 2.1 kg and in Europe is 6 kg. Currently, Brazil accounts for some 60% of Unilever's profits, Mexico and Colombia both contribute 10% each, and eight other countries account for the rest.[48]

Unilever has expanded its margarine businesses beyond Brazil and Argentina through acquisitions. Unilever acquired full control of Panama's Compaceites in 1995 and Paraguay's CAPSA in 1996. Unilever has taken a 50% equity position in Peru's Industrias Pacocha in 1996. In countries where its presence does not correlate with the country's potential, Unilever has acquired several local companies. In Mexico, for instance, Unilever has increased the capacity of its local operating company, Anderson Clayton, through acquisitions of Iberia, the leading yellow fats producer in Mexico, and Carrancedo. Unilever acquisitions in Mexico offer the potential to increase this country's contribution to regional revenues to the level of Mexico's share in the region's economy.[49]

In response to the differences in regional consumption, Unilever uses different brand names. Dorina is the brand name for Brazil,

Paraguay, and Argentina. Brazil is the sole supplier of margarine for Mercosur countries. Doriana is the brand used in Chile, Peru, and the Caribbean area. Unilever in Colombia markets margarine under the name Rama, and in Mexico under the Primavera brand name.

With income levels rising, the demand for other spreads, such as cream cheese, is increasing at a fast rate, especially in Argentina and Chile. Thus, the industry has been challenged to develop premium products. One trend in particular is the emergence of more health conscious consumers, who demand low-fat products, especially those of yellow fats. The industry has responded with a variety of new products, and major competitors have introduced a variety of cholesterol-free, fat-free, heart-healthy spreads. To maintain its market leadership in yellow fats and in margarine in particular, Unilever depends on its ability to innovate and develop better products. In recent years, Unilever has introduced local adaptations of product innovations made by subsidiaries outside the region. One new product is a successful combination of margarine and yogurt first introduced in the United States and later in the Southern Cone as Doriana Yoffresh.[50] Another effort includes the firm's decision to locate one of their four worldwide research centers for margarine product development in Brazil. This research center is designed to support the entire region and to develop products that meet the needs of Latin American consumers.

Unilever faces tough competition in Latin America in the yellow fats business. Most of Unilever's key competitors have either a subregional or strong national presence. One such competitor is Venezuela's Mavesa, which competes directly with Unilever in the margarine market. Mavesa targets primarily the Caribbean, Colombian, and northern Brazilian markets.[51] Unilever disputes the large Brazilian market with Santista-Ceval and Sadia. Unilever and Santista-Ceval are the market leaders, with a 35% market share each. Sadia holds about a 20% market share. Sadia has gained an edge in yellow fats based on its strength in commodity and poultry processing. Sadia's vertical integration provides this firm with a low-cost source of high-quality oil, the main ingredient in yellow fats. Sadia also has an impressive distribution network of more than 300,000 points of sale in Brazil that they serve through a fleet of refrigerated trucks. Argentina's Bunge & Born also presents a challenge to Unilever with its highly diversified agribusiness operations and geographical spread. Bunge & Born owns 50% of Brazil's large food conglomerate Santista-Ceval. Although Bunge & Born made a name for itself in grain and meat commodities, it also built up very efficient distribution networks. Currently, in an attempt to slim down and refocus on its key competencies, Bunge & Born is selling off many business units. In Chile, Unilever faces strong competition from the leading company, Watts, which holds 37% of the market to Unilever's 35%. In Venezuela, Mavesa has gained a foothold in the Colombian and northern Brazilian markets and is poised to do the same in Ecuador and Peru. The challenge in Mexico comes from U.S. market leaders that wish to penetrate the Mexican market through exports to this country.

As with the rest of the food industry in Latin America, the yellow fats segment has also undergone significant consolidation, although not enough to create a regional market. Unilever's domestic competitors also have been buying up small producers, either to integrate vertically or to expand horizontally. Thus far, Unilever has focused on competing in local markets. Other than the centralized R&D center for yellow fats in Brazil, their operating companies have focused on local markets only. The economics of margarine and butter production force the company to serve the market with local production only. Excess capacity in one country does not help with another country's excess demand potential.

STRATEGY IN THE ICE CREAM MARKET

Unilever's ice cream global brand portfolio includes national brands in key markets such as Breyers and Klondike in the United States, regional brands such as Watts in Asia, and global brands such as Cornetto and Magnum. Its acquisition of Ben & Jerry's has further increased Unilever's strong market power in the ice cream business. The ice cream and beverages category accounts for 31% of the corporate food business revenues and 23.5% of its profits.

Annual ice cream per capita consumption in Latin America pales with that of more developed countries. Ice cream consumption per capita in Latin America ranges from 0.3 kg in Mexico to 3.2 kg in Argentina. The annual per capita consumption of ice cream is 12.3 kg in the United States and 5.7 kg in Europe.[52] On a value basis, Latin America is a poor market base. Ice cream sales per capita in the United States and Europe reach $23.26 and $30.11. Unilever has certainly made sure that they have market presence and control of this promising regional opportunity. Since 1993, Unilever has spent more than $1.5 billion building up its ice cream business to establish ice cream operations in 12 Latin American countries.[53]

Unilever has used acquisitions to build its ice cream business in Latin America. The firm's expansion strategy began in Chile with acquisitions of Helados Panda and Helados Bresler. During the period

1994–1996, Unilever acquired ice cream businesses in Venezuela, Colombia, Ecuador, and Peru. In 1997, Unilever focused on the large Argentinean ice cream market, the second largest in the region after Brazil, with acquisition of Monthelado from Philip Morris. In 1997, Unilever acquired Brazil's ice cream market leader, Kibon, from Philip Morris. Brazil, with a low average per capita consumption of only 1 kg, offers a great potential for growth. Unilever entered Mexico in 1997 through a joint venture with two Mexican companies, Helados Holanda S.A. and Helados Bing S.A. By the end of 1998, Unilever had bought out its joint-venture partners and had become the leader in the Mexican ice cream market. With the acquisitions in Mexico, Unilever virtually shut down local competition. In a very short time, Unilever has become the ice cream market leader in Latin America. Its nearest rival is Nestlé.

Other areas where Unilever has a strong ice cream presence include Bolivia, Chile, Colombia, Costa Rica, Mexico, Peru, and Uruguay. The annual average per capita consumption of ice cream is highest in Chile, at around 5 liters. In Peru, a country to which Unilever exports some of its ice cream products from Chile, average per capita consumption is slightly less than 1 liter. Furthermore, local competition can be strong, especially since ice cream is no longer seen as something only for the summer months. Unilever faces Soprole in Chile, D'Onofrio in Peru, Oasis and Alpha in Uruguay, and Dos Pinos in Costa Rica.

Unilever's ice cream competition comes from global companies and few local champions. In Argentina, Unilever faces stiff competition from market leader Freddo. Freddo, which uses ice cream parlors, has expanded throughout the country and plans to enter the ice cream market in Chile and Brazil. Until 2001, Freddo was part of the Argentinean investment group Exxel, which financed its expansion.[54] Another global competitor is Häagen-Daz, owned by UK-based Diageo. Häagen-Daz entered the Argentina market in 1996 quickly and opened 15 ice cream shops around the country and expanded distribution of its products through video stores, supermarkets, and convenience stores. Häagen-Daz has been very successful in introducing local flavors. In fact, the company created a global market for the Argentinean flavor *dulce de leche,* caramelized milk. Within a year of its inception, *dulce de leche* had become Häagen-Daz's best-selling flavor.[55] Since its entry into Argentina, Häagen-Daz has expanded its product line to frozen desserts through its bakery chain subsidiary, Delicity. Another global competitor of Unilever is Parmalat. The Italian company entered Argentina in 1999 through the acquisition of Lactona and opened as many as 15 ice cream shops. A large Italian multinational, Parmalat's strengths lie in its strong ties to the dairy industry. Its dairy tradition is reflected in the quality of its ice cream, which is made daily in small batches, guaranteeing a fresh and creamy product. The Argentinean venture was Parmalat's second Latin American investment after entering Brazil in 1996. Parmalat has also expanded into Colombia and Venezuela.[56]

Charles Strauss, president of Unilever's Latin American Business Group, identified Latin America as a region with high growth potential for Unilever, and ice cream is a priority category.[57] Unilever's strategy entails buying local competitors with strong market shares. Unilever then builds upon the existing brand by bringing in Unilever's technological and innovative expertise. In conjunction with building on the existing product, Unilever introduces global premium brands to complement its ice cream portfolio.

STRATEGY IN EMERGING MARKETS: TEA

Unilever is a formidable participant in the production and marketing of tea. The firm commands approximately 20% market share of the world market for tea products and purchases 25% of the world's tea production. Its Lipton tea brand is indisputably the leading brand in many markets worldwide. Latin America is not a tea culture and accounts for very little of the world's tea sales. Tea consumption per capita ranges from 0.1 kg in Brazil to 0.4 kg in Argentina. High beverage consumption patterns and an increasing concern about health in the region may increase tea-based beverages in the future.

Unilever has marketed Lipton brand tea in Latin America for many years. It has only recently made an effort to test the market for cold iced-tea beverages. Unilever targeted Brazil as the market for new ventures for tea-based beverages. The firm initially franchised the Lipton brand to PepsiCo in Brazil to test the market for iced-tea beverages. As this arrangement proved unsuccessful, Unilever terminated the partnership and formed a joint venture with Brahma, now part of AmBev. The new company, named the Ice Tea Co., combined Unilever's Lipton tea reputation and Brahma's bottling capacity and distribution. Each partner holds 50% of the new venture. The arrangement with Brahma has proved successful. Lipton Iced Tea is the second brand in the Brazilian market, with a 35% market share.

In Brazil, Unilever faces the challenge of local and global competitors. The market leader is Leão, a local company, with a 40% market share. Leão's strength lies in its distribution networks.

Unilever also faces competition from Parmalat, which currently holds 20% of the Brazilian tea market. However, Parmalat's weakness is distribution. Parmalat has not developed an efficient distribution system, nor has the firm made alliances to move toward this goal. Another strong competitor in the iced-tea market is Nestlé with its Nestea brand.

The Latin American tea market is promising but unproven. Unilever is taking a cautious approach to market development and is making sure that they have the right formulation, packaging, and distribution strategy mix that will help develop the market potential for tea products in Latin America. By testing their products in Brazil, the company seeks to create a market strategy that can be used throughout Latin America. The joint venture with Brahma may help expand to other countries in the region where Brahma expands. Under Unilever's strategy of decentralizing innovation centers, the firm has designated Chile as the regional innovation center for this category. Also, Unilever can leverage its large global buying power of raw tea and tea syrups.

MANAGING DIFFERENT STRATEGIES

The Unilever case illustrates the challenge of building regional market platforms to respond to present and future opportunities in Latin American consumer markets. In mature markets such as yellow fats, idiosyncratic differences in Latin American markets require a differentiated and national approach. This strategy seems to be working for Unilever and has helped the firm become the market leader in this food category. Unilever has acquired local companies to increase capacity to serve the market. In countries with advanced levels of demographic transformation, such as Argentina and Chile, consumption patterns seemed to be changing faster. For this advanced market, Unilever has introduced product innovations (spreads) and specialty products such as low-calorie formulations.

In the growing market for ice cream in Latin America, Unilever uses acquisitions for quick entry and uses a combination of local brands for mass markets and global brands for niche upscale-market segments. In a short span, competition in the Latin American ice cream market has shifted from local to global. The future of this market is uncertain, however. Ice cream may be one of those categories that Latin American consumers may decide to eliminate, or it may become a small self-gratification item that would increase consumption. Each of these consumption trends leads to different product positioning and pricing strategies for ice cream.

In the case of tea, the challenge is to shape and develop a new product category in Latin America. Unilever's powerful Lipton's global brand image provides a unifying approach to the region. The joint venture with Brahma will leverage the assets and experience of Brahma in Brazil, but the expansion to other Latin American markets depends on Brahma's intent for the region. As we mentioned earlier in this chapter, AmBev's global market ambition for Brahma may limit the Latin American expansion.

Retail Metamorphosis in Latin Markets

Modernization, new retail technology, the entry of global players, and consolidation have played important roles in changing the face of Latin American retail. We explain below how these drivers are shaping the retail landscape.

Migration to Self-Service Retail

The increased penetration of self-service formats is the result of modernization and demographic transformation in Latin America.[58] The highest level of penetration of self-service retail formats is in Brazil, Argentina, and Chile. The drivers of retail transformation in these countries are consolidation, more intense use of information technology in retail processes, and expansion to second- and third-tier metropolitan markets. In other countries, such as Mexico, Colombia, and Peru, traditional shops remain the most important retail channel. Figure 5.6 shows the levels of penetration of various retail channels in major Latin American countries. With the exception of Brazil, the level of penetration of supermarkets corresponds to the patterns of demographic transformation shown in Figure 2.1. Argentina and Chile are countries with advanced levels of transformation, whereas Mexico and Colombia are countries undergoing full transformation. Brazil, an outlier in this case, may have experienced an earlier retail transformation because of early investments in this country by European retailers, which helped introduce the concepts of self-service and discount in Brazil in the 1970s.[59]

The market potential for self-service in Latin America depends on household buying power, percentage of household food expenditures, and size of the market. As discussed in Chapter 2 (see Table 2.4), the average percentage of household food expenditures in Latin

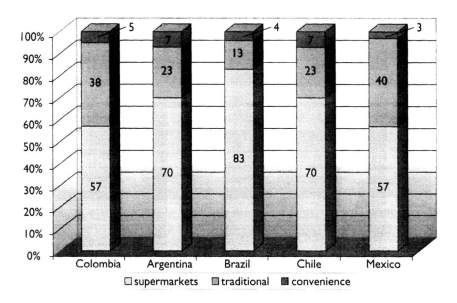

FIGURE 5.6
Retail Channel Penetration in Latin America

America is 35%; the highest percentages of food expenditures were in Peru, Argentina, Venezuela, and Chile. Food expenditures in the largest markets of Brazil and Mexico were below the region's average. In terms of household buying power, one indicator of market potential is consumer expenditures in self-service stores. Since food comprises the bulk of consumption expenditures, per capita expenditures in supermarkets is a good surrogate of self-service market potential. According to a survey of supermarket consumption patterns in 17 large metropolitan Latin American markets by AC Nielsen, the average Latin American household expenditure is $161 per month. Argentinean households have the highest expenditures per capita, with $232, followed by Chilean households, with $159. Household expenditures in the two largest consumer markets in Latin America, Brazil and Argentina, were lower than the average for the region, with $144 and $121, respectively. Based on these indicators, the market with the highest level of retail activity is Argentina.

MARKETING TO GOAL-ORIENTED LATIN AMERICAN SHOPPERS

Economic uncertainty drives consumers of all socioeconomic classes to patronize all types of retail formats in search of economic value. An AC Nielsen retail shopping study shows that 54% of regular users of supermarkets are middle class and young. The same study shows that the two most important factors determining shopping preferences are low prices and sales promotions.[60] Retail strategies need to address the important consumer goals emerging from new economic realities. We explain these goals below.

The first goal relates to consumer economic value. For retailers, offering competitive prices is central to their strategy, but this factor alone does not guarantee success. To avoid predatory price competition, large format retailers should focus on understanding the impact of economic uncertainty and volatility on two aspects of shopping behavior: efficiency and convenience. Latin American consumers are increasingly pressured for time. As explained in Chapter 2, demographic shifts, economic pressures, more working family members, and lifestyle changes have forced Latin American consumers to make fewer shopping trips, visit fewer stores, and plan shopping trips around sales promotions. Latin American consumers favor one-stop full-service shopping. Retailers are increasingly offering a range of services, from banking to telecommunications, under one roof. Convenience stores also meet consumers' need to save shopping time. Convenience stores complement weekly trips to a large-format store.

The second Latin American consumer goal relates to self-gratification and security needs. Latin American consumers derive a great deal of satisfaction from shopping. An intrinsic part of Latin American culture is close and frequent interaction with family and friends, and shopping is a means to achieve social interaction. A retail trip becomes a source of entertainment and socialization, a destination in itself. Most Latin American cities suffer from high crime, traffic congestion, and environmental pollution. Latin Americans find shopping a way to reduce the stress. In this context, a shopping experience that provides high levels of security, cleanliness, entertainment, and the opportunity for a social gathering becomes an escape from life's harsh reality.[61]

Supermarkets have also responded to the need for emotional shopping needs with a rich variety of prepared foods, eating corners, and special events such as book signings. Brazil's Pão de Açúcar is a leader in this respect. The retail chain assigns a dedicated food consultant to registered customers. The consultant reviews shopping needs, provides information on new items and changes in the store, and advises the customer on menus and special promotions. Pão de Açúcar's personalized service is driven by the firm's 1-million customer database, which stores individual shopping profiles. Key aspects of success in implementing such an information-driven strategy are the consultant's immediate access of customer information at any store location, the ability to tailor store promotions and service to individual customers, and customers' trust in sharing such information with Pão de Açúcar. The Brazilian firm's core retail competence is its ability to deliver fresh produce and information. The firm's large investment in technology is working to supply both.[62]

EFFECTIVE RETAIL STRATEGIES FOR THE FUTURE

Retail brand strategy is the core of effective retail strategies in Latin America. It is clear from our review of the transformation of the Latin American retail sector that the emphasis is shifting from efficiency and scale to customer relationship-building efforts. In the future, the retail value proposition should address the economic and emotional goals of retailers.

Two strategic options are a focus on a single retail brand or on multiple brands for multiple formats and segments. Format alone may not be a differentiating factor. In the past, Latin American retailers have favored using multiple formats and retail brands for different social classes. For instance, the largest supermarket in Chile, Distribucion y Servicio (D&S), operates four retail brands that combine two formats (supermarket and hypermarket) and two class segments (ABC1 and C2–C3). By contrast, Chilean Santa Isabel targets middle and lower socioeconomic classes under a single brand and multiple formats (supermarket, hypermarket, and convenience).

A single retail brand increases shopping efficiency. Consumers become familiar with store layouts and private brands, and take advantage of store promotions regardless of location or format. A single brand also builds on and improves the opportunity to build better customer relationships as retailers offer the same consistent shopping alternative under any format, location, and time. In the United States, Wal-Mart is experimenting with the concept of a neighborhood market, tentatively named Market Express.[63] In Latin America the newly merged Colombian supermarket Carulla-Vivero is also testing small supermarkets formats in the northern part of the country.[64]

We believe that a single brand retail strategy will work better in Latin America. Large-volume operators should aim at conquering all socioeconomic segments with all types of formats and location with the best value-to-price proposition and integrating all sorts of services under one shopping solution. Small retail specialists should also succeed with a single brand strategy by focusing on a single market niche. Upscale specialists might target affluent consumers, such as those of Banco Itaú's Personalité; low-income market specialists such as Mexico's Elektra, which offers low-price electronics and consumer credit services for low-income consumers, are also more likely to be successful.

Another strategic aspect of future retail strategies in Latin America is the centralization of core competencies, and sharing them with all parties: suppliers, customers, alliance partners, or employees. These retail core competencies include customer response systems, consumer credit, and merchandising. Sharing these competencies will enhance the retail customer experience, as illustrated by Brazil's Pão de Açúcar.

Pan-regional expansion strategies will depend on the ability of a firm to replicate in various countries the core competencies discussed above. More effective replication will be possible among countries that offer similar levels of retail infrastructure and government regulations. In this context, retail strategies based on the use of information systems will travel well in such countries as Chile, Argentina, Uruguay, and Brazil, which have greater levels of connectivity in the region. Chile's Falabella has used this approach to expand within this subregion, with the exception of Brazil. Retail regulations, on the other hand, may affect the exportability of the retail format regionally and even within a particular country. Regulations affecting location and hours of operation tend to be enforced by local rather than central governments. Thus, regulations may affect the depth of expansion from first-tier to second-tier city markets for certain formats, such as hypermarkets and large-store formats.

Another dimension of future retail strategy is the effort of consumer package firms to establish direct contact with consumers. Transformation of the Latin American retail industry has shifted customer influence to retailers. Consumer goods manufacturers are trying to gain back some of that influence by experimenting with alternative ways to reach consumers directly. Nestlé is considering this approach for particular food categories where its brands may have enough power to attract consumers. The company has opened small stores under the brand Frigor in Argentina that feature exclusively Nestlé's ice creams and Nescafé coffee. The small store formats can be replicated in many ways, inside hypermarkets or high pedestrian traffic locations. A similar approach is used by CCU, the Argentinean brewery, which has opened beer bars that offer special beers.[65]

INTEGRATORS AND SPECIALISTS IN CONSUMER MARKETS

The periodic crises in Latin American markets may have slowed the expansion of global retail chains, but they have not stopped their transformation. Whether it is consolidation or retail innovation, Latin

American industry continues to reinvent itself. Global and national competitors are working hard to fine-tune their strategic plans to address the goals of consumers in volatile times. Out of this process, a few integrators and specialists will emerge as dominant actors. In this final section, we examine the strategies of the largest firms in Latin American consumer markets, including retailers.

Table 5.2 shows the strategies of firms in consumer markets with annual revenues greater than $1 billion in 2000, and Table 5.3 provides a summary of key indicators of performance by sector, strategy, and country.[66] Financial returns for all firms were low for all consumer market sectors reported in Table 5.3. Firms in the consumer beverage markets had strong growth in 2000. Beverage firms had stronger revenue growth than firms in other consumer categories due to greater margins and strong market growth. Firms in other consumer sectors, such as automobiles, consumer electronics, and consumer food, had low revenue growth in 2000. Beverage firms were able to show better returns.

Firms based in Mexico performed much better than did firms based in other countries. Fueled by a stronger U.S. market in 2000, Mexican firms showed greater average annual revenues, revenue growth, and net profits than did any other Latin American firm in this group. Firms based in Brazil were second to Mexican firms. Firms based in Argentina, Chile, Colombia, and Venezuela clearly suffered the impact of economic recession and price deflation in their countries. As Table 5.3 shows, these firms had declining revenue growth and meager profits. Interestingly, greater returns on net worth among firms in these countries may indicate greater emphasis on leveraging financial resources to confront economic crises.

Broad regional integrators such as Carrefour developed strategies to reach mass markets throughout the region. Other companies using a broad regional integration approach include large diversified multinationals such as Nestlé, Unilever, P&G, and Sony. Examples of narrow integrators include automobile manufacturers and consumer electronic firms. Narrow integrators tend to rationalize production in either Brazil or Mexico or in both.

Specialists concentrate on a narrow consumer category. Some specialists, such as Mexico's FEMSA, have broad geographic presence and a presence in several Latin American countries. Other specialists, such as Brazil's AmBev, operate in several Latin American markets but have global ambitions for their brands.[67] An essential element of their strategy is to form alliances with global leaders such as Coca-Cola and PepsiCo. Another category specialist with broad presence is Mexico's Bimbo, which focuses on industrial bread and

TABLE 5.2 Top Consumer Goods Firms in Latin America by Type of Strategy, 2000

COMPANY	SECTOR	COUNTRY	STRATEGY[a]	TOTAL ASSETS ($ MILLIONS)	EMPLOYMENT
Wal-Mart Mexico	Retail	Mexico	BRI	5,192	7,479
Carrefour Brazil	Retail	Brazil	BRI		44,571
Gessy Lever	Consumer products	Brazil	BRI	1,097	12,369
Nestlé Brazil	Food	Brazil	BRI		8,602
Sony Mexico	Consumer electronics	Mexico	BRI		11,646
Sam's Club	Retail	Mexico	BRI		8,810
Nestlé Mexico	Food	Mexico	BRI	1,161	6,990
Nestlé Brazil	Food	Brazil	BRI	507	12,369
Phillips Mexico	Consumer electronics	Mexico	BRI		12,743
Carrefour Argentina	Retail	Argentina	BRI		
P&G Mexico	Consumer products	Mexico	BRI		6,390
Bompreco	Retail	Brazil	BRI	981	14,265
Wal-Mart Supercenters	Retail	Mexico	BRI		11,435
Makro	Retail	Brazil	BRI		2,466
FEMSA	Beverages	Mexico	BRS	4,719	42,594
Bimbo	Food	Mexico	BRS	2,569	61,822
Modelo	Beverages	Mexico	BRS	4,732	45,582
Sabritas	Food	Mexico	BRS	1,614	17,000
AmBev	Beverages	Brazil	BRS	4,418	17,000
Coke–Femsa	Beverages	Mexico	BRS	1,334	15,273
Panamco	Beverages	Mexico	BRS	3,026	
Sanborns	Retail	Mexico	NC	4,014	50,125
Pão de Açúcar	Retail	Brazil	NC		50,000
Comercial Mexicana	Retail	Mexico	NC	2,115	35,322
Savia	Food	Mexico	NC	6,598	15,947
Gigante	Retail	Mexico	NC	1,829	34,046
Soriana	Retail	Mexico	NC	1,814	30,184
Norte	Retail	Argentina	NC	1,961	
FEMSA Montezuma	Beverages	Mexico	NC	2,245	17,398
CBD Extra	Retail	Brazil	NC		
Casas Bahia	Retail	Brazil	NC		13,296
Casa Saba	Retail	Mexico	NC	627	
Liverpool	Retail	Mexico	NC	1,712	18,006
Coto	Retail	Argentina	NC	622	16,616
Sadia	Food	Brazil	NC	1,677	28,845

Market Capitalization ($ millions at 12/31/2000)	Net Worth ($ millions)	Revenues ($ millions)	Revenue Change (%)	Net Profits ($ millions)	Net Profits/ Revenues (%)	Net Profit/ Net Worth (%)
10,112	3,212	7,725	21	373	4.8	11.6
		4,868	12			
		2,634	−8.9			
	378	2,575	−2.8	107	4.1	23.2
		2,393	9.2			
		2,240	33.7			
	564	2,135	16.7			
	316	1,685	0.2	50.6	3	16
		1,670	12.5			
		1,538	−6.3	−3.4	−0.2	
		1,515	28.5			
	272	1,337	4.9	1.8	0.1	0.7
		1,236	18.7			
	234	1,101	−1.8	33	2.9	131
3,432	1,828	4,748	19	265	5.6	14.5
1,999	1,606	3,288	11.2	191	5.8	11.9
7,933	2,764	3,064	18.6	341	11.1	12.3
		2,807	10.7			
9,385	1,573	2,685	93.4	240	9	15.3
3,432		1,733	18.5	135	7.7	
	1,195	2,416	7.6	−505	−19.4	−42.2
1,348	926	5,707	338	113	2	12.2
3,944	1,600	4,346	8.7	135	3	7.9
1,013	1,010	3,302	15.7	115	3.5	11.4
2,099	1,312	3,220	22.3	−319	−9.9	−24.3
1,792	1,132	2,842	17.7	106	3.7	9.4
1,457	1,047	2,649	22	156	5.9	14.9
	584	2,037	−5			
	1,736	1,962	6.7	185	9.4	10.7
		1,910	24.1			
	1,025	1,746	9.7	−36	−2.1	−3.5
		1,627	17.8	41.6	2.5	
2,266	934	1,639	28.1	123	7.5	13.2
	176	1,486	12	35.1	2.4	19.9
	485	1,473	−5.1	57.7	3.9	11.9

(continued)

TABLE 5.2 Top Consumer Goods Firms in Latin America by Type of Strategy, 2000 (Continued)

COMPANY	SECTOR	COUNTRY	STRATEGY[a]	TOTAL ASSETS ($ MILLIONS)	EMPLOYMENT
Ponto Frio	Retail	Brazil	NC		7,154
D&S	Retail	Chile	NC	1,018	12,442
Sendas	Retail	Brazil	NC		14,382
Exito	Retail	Colombia	NC	843	
GM Mexico	Automobile	Mexico	NRI	4,145	14,968
Daimler-Chrysler	Automobile	Mexico	NRI	3,688	12,500
VW Mexico	Automobile	Mexico	NRI	3,191	16,456
Ford Mexico	Automobile	Mexico	NRI	1,519	9,442
GE Mexico	Consumer electronics	Mexico	NRI	1,096	32,000
Disco	Retail	Mexico	NRI	1,601	17,600
Gruma	Food	Mexico	NRI	2,294	16,150
Bunge Alimentos	Food	Brazil	NRI	1,724	12,340
Polar	Beverages	Venezuela	NRI		14,832
Kimberly-Clark Mexico	Consumer products	Mexico	NRI	2,170	7,669
Ford Brazil	Automobile	Brazil	NRI	1,502	6,975
Sonae	Retail	Brazil	NRI		
Elektra	Retail	Mexico	NRI	1,514	19,442
MABE	Consumer electronics	Mexico	NRI	1,665	18,000
Falabella	Retail	Chile	NRI		13,000
Ford Argentina	Automobile	Argentina	NRI		330

has established a broad regional presence through joint ventures and acquisitions. A few regional specialists operate in narrow subregional market corridors. Examples of the few include Chile's department store specialist Falabella, Mexico's tortilla maker Gruma, and Venezuela's beer giant Polar.

National champions are category leaders in their countries. Argentina's food retailer Coto and Brazil's Pão de Açúcar are examples of firms in this group. Most national specialists in this group have broad business scope. In terms of returns, the broad regional specialists clearly outperformed companies using other strategies. The good performance of regional specialists can be attributed to strong revenue growth and greater revenue margins, which result in greater average profits for the group. Despite their large fixed asset and

Market Capitalization ($ millions at 12/31/2000)	Net Worth ($ millions)	Revenues ($ millions)	Revenue Change (%)	Net Profits ($ millions)	Net Profits/ Revenues (%)	Net Profit/ Net Worth (%)
887	271	1,435	16.6	10.2	0.7	3.6
1,557	437	1,398	−8.9	50	3.6	11.4
	146	1,325	−5.3	10.6	0.8	6.9
		1,278	−2.8	40.4	3.2	8.1
	631.5	9,648	30			
		9,084	24			
	1,519	7,631	10.6			
	460.8	5,964	47.6	31.8	0.5	6.9
	929	2,629	6.3			
	407	1,987	13.6	9.9	0.5	2.4
	988	1,901	18.7	27.4	1.4	2.8
	398	1,839	13.5	−27.1	−1.5	−6.8
		1,719	4.2			
3,434	1,186	1,661	14	317	19.1	26.7
	−10.3	1,649	−5.7	−165	−10	
20,396		1,561	−1.4			
1,068	571	1,538	27.6	117	7.6	20.6
	421	1,391	16.8	40	2.9	9.5
1,758	680	1,109	4.2	86	4.9	12.6
		1,080	−14.4			

Source: Compiled by the authors from América Economía, 500 Largest Latin American Firms; Financial Times, 100 Largest Firms in Latin America.
[a]BRI, broad regional integrator; BRS, broad regional specialist; NRI, narrow regional integrator; NRS, narrow regional specialist; NC, national champion.

employment base, these companies had an impressive 22.6% return on net worth.

Broad regional integrators have large average profits but sluggish revenues, and margins were less than the average for all firms in 2000. National champions had the largest revenue increase but failed to turn strong profits and returns. Narrow regional specialists manage to have average growth and return performance. Narrow regional integrators also had disappointing results. As expected, size helps companies achieve a greater customer base but not necessarily a greater profit margin. Narrow regional specialists have a small revenue base but generate greater margins than do integrators and na-

TABLE 5.3 Performance of Top Latin American Firms in Consumer Markets by Industry, Strategy, and Country[a]

SPLIT BY:	TYPE	TOTAL ASSETS ($ MILLIONS)	EMPLOYMENT	MARKET CAPITALIZATION ($ MILLIONS)	NET WORTH ($ MILLIONS)	REVENUES ($ MILLIONS)	REVENUE CHANGE, 2000/1999 (%)	NET PROFIT ($ MILLIONS)	NET PROFIT/REVENUE (%)	NET PROFIT/NET WORTH (%)
Sector	Automobile	4,145	10,111		631.5	5,842	15.3	n.a	n.a	n.a
	Beverages	3,412	25,446	6,045	1,819	2,618	24.1	110	3.9	2.1
	Consumer electronics	1,380	18,597	n.a.	675	2,020	11.2	n.a.	n.a.	n.a.
	Food	2,268	20,007	2,049	755	2,324	9.5	12.5	0.9	4.9
	Consumer products	1,633	8,809	n.a.	n.a.	1,936	11.2	n.a.	n.a.	n.a.
	Retail	3,653	21,001	5,562	814	2,344	23.6	75.8	2.8	10.5
Strategy	Broad regional integrator (BRI)	1,787	12,318	10,112	829	2,475	9.8	93.6	2.45	12.8
	Broad regional specialist (BRS)	3,201	42,594	3,432	1,511	2,963	25.5	120	3.3	-13.8
	Narrow regional integrator (NRI)	2,175	14,113	6,664	681.7	3,274	13.1	48.5	2.8	9.3
	National champion (NC)	2,082	24,554	1,818	854	2,299	28.4	51.4	2.5	7.6
Country	Brazil	1,700	17,473	8,653	557	2,135	9.5	34.8	1.1	7.5
	Mexico	2,663	21,264	12,490	1,236	3,378	29.6	97.5	3.7	7.18
	Argentina	1,961	11,515	n.a.	299	1,625	-0.02	13.8	0.9	11.1
	Chile	n.a.	12,721	1,657	558	1,253	-2.5	68	4.2	12
	Colombia	843	n.a	n.a.	n.a.	1,278	-2.8	40.4	3.2	8.1
	Venezuela	n.a.	14,832	n.a.	n.a.	1,719	4.2	n.a.	n.a.	n.a.
Average	All firms	2,284	19,087	3,723	919	2,712	18.8	67.2	2.7	11.5

[a] n.a., not available or not enough firms to calculate average.

tional champions. Broad regional specialists leverage this strategy with size. By operating at a larger scale, broad regional specialists produce higher margins and returns on net worth. Large scale alone is not a strategy for broad integrators. Large scale, however, protects these firms as the market consolidates. Firms that lack either scale or specialization are the most vulnerable.

6

FUNDING THE LATIN MARKET GROWTH

No sector has been so affected by the sweeping economic, legal, and regulatory reforms of the 1990s as financial services. At the same time, no sector has affected as extensively the economic liberalization process that has been the hallmark of Latin American development from the late 1980s through the present. In this chapter we highlight trends in the financial services sector, discuss the key drivers of change both globally and regionally, illustrate how three of those drivers—mergers and acquisitions, technology, and customer demand—are revolutionizing this sector, and review the organizational and strategic responses by financial firms to the increasingly competitive environment.

TRENDS IN THE FINANCIAL SERVICES SECTOR

During the last decade, all of the big emerging markets of Latin America introduced amendments to their banking legislation, and in 90% of the cases the changes have been substantial.[1] These reforms were a response to crises or significant problems in the banking systems or were influenced by them. The relationship between the crises and the reform processes has been well documented.[2] The most important changes in the financial services sector include macroeconomic liberalization, the expansion of technology, development of new products and services, decline in state ownership, and the modernization of financial regulations.

THE BANKING ENVIRONMENT IN THE REGION'S BIG EMERGING MARKETS

Given these distinguishing trends in the modernization of financial regulations, it is important to note the specific characteristics and condition of the banking environment in Latin America's big emerging markets of Argentina, Brazil, and Mexico.[3]

Argentina. The nation's economic crisis that began in 1997 and resulted in collapse in 2002 has significantly affected all of Argentina's 93 banks and 24 nonbank institutions, strong as well as weak. A lack of loan activity, withdrawls by depositors, and most important, problem loans have dealt a major blow to the banking sector. Despite higher profit margins and the increased yield of government securities due to higher sovereign risk, bank profitability has suffered. Problem loans have grown, despite improved risk evaluation and recovery activities of the major banks.

Banks' exposure to Argentine government and overall public-sector debt poses a significant risk that was reflected in the May 2001 downgrade by Moody's Investors Service of five leading banks: Banco Río de la Plata, BBVA Banco Francés, Banco Galicia, HSBC Bank Argentina, and Banco Provincia. This move reflected the rating agency's concern that a change in public-sector debt maturity might harm their stand-alone strength. The downgrades do not reflect institution-specific credit deterioration but rather, changing government policies (and the prospect of changes in—and now abandonment of—the currency board arrangement) that have increased generic risks systemwide. In fact, the five banks cited above are the

Argentine banks that have the highest financial strength ratings in the system. The downgrades do not reflect institution-specific credit deterioration but the higher generic risks in the banking system associated with changing government policies. For example, rating agencies are concerned that recent modifications of the banking law, particularly the lowering of reserve requirements and their redefinition to include government bonds, could diminish the system's liquidity cushion.

Most major local banks are owned by foreign institutions that maintain important networks in many other countries of the region. Sovereign default has had a negative effect on the perceived franchise value in the entire region. Banco Santander Central Hispano, Banco Bilbao Vizcaya Argentaria, HSBC Holdings, and Bank of Nova Scotia are some of the major banks that have been forced to manifest their level of support for their subsidiaries following sovereign default. Since weak support could damage their image, many will feel encouraged to demonstrate their serious commitment to their local banks.

Within this turbulent milieu, Argentine banks, like banks elsewhere in Latin America, have witnessed ongoing market concentration and consolidation, increasing foreign participation, and broadening distribution channels. Once economic recovery sets in, one may expect further privatizations of provincial banks and financial institutions and an upswing in institutional lending and consumer borrowing, but this may be several years away.

Brazil. The Argentine economic collapse crisis, energy shortages, and home-grown political problems have curtailed the rapid growth and expansion of banking in Brazil. Most private banks are well capitalized and well provisioned, however, to insulate themselves from an economic downturn. High interest rates and high yields on government securities continue to dampen lending activities. Instead of intermediating credit to the private sector, banks mainly engage in short-term treasury operations. Also, public debt servicing needs have crowded out private borrowers. Additional impediments include the lack of secured lending and lack of effective bankruptcy procedures, the high reserve requirements on demand deposits (raising banking spreads even higher), and the distorting factor of compulsory credit to agriculture and housing.[4]

Brazil's financial system is largely bank-dominated. While assets of the banking system, at about $500 billion, or 95% of gross domestic product (GDP), are high, credit to the private sector accounts for only 35% of GDP, or only 33% of banking system assets. A large part—about one-half—of bank credit to the private sector is provided by state-owned institutions. The share of the foreign capital in the total of assets of the Brazilian financial system has now increased to 27.8%. In December 1995, by comparison, this share was of 8.96%. Foreign banks are now owners of approximately $120 billion of the total amount of $415 billion in assets. Brazil's banking system is highly concentrated and still dominated by public (mainly federal) banks, although foreign bank presence has risen significantly in recent years. On average, Brazilian private banks appear profitable, liquid, and well provisioned and capitalized. Risks to systemic stability in the Brazilian banking sector are considered low. In addition, the unsound major private banks were already removed in the context of the 1995–1996 wave of bank failures.

The Brazilian financial market has been experiencing great changes since 1994, with the increase in privatizations of state financial institutions and mergers and acquisition of private agencies. Government-owned Banco do Brasil is still the largest Brazilian bank, with 17.6% of all the assets, followed by the Caixa Econômica Federal, another federal institution, with 15%. After Bradesco, the largest private bank, Banco Itaú holds second place. Itaú won the auction for the Banestado (Bank of the State of Paraná), paying approximately $800 million, a premium of 303% over the minimum price, in the auction held in October 2000. A month later, Banespa (Bank of the State of São Paulo) was purchased by BSCH for $3.6 billion, a premium of 281% over the minimum price established by the federal government. With the acquisition of Banespa, Santander is now the third-largest private bank in Brazil.[5]

Bradesco, Banco Itaú, and Unibanco are especially well capitalized. While an individual or group/family of shareholders can halt or at least derail a hostile takeover, due to share concentration and weak corporate governance laws in Brazil, smaller and medium-sized Brazilian banks will be among the most vulnerable as acquisition and consolidation activity continues. These banks tend to be highly inefficient, with productivity levels 60% less than that of American banks and 73% less than that at some European banks.[6] Unless these banks take measures to boost profits other than through raising charges to their customers, they will not be able to survive.[7] Large players such as BSCH, BBVA, and Citigroup will need acquisitions if they want to expand into retail activities. This consolidation (shrinking) of the number of banks should not pose a problem, as it does not in Germany, where the three biggest banks maintain 90% of the capital, as long as there are sufficient and geographically dispersed branches and an extensive and varied menu of banking products and services.[8]

As for the capital markets, stock market capitalization amounts to some $230 billion or about 40% of GDP, while debt securities on issue amount to around $270 billion or 50% of GDP. Outside the banking system, the largest holders of financial assets in Brazil are pension funds, either directly or through their mutual funds. Total assets of pension and mutual funds are estimated at about $120 billion (22% of GDP).

Although the outstanding volume of securities on issue in Brazil is large, the role of securities markets in mobilizing nonbank finance for private businesses is limited. The bulk of debt securities outstanding (over 80%) is comprised of government bonds. Nevertheless, the potential for further development of securities markets in Brazil appears substantial, especially in view of the huge size and rapid pace of growth of institutional investor funds. Total assets of institutional investors are estimated at about $120 billion or 22% of GDP, the highest among Latin countries excepting Chile. Development of securities markets is constrained by a number of factors: corporate governance, transactions costs (the imposition of a financial transactions tax), and scattered regulatory responsibilities.[9]

Mexico.   The implementation of NAFTA and the 1994–1995 financial crisis radically altered the Mexican banking sector. Under NAFTA, foreign financial affiliates (basically wholly owned U.S. and Canadian subsidiaries) are permitted to engage in a full range of banking activities. NAFTA-based banks may acquire Mexican-controlled financial institutions regardless of individual and aggregate market share limits.[10] As a result of the 1994–1995 financial crisis, Mexican banks were swamped with a dramatic increase in their overdue loans and a serious capital drain. The Mexican government came to the aid of the banks through a number of capitalization and debt-relief programs.[11] Subsequent financial reform legislation liberalized foreign ownership and capital limit requirements for banks.

Mexico has made significant progress in strengthening its banking sector, which practically collapsed with the 1994–1995 peso crisis. In 1998, Congress passed a law creating the Institute for the Protection of Bank Savings (IPAB), an organism created to take over the assets and liabilities formerly held by the now-defunct FOBAPROA and to act as a deposit insurance fund. By June 1999, IPAB had assumed control of $65 billion worth of liabilities and has since begun selling off FOBAPROA's former assets. The government also eliminated restrictions on foreign ownership of the largest banks, a move that has borne fruit, as foreign banks are moving to acquire controlling interest and to inject needed capital in some of Mexico's largest banks.[12]

The Mexican banking system is on the verge of a new stage of consolidation. Banks' performance results show that Mexican banks have finalized their process of recovery.[13] In 1999, nonperforming loans fell 36% in real terms, largely as a result of a debtor-relief program known as Punto Final and a reduction in interest rates. Loan-loss reserves in the banking system averaged 95.6% of past-due loans by the beginning of 2000. Mexican banks have consistently improved their capitalization index and earnings since 1995.

Although the Mexican government argues that economic growth in Mexico has not been constrained by a lack of credit (although in 2001 bank credit contracted 6.6%), all but the largest corporate borrowers complain vehemently about credit availability under *reasonable terms and conditions*. Recognizably, however, the scarcity of domestic credit was replaced by other credit sources, such as domestic and foreign companies' suppliers, savings associations, commercial credit from chain stores, debt issued in the domestic and international markets, and financing from foreign banks as well as from reinvested earnings.

Despite banks' reentry into the consumer sector, lending is weighted more toward the commercial and government sector, and this will continue. Nevertheless, credit card lending has posted the largest growth during the past two years, albeit from a small base. Internally, Mexican banks are strengthening their credit risk management and witnessing marked improvements in their asset quality ratios.[14]

Merger and acquisition activity has also been a key feature of the Mexican banking panorama. Several Mexican banks have merged over the last two years, and the trend is expected to continue. Spain's largest bank, Banco Santander Central Hispano (BSCH) purchased Mexican Grupo Financiero Serfin in April 2000 for $1.6 billion. Rival BBVA has been one of the most aggressive investors in Mexico, acquiring Bancomer in June 2000 for $2.5 billion. Canada's Bank of Nova Scotia (Scotiabank) increased its holdings in Inverlat in November 2000 from 10% to 55%, paying $145 million for the increased shares.[15] In 2001 Banorte, Mexico's fifth largest bank, bought state-owned BanCrecer for $175 million.

In the biggest deal of all, in May 2001, Citigroup, North America's biggest financial services company, acquired Banamex–Accival, the second-largest Mexican bank, known as Banacci, for $12.5 billion in cash and stock. The biggest Latin American acquisition by a U.S. company, the purchase marked the first takeover of a large

Mexican bank by a U.S. financial institution. Citigroup officials said they saw tremendous lending potential in Mexico and hoped to use the company's Banamex brand name to serve the fast-growing Hispanic population in the United States as well.

With the quality of operating income up considerably and core bank earnings strong, the future profitability of Mexican banks looks bright. However, a marked increase in interest rates would affect negatively both net interest margins and the valuation of securities portfolios, as would sluggish growth of the U.S. economy.

STRATEGIC RESPONSES OF FINANCIAL INSTITUTIONS

As banking and investment institutions position themselves to achieve success in Latin America's competitive business environment, they must contend with the endemic challenges of economic and political volatility, instability, and uncertainty. These include fluctuating commodity prices, debt-servicing problems, a lack of domestic savings, growing income inequality, and weak and inefficient legal and administrative institutions. On the other hand, this environment is also characterized by the best demographics in the world, an expanding consumer base, increasing acceptance of market capitalism and its accompanying institutions, prudent monetary policies, privatization, and the continued liberalization of trade, investment, and finance. Within this milieu, the key drivers of financial institution strategies have been and will continue to be (1) the need for consolidation, (2) the expansion of technology, and (3) greater emphasis on customer service, both retail and corporate.

EXPANSION OF INFORMATION TECHNOLOGY AND THE INTERNET

The growth and expansion of information technology and the Internet as drivers of financial products, operations, and services are having a major impact on the financial industry. Among the technological resources that are proliferating are financial cryptography hardware, biometrics security, interactive voice response systems, gateway and interface software, call center system hardware, ATM-related software, smart cards, credit scoring systems, and reconciliation systems. Unquestionably, technology's most sweeping impact has been in the area of online banking, both corporate and personal. While consumer demand may be driving part of this movement, it is the banks' competitive interests that are the real forces for change. These include lower transaction costs (although this is mitigated by the need for both online and off-line infrastructures), defensive positioning (vis-à-vis other banks seeking prime clients), market share, and business opportunities [e.g., handling security and payment in business-to-consumer (B2C) operations].[16]

In most of Latin America, the postal system is neither secure nor dependable, and consumers lose hours of time waiting in line to pay utility, credit card, and other bills at banks or the branches of utility companies. Online banking has great potential in Latin America, even though the vast majority of people do not own personal computers (PCs). Decentralized locales such as kiosks, as well as PCs installed in banks, can serve their needs. Since banks spend heavily to staff numerous neighborhood branches, customers are not the only ones to gain from online banking; the banks will be able to save considerably on transaction costs. The cost of delivering bank service through the Internet is approximately 10 cents per transaction versus 60 cents at an ATM and $1.53 with a teller.[17]

Brazil is clearly the leader in online banking in Latin America, a model for other countries both within and outside the region. Brazil's unstable economic environment from the late 1970s to 1994 actually contributed to the use of technology by the banking system. Since unstable money created an opening for huge gains through overnight interbank trading in Brazil's currency, efficient electronic clearance systems were established quickly, creating a strong technological base that later eased the path to online banking.[18] Today, the use of the Internet for consumer banking in Brazil is much more common than it is in Asia and even approaches the level achieved in the United States (see Table 6.1).[19] Nevertheless, to maintain their level of success, Brazilian banks will have to satisfy the demands of "increasingly sophisticated and decreasingly loyal" customers.[20] Internet banking in Brazil approximates telephone and traditional banking penetration levels.

Large Brazilian financial institutions are the leaders in online banking: Bradesco, Unibanco, Banco Itaú, and Banco do Brasil. To illustrate, Banco do Brasil, Banco Bradesco, and Banco Itaú each has over 2 million Internet clients, between 14 and 17% of their total customer base. Bradesco inaugurated Brazil's first free Internet service provider (ISP) service with an incentive to use online banking. It has expanded its customer base by 65% over the past two years while increasing the number of branches by only 4%. A number of

TABLE 6.1 Banks Offering Internet Banking Services in Brazil, 2001

Banco 1	Banco Real (ABN AMRO Bank)
Banco Bandeirantes	Banestado
Banco Boavista	Bannisul
Banco de Boston	Banco Safra
Banco Bradesco	Banco Santander Brasil
Banco do Brasil	Banco Sudameris
Banco de Crédito Nacional (BCN)	Caixa Econômica Federal
Banco do Estado do Ceará	Citibank
Banco do Estado de Santa Catarina	HSBC Bamerindus
Banco Indusval	Nossa Caixa Nosso Banco
Banco Itaú	Unibanco

Source: eMarketer, *2001.*

Brazilian banks plan to offer consumers reasonable PC financing and free Internet access to increase use of the online channel.[21] (Outside Brazil, Banco Río de la Plata introduced online banking in Argentina in 1999; in Chile, Banco de Crédito, and in Mexico, BBVA–Bancomer, have aggressively rolled out online services.)

Medium- and high-income Brazilian customers are eager to embrace automated and remote banking channels. A young (under 40), wealthy, tech-savvy, mobile professional class is on the rise, regardless of the perennial ups and downs of Latin American economies, and to the fear and consternation, as well as hope and joy, of banks, they can (and do) switch banks with the click of a mouse. These consumers are drawn to online banking in search of convenience, security, choice, and a wide array of services. According to the Info-Americas market research organization, there are more than 10 million customers in Latin America in the 20–39 age group who consume an average of $50,000 per year of their own money or that of their parents. They are heavy spenders and frequent travelers— the first generation of the neoliberal Latin American experiment— and are courted by every major consumer product and service company in the region.[22]

Results of a McKinsey survey on Internet banking in Brazil provide some sobering insights. First, there is a concern among 80% of the respondents about Internet security: they have a real worry about sending financial information over the Internet. Additionally, government regulations, such as requiring people to open financial accounts in person or to use an independent broker for insurance deals, could limit the expansion of online banking; nevertheless, it has achieved a 41% penetration rate among the survey's respondents. Finally, customers of Brazilian banks seem to be less loyal than in the past. Although most respondents expressed satisfaction with their current financial institutions, almost 30% said they would move to another institution for a small advantage in interest rates or service fees.[23] Promising though online banking may be, bank branches will remain customers' first choice: 80% of transaction volumes and 70% of all channel spending are done via branches.

For those banks that have been reticent to embrace the Internet and are just now coming to realize the need to go high-tech, alliances provide a feasible avenue. For example, UnoFirst struck up an alliance with BBVA and Terra Networks with First-e, an Irish Internet bank. BSCH, Banco Itaú, and Argentina's Banco Galicia have been particularly active. Itaú plans to use its investment in AOL Latin America to sell financial services online in other Latin American countries. BSCH, already a powerhouse in the region, is inclined to take a more integrated approach, as exemplified by its $540 million purchase of 75% of Patagon.com, an Argentine online securities sales service. Banco Galicia, with subsidiaries in Uruguay and Paraguay, is beefing up its presence in Mercosur via a $60 million business-to-business (B2B) joint venture with Brazil's Unibanco and Portugal Telecom. To reach greater numbers of home users, banks are also turning to alliances with mobile operators and Internet portals. Prepay mobile phone users are huge in number; in fact, they may be among the 70% of Latin Americans that do not yet have bank accounts. Bradesco teamed with Telefónica Celular and Telesp Celular to develop a product even before network capability was in place.[24]

Be that as it may, the Internet also poses competitive challenges to banks' very operations. First, it lowers barriers to entry (since technology is widely diffused) and compresses operating margins of the banks. Once a client is on the Internet, he is only a click away from the bank's competitor; and more and more financial sites, search engines, and portals will continue to push competing products, squeezing margins further. A new breed of firms, such as E*Trade and Charles Schwab, discount stockbrokers, have positioned themselves to take on both commercial banks and brokerage firms.[25]

Not surprisingly, many banks are becoming increasingly aggressive in their online business. Banco Mercantil in Venezuela teamed with McKinsey to create a joint venture online bank. Bancolombia is using its Internet strategy to raise $200 million through a new share issue: Their objective is to double the number of Internet transactions from the current level of nearly 400,000 per month. Colombia's leading financial services group, Grupo Aval, signed a $40 million contract with AT&T Latin American to connect their 800 communications portals among different banks using fiber-optic links.[26] As part of its regionwide approach to business, Citibank boosted its online presence through a five-year agreement signed in 2000 with ZonaFinanciera.com, a financial Web site for Spanish- and Portuguese-speaking people, to let its customers throughout Latin America do banking and brokerage transactions online.[27]

However, it is Bradesco, as Fernando Amandi, an Internet consultant at PriceWaterhouseCoopers notes, that is the benchmark—a Web-centric company offering connectivity, commerce, content, and consumer financial services.[28] Through its portal, consumers may purchase goods directly from merchants or on Bradesco's site. In both the B2B and B2C arenas, Bradesco is using the Internet in creative ways to boost bank revenues. For example, the bank links 500 trucking companies and 50 gas stations nationwide via an automatic billing arrangement through its Controle Telefrotas (CTF) portal launched in 1995. As Cândido Leonelli of the bank points out: "It's a no-fraud transaction. No tickets, no cards, no paper, no invoices.... These are 100% Bradesco accounts; we then sell the companies leasing, payroll and credits. We even invest their money."[29]

Three areas relevant to online banking pertain to security in transactions, payment processing, and electronic trading. In the first instance, it is common knowledge that Latin American consumers were more concerned about security than their North American counterparts. For example, the mere presence of the Visa brand, although significant, is not enough to calm consumers' fears that their card number will somehow be compromised when shopping online.[30] Consequently, the company has committed to advancing the use of a new, user-friendly, server-based version of the latest encryption technology—SET (Secure Electronic Transaction). SET ensures authentication between buyer and seller in an Internet environment. Additionally, with its member banks in Brazil, Visa employs this technology as part of its Risco Zero (zero liability) program.

In terms of payment processing, information technology has brought banks and companies much closer together: They can communicate more quickly and securely. In the past, U.S. firms with Latin American offices and operations would normally process all payables within each country. This was because a lack of technology and restrictive and parochial business regulations within individual countries forced U.S. firms to use local banks for payments. It was simply easier to handle disbursements locally.[31] Today, however, the Latin American business environment has changed, especially with respect to telecommunications infrastructure and systems. Transmission of financial and disbursement information is far more reliable and secure.

Banks are now using enhanced Society for Worldwide Interbank Financial Telecommunications (SWIFT) format to share information; increasing their use of electronic data interchange with their corporate clients; and introducing enhanced local automated clearinghouse equivalent payment systems. More banks are able to provide the types of products and services necessary for regionalizing payments, including centralized payables, either through their own branches or through strategic partnerships.[32] Newer banking systems also permit access to information on all activities. Corporate treasury professionals can receive consolidated reports on their company's cash position throughout Latin America—all from U.S. banks. The advancements combine to make it possible for a single payment system that can offer a number of benefits and advantages in addition to efficiency.

Finally, internationally electronic trading is altering the landscape of banking and finance in Latin America. There are thousands of B2B e-marketplace sites in operation today, trading bananas, zinc, coffee, metals, and other commodities; competitive sites (those that will survive) will be those that have strong logistical support and involvement from producers, traders, or financiers.[33] Two of the best-known trading platforms, Bolero.net and TradeCard, have worked assiduously to improve their systems. The former was created in 1999 as part of a global initiative to move trade onto the Internet. Bolero offers secure electronic transmission of business data and documents through the entire chain, from order processing and management to back-end trade document exchange. TradeCard, a B2B e-commerce infrastructure, allows buyers and sellers to carry out international trade transactions securely over the Internet. Through an aggregation of buyers, sellers, and separate trade service providers, the company automates and streamlines typical international trade transaction processes—processes that are complex, paper-based, time-consuming, and expensive.[34]

There is a growing trend among international banks to become involved in trade as partners with such trading platforms or at least to monitor developments and be prepared to embrace these electronic transactions. Banks that have made great progress in this regard include ABN AMRO, Bank of America, Barclays, BNP Paribas,

Citibank, Deutsche Bank, HSBC, and Standard and Chartered. In 2000, Deutsche Bank launched eCash Solutions, one of its e-commerce initiatives. The department that oversees this is responsible for e-commerce product development for cross-border payments, liquidity management, deposit services, image archive, and trade-related products for both financial and nonfinancial institutions.

As for investment banks, they are picking up the pieces from the dot-com meltdown which began in 2000 and are exercising greater selectivity and prudence and opting for established firms, or at least Internet-related firms that appear to have both strong linkages to bricks-and-mortar firms with proven managerial sustainability. Investment banks are especially cautious now: They feel positive about technology and telecommunications firms, but they are avoiding Internet startups. For example, in March 2001, Warburg Pincus invested $35 million in ebX Express Brasil, a private logistics and package delivery company based in São Paulo. EbX Express Brasil is a division of EBX Capital, a closely held Brazilian investment company founded in March 2000 through the acquisition of several packaging delivery companies. Again, *management* is key. Varel Freeman, a senior partner in Baring Latin American Partners, a private equity fund, asserts that a company's leader and management team are the sine qua non of financial success. In addition to "great management," he looks for companies whose scale is such as to be listed in the United States or eventually, to be involved in a strategic purchase: high-growth companies that are cash generative and players in a huge marketplace.[35]

Emerging trends that will link financial institutions and technology during the coming years will include virtual currency (e.g., stored value cards, also known as "smart card money"); specialized service providers, such as Patagon and Zona Financiera; wireless growth, expected to increase to 100 million customers by 2003; and a broadening market base, to both the very wealthy in the region and the working poor.[36] Anticipating and responding to these developments will weigh heavily in determining the competitive advantages of both commercial and investment banks.

CONSOLIDATION AND THE GROWTH OF MERGERS AND ACQUISITIONS

Another driver of financial service firm strategies in Latin America is the need to consolidate, through internal efficiencies and reorganization, and on a larger plane, mergers and acquisitions. As mentioned above, information technology has been a critically important vehicle for banks, in particular, to increase productivity, efficiency, customer service, and product development—controlling/curtailing costs and increasing profitability. Investment banks also are under pressure on a global basis to both consolidate internally and to seek alliances, mergers, or acquisitions to strengthen their competitiveness.

The trend toward the emergence of strong regional players has been spreading during the last half-decade. Fewer commercial and investment banking houses will dot the financial landscape; the remaining "champions" will possess a breadth and depth of capability and services that will assuredly bring a greater array of financing choices for consumers and companies than those available previously. As Michael Contreras, executive vice-president for Latin America at Citibank International's Corporate and Investment Bank observes, consolidation has resulted in a number of foreign banks

TABLE 6.2 Top Latin American Financial Institution Mergers and Acquisitions, 2000–2001

TARGET NAME	BIDDER NAME
Banco do Estado de São Paulo (30%)	Banco Santander Central Hispano
Grupo Financiero BBVA Bancomer (32.2%) (Bid No. 1)	Banco Bilbao Vizcaya Argentaria
Grupo Financiero Serfin	Banco Santander Central Hispano
Banco do Estado de São Paulo (63.72%)	Banco Santander Central Hispano
Grupo Financiero Meridional (97%)	Banco Santander Central Hispano
Banco do Estado do Paraná (88.04%)	Banco Itaú
Seguros Comercial America (41.5%)	ING Groep NV
Banco de Galicia y Buenos Aires (46.89%)	Grupo Financiero Galicia
Banco Río de la Plata (26.5%)	Banco Santander Central Hispano
Seguros Bancomer, AFORE Bancomer Pensiones Bancomer (49%)	Banco Bilbao Vizcaya Argentaria
Banco Bandeirantes, Trevo Seguradora	União de Bancos Brasileiros
Grupo Financiero BBVA Bancomer (9%)	Banco Bilbao Vizcaya Argentaria
Banco de Chile (35%)	Luksic Group
Banco Boavista Interatlântico	Banco Bradesco
Banco de Caracas SACA (93.1%)	Banco Santander Central Hispano
Banca Promex	Grupo Financiero BBVA Bancomer
Siembra AFJP (50%)	Citigroup
Banco Río de la Plata (18.5%)	Merrill Lynch & Co.
Banco Fininvest (50%)	União de Bancos Brasileiros

either closing their operations or scaling back on the products and services they offer. Foreign banks in the region have reassessed their international presence, and a number have opted to focus only on markets that have critical mass.[37]

Consolidations among Latin American banks are occurring more frequently than consolidations in Europe and Asia; the pace is more akin to that of the United States (see Table 6.2). Foreign banks have been buying aggressively into local Latin American banks. Mexico provides a prime example. In May 2001, Citigroup bought Grupo Financiero Banamex–Accival, Mexico's second largest bank, for $12 billion in cash and stock—in the process putting Mexico's top three banks in foreign hands.[38] Mexico's fourth-largest bank, Banorte, purchased Bancrecer for $175 million later that year. Bital, Mexico's fifth-largest bank, has 8% of the market share, compared to 6.7% for Banorte and 1,387 branches versus 452 for Banorte. Consequently, Bital remains an excellent acquisition for a foreign bank that has a strong business focus on consumer lending.

TARGET NAME	BIDDER NAME
Interbank-Banco Universal (97%)	Mercantil Servicios Financieros
AFORE Bital (51%)	ING Groep NV
Profuturo GNP (44.62%)	Grupo Nacional Provincial
Grupo Financiero Inverlat (45%)	Bank of Nova Scotia
Previnter AFJP S.A. (55%)	Grupo Bapro, Banco Santander Central Hispano
Banco Suquia S.A. (60%)	Caisse Nationale de Credit Agricole
Grupo Financiero Serfin (19.9%)	Government (Mexico)
Banco Sud Americano (39.1%)	Bank of Nova Scotia
Grupo Financiero Banamex–Accival	Citigroup
Seguros Comercial America (45%)	ING Groep NV
Caixa Seguros (50.75%)	Caisse Natl. de Prevoyance Assrs.
Banco del Nuevo Mundo	Banco Interamericano de Finanzas, NBK Bank, Banco Fin. del Peru
Generar AFJP	Citigroup
Banco Itaú (data network business)	Telefónica
Banco Bradesco (16%)	Banco Espírito Santo
BBV Banco Ganadero (14.88%)	Banco Bilbao Vizcaya Argentaria
Banco de Chile (5%)	Luksic Group
BanCrecer (portfolios of past-due home loans)	Grupo Financiero Banorte

Source: Latin Finance, Aug. 2001.

The Spanish banks, BSCH and BBVA, have led the charge in merger and acquisition strategies in Latin America and now have a host of Latin American subsidiaries throughout the hemisphere. These two banks, arch rivals, vie for everything from consumer deposits and pension-fund management to corporate lending and wholesale banking. Together they account for more than 30% of loans and 40% of the mutual fund market in Spain's private banking sector. BSCH's assets exceed $320 billion, and BBVA's total $280 billion. They each boast market capitalizations in excess of $42 billion. BSCH came into the Latin American market in 1983, and $15 billion later, it owns 10% of the banking market, with banks in 12 countries. A decade afterward, BBVA entered the market and has spent $8.2 billion for just under 10% of the Latin market. It is the leading bank in pension fund management with nearly a 29% share.[39] Although Mexico has been a priority market, other large emerging markets in the Americas have also been targets of the Spanish banks. In Venezuela BSCH acquired Banco de Venezuela in 1999, turning it into the nation's largest bank. Banco Provincial, a close rival of Banco de Venezuela, is controlled by BBVA. The bank also holds a 65% share in Banco Francés in Argentina, while BSCH has acquired or increased its stakes in other major Latin American banks, including Banespa in Brazil and Banco Río de la Plata in Argentina.

The Spanish banks' acquisition binge, however, has not been an easy row to hoe, and unforeseen problems—most notably, in Argentina—will take a toll on profitability. Some analysts believe that the Spanish banks may well have been overpaying for their acquisitions in the Americas. Business writer Jonathan Wheatley, commenting on the aftermath of BSCH's $3.55 billion purchase of a 30% controlling stake in Banespa, the former São Paulo state bank, notes: "Deposits are leaking, account holders are heading for the door and the scale of Banespa's potential bad debts has led to an unexpectedly large write down of asset value."[40] More than one-third of account holders left or were expected to leave after the sales. Under payroll deals with banks, Brazilian employers stipulate where employees must open accounts. Many public-sector employers in São Paulo switched to Nossa Caixa Nosso Banco, a savings bank under state control that the government has no plans to sell. In addition to the premium prices paid by the Spanish banks, they are faced with the need to spend hundreds of millions of dollars on marketing and investments in technology. Still another problem—perhaps the biggest—is the difficulty in integrating the banking culture/national culture of a country into that of Spanish banks and Spanish culture.

A major impact of Latin American mergers and acquisitions is that financial institutions have been forced to define their strategies to keep up with heightened competition. In the case of Venezuela, government protection contributed to a proliferation of banks, particularly smaller ones—too many, in fact, for the size of the country. It is estimated that in the next few years there will be a 30% reduction of the banking system due to future acquisitions of small banks by larger institutions and the collapse of marginal players.[41] It is necessary to point out that only 50% of merging companies have outperformed their immediate competitors. The problems with mergers are numerous and complex. Emilio Botín, cochairman of BSCH, asserts that managing a merger is as important as the decision to merge itself. Setting the time frame, creating a new corporate culture, encouraging staff, and offering credibility to investors are all crucial. He emphasizes that the successful merger is one whose aim is to generate increased shareholder value, quality and efficiency in customer service, and career opportunities for staff, as well as greater competitiveness in the financial sector and the economy as a whole.[42]

For BSCH and many other firms, acquisitions often offer a more attractive option. Buying a company that best complements the acquirer's own competitive advantages, or which allows it to build these advantages in other markets and businesses, is deemed a better move. Additionally, acquisitions are the best option for growth and the only one that allows for building a compatible if not identical corporate structure, especially where acquisition means not just control but also a clear majority stake. The acquisitions that have occurred during the past decade have carried with them very high price tags, far exceeding book value. Consequently, acquiring institutions have been forced to extract considerable cost savings. Moreover, the challenge becomes all the more daunting since the banks must compete not just with other banks but also with brokerage houses, mutual funds, and insurance companies.

Megabanks such as Citigroup have been able to meet this challenge successfully by offering a wide array of bank and nonbank services that go head to head against those of brokerage firms, investment banking houses, insurance providers, and e-commerce intermediaries. Illustrative of Citigroup's tremendous ability to seize leadership opportunities in high-growth emerging markets and make a massive commitment to the business is its acquisition of Banamex. The first big acquisition in Mexico by a U.S. bank, the deal catapulted Citigroup into the largest private sector financial institution in Latin America, with $49 billion in assets in the region. Investing in a partnership with Mexico's premier banking institution, Citicorp sees the acquisition as a means of challenging the Spanish banks' strong presence in the market; offering an even wider spectrum of financial services; bringing cost-efficiency, technology, and top drawer financial management to its Mexican partners; and using the Banamex brand to crack the U.S. Hispanic market. (Banamex is a highly regarded brand name among Mexicans residing in the United States.) As a "reverse acquisition" (Banamex is larger than Citibank's Mexico operation), only the Banamex logo will be used in Mexico, and the bank will remain under Mexican management. Moreover, Banacci chairman Roberto Hernández and CEO Manuel Medina-Mora will stay on to run the merged entity, and Hernández will take a seat on the Citigroup board. Whether one chooses to call this "cultural sensitivity," good corporate citizenship, or just good business sense, Citigroup's acquisition of Banacci changes the rules of the game in Mexico's banking industry.[43]

Investment banking groups, including the big guns of Merrill Lynch, Morgan Stanley Dean Witter, and Goldman Sachs are also consolidating to strengthen their core competencies as their industry becomes more concentrated. Regardless of the whims of the global economy, the market for investment banking services is certain to expand as a result of globalization, deregulation, economic restructuring, the growth of managed assets, and increased investment in equities. However, in addition to the three firms cited above, only a handful of other leviathans have the resources and scale to dominate business in global investment banking: J.P. Morgan Chase, Credit Suisse First Boston, Deutsche Bank, and UBS.[44] That line of business will include complex cross-border mergers and acquisitions, requiring a necessary pool of expertise and global reach to put together such sophisticated deals. These banks will have to pay top dollar to identify, recruit, and select the talent necessary to bring in the business and work the intricacies of the deals.

Consolidation in investment banking is occurring in tandem with consolidation in the corporate sector as well. Although mergers and acquisitions dropped by over a third in 2001, the decline is far less than expected given the negative economic and political events affecting the region (e.g., Argentina's economic crisis, Brazil's energy problems, instability in Venezuela and Colombia, and the fallout from global terrorism). On the positive side, private equity experts assert that down cycles provide excellent buying opportunities; and multinationals with a pan-regional versus single-country focus (e.g., banks, telecoms, and media and entertainment firms) view consolidation as an integral part of their long-term strategies.

Latin America generated nearly $38 billion in merger and acquisition volumes during the first half of 2001, a slight drop only from $40.8 billion during the same period a year earlier. Telecoms accounted for a significant share of this activity. For example, Portugal's Telecom, Spain's Telefónica and pan-regional Telecom Américas, a joint venture with Mexico's América Móvil, Bell Canada International, and SBC International have all been acquiring smaller Brazilian cellular companies.[45] Other major areas of merger and acquisition activity, in addition to banks and telecoms, include oil and gas, electricity, media, Internet, food, mining, and funds management. Unquestionably, market leaders and conglomerates continue to acquire assets aggressively in the region. Cemex, the Monterrey-based cement multinational owned by the Zambrano family, has evolved from an inward-looking Mexican firm to the third-largest cement company in the world. Since NAFTA came into being in 1994, Cemex has pursued a global expansion strategy, acquiring 21 companies: 13 in Latin America and 8 in the United States, western Europe, Asia, and Egypt. In addition to this $4.4 billion in acquisitions, Cemex acquired Houston-based Southdown in November 2000 for $2.8 billion, the largest acquisition of a U.S. firm by a Latin American company to date.

In Brazil, Gerdau, the biggest long-products steelmaker, aquired a 75% stake in Tampa, Florida–based AmeriSteel Corp, the second-largest rebar producer in the United States. In North America, Gerdau owns Canada's MRM Steel and Courtice Steel. Gerdau has also been acquiring firms in Chile, Uruguay, and Argentina. Selling steel in regional markets saves transportation costs, which fits Gerdau's business strategy.

The quest for consolidation to increase market share, profitability, and sustainable competitiveness will continue to shape the internal operations and merger and acquisition policies of commercial and investment banks as well as their corporate clients in Latin America (see Table 6.3). The networks of relationships produced by these new arrangements and the management challenges inherent in the new organizational structures that emerge will occupy (and preoccupy) banks' time, attention, and resources for the foreseeable future.

MEETING CUSTOMER NEEDS

Still another driver of financial institutions' strategies operating in the Americas is the need to focus on actual and potential customers, both corporate and retail, in the areas of products and relationship management. Consumer, or retail, banking has never been a priority for the international expansion of most banks. Compared to corporate banking, barriers to entry are high and economies of

TABLE 6.3 Top 50 Latin American Banks

RANKED BY TOTAL ASSETS AS OF DEC. 31, 2000

	INSTITUTION	COUNTRY	TOTAL ASSETS US$ MILLION 2000	TOTAL ASSETS % CHANGE 99/00	LOANS US$ MILLION 2000	LOANS % CHANGE 99/00	DEPOSITS US$ MILLION 2000	DEPOSITS % CHANGE 99/00
1	Banco do Brasil	Brazil	71,232.5	1.9	20,175.9	-9.7	33,819.8	-15.6
2	Caixa Econômica Federal	Brazil	64,491.2	-5.8	36,142.9	-12.6	32,286.8	-6.1
3	BBVA Bancomer	Mexico	39,889.7	45.2	27,370.1	39.8	31,267.0	58.4
4	Bradesco	Brazil	32,929.7	4.8	15,866.6	31.3	15,890.3	-13.4
5	Banamex	Mexico	31,280.8	7.1	21,771.5	15.4	20,936.4	7.4
6	Banco Itaú	Brazil	29,542.0	18.1	8,876.2	16.0	13,388.7	2.6
7	Unibanco	Brazil	21,252.9	22.0	8,366.9	13.0	5,937.2	3.8
8	Banco de la Nación Argentina	Argentina	17,872.9	0.7	9,946.2	9.1	13,223.1	5.4
9	Banco de Galicia y Buenos Aires	Argentina	15,323.5	14.8	7,746.9	6.2	8,739.6	14.6
10	Banespa	Brazil	15,080.8	-3.4	2,928.8	-9.2	6,164.9	-2.0
11	Banco Santander Chile	Chile	14,794.5	6.5	4,857.5	-8.3	6,425.6	-4.1
12	Banco de la Provincia de Buenos Aires	Argentina	14,457.0	2.0	8,325.2	-3.9	8,821.6	-1.9
13	Banco Río de la Plata	Argentina	14,087.6	19.4	6,210.2	8.2	7,024.6	17.1
14	ABN AMRO Bank	Brazil	13,781.4	153.3	6,198.2	463.2	4,039.0	369.9
15	Banco Santiago	Chile	13,483.7	-6.3	7,052.1	0.9	7,258.1	-1.8
16	Banca Serfin	Mexico	13,001.4	-31.6	8,616.1	-41.9	8,560.5	-28.9
17	Bital	Mexico	12,282.3	-7.2	6,323.7	0.3	9,726.5	3.5
18	Banco del Estado de Chile	Chile	12,162.8	0.1	5,667.5	-4.8	7,523.5	-4.8
19	BBV Banco Francés	Argentina	12,004.2	23.6	5,848.3	5.1	7,424.6	20.8
20	Banco Safra	Brazil	11,934.4	19.2	3,675.3	24.1	2,424.0	9.2
21	Banco de Chile	Chile	11,327.0	10.3	5,333.0	-1.5	6,756.4	10.3
22	BankBoston	Argentina	11,130.4	-1.9	4,914.9	-13.9	4,989.6	1.7
23	Banorte	Mexico	10,685.6	-19.2	8,299.1	-7.3	7,012.2	-28.1
24	Banco Santander Brasil	Brazil	10,449.2	48.0	2,980.8	-3.9	2,224.4	5.8

25	Citibank	Argentina	10,343.9	-0.8	4,600.1	-3.0	4,617.3	-16.2
26	Banco Santander Mexicano	Mexico	10,330.0	39.3	5,859.7	11.0	6,884.7	16.9
27	Nossa Caixa	Brazil	9,450.6	9.4	1,175.9	20.0	6,050.6	-2.8
28	Citibank	Mexico	9,168.0	20.8	2,561.0	-5.0	5,069.7	-10.4
29	Banco de Crédito e Inversiones	Chile	8,970.2	5.4	3,573.3	-1.8	4,364.4	8.1
30	HSBC Bank Brasil	Brazil	8,693.3	19.2	3,629.2	45.5	4,151.6	15.5
31	Citibank	Chile	8,310.6	34.8	1,782.2	3.7	2,131.9	-8.2
32	BankBoston	Chile	8,064.1	20.4	758.6	37.3	987.1	17.6
33	Citibank	Brazil	7,242.6	13.4	3,460.5	26.6	2,745.7	25.5
34	Banco Sudameris	Brazil	7,214.7	20.4	3,086.3	8.1	2,164.2	44.0
35	Banco de Crédito Nacional	Brazil	6,716.2	-1.7	2,777.5	5.8	2,326.0	5.6
36	Banco de A. Edwards	Chile	6,704.4	8.4	3,653.8	5.1	3,785.0	7.6
37	HSBC Bank Argentina	Argentina	6,674.6	33.1	2,155.5	-5.6	2,977.8	8.2
38	BankBoston	Brazil	6,597.3	5.7	1,672.0	38.4	2,284.5	4.2
39	Banco BBA Creditanstalt	Brazil	6,457.8	-1.2	2,410.6	-16.3	1,894.1	-7.1
40	Scotiabank Inverlat	Mexico	6,373.9	N/A	4,537.3	N/A	5,052.1	N/A
41	Bladex	Panama	5,660.7	9.4	4,927.5	7.3	313.4	-18.7
42	BBVA Banco BHIF	Chile	5,524.9	16.1	2,597.6	7.5	2,553.4	2.9
43	Banco Hipotecario	Argentina	5,200.9	-0.4	2,996.9	-16.6	426.2	29.2
44	Banco Bilbao Vizcaya Brasil	Brazil	5,107.7	8.0	1,567.0	57.2	2,621.0	3.8
45	Banco de Crédito	Peru	4,995.7	-1.1	2,523.3	-8.1	3,830.3	-0.2
46	Banca Nazionale del Lavoro	Argentina	4,987.7	40.6	2,770.8	31.0	2,630.7	22.2
47	BankBoston	Brazil	4,872.9	15.2	1,426.4	26.7	8.8	-93.9
48	Banco Provincial	Venezuela	4,770.8	26.9	2,043.4	43.2	3,835.8	30.8
49	Banco de la Republica Oriental del Uruguay	Uruguay	4,728.8	-7.2	3,447.8	-13.4	4,006.9	-1.3
50	Inbursa	Mexico	4,626.8	12.5	2,870.7	33.3	1,285.9	-27.5

Source: Latin Trade, September 2001.

scale are challenging to achieve. In a consumer banking business, acceptable economies of scale come from having tens of thousands (and millions in mass retail) rather than hundreds of clients. P. J. Kalff, former chairman of the managing board of ABN AMRO, notes that it is expensive to accumulate these numbers and build proper distribution networks to serve them. "Although acquisitions may seem to provide a shortcut, they often come at the price of integration costs, including those of adjusting brand image and performance."[46]

Other barriers to entry include the "foreign" image of an international bank. It requires a huge financial commitment to public relations and marketing by a bank to be accepted as a domestic service provider. Foreign banks, more than domestic ones, are often seen as transient players, looking for quick profits and a quick exit strategy. As a relatively underdeveloped phenomenon in emerging markets, consumer banking is considered high-risk in credit terms; moreover, foreign banks' management expertise in consumer banking in Latin American markets is scarce.

As international banks increase their added value through structuring, transactions, and advice, and engage in investment banking activities as well, they increase their competitiveness by offering a complete array of financial services to their clients. But at the same time, this adds volatility to their operations and resulting performance. Consequently, by adding consumer banking to their portfolio of activities, they gain a potentially stable earnings stream.

Since consumer banking is a relationship business, foreign banks that move into emerging markets are faced with major human resource challenges: identifying, selecting, and recruiting host country nationals who, after training, can build the kind of confidence, trust, and reputation for responsiveness among the bank's customers necessary to secure new accounts and service existing ones effectively. This is all the more important since nonbanks are starting to play a larger role in international financial consumer services. This is becoming visible in the card business with the increasingly widespread use of telecom cards, airline-related cards, and other products. Global challengers such as Microsoft, IBM, or Quicken could take a share of the business away from traditional banks. Consumer finance, fast becoming a huge international business, as well as nonbank firms dedicated to marketing mortgages, investments, and savings, also pose serious challenges.

As Latin American consumers' access to personal credit increases, and as the region's middle class grows, banks—both foreign and domestic—will be competing tenaciously for their business. The demands for most of the same services found in industrialized nations—checking accounts, savings accounts, checking/savings combinations, certificates of deposit, and loans—are driving banks to offer a broad package of products and services to a growing base of consumers. For example, the Brazilian credit market has a huge potential; it presently represents 30% of GDP, whereas the same ratio in developed countries is 70%.

However, banks are conservative institutions, and those that operate in Latin America are particularly wary of lending to consumers, despite the great potential (profitability) of doing so. The question they face is: How can the need to mitigate credit risk be reconciled with the need to increase both customer base and profitability? Brazil's Banco Itaú, the country's second-largest private bank, provides a vivid example of how to overcome this dilemma. Anticipation and control are the principal drivers of its credit control system, one that began to be shaped more than a decade ago when Brazilian financial institutions earned the largest part of their income from public bonds and notes and paid little attention to the credit market.[47] Itaú's integrated credit control system uses advanced technology and a centralized information structure to enhance the credit approval process. It depends heavily on credit and behavior scores for retail customers, and for both the middle and corporate markets, the bank relies on proprietary rating models. Retail customers in particular benefit from Itaú's aggressive use of preapproved credit limits. With this system, loans are even being contracted at ATMs. For corporate clients, the client's rating and size of deal are key factors.

Itaú's credit monitoring system allows for rigorous and continual evaluation of its borrowers. This has been invaluable in allowing the bank to land new customers and clients; most of the bank's new loans are for clients with little or no track record with the bank. Banco Itaú's "red flag system," based on an internally developed computer system, tracks all deals in which the borrower shows any sign of quality deterioration based on the bank's internal parameters.[48] This system runs daily, and it is one of the bank's most effective tools used to monitor mass transactions.

On the corporate side, banks are realizing increasingly that as the number of banks serving the Latin American market shrinks, relationships with local companies take on added importance. Foreign banks that enter the local market can have a profound influence on relationship management practices by local banks operating in their own corporate or wholesale markets. Although local banks dominate the domestic lead relationship of Latin American corporations, Latin firms with genuine international business activities choose foreign banks, especially large global ones, such as Citicorp, BSCH, and ABN AMRO, to handle their business. One of the main reasons is the panoply of services that only large foreign banks can offer, especially that of advisor as well as provider. In a survey of senior financial officers of Latin American companies, three attributes were mentioned as most important: prompt follow-up on requests for information, provision of creative ideas and solutions, and knowledge of credit needs. Nearly 32% of senior financial officers claimed that "creating ideas and solutions" is an area in which their relationship managers must improve. Among banks competing in Latin America, foreign bank relationship managers receive the highest evaluation on this attribute.[49]

One increasingly important area where corporate customer needs are great is trade finance, given the explosion of trade in recent years, both intra- and extraregional. The structures of trade finance deals are becoming bigger and more sophisticated, resulting in close cooperation among export credit agencies, multilateral lending organizations, private insurers, and commercial banks. Responding to customer needs (locally owned medium-sized to large firms in particular) is necessary but risky. Therefore, as existing financiers need to absorb greater exposure and constantly introduce innovative risk mitigation solutions, banks and insurers have come closer together. A prime example of a deal that permitted the borrower to access funds at much lower rates than it would have been able to without support was a $200 million, five-year syndicated loan facility for Light Serviços de Eletricidade (Light), one of Brazil's largest privately owned power utilities. Three political risk insurance agencies supported a deal jointly involving ABN AMRO, BSCH, Citicorp, and FleetBoston. Reduced costs for the borrower is a selling point that the arranging banks have been using with other key clients in the region.[50]

As for investment banks, pressure is mounting on these institutions to go further in meeting the needs of their current and potential customers. The driving force behind this is the aggressive pursuit by commercial banks to cut into their business by offering low-interest loans (which can be unprofitable) along with underwriting and merger advice.[51] The banks are using "loss leaders" to get the lucrative investment banking business that is the bread-and-butter of such firms as Merrill Lynch and Goldman Sachs.[52]

Many investment banks are taking stock of challenges facing them and developing strategies with a greater customer-oriented focus in mind. This includes establishing relationships with, and developing a deeper knowledge of, their middle-market customers; becoming more aggressive in accessing rich retail customers; and building local product expertise and execution capabilities.[53] Investment banks face the dual challenge of developing standardized products while shunning a one-size-fits-all business model.

In Latin America, investment banks' customer focus on the institutional side is based on the hope that private equity can offer a growing and profitable avenue of business, even though it accounted for less than $2 billion in funds raised in 2000.[54] The industry turned to Latin America in the early 1990s when private equity firms banded together with local and foreign partners to join privatizations. In Argentina, for example, J.P. Morgan Partners joined France Télécom, Telecom Italia, and Techint, a local construction company, to buy a telephone concession in Buenos Aires. More recently, private equity investors have targeted early-stage venture capital opportunities in the region. Chase touched off the mania through its involvement with StarMedia, the Spanish- and Portuguese-language Internet media company, one that experienced an enormous run-up, then a spiraling decline when the dot-com bubble burst in late 2000–early 2001. The biggest remaining hurdle for the expansion of private equity is the incapacity and unreliability of the region's local financial markets and institutions, which make it difficult for investors to cash out. Capital market reforms in Mexico and Brazil will do much to improve the situation.

As for asset management, a core business of investment banks, great expectations have failed to materialize. U.S. and European asset management companies such as Alliance Capital, Franklin Templeton, Merrill Lynch, Bankers Trust, Mellon (Dreyfus), and Schroders were attracted to the Brazilian market in the mid-1990s following the success of the Real Plan. It was thought that the end of high inflation and high domestic interest rates would lead to a major reallocation of assets to the local equity market by both individual and institutional investors such as pension funds. However, the experience of these companies to date has been very disappointing. Not only has the Brazilian equity market stagnated due to poor economic performance, continued high real interest rates, and the failure of pension fund assets to grow as projected, but the barriers to entry for nonbank foreign financial institutions have proven to be very high.

In the case of companies entering the market on their own, the lack of domestic distribution via a local banking network frustrated their marketing efforts. Companies such as Alliance, Franklin Templeton, and Bankers Trust, which established joint ventures with large local banks such as Bradesco and Itaú, were able to raise substantial assets; but they were then driven out of the market when their Brazilian partners decided unilaterally to terminate the joint-venture relationships. Modest success has been achieved only by foreign asset managers who established joint ventures with medium-sized but well-positioned local partners (e.g., Dreyfus Brascan Asset Management). For all the players in this market, a sharp decline in asset management fees due to increased competition has made this business very unattractive.

Turning to the wholesale side of the financial services industry—mergers and acquisitions, advice, foreign exchange, and underwriting of derivatives, bonds, and equities—this segment of the industry is thoroughly globalized; however, personal financial services is still largely a local game.[55] This part of the industry includes services such as life and accident insurance, brokerage, and investment management. Technological innovation has sharply cut interaction costs and enabled investment firms to roll traditionally local products out into global markets. Consequently, they can now provide local customers with a greater choice of personal financial service products and bring their strong suits/specializations to developing country markets. For example, Merrill Lynch has acquired local investment-oriented nonbanking institutions around the world. It subsequently transferred specialized skills, products, and capabilities, including its brand name, many of its leading U.S. products, and its "high-touch" advice-based model for high-net-worth customers.[56]

FINANCIAL FIRM STRATEGIES: FROM DIVERSIFIED COMPETITORS TO NICHE PLAYERS

In the volatile and highly competitive world of financial services, both commercial and investment banks have had to seriously assess and reassess their global, regional, and country-specific strategies and structures. In a challenging environment that has provided both winners and losers (see Figure 6.1), some firms, particularly mega-banks and the big investment houses, have opted for broad, diversified business lines to grow their institutions and market share. Others, such as strong local banks, have chosen to become highly competitive niche players.

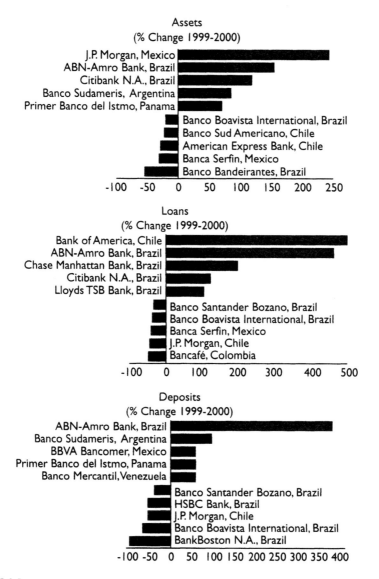

FIGURE 6.1

Winners and Losers

Source: Banking authorities of Argentina, Colombia, Chile, Costa Rica, Dominican Republic, El Salvador, Panama, Peru, Mexico, Uruguay, and Venezuela, *Latin Trade.*

Presented below are brief overviews of six financial institutions, each with a different philosophy, approach, and response to the changing Latin American financial environment.

BBVA (Banco Bilbao Vizcaya Argentaria). Along with BSCH, BBVA accounts for more than 30% of loans and 40% of the mutual fund market in Spain's private banking sector. Both on the continent and in Latin America these two financial powerhouses vie for everything from consumer deposits and pension fund management to corporate lending and wholesale banking.[57] With a reputation as the more traditional and conservative of the two rival banks, BBVA did not become a global company until after 1994. Its presence in Europe, North Africa, and Japan was minimal, and it served Latin America through a small network of representative offices. The prospect of European monetary union and deepening trade and investment integration, resulting in intensified competition in banking along with lower interest rates and slimmer profit margins, impelled BBVA to make two major strategic moves.[58] The first was to cut costs and acquire significant stakes in key industrial corporations; the latter was to diversify internationally, focusing on the growing markets of Latin America.[59]

BBVA moved with alacrity in implementing its new strategy. It gained control of major banks in Mexico and Peru in 1995, in Colombia and Argentina in 1996, and in Venezuela in 1997. It followed with acquisitions of Brazilian, Chilean, and Puerto Rican banks in 1998; and in 2000, BBVA purchased a controlling minority stake of Mexico's Bancomer for $1.2 billion in stock and debt convertible to stock.[60] With deep pockets and a focus on commercial banking and pension fund management, BBVA has shunned mergers in favor of acquisitions and controlling stakes in top banks throughout the region. It expects that the demand for banking services among the people of Latin American will rise rapidly, simultaneously with consolidation and the collapse of small domestic players in the financial services market. Where large domestic banks are not available for acquisition, BBVA will target medium-sized ones with solid brand names to serve as a nucleus and within a short period of time, transform them into market leaders.[61] A good example is Banco Francés. BBVA entered Argentina in 1996 by purchasing a controlling interest in the bank, and in 1997 BBVA Banco Francés, as it is now called, purchased a 72% stake in Banco del Crédito Argentino. In 1998 it took 100% control, and shortly thereafter the two acquisitions were merged, making BBVA Banco Francés the second-largest private bank in Argentina.

Turbulent economic conditions in Latin America in recent years have caused BBVA to moderate its acquisition campaign. In fact, in July 2001 it canceled its offer to buy the 32% of Banco Francés that it doesn't already own, citing market conditions. On the other hand, BBVA announced in September 2001 that it planned to increase its stake in Bancomer from 49% to 65%, a sign of its faith in the future of the Mexican economy.[62] The bank will gradually increase its ownership from its current $2.5 billion position. The shares will come from the Mexican government's placing its 17% stake up for auction. Bancomer has turned out to be one of the best investments that BBVA has ever made. *The Banker*, a London-based international banking publication, chose BBVA–Bancomer as the "Best Mexican Bank" of 2001. The award was given in recognition of Bancomer's ability to generate savings in expenses and economies of scale and integrating and expanding its commercial and investment banking operations.[63]

According to BBVA co-chairman Francisco Gonzalez, BBVA's team-driven culture and aggressive forays into new markets has positioned the bank to withstand the volatility in the Latin American political and economic landscape.[64] Like rival Citicorp, BBVA has its eye on Mexicans and other Spanish-speakers living in the United States and could well establish a presence north of the border in the very near future. While BBVA has been faulted for making very few loans in Latin America and having failed to secure returns from its investment in e-banking, BBVA and its rival BSCH will be hard to dislodge from their preeminent position in the financial services sector in Latin America.

Banco Espírito Santo.   The Banco Espírito Santo is an integral part of the Espírito Santo Group, a Portuguese-owned, diversified, international conglomerate with operations throughout Europe and the Americas. Begun in Portugal with a bank founded in 1884, the group today has consolidated assets worldwide exceeding $40 billion. Espírito Santo Financial Holdings S.A. (ESFH) is the Luxembourg-based holding company of the group's financial interest. With a capitalization of over $400 million, ESFH is a public company whose shares are listed on the New York, London, and Luxembourg stock exchanges.

Apart from the Banco Espírito Santo, ESFH has banks in Portugal, Spain, Macau, France, Switzerland, the Cayman Islands, and Brazil. Its flagship bank, Banco Espírito Santo, has nearly 480 branches in Portugal and in such financial centers as New York, Miami, London, and Madrid. Another ESFH bank in Portugal, Banco

Internacional de Crédito, has 120 branches. Espírito Santo came to Brazil in 1975 after the Portuguese revolution when the government nationalized the banking system. It began with a small investment bank in Brazil in 1976 and evolved into commercial banking, as well. In 1982, J.P. Morgan purchased 50% of the Brazilian banking operation. From 1987 to 1997, Espírito Santo, Monteiro Aranha, and Crédit Agricole shared ownership of Banco Inter-Atlântico, which subsequently merged with the local Banco Boavista, a bank with a strong presence in the retail market. In September 1997, the share control of Banco Boavista in Brazil was transferred to Banco Espírito Santo, Monteiro Aranha S.A., and Caisse National de Credit Agricole, resulting in a new financial institution: Banco Boavista Inter-Atlântico.

Unfortunately, financial crises in 1997 (Asia), 1998 (Russia), and 1999 (Brazil) took their toll on the performance of the new bank. In essence, the timing was wrong. Consequently, in 2000, the Espírito Santo Group shareholders decided to sell Boavista Inter-Atlântico to Bradesco. The deal was done through an equity swap rather than a direct sale. Today, Espírito Santo's presence in Brazil—its only significant operations in Latin America—consists of a small investment bank (owned jointly with Bradesco, although that bank intends to reduce its ownership from 50% to 20% in the near future) and a brokerage firm.

As a niche player, or specialist, Banco Espírito Santo's bread-and-butter business is service intermediation, an appropriate activity given the small capitalization ($30 million) of its Brazilian operations. It provides advisory services for Portuguese and Spanish firms seeking to do business in Brazil and for Brazilian firms in the Iberian Peninsula or seeking business there. Although it doesn't always lead in syndicated loans, it does participate in many of them; and its activities in stocks and debentures, mergers and acquisitions, corporate services, and treasury functions (derivatives and hedging for customers) generate significant fee income. With a solid research department, Espírito Santo plays an important role in initial public offerings (IPOs), share buybacks, and mergers and acquisitions. Its strategy for the future is to add fund management as a major line of business.

How does this David among Goliaths in the investment banking and brokerage businesses manage to perform so well? Board member Ricardo Espírito Santo sums it up quite well: "We take an entrepreneurial approach to finance. We identify equity investors and other potential business clients through 'teaser' presentations. We follow up tenaciously; and we are innovative and creative in the intermediation transactions and investment deals we undertake. Since we are not a global institution, despite our stellar reputation in Portugal, Spain and Brazil, we have to take the initiative and look for the deals. We can't sit by the phone and wait for the calls to come in like Merrill Lynch or Lehman."[65]

Banco Itaú.   With the largest profits in Brazil's banking sector and a 10-year increase of more than 7,000% in its stock price, Banco Itaú is a formidable player among Brazilian banks.[66] In an environment of consolidation, efficiency and scale are paramount; and since 1994, when CEO Roberto Setúbal took the helm, Itaú has been on a constant course of expansion, netting one new bank per year. In 2000, Banco Itaú earned $954 million, with a customer base of nearly 8 million depositors. Its strong position in U.S. dollars has insulated the bank, to a great extent, from the economic turmoil in the region and enabled it to zero in on its plan to unseat Banco Bradesco as Brazil's largest private bank. Since 1994, Itaú has revamped its corporate structure, doing away with rigid hierarchies and recruiting executives from outside the bank (a new point of departure). It also developed an incentive system as part of its compensation policy, performance-based salaries, and stock options. Maintaining and increasing shareholder value were adopted as guiding principles of the bank's policies and operations.

Banco Itaú's acquisition campaign began in 1995 with the purchase of Banco Francês e Brasileiro (BFB) for $476 million. Renamed Itaú Personnalité, it caters to high-end clients through 33 branches, with another 17 planned for the near future. In 1997, Banco Itaú purchased the State Bank of Rio de Janeiro for $290 million and the following year bought the State Bank of Minas Gerais for $494 million. In 2000, the bank also successfully bid $1 billion, 303% above the minimum bid, for the State Bank of Paraná. This acquisition allowed Itaú to increase its branches in the state with the fifth-largest economy from 49 to 425 and to gain $2.58 billion in deposits.

The present strategy of Banco Itaú is to expand its client base by means of better service and a wider array of offerings. With only one in three Brazilians possessing a bank account and the number of bank accounts projected to grow by 33% in the next five years, Itaú is betting that the retail market will be a lucrative source of business. Itaú has been adding over half a million new account holders per year and expects to increase that to 800,000 in 2002. Nevertheless, Bradesco expects to add over 1 million customers and aggressively market its products and services to stem the advance of Itaú in retail banking.

In a move to bolster its competitiveness in the Brazilian market, Itaú bought Lloyds TSB Group Plc's Brazilian asset management unit and private banking business in order to expand its fund management business for institutional investors. With the acquisition, Itaú will more than double its number of private banking customers to 7,000. It also becomes Brazil's second-largest asset manager, overtaking rival Banco Bradesco S.A. The leading bank remains Banco do Brasil.[67] Although a latecomer to online banking—Bradesco and Banco do Brasil got there first—Itaú successfully played catch-up by launching a joint venture with America OnLine (AOL) Latin America to bring its customers to AOL's pay service. Itaú received 12% of AOL Latin America; the bank's clients received three months of free Internet service and other benefits, including future e-mail access. Presently, 60% of AOL Latin America's 500,000 subscribers are Banco Itaú customers.

Having invested nearly $500 million in automation, Banco Itaú is reaping the rewards of online banking—its customers made more than 87 million online banking transactions in 2000, at a cost of 10 cents per transaction versus $1 by teller and 54 cents by phone. In addition to reducing costs, electronic banking is increasing the amount of business that customers do with the bank. They can now buy stock, take out loans, pay bills, and print checks, all at the ATM. Itaú's Investnet enables customers to access online real-time information on stocks and mutual funds, chat with a broker, buy insurance, sign up for a retirement fund, and get a mortgage.[68]

Banco Itaú was named "Best Domestic Bank in Brazil" by *Euromoney* in 2000. As one writer noted: "Pick almost any measure of a bank's performance and Itaú tends to come out on top. Take return on average equity: Itaú's is 31.5% while the other leading private Brazilian banks Bradesco and Unibanco clock up 16% and 15.4% respectively.... The secret of Itaú's success has been its ability to operate profitably and safely in Brazil's often volatile environment. It has been a cautious lender, maintained strong capital ratios and played major upheavals such as [the 1999] *real* devaluation to its advantage. Itaú is noted for its transparency in accounting and its good relationship with investors and analysts."[69]

ABN AMRO. The history of ABN AMRO spans more than 175 years. The Dutch multinational bank has a presence in 70 countries, including many in Latin America and the Caribbean. Brazil has always been a prime market for ABN AMRO; it has been operating there for nearly 85 years. In addition to ABN AMRO Bank, affiliates include Banco Real (its flagship commercial bank in Brazil, purchased in July 1998 for $2 billion), ABN AMRO Asset Management, BANDEPE, and Real Seguros.

In 2001 the bank embarked upon a new strategy, with the aim to maximize value creation for shareholders, clients, and staff. The bank is now organized around clients rather than countries. It operates in three new globally organized and largely autonomous strategic business units, each serving distinctive client groups: wholesale clients, consumer and commercial clients, and private clients and asset management. Each strategic business unit runs its own business. The managing board focuses on governance and policy and promotes synergy between the businesses. A new management framework—managing for value (MFV)—underpins the implementation of the new strategy across the group, ensuring that every management decision made within every part of ABN AMRO will be focused on maximizing returns for its shareholders.

The bank's new strategy will have a dramatic impact on ABN AMRO's pan-regional presence in the Americas. New performance targets will require the bank to reallocate capital and resources to businesses that promise higher returns. As a result, ABN AMRO is strengthening its presence in certain key markets, exiting a limited number of countries, and discontinuing nonpriority (predominantly retail) operations in several locations to create a more profitable and effective global network.

As part of its Latin American and Caribbean exit/reorientation strategy, ABN AMRO is withdrawing from consumer banking in markets where it does not enjoy a sizable share (it has also sold units in Aruba, Bolivia, Ecuador, Panama, and Surinam). It sold its Argentine consumer banking business (26 branches and $600 million in assets) to Banco de Galícia y Buenos Aires, which will make the latter the largest private bank in the country. ABN AMRO will continue to maintain corporate, investment, and private banking services in Argentina.[70] At the same time, it will be opening an additional 50 branches in Brazil, where it owns the country's fifth-largest private-sector bank.

While ABN AMRO's presence has been diminished in the region in terms of coverage, its reorientation ensures a lasting presence. Pretax profit increased in 2000 from ε576 million to 633 million, an increase of nearly 10%.[71] The bank completed its planned IT integration of Banco Real, ABN AMRO, and BANDEPE. It also upgraded and streamlined its distribution platform, partly by introducing state-of-the-art home, office, and Internet banking. The bank also opened call centers in São Paulo and Rio de Janeiro.

ABN AMRO sees the principal factors and forces shaping the financial services market in Latin America as consolidation of the banking system, general reduction of country risk, and the rapid commodization of products and services. This last trend will be especially problematic, as banks offering the same services will be subjected to intense competition. AMN AMRO's corporate energies vis-à-vis the region will focus on institutions (investment banking and corporate finance) and private banking, with the greatest attention to Brazil. Private banking could provide an especially attractive avenue of profitability. As Bruce Kelley, group vice-president in the Miami agency of ABN AMRO notes: "We foresee a reduction in country risk, leading to more stable and higher growth rates which, in turn, will generate wealth for off-shore as well as on-shore deposits. On the private banking side we will continue to refocus our strategy on the market niches that we think offer the best growth opportunity within and across countries. In addition, we will deepen the relationship we have with our clients and try to sell a variety rather than one or two products. Brazil will be the most attractive given its size, growth, prospects and most importantly our position in the country via Banco Real."[72]

The bank's forte in investment banking and corporate finance should provide a steady stream of business, whether through loan syndications, placements, or trading. Private banking will rely less on local presence, knowledge, and services and replace these with international coverage. Although this may appear counterintuitive at first (e.g., private bankers *not* stationed in-country), the "Swiss approach" to private banking has proven to be a feasible and profitable alternative. Under this arrangement, private banking relationship managers fly in for a week or two at a time. Many clients want their nonlocal assets handled in strictest confidence by savvy advisers in Switzerland or Miami. Also, from the bank's standpoint, there must be a "critical mass" of income and assets to justify a full-time local presence.

Technology will be critical as ABN AMRO seeks to improve service and provide a platform from which to better serve clients and differentiate its product. As Bruce Kelley notes: "More attention will be paid to MIS issues, since our deployment of technology is of critical importance in our providing top quality service for our customers."[73] The bank believes that its name and reputation are its strongest assets. However, it recognizes as well that the broadening and deepening of economic reforms and attention to improving the socioeconomic condition of the region is of fundamental importance if ABN AMRO is to realize its full potential in Latin America and the Caribbean.

Merrill Lynch. This firm is one of the world's leading financial management and advisory companies, with offices in 44 countries and total client assets of about $1.6 trillion. It has the largest equity research department in the world, with more than 600 fundamental equity analysts in 26 countries covering more than 3,600 companies. In 2000, for the sixth straight year, Merrill Lynch ranked as the leading firm in *Institutional Investor's* All-America Research Team, capturing 55 team positions. The following year, Merrill Lynch won top *Euromoney* awards for Best Investment Bank and Best Equity-Linked House.

As an investment bank, Merrill Lynch is the top global underwriter and market maker of debt and equity securities and a leading strategic advisor to corporations, governments, institutions, and individuals worldwide. The firm benefits from a global network of relationships, focusing on three primary businesses—corporate and institutional, private client, and investment managers—and the synergies that result. For example, private clients benefit from the availability of securities and solutions that may better satisfy their needs, while institutional and corporate clients benefit from liquidity created through diverse distribution channels. Combining local client relationships with global resources has enabled Merrill Lynch to provide integrated solutions both within and across geographic borders—a boon to its equity, debt, and advisory businesses, which increasingly are serving corporations doing business in multiple markets.

Merrill Lynch has been a presence in Latin America for more than 30 years and is today a leading underwriter of Latin American debt and equity offerings, with the top-ranked research team in the region. The firm maintains investment banking offices in Buenos Aires, Mexico City, and São Paulo and has built a vast distribution system for Latin American securities, offering issuers access to managed offshore funds, traditional institutional investors, and high-net-worth individual investors. Merrill Lynch is the leading trader of Latin American ADRs (American Depositary Receipts) and is an active member of the Mexico City and São Paulo stock exchanges.

The firm regards Brazil, Mexico, and Argentina as their prime markets in Latin America for their debt business (centered in New York), corporate offerings, and wealth management. Senior management at Merrill Lynch regards Mexico's proximity to the United States, the deepening of NAFTA, and the Mexican presidential election of 2000, in which a non-PRI candidate won for the first time in 71 years, as huge pluses. Merrill Lynch's unique advantage in the region, in addition to its three-decade presence, is an exceptional infrastructure in-country in both physical offices and in talent. Because of its global capabilities, the firm is very strong in mergers and acquisitions. The Repsol–YPF deal in Argentina and a host of other M&As in Brazil and Mexico have been very significant transactions for Merrill Lynch. The automotive and retail sectors have generated substantial business for the firm, and foreign direct investment traditionally has been a strong catalyst for growth of Merrill Lynch in Latin America.

Despite the region's attractiveness in many ways, Merrill Lynch does not look at Latin America through rose-colored glasses. Corporate executives are concerned about political and economic volatility; a lack of liquidity, indigenous financial systems, and depth of markets; and the paucity of large domestic corporate borrowers and issuers of equity. Firms such as Cemex, Televisa, and Petrobrás are still few and far between. Moreover, the spate of acquisitions in recent years, although beneficial to investment banking firms like Merrill Lynch that advise and structure such deals, has resulted in a shrinking of local stock markets, due to de-listings (e.g., Spanish oil company Repsol's purchase of Argentina's YPF). In fact, Merrill Lynch joined five other firms in closing its Argentine brokerage operations in 2001, due to low trading volumes. Trading volume on the Buenos Aires Stock Exchange has dwindled from $100 million per day in 1993 to less than $16 million in 2001. Merrill Lynch continues to offer market research, investment banking, and private banking services; in fact, its most successful client office in Latin America is Buenos Aires.[74]

Although a number of capital market firms are pulling back from the region, Merrill Lynch is not following this trend. According to Jeff Hughes, managing director and chairman of Latin America and Canada for Merrill Lynch's Corporate and Institutional Client Group: "We're not pulling back but refocusing our resources. We have had a long-term involvement with the region and will continue to do so. Despite a higher cost basis than elsewhere, we have the expertise—the products, service and relationships. We are ideally positioned to do well, regardless of the whims of local market conditions; for the long-term macroeconomic picture and the demographics, especially for Brazil and Mexico, look very favorable, for both the retail and institutional sides of our business."[75]

Not resting on its laurels as the premier investment banking organization, Merrill Lynch is designing new products and launching new initiatives to strengthen its competitive advantage. In 2000 it implemented a client segmentation strategy and intensified its client focus with two key launches: Private Wealth Services and an online joint venture with HSBC aimed primarily at mass affluent self-directed investors. This emphasis is part of a new, narrower focus for Merrill Lynch under the leadership of president Stanley O'Neal, one that intends to move the firm from financial supermarket to a more specialized firm serving clients with more than $100,000 in assets.[76]

In another major development sure to have a positive impact on Merrill Lynch's Latin American business, the Corporate and Institutional Client Group, a $12.5 billion division that accounts for almost half of Merrill's revenue, has undertaken a major initiative in e-commerce. The group wants to expand Merrill's base of institutional clients while giving them more personalized information; create a flow of real-time information to all clients; give institutions access to research and other information produced by competing firms; boost demand and liquidity for existing debt and equity instruments; and create new venues for issuing securities.[77] With a truly global reach and long-standing relationships in Latin America, Merrill Lynch is sure to capitalize on these sustainable assets vis-à-vis its Latin American clients located within as well as outside the region.

Citigroup. With a relentless focus on growth and earnings, a global orientation, highly diversified products and services, and a client-centered approach to all segments of its business, Citigroup is one of the most successful financial services companies in the world. Emerging markets is one of Citigroup's principal arenas of business, and it leads all other banks in this field, accounting in 2000 for $11.3 billion in revenues and $2.7 billion in net income (see Figure 6.2).

Operating in 80 countries, Citigroup's 55,000 employees serve a customer account base of 20 million.[78] Presently, the bank's emerging market organization encompasses three global product businesses: e-business, worldwide securities, and sales and trading. Citigroup's consumer franchise entails retail banking, credit cards, and investment services.[79]

Citigroup's presence in Latin America dates from 1914. In addition to the services mentioned above, the region has proven to be fertile ground for the bank's work in M&As, insurance, and online banking. In Latin America, the bank produced $4.4 billion in revenue and $956 million in earnings in 2000. With 29,000 employees and $50 billion in assets, Citigroup's Latin American business involves a physical presence in 24 countries and over 10 million accounts. Its 2000 market share ranking (excluding Banamex)

1999
Revenues* ($B)

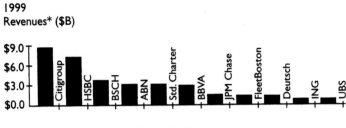

*Corporate and Consumer Bank. Market Share excludes China.

FIGURE 6.2
Performance of the Leading Emerging Market Banks

included: number 1 in syndicated loans, number 2 in both debt and equity, and number 5 in M&A.[80]

The bank is especially bullish on its transactional business with Latin America: cash management, securities, trade finance, treasury operations, and pension funds. At the same time, Citigroup regards the development of local capital markets in countries such as Mexico and Brazil as extremely promising for its business. It is also enthusiastic in its belief and commitment to the Internet. In fact, e-business is a line of business in which Citigroup hopes to dominate. According to Rajesh Mehta, Citibank's e-business manager for Latin America, the bank plans to build an online pan-regional system for buyers, sellers, and distributors to manage transactions online using a common tool: an Internet browser.[81] Citibank's system—CitiCommerce—includes electronic billing, transaction management, a secure Internet-based billing service, and a procurement platform that connects buyers and sellers worldwide. Up and running in Argentina and Brazil, CitiCommerce is next slated for Mexico and Colombia.

The term *strategic vision* most aptly describes the guiding principle behind Citigroup's activities in Latin America. As Victor Menezes, chairman and CEO of Citibank N.A. cogently asserts: "Citigroup has always taken the long view—we get in local all the way, whether retail or corporate. We strive to maintain continuous growth and expansion of market share, with a long-term commitment as a local player. Building a global network and technical platform with high quality local staff is paramount to our future business in Latin America."[82]

As mentioned earlier, Citigroup's $12.5 billion acquisition of Banamex—Mexico's second-largest but most profitable financial group—aptly illustrates Citigroup's strategic long-term vision. Convinced that Mexico will continue to be a solid, fast-growing economy and a nation committed to political reform as well, chairman and CEO Sandy Weill structured an ingenious deal that "changes the rules of the game in Mexico's banking industry."[83] The acquisition of Grupo Financiero Banamex–Accival will enable Citigroup to expand significantly its retail banking, trade finance, pension fund, and investment banking activities in Mexico; fold its local operations under the Banamex logo, thereby boosting its marketing position both in the local Mexican market and among the large and growing Hispanic market in the United States; and smoothly integrate two strong and profitable institutions that have very little overlap in their products, services, and operations. Citigroup's philosophy of long-term commitment is enhanced by the bank's staying power—its ability to withstand crises, compared with many local banks that cannot weather the storm of economic volatility and recent financial downturns. Additionally, the bank is known for steering a careful path between risk taking and risk aversion.

Citigroup's Latin America Global Corporate and Investment Bank is illustrative of the principles of diversity of product and service offerings, sound management, and carefully managed risk.[84] Headquartered in Miami with a staff of 35, the Latin America Corporate and Investment Bank handles the countries of the region on a portfolio basis. The operation is managed as a cluster, not on an individual country basis. For example, Bolivia, Ecuador, and Peru are one cluster, managed out of Peru. Although the operation is managerially centralized, it has a strong "front end" in-country—Citibankers on the ground stay closely in touch with customers and ensure a high degree of responsiveness to client needs. Thanks to its joint venture with Salomon Smith Barney (SSB), Citigroup can handle Latin American clients' complete investment banking needs. Since SSB does not have resources in-country, Citigroup leverages its 500 relationship managers for SSB in an effective cross-selling operation.

On the lending side, the Corporate and Investment Bank's policies are not so much conservative as they are prudent. Preclearance of potential borrowers is a rigorous process. As Citigroup executive Michael Contreras points out: "We don't lend our balance sheet easily. When we lend to a customer, it is a mutual commitment. Citigroup works with borrowers who develop financial problems, including restructuring and rescheduling loans and, when necessary, bringing in a strategic investor."[85]

Although Citigroup does not hesitate to acknowledge that it faces competition from well-managed and strategically astute local banks as well as J.P. Morgan Chase and the Spanish banks (BSCH and BBVA), it nevertheless proclaims with confidence that "nobody has the breadth and depth we do in all 24 countries across the spectrum of products and services we offer—ones which are truly globalized. We can deliver seamlessly to top-tier as well as medium-size firms when they relocate or expand from one market in the region to another. They regard us as integral to their regional strategy.[86]

Citigroup's uniqueness and incomparable standing in the world of global financial services is poignantly described by former *Wall Street Journal* reporter and author Philip Zweig: "In evolving over the last century into what is arguably the only truly global financial services organization, Citigroup has generally been a major force for financial market reform, modernization and efficiency.... Citi has promulgated free-market competition, innovative financial products and greater access to capital wherever it has managed to gain a foothold."[87]

GROUPING STRATEGIC RESPONSES

As the rules of the game have changed in global finance, so have the approaches, strategies, and responses of financial institutions.[88] The six financial institutions highlighted above have followed distinctive paths by which to grow their business and increase profitability and market share. Their strategies, however, may be clustered according to the categories cited and illustrated in Chapter 4. Three institutions—Citicorp, BBVA, and Merrill Lynch—can be considered broad regional integrators. These financial institutions are builders of pan-regional networks of banking and financial operations. They are guided by a long-term vision and maintain a singular focus on global competitiveness. They offer a wide range of products and services, effectively utilize information technology, and regard mergers and acquisitions as feasible vehicles for consolidation of their regional and in-country market positions.

ABN AMRO falls into another category: narrow regional integrator. Organized around clients rather than countries, it scaled back its consumer banking operations in the region, preferring instead to concentrate on its highest-priority market, Brazil, through its commercial bank (Banco Boavista), and on its highly successful private and investment banking and corporate finance activities. Banco Itaú is clearly a national champion, its forte being the ability to compete successfully in its home market. Strong in commercial banking, with a growing and loyal customer base, Itaú aspires to be the dominant player in the local Brazilian market. Tight management, an emphasis on customer service, the pursuit of acquisitions, and an emphasis on online banking are defining characteristics of this national champion. Finally, Espírito Santo's role in Latin America is that of a specialist, focusing on two areas: intermediation and private banking. Advisory services, participation in syndicated loans, and M&A work define the bank's presence in Latin America, one in which Brazil accounts for the overwhelming majority of Espírito Santo's activities in the region.

The economic turbulence that buffets the region periodically, due to global factors (worldwide attacks by global terrorists, economic recession in industrialized nations), regional ones (debt crises, droughts, and floods), or country-specific problems (political turmoil, economic mismanagement), will continue to define the business landscape in the Latin America. Financial institutions, in particular, will be affected strongly by political and economic events; in turn, the effects upon them, as well as their responses, will have repercussions throughout every sector and industry in the region. How financial institutions face and respond to crises—perhaps even enhancing their positions in the process—will surely weigh heavily in determining their long-term competitiveness and sustainable profitability in the Latin American market.

IMPROVING HEALTH SERVICES AND PRODUCTS

B uilding the Latin world's physical, electronic, and financial infrastructure, as shown previously, is essential to the region's further development, but the most crucial drivers of global competitiveness are undoubtedly health care and education. These are the twin foundations of a workforce with world-class skills and are also important factors of economic and political stability. Although significant progress has been made in this area in major countries, challenges remain, and the region's performance gap with emerging Asia has widened in the past decade. In addition, broad discrepancies persist between the least and most developed countries, and health systems are quite dissimilar. Although total expenditures on education are similar between emerging Latin and Asian markets, their allocation varies markedly; studies by the World Bank and other agencies have found it to have a major impact on competitiveness. Southeast Asian countries have generally stressed primary education, which has positively affected their workforce skills and spurred both exports and foreign investment; by contrast, Latin countries have tended to privilege higher education, and their universities have remained largely isolated from industry, which has hindered innovation.

The region is also highly heterogeneous in both its health and education levels. Whereas in 1998 adult illiteracy was almost eradicated in the South Cone (except for Paraguay), it remained at 16% in Brazil and reached 40% for women and 25% for men in Guatemala.[1] This reflects income inequalities, high throughout the region, but reaching a world-record level in Brazil. By 1999, the richest 10% of the population accounted for 47% of the total income in Brazil, whereas it was 37% in Argentina and Mexico. Income distribution actually worsened in the past two decades, since the income of the wealthiest 10% went from 39 to 47% in 1997–1999 in Brazil, 30 to 37% in Argentina, and 26 to 37% in Mexico. The region's income distribution is still considered to be the world's most unequal. Paradoxically, its negative trend is due in part to Latin America's economic liberalization. In the 1990s, privatization and industry consolidation led to massive layoffs, especially in Argentina. The region's unemployment rate rose by over 10% annually in the 1997–1999 period alone. This was also due to demographic trends: The workforce, composed of 212 million people by the late 1990s, grew by 44 million in the decade, and this was not matched by the increase in available jobs. As a result, almost 44% of Latin Americans were still living in poverty at the end of the 1990s. The UN objective of halving extreme poverty rates by 2015 will require an average increase in per capita output of 2.3% annually.[2]

REGIONAL HEALTH PROFILE

HEALTH INDICATORS

Income and education inequalities also apply to health care, but the region has still made significant progress. By the end of the 1990s, the Latin America/Caribbean region devoted 7.3% of its gross domestic product (GDP) to financing health services, representing annual expenditures of about $114 billion. This had some positive results: Life expectancy at birth rose from 69 years in the early 1990s to 71 years today. The average annual infant mortality rate (deaths of children under 1 year of age) for Ibero-America decreased from 38 in 1990 to 26 deaths per 1,000 live births in 2000; maternal mortality fell by 26% in the same period. Access to drinking water improved sharply, with the percentage of people without access falling by about half (from 31% to 16%). Immunization was also a success story: In 1999, vaccination coverage (TBC, DPT3, polio, and measles) reached 90% of 1-year-olds. Overall spending on health care grew more unevenly, rising most in Argentina, Chile, and Colombia.[3]

As in education, however, there are massive variations among countries. The infant-mortality rate ranged in 1998 from 10 deaths per 1,000 live births in Chile to 19 in Argentina, 30 in Mexico, 33 in Brazil, and as high as 60 in Bolivia. Average life expectancy also varied from 76 in Costa Rica to 73 in Argentina, 72 in Mexico, 67 in Brazil, and only 62 in Bolivia. This was closely correlated to public expenditure on health. In 1990–1998, public spending reached 6.9% of GDP in Costa Rica and 4% in Argentina, versus 3.4% in Brazil, 2.8% in Mexico, and only 1.1% in Bolivia. Access to health care played a similar part: In the same period, physicians per 1,000 inhabitants ranged from 2.7 in Argentina to 1.3 in Brazil and 1.2 in Mexico.[4]

DEMOGRAPHIC TRENDS

These health inequalities will become more acute as the region registers a rapid aging of its population. In the next two decades, the over-60 group in the region is projected to grow from 7.3% to 12.2% of the total population. Issues that will become key include the less-than-universal coverage by social security systems and the inadequacy of pensions and retirement income to meet basic needs, which in small part may be offset by the continued participation of older adults in the labor force.[5] Aging will not be uniform, and Latin countries fall into three tiers in this regard. The South Cone (minus Paraguay) falls into the low birth/low death rate pattern of Spain, Portugal, and most other developed countries. Transitional countries, with a declining birth rate and low death rates, include Mexico and Brazil; these will have the hardest task ahead, as their populations are aging the most rapidly. In the third tier, the poorest countries, such as Bolivia, Paraguay, and Nicaragua, have the young population profile of the least developed world (see Table 7.1).

EPIDEMIOLOGY PROFILE

Differences in economics and demographics are reflected in epidemiology; most of the South Cone is close to Iberia and OECD countries, with a prevalence of age-related chronic diseases, but countries with a young population are more skewed toward acute

TABLE 7.1 Health Indicators in Latin Markets

COUNTRY	TOTAL POPULATION (THOUSANDS), 2000	POPULATION GROWTH RATE (%), 1990–2000	POPULATION 60+ YEARS (%), 2000	LIFE EXPECTANCY AT BIRTH (YEARS), 2000		TOTAL EXPENDITURES ON HEALTH (% OF GDP), 1998	PUBLIC EXPENDITURES ON HEALTH (% OF TOTAL), 1998	PRIVATE HEALTH INSURANCE (% OF PRIVATE HEALTH SPEND), 1998
				MALE	FEMALE			
Canada	30,757	1.1	16.7	76	81.5	9.3	70.1	37.5
U.S.	283,230	1.1	16.1	73.9	79.5	12.9	44.8	60.7
Spain	39,910	0.2	21.8	75.4	82.3	7	76.8	23.6
Portugal	10,016	0.1	20.8	71.7	79.3	7.7	66.9	5.3
Argentina	37,032	1.3	13.3	70.2	77.8	8.1	55	24.8
Brazil	170,406	1.4	7.8	64.5	71.9	6.9	48.2	53.2
Mexico	98,872	1.7	6.9	71	76.2	5.3	48	4

Source: Adapted from World Health Organization, The World Health Report 2001, Geneva, 2001, pp. 136–167.

conditions. In Mexico, for instance, the second largest prescription drug category is infectious disease, whereas it is only in fourth place in Argentina.

In major markets, however, the epidemiological profile is converging with that of Europe and North America, especially in urban populations. For instance, about 300,000 Latin Americans now have type 1 diabetes, but this is projected to have grown by 60% in 1995–2010, versus less than 40% in North America and less than 10% in Europe.[6] Type 2 diabetes is also expected to follow the growth pattern of Europe and North America, in keeping with urban lifestyle changes; metabolism is already the top category for prescription drugs in Argentina, Brazil, and Mexico. Similarly, the top two therapeutic areas in the United States (neuroscience and cardiovascular), which are age-related, are also among the top three categories in the major Latin markets (see Table 7.2).

However, any marketer concluding from this converging epidemiology profile that a one-size-fits-all strategy is appropriate would be mistaken. There are significant differences between North and South America in terms of health products consumption, which can be explained by three factors: history, culture, and brand loyalty. Latin American markets were closed for many decades prior to the 1990s, which led to the rise of local brands. In addition, physicians as well as consumers in the region tend to be brand-loyal and conservative, which explains the greater local longevity of mature brands. Finally, culture plays a part: Even though most countries (except for Argentina) do not have comprehensive drug reimbursement, the upper-income tier of the population manages to pay for top brands, including lifestyle drugs such as Viagra (erectile dysfunction) and Xenical (antiobesity).

These trends are reflected in overall sales patterns in the top seven markets of the region. Among their top 10 products, only one, Lipitor (a cholesterol reducer), is also represented in the top 10 worldwide list. Among others, three are very mature brands: Voltaren (antiarthritis) is long off-patent and is being replaced in North America by newer drugs (Enbrel and cox-2 inhibitors Celebrex and Vioxx); Bayer aspirin was launched in 1897 and the antibiotic Amoxil is also an older drug. Two products are specific to the region—the analgesic Novalgina and Celestone, sold by Brazil's top local producer, Aché Labs.

By contrast, the top 10 products worldwide are largely driven by age-related chronic conditions. Top categories are cardiovascular (Lipitor, Zocor, Norvasc), neuroscience (Prozac, Paxil, Zyprexa, Zoloft), gastrointestinal (Losec and Prevacid), and musculoskeletal

TABLE 7.2 Leading Therapeutic Areas (Sales in 2000)^a (Millions of Dollars)

	U.S.	SPAIN	BRAZIL	MEXICO
Neuroscience	9,904	517	716	365
Cardiovascular	7,778	563	768	389
Respiratory	6,137	266	529	545
Oncology	5,586	n.a.	n.a.	n.a.
Women's health/ genitourinary	5,091	259	555	341
Metabolism	4,336	611	856	919
Infectious disease	1,589	349	451	851
Dermatologicals	n.a.	214	389	297
Vaccines	1,425	n.a.	n.a.	n.a.
Musculoskeletal	1,397	269	436	365
All other	102,808	n.a.	n.a.	n.a.

Source: IMS/MIDAS (2001) for United States; IMS Health, Pharma Prognosis Latin America, *2001, for other countries (p. 55).*
^{a}*n.a., not available.*

(Celebrex). This discrepancy leads to a challenge for multinational manufacturers, who must balance their global branding objectives against this mixed pattern of regional preferences (see Table 7.3).

HEALTH REFORM

Latin America's health systems still have significant differences, but they are partly converging due to a health reform movement which is the most significant since the region's social systems were set up in the 1940s. Common threads in the region are a move toward decentralization and broader coexistence of the public and private sectors. However, progress has been hindered by economic constraints as well as by public opposition to cost-shifting from government to consumers. In addition, all health systems suffer from underfunding and chronic mismanagement. Argentina, for instance, spends over 8% of its GDP on health—more than Spain—but one-third of its population lacks health insurance coverage, whereas Spain meets the European norm of universal access to basic care.

Regional health systems are now hybrids—structurally akin to the European model of government-driven care, but financially closer to the American model. Whereas in Spain, public expenditure on health accounts for almost 80% of the total, it ranges from only 48 to 55% in Mexico, Brazil, and Argentina, closer to the U.S. propor-

TABLE 7.3 Leading Products: Latin America Versus World

RETAIL MARKET SALES AT EX-MANUFACTURER PRICES[a]

PRODUCT (COMPANY)	($ MILLIONS)	MARKET SHARE (%)	WORLDWIDE LEADING PRODUCTS[b]
Voltaren (Novartis)	218.3	1.4	1. Losec (Astra Zeneca, antiulcerant)
Novalgina (Aventis)	90.5	0.6	2. Lipitor (Pfizer, statin)
Viagra (Pfizer)	81.8	0.5	3. Zocor (Merck, statin)
Celestone (Aché Labs)	79.6	0.5	4. Norvasc (Pfizer, calcium antagonist)
Xenical (Roche)	76.1	0.5	5. Prevacid (Takeda, antiulcerant)
Bayer Aspirin (Bayer)	73.7	0.5	6. Prozac (Lilly, antidepressant)
Lipitor (Pfizer)	73.3	0.5	7. Paxil (GlaxoSmithKline, antidepressant)
Lexotan (Roche)	67.6	0.4	8. Zyprexa (Lilly, antipsychotic)
Amoxil (GlaxoSmithKline)	65.1	0.4	9. Celebrex (Pharmacia, antirheumatic)
Tegretol (Novartis)	63.4	0.4	10. Zoloft (Pfizer, antidepressant)

Source: IMS Health, Pharma Prognosis Latin America, 2001, p. 24 (Latin America); IMS Health, World Review 2001, p. 116 (worldwide sales).
[a]*MAT, Sept. 2000; sales in top seven countries (Mexico, Brazil, Argentina, Venezuela, Colombia, Chile, Peru).*
[b]*Year-end 2000 sales, worldwide.*

tion of 45%. Health systems currently consist of dual structures, including, as in Europe, social security programs partly funded by compulsory payments from companies and employees, supplemented by "solidarity" funds for the poorest tier of the population.

ACCESS AND REIMBURSEMENT

In Mexico, about two-thirds of the population are covered by the social security system. The government-controlled IMSS (Social Security Institute) covers 44 million private-sector employees against payroll contributions and administers a solidarity program for 11 million unemployed and elderly. A government-run insurance fund, ISSTE (Institute of Social Security and Services for State Workers), covers state employees. Only 3 million people have private health insurance (mostly funded by employers), and any development of a private managed-care sector will depend on an increase in consumer purchasing power. Under the former government, a reform program had been initiated with a $700 million World Bank loan to improve the quality of health care provision and increase social security coverage. Some 30 million uninsured poor now depend on basic health care at Department of Health (SSA) hospitals and clinics, and 3 to 6 million rural Mexicans still have little or no access.[7]

Brazil faces worse inadequacies. Its public health system, SUS (Sistema Unica de Saúde) covers only one-third of the population; while 43 million people have private coverage, as many as 70 million have little or no access. As in Mexico, primary and preventive care are generally lacking (see Figure 7.1). Brazil has a disproportionate number of specialists versus general practitioners, and the system tends to be led by secondary care. Reform efforts include decentralization, development of primary care, and some privatization, but they remain insufficient. Following a mid-2000 senate ruling, the federal health budget was to rise 5% in 2001 and follow GDP growth thereafter; the states were also required to allocate a minimum of 7% of their budgets to health in 2001, and 12% in the next four years.

Primary care promotion is sporadic. The Family Health program has created primary care teams, but so far, covering less than 10% of the population. In the poor northeast, initiatives to provide basic care and promote self-help in disease prevention have reduced mortality levels, but also on a small scale. In a partial privatization, public hospitals have remained under government control but are managed by private companies. HMOs are also widespread in the private sector, covering over 44% of the 43 million people with private insurance, but as in the United States, their growth has slowed

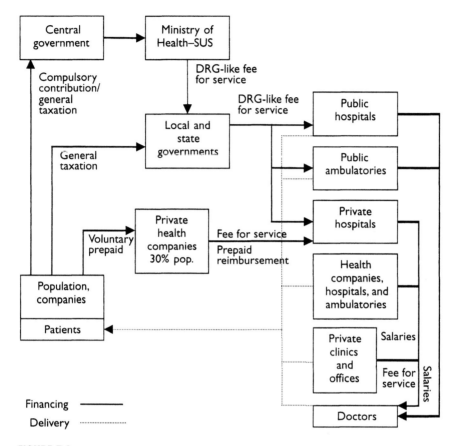

FIGURE 7.1

Brazil Health System

Source: Sonia Fleury et al., eds., *Reshaping Health Care in Argentina, Brazil and Mexico*, International Development Resource Center, Apr. 2000, p. 122.

from 5% to less than 3% in the late 1990s. Nearly 11 million people are also covered by Unimeds (HMO-like groups contracting doctors), and another 4 million by health insurance networks.

In Argentina, health care inequalities are less pronounced than they are in Brazil, and the country has more comprehensive drug reimbursement, reaching about two-thirds of the population.

Basic health is covered for 45% of the population by the OS (Obras Sociales, independent insurance funds) against compulsory employer and employee contributions. Another 10% are covered by PAMI, a state insurance program for retirees, but the program suffers from mismanagement and heavy debts. Many people supplement the

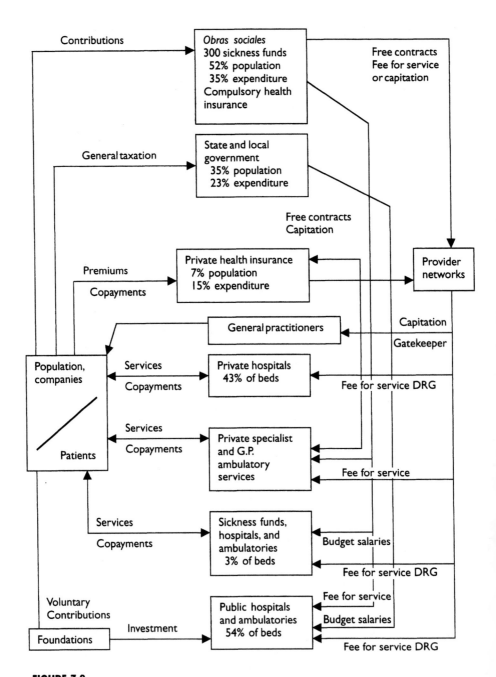

FIGURE 7.2

Argentina Health System

Source: Sonia Fleury et al., eds., *Reshaping Health Care in Argentina, Brazil and Mexico,* International Development Resource Center, Apr. 2000, p. 65.

Obras Sociales basic coverage with additional premiums to Prepagas, prepaid private insurance groups. Legislation effective in January 2001 has partially deregulated social security, allowing the private companies (Prepagas) to compete in Argentina. Private health providers also started to expand in the early 1990s, accounting for over 40% of the hospital bed capacity by the end of the decade—but less than 10% of the population now has private insurance (see Figure 7.2)

As in Brazil, managed care is spreading, and Blue Cross Blue Shield has a presence in the private insurance sector. HMO-like groups are pooling resources with hospitals for computerized databases, and Prepagas as well as some large companies are using disease management, with employee education and monitoring. Economic constraints will probably accelerate health insurance consolidation, leading to fewer, stronger Obras Sociales and to a few key players in the private sector, including some American HMOs if the investment climate improves. Private insurance is likely to remain much stronger in the South Cone than in Mexico, where cross-border HMO coverage has helped a few managed care groups, but where the market remains limited. A summary of health policy reform is provided in Table 7.4.

REGULATION

Drug Approvals. One area in which reform has been relatively uniform and successful in major markets is product registration. New agencies modeled after the U.S. Food and Drug Administration (FDA) were set up, and the acceptance of foreign clinical trials data has generally reduced approval times to less than a year. In Mexico, the registration period now averages six to seven months for new compounds. In Brazil, the ANVS (Agencia Nacional de Vigilancia Sanitaria), set up in 1999, has reduced the marketing approval time for products already registered in other markets to one year or less. In Argentina, the ANMAT was also set up in 1992 as an FDA-type regulatory agency and has led to an efficient process with approval times from six to nine months and fast-track registration for lifesaving drugs. However, full regional harmonization of approvals is not expected in the next several years.

Although all regional regulators have tightened manufacturing requirements, GMP (Good Manufacturing Practices) standards are uneven, which is a barrier to foreign investment. In Brazil, large local companies such as Aché are compliant, and better enforcement is expected under the new ANVS agency. Brazil is now emerging as a major production site for multinationals. Companies such as

TABLE 7.4 Key Health Policies

Argentina	• Reform efforts to focus on the health insurance sector (more direct competition will aim to increase efficiency and quality). • Broader integration of the public and private health care sectors; public hospital finance problems may persist. • Tighter payer control on prescribing and reimbursement; this will limit price growth. • Implementation of patent legislation in November 2000; copy products will retain substantial market shares for several years.
Brazil	• Tight fiscal policies will continue to limit public health funds; broader access to basic health care will require cost containment, targeting pharmaceutical prices. • The government will continue to promote generic drugs; pro-generic policies will benefit copy products until more generics are available. • Pharmacy benefits will develop, following a return to growth in the private health insurance market. • Prices will remain subject to government control; price growth limited by tighter hospital formularies and cost containment policies by private payers.
Mexico	• No major increases in government health care spending; additional moves to encourage contracting of private services. • Pro-generic policies undermined by the activities of some copy product manufacturers; sales of generics to take off by 2005. • Some government price control will be retained; recent rapid price growth will not be sustained.

Source: IMS Health, Pharma Prognosis Latin America, *2001, pp. 11–12.*

Novartis, Aventis, and Johnson & Johnson have their regional headquarters there, and Pfizer has consolidated some of its production in Brazil. On the other hand, Mexico's NAFTA membership as well as its trade pact with Europe will give it significant advantage in the coming years.

The regulation of advertising and promotion in Latin America closely follows European policies. In Mexico, the advertising of prescription drugs is restricted to medical publications. Similar policies exist in Brazil and Argentina. However, these restrictions are countered, as in Europe, by direct-to-consumer communications on the Internet. Regulation in this area is still largely in the planning stage. In Brazil, the Ministry of Health proposed in early 2001 to introduce legislation on criteria for electronic pharmacies; these would need to obtain operating licenses from the ANVISA agency to meet minimum IT standards and to provide drug information to consumers. So far, virtual pharmacies have competed aggressively, offering discounts of 20% on brick-and-mortar retail prices, but their business models rely too much on advertising income from manufacturers, who by now have their own Web sites. In addition, the regional e-commerce constraints (i.e., poor infrastructure and logistical problems) apply to virtual pharmacies. These regulatory trends are summarized in Table 7.5.

Pricing.   Although cost containment is a worldwide factor in health care, drug pricing policies vary significantly throughout the region, with Mexico as the most benign location and Brazil as the most threatening environment for manufacturers. Governments are divided on issues such as pricing and patenting, since the ministries of health see broad access and low price as their main objective, while the ministries of finance or trade departments want to attract foreign investment and protect the profitability of domestic manufacturers. In Mexico, price controls are relatively relaxed, as most launch prices for new drugs are approved by the Department of Trade. First-in-class products tend to follow international prices, so as to limit "gray market" trade with the United States.

TABLE 7.5 Key Regulation Trends

	REGISTRATION	GMP[a]	OTHER ISSUES
Argentina	Fast and efficient for both original brands and copy products. Fast-track authorization for some lifesaving drugs.	Regulation based on 1992 WHO guidelines; introduction of GMP standards, but tighter policing required.	Tighter bioequivalence regulations to be enforced; like GMP, their impact will depend on levels of enforcement.
Brazil	Progress due to establishment of FDA-type agency (ANVS). New products given priority; backlog still a problem.	Larger local companies moving toward compliance; better policing expected under the new ANVS agency.	Lack of centers qualified to undertake bioequivalence studies has hampered generic entries; foreign studies now accepted.
Mexico	Acceptance of foreign trial data helped speed registration (now averages 6–8 months for new drugs).	Regulations in place but enforcement is lax; may be stepped up to support interchangeable generics.	Bioequivalent generics approved under 1998 legislation. Promotional activity policed strictly.

Source: IMS Health, Pharma Prognosis Latin America, *2001, p. 27.*
[a]*GMP = Good Manufacturing Practices.*

By contrast, Brazil has seen two waves of price freezing, in 2000 and from February 2001 to year end. This was interpreted as a prelude to the reintroduction of price controls, which were liberalized in the early 1990s. An aggressive cost-containment effort under health minister José Serra included a cut in federal taxes on many chronic disease therapies, with a demand by the government that reductions be reflected in retail prices. In the public system, chronic disease drugs are free of charge, and since over half of the drug budget is devoted to the AIDS program, HIV drugs have become a recent cost target. Cost-saving measures include the accelerated production of antiretrovirals at state-owned laboratories, with the ultimate objective to fulfill up to 75% of domestic demand. This concerns the first generation of HIV drugs, such as AZT (now genericized worldwide), which were never patent-protected in Brazil.

In addition, a major effort to encourage generics led to approval for over 300 generic drugs by July 2001, only 16 months after the 1999 new generic law. Generics were expected to account for 10% of the market by 2002, and possibly 30% by 2004. Novartis invested in a dedicated plant and intends to launch over 100 generics in Brazil in the next two years. Local companies such as Cristalia are also investing in generic production and entering joint ventures; Biosintética and Israel's Teva have set up a joint venture to distribute generics supplied by Teva. The lack of local facilities to perform bioequivalence studies is alleviated by two strategies: the acceptance of foreign bioequivalence studies and—more problematic—the sourcing of generics from markets with loose criteria, such as India. Indian producers, including Ranbaxy, are making significant investments in this area.

Similarly, Mexico introduced in 1998 a new "interchangeable" (bioequivalent) generic category, for which pharmacy substitution is allowed. However, generics still account for less than 1% of market value and less than 3% in Argentina and Brazil. In the latter (the largest generic market), sales are just over $100 million. While the Brazilian government is pressuring public-sector physicians to prescribe generically, and Mexico is following suit, the private sector is still largely immune. Mexico abandoned its planned generic prescribing requirements for private physicians and replaced it with an "encouragement" policy.

In Argentina, economic problems and government efforts are also affecting prices negatively, but the market situation is quite different, as generics face strong competition from local copy products. These had a market share of over 44% in 2000 versus shares of 22% and 28%, respectively, in Mexico and Brazil. Mexico's low share pertains to NAFTA's patent protection clauses. By contrast, the Argentinean market is led by local copy producers such as Roemmers, who wield considerable lobbying power and were instrumental in delaying the enactment of an intellectual property law.

An additional problem is specific to the region: under-the-counter drug dispensing, that is, pharmacy sales of ethical drugs without prescriptions. Given that consumers tend to be brand-loyal and conservative, this militates against a rapid spread of generics and pharmacy substitution. The two key issues in the region from the viewpoint of multinationals remain pricing and especially, patent protection.

Patent Protection. Intellectual property (IP) is a key negative differentiator between Latin America and some other emerging markets, and it has far-ranging implications. Historically, the lack of it has stymied both foreign investment and domestic innovation, and current conditions are still suboptimal and highly uneven. A key part of the 1994 World Trade Organization (WTO) agreement on trade was trade-related intellectual property provisions (TRIPS), which gave emerging markets a five-year period to establish regulations. Two years after the January 2000 deadline, most of Latin America is still not fully compliant, and the countries closest to it will gain a competitive advantage.

Due to its NAFTA membership, Mexico has the most favorable IP environment, with patent legislation that actually exceeds TRIPS and with GMP requirements, although the latter are not fully implemented. An important feature is a ban on compulsory licensing (i.e., the obligation for foreign patent holders to license production to local companies for lifesaving drugs in situations of "national emergency"). Brazil passed a good patent law in 1996, with a 20-year patent life, pipeline protection, and basic protection for biotechnology, as well as a ban on parallel imports. The law's clause on local production within three years led to a WTO case by the United States against Brazil, which has since been dropped. Its compulsory licensing provision presents a much greater problem and has been used as a threat by health minister Serra to obtain lower prices on HIV drugs.

The most problematic market remains Argentina. It finally passed a patent law in 2000, but the prior lack of protection was estimated to cost U.S. manufacturers about $500 million a year in revenues lost to copy products. This situation comes from the unique strength of local copy manufacturers, which hold commanding market shares. The variance between major markets can be summarized as follows for 2000:[8]

	COPY PRODUCTS (% OF TOTAL)	GENERICS (% OF TOTAL)
Argentina	44.1	2.3
Brazil	27.5	2.8
Mexico	21.5	0.1

Although copying is trending downward as a result of tighter IP protection, it is expected to remain a significant factor in Argentina for several years. In Brazil, generics are expected to play an increasing role due to the government's strongly proactive stance. According to the domestic producer association Alanac, generics already had a 5% market share by mid-2001 and were projected to double it by year end 2002.[9] However, 50% of those were imported from companies in Israel (Teva), Canada (Apotex), India, Portugal, and Germany.

Although about 160 pharmaceutical companies are now operating in Brazil, only 25 are generic producers (16 of which are domestic). However, the 1999 law includes promotion and development measures: The National Bank for Economic and Social Development (BNDES) is to provide financing to generic producers and distributors, and pharmacists must display information on generic products. Generics are priced, on average, at a 40% discount and have started to erode some competitive categories. Antihypertensive sales include up to 50% of generics, and these are also present in the antibiotic and antiulcer categories.[10] A summary of patent and pricing issues is provided in Table 7.6.

THE HIV DRUGS DEBATE

The intellectual property area has seen its sharpest dispute in the area of HIV drugs, with the widely publicized lawsuit brought by 39 pharmaceutical companies against the South African government—then dropped due to public pressure. The dilemma of providing broad access to lifesaving drugs (while respecting a patent system that offsets the $800 million development cost of a new drug) goes well beyond Latin America. When the WTO's 142 members agreed in November 2001 to launch a new round of trade talks, they issued a declaration that IP rules should not block poor

TABLE 7.6 Key Patent and Pricing Issues

COUNTRY	KEY PATENT ISSUES	KEY PRICING ISSUES
Argentina	• Applications for 20-year product patents (calculated from date of filing) considered from November 2000 under 1996 law • New law fails to comply with several TRIPS requirements: lack of pipeline protection, compulsory licensing provisions, and failure to protect biotech products • Legislation subject to U.S. complaint at WTO level	• Direct controls lifted by early 1900s • Recent price growth curbed by low patient purchasing power and government/industry risk-sharing agreement • Tighter price control under new risk-sharing agreement in 2000 • Market forces (competition, patient ability to pay, and stronger insurance sector) plus threat of reregulation will limit price growth
Brazil	• 1996 law provides 20 years of protection for pharmaceutical products, pipeline protection, basic protection for biotechnology and a ban on parallel imports • Local manufacturing requirements contravene TRIPS; WTO case against Brazil by the U.S., dropped in 2001 • Possible compulsory licensing provision also a threat to multinationals • National patent office (INPI) is underresourced and faces a backlog of pending patent applications	• Controls lifted in 1992, but prices frozen in second half of 2000 following recent rapid increases • Negotiations by Ministry of Health led to forced decrease in price of patented HIV drugs
Mexico	• 1994 patent law provides 20 years of protection from filing for both products and processes; pipeline protection also recognized, and compulsory licenses outlawed; patent holders entering comarketing agreements with local companies gain an additional three years of protection • Data protection remains an issue; some copies authorized by Ministry of Health without patent verification	• Controls relaxed significantly; proposed launch prices for new drugs seldom refused • Prices generally accepted by department of trade if do not exceed prices in major markets (e.g., U.S.) • Broader use of pharmacoeconomic data by companies for new products

Source: IMS Health, Pharma Prognosis Latin America, 2001, pp. 30–31.

countries from access to lifesaving drugs. Although not legally binding, it signals a possible future change in public policy.[11]

Minister Serra placed Brazil at the forefront of this debate. The October 6, 1999 Presidential Decree on the implementation of Article 71 of Brazil's IP law allowed compulsory licensing in national emergencies. The government announced in September 2000 that it would enforce this decree if it were unable to produce 80% of its required AIDS drugs by 2002.[12] Due partly to the strength of the consumer AIDS lobby, HIV drugs hold a very high share of Brazil's government expenditures. By 1999, AIDS and STD drugs amounted to 46% of the federal drug budget.[13] HIV drugs alone accounted for about one-third, as approximately 100,000 Brazilians now have the condition.

The government's aggressive policy of free distribution of antiretrovirals has been a medical success, halving AIDS mortality in 1996–1999 and saving about $400 million in hospital costs in that period. But Brazil falls short on prevention and education, since incidence (number of new patients) is still over 2,000 per month and the distribution program costs over $400 million per year. Consequently, the Health Ministry announced in November 2,000 that unless multinationals slashed their HIV drug prices, Brazil would start manufacturing them, including those under patent. By early 2001, state laboratories were already producing eight of the 12 off-patent drugs. In February 2001, Minister Serra announced that if prices were not lowered, he would override the patents of two drugs (efavirenz, branded as DuPont's Sustiva and Merck's Stocrin, and nelfinavir, distributed by Roche as Viracept), since these accounted for 36% of the $305 million federal HIV drug budget. Multinationals first threatened to suspend investment in Brazil if it broke patents, then they negotiated. Merck agreed in April 2001 to cut the prices of Crixivan and Sustiva/Stocrin by almost two-thirds in exchange for continued patent protection (representing savings of $39 million annually), and Roche also negotiated on Viracept.[14]

IMPACT ON INNOVATION

Although Brazil's AIDS policies have been strongly supported by NGOs (nongovernmental organizations), including Doctors Without Borders and Oxfam, they are not without risk. A major weakness of the region is its innovation lag, and any retreat from patent protection will not only shift away foreign investment but also prevent domestic companies from increasing their own R&D. Should Brazil institute a steady policy of forced price cuts and IP threats, it will only increase Mexico's attractiveness as an alternative investment site. In a May 2001 report entitled "Drug Companies vs. Brazil: The Threat to Public Health," Oxfam advocates price controls and compulsory licensing as the key to improved access for all essential medicines, and most other NGOs take similar positions.[15] However, inadequate drug access in emerging markets involves many factors beyond pricing, including inadequate education and prevention, poor distribution systems, and corruption.

A 2000 study by Michael Porter and Scott Stern for the National Bureau of Economic Research placed not only Latin America but also Spain at the bottom of worldwide innovative capacity. The study stressed the importance of factors such as government policies, workforce quality, aggregate R&D expenditures, openness to international competition, spending on higher education, and IP protection. It chose as a measure of innovation output the number of U.S. patents granted to inventors from a country, expressed on a per capita basis to control for country size; U.S. patenting was chosen because it signaled the innovation's economic potential (given the costs involved) and its world-class technological level. By that measure, Spain was consistently last among OECD countries during the 1975–1996 period. The top innovation tier was Japan, the United States, and Switzerland; a second tier was led by Sweden, Finland, and Germany. Since the mid-1980s, Finland and other Scandinavian countries have increased their scientific workforce, raised R&D investment, opened their markets to competition, and provided strong IP protection.[16] While Sweden led OECD countries with a 1999 R&D spending of almost 4% of GDP (versus a 2.2% OECD average), Spain was in the lowest tier with less than 1% of GDP.[17]

A related factor is the structure of research. Silicon Valley–type innovation clusters in the United States and northern Europe closely link local universities, startups, and venture capital firms. By contrast, in the Latin world, universities have historically been isolated from the private sector; in addition, Latin American markets were for decades closed to outside competition, IP protection was weak to nil, and venture capital was unavailable. A worrisome trend is the further erosion of Latin America's innovative competitiveness in the last decade. In the late 1970s, Mexico and the South Cone were on a par with Taiwan in terms of their U.S. patents. By the late 1990s, Taiwanese and South Korean patents dwarfed those from Brazil and Mexico—almost 16,000 patents from Taiwan versus less than 500 for Brazil and Mexico (see Table 7.7).

TABLE 7.7 Latin American Innovation

Innovative Performance: Latin America Versus Asia

	1976–1980[a]	1995–1999[a]	GROWTH RATE
Emerging Latin American economies			
Argentina	115	228	0.98
Brazil	136	494	2.62
Chile	12	60	4.00
Costa Rica	22	48	1.18
Mexico	124	431	2.48
Emerging Asian economies			
China	3	557	191.33
Hong Kong	176	1,694	8.63
Singapore	17	725	41.65
South Korea	23	12,062	523.43
Taiwan	135	15,871	116.56

Some Factors of National Innovation, 1998[b]

	FULL-TIME EQUIVALENT R&D WORKERS PER MILLION POPULATION	R&D EXPENDITURE ($ MILLIONS) PER MILLION POPULATION	STRENGTH OF INTELLECTUAL PROPERTY PROTECTION[c]	OPENNESS TO INTERNATIONAL COMPETITION AND TRADE[d]
Argentina	1,212.2	32.8	4.7	8.5
Brazil	433.7	35.3	3.3	5.4
Chile	639.2	32.0	6.1	8.8
Colombia	—	9.0	5.0	5.0
Costa Rica	557.0	32.2	6.0	6.0
Mexico	365.3	15.2	6.1	7.9

Source: Michael Porter and Scott Stern, "Innovation: Location Matters," MIT/Sloan Management Review, Summer 2001, p. 33. By permission of the publisher. © 2001 by Massachusetts Institute of Technology. All rights reserved.

[a]*Total number of U.S. patents in each country during each five-year period.*
[b]*Calculations are based on data from the Ibero American Network of Science and Technology Indicators, 2000, and the World Competitiveness Yearbook (Lausanne, Switzerland: IMD, 1998).*
[c]*Ranking is based on a 1 to 10 scale, where 1 = weakest and 10 = strongest.*
[d]*Ranking is based on a 1 to 10 scale, where 1 = least open and 10 = most open.*

Paradoxically, innovation leadership in Latin America may come from outside the major countries: namely, from Costa Rica, Uruguay, Chile, and Cuba. The Costa Rican government, in partnership with companies such as Hewlett-Packard, is spurring the development of an information technology cluster. Uruguay has a growing software cluster, and Chile, besides being a global trader and the most open country in the region, is gradually shifting its export portfolio from commodities like copper to technology products and services.

The region's only well-developed biotech industry is located in Cuba, where it has benefited from four decades of government priority funding, a world-class scientific labor force, and a long tradition of medical research. The National Center for Scientific Investigation, established in 1961, has set up a network of 53 public biotech research facilities, which has drawn up to $1 billion of foreign investment in the last decade—in an economy estimated at less than $20 billion.[18] Cuba's discovery heritage goes back to medical pioneer Dr. Carlos Finlay, who is said to have first traced yellow fever to its mosquito vector in 1881. Present institutes have produced over 160 new products with an estimated sales revenue of $100 to $200 million annually; these are undercommercialized, due to the relative lack of international marketing partnerships. The portfolio includes products for local consumption, such as a dengue fever vaccine spurred by a 1980s epidemic in Cuba, but also several products with global market potential in areas such as vaccines (recombinant hepatitis B and meningitis B vaccines), thrombolytics (recombinant streptokinase), and oncology (range of monoclonal antibodies that could be developed as anticancer vaccines, especially those targeting epidermal growth factor).

A product already exported by Laboratorios Dalmer to Europe and across Latin America is PPG (Policosanol), a sugar cane–derived oral therapy approved as a reducer of both cholesterol and atherogenic lipoproteins; a frequent side effect is heightened libido, which is well known in Latin America and undoubtedly helps sales. On the services side, Cuba is also unique in the region for its "medical tourism" sector. Its top-tier physicians are world class and have unique expertise in areas such as vascular surgery and ophthalmology, and draw medical tourists, who constitute the most upscale tier of its 1 million annual visitors.

Since Cuba has no IP infrastructure and little marketing experience, commercialization has started through joint ventures. Major partnerships were set up with Canada's York Medical and SmithKline Beecham (now GlaxoSmithKline). York set up joint ventures with five research institutes and invested in clinical trials leading to four anticancer molecules, all monoclonal antibodies. In 1999, the U.S. Treasury allowed a SmithKline joint venture with the Finlay Institute, leading to the licensing of Finlay's recombinant meningitis B vaccine, against initial payments in food and medicines and post-launch cash royalties. It is patented in 17 countries and sold in 10 Latin American markets, including Argentina and Brazil. Multiyear trials are needed before launch in the United States and Europe, but the vaccine is expected to be available in the United States by 2005.

In the rest of Latin America, local copy companies have weak R&D, and foreign investment has been blocked by the lack of IP protection. In Brazil, total R&D spending by multinationals remains below $100 million. However, the government is providing some financial support for biomedical research, and the largest local companies are beginning to invest. Aché has formed a joint venture with Merck, and Biosintética is spending R5 million on university alliances.

Clinical trials are now conducted in Brazil by companies such as Aventis, Novartis, Pfizer, and Roche, but these are most often phase III trials. Increased investment will be linked to the implementation of GCP (Good Clinical Practices) standards at more trial centers.[19] Given the region's massive innovation lag, any significant progress is likely to come from acquisitions and alliances initiated by foreign multinationals, and this will not take place unless governments commit to patent protection in major markets, especially in Brazil.

PHARMACEUTICAL MARKETS: SCOPE AND GROWTH

While the health services sector, in the United States as well as in Latin America, has remained largely local (with the exception of some cross-border HMO investment), the manufacturing sector has been global for decades. In Latin America, however, investment patterns have been volatile. In the "lost decade" of the 1980s, most U.S. companies and a few European firms left the region, including Merck, Lilly, Searle, and Astra. They have now returned, often via acquisitions, and are rebuilding a presence in the region.

REGIONAL TRENDS

Latin American markets are still limited in value, if not in volume. The top seven markets totaled over $20 billion in sales in 2000 versus global sales of $221 billion, including $96 billion in the

TOTAL PHARMACEUTICAL MARKET SIZES AT ACTUAL PRICES (2000–2005) ($ MILLIONS)[a]

COUNTRY	2000[b]	2005	2000–2005 CAGR	PER CAPITA SALES AT ACTUAL PRICES ($)[b] 2000
Argentina	3,756	4,523	3.8%	101.8
Brazil	6,726	8,427	4.6%	38.9
Chile	697	852	4.1%	45.9
Colombia	1,296	1,717	5.8%	32.6
Mexico	6,041	11,081	12.9%	60.2
Peru	380	531	6.9%	14.1
Venezuela	1,472	2,492	11.1%	62.4
7 countries	20,368	29,623	7.8%	50.8

[a]At ex-manufacturer's prices.
[b]Forecast values.

Market Shares by Country, 2000

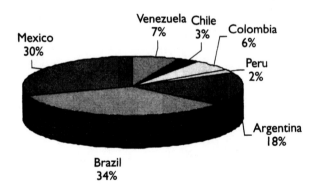

FIGURE 7.3
Pharmaceutical Markets, Latin America
Source: IMS Health, *Pharma Prognosis Latin America,* 2001, pp. 15–17.

United States, $52 billion in Japan, and $51 billion in the top five European markets. This makes Latin America the fourth-largest region worldwide. A distinction should be made between unit volume, which is almost at parity between Latin America and the United States, and dollar sales, which are affected by lower prices in Latin markets.

The top seven markets were projected to grow at a 7.8% compound rate in the 2000–2005 period (an improvement over the 5.6% rate of the 1995–2000 period). By comparison, U.S. sales grew by 14% in 1999–2000, the European top five markets by 8%, and Japan by

4%. Growth is highly variable among the top three markets (Argentina, Brazil, and Mexico), which account for 76% of the region. Mexico is projected to be the most dynamic by far, with a compound average growth of almost 13% in the 2000–2005 period versus less than 5% in Brazil and only 3.8% in Argentina (see Figure 7.3).

While price growth will be severely constrained by government actions and low consumer purchasing power, volume growth is only expected to rise slightly (in a 0 to 3% range) in most markets in the next five years. Drivers and constraints of volume growth may be summarized as follows:[20]

Drivers

- Favorable demographics (aging population + young people coming into the workforce)
- Government actions to broaden health coverage
- Growth of generics, increasing market penetration

Constraints

- Purchasing power of most of population expected to remain low
- Tighter controls on prescribing in public sector and prescription monitoring in private sector
- Self-medication to remain high in most markets

The main driver of price growth will be new product launches, especially those of breakthrough drugs, but a key factor of uncertainty will be the Brazilian government's stance on HIV drug price cuts and a possible extension of these to all essential drugs. Therapeutic class sales show the gradual convergence of the region with the therapeutic profile of developed markets. In 2000, the three leading categories for the top seven markets were gastrointestinal/metabolism, central nervous system, and cardiovascular, reflecting the chronic disease pattern of OECD countries. Systemic anti-infectives came only in fourth position regionally.

The best growth is projected to come from musculoskeletal and cardiovascular drugs, reflecting the aging of populations in major markets and the availability of new drugs (the cox-2 inhibitors Vioxx and Celebrex and the anti-TNF Enbrel and Remicade in the musculoskeletal area). Cardiovascular dollar sales will be limited by the growth of generics in Brazil and Mexico, but spurred by broader use of lipid reducers and angiotensin II blockers (see Table 7.8). The evolution of the main markets largely reflects their macroeconomic environments, with Mexico in the lead and Argentina in the most difficult position.

TABLE 7.8 Therapeutic Class Profile: Retail Sales Forecast, 2000–2005 (Millions of Dollars)

Anatomical Classification	2000 SALES	2000 % SHARE	2005 SALES	2005 % SHARE	CAGR (±%), 2000–2005
A Alimentary tract and metabolism	2,915	17.7	3,960	17.1	6.3
C Cardiovascular system	2,045	12.4	3,050	13.2	8.3
D Dermatologicals	1,121	6.8	1,524	6.6	6.3
G Genitourinary system/sex hormones	1,404	8.5	2,017	8.7	7.5
J Systemic anti-infectives	2,018	12.3	2,225	9.6	2.0
M Musculoskeletal system	1,317	8.0	2,003	8.7	8.8
N Central nervous system	2,144	13.0	3,122	13.5	7.8
R Respiratory system	1,669	10.1	2,404	10.4	7.6
All others	1,810	11.0	2,788	12.1	9.0
Total	16,443	100	23,093	4.9	7.0

Country	Year	A	C	D	G	J	M	N	R
Argentina	Sales, 2000	611	563	214	259	349	269	517	266
	Sales, 2005	703	765	250	320	341	345	657	320
	CAGR (%)	2.8	6.3	3.1	4.3	-0.5	5.1	4.9	3.8
Brazil	Sales, 2000	856	768	389	555	451	436	716	529
	Sales, 2005	1,040	1,027	481	715	338	578	949	663
	CAGR (%)	4.0	6.0	4.3	5.2	-5.6	5.8	5.8	4.6
Mexico	Sales, 2000	919	389	297	341	851	365	569	545
	Sales, 2005	1,463	724	480	610	1,138	683	1,000	927
	CAGR (%)	9.7	13.2	10.1	12.4	6.0	13.4	11.9	11.2

Source: IMS Health, Pharma Prognosis Latin America, 2001, pp. 48, 55.

MEXICO: MOST DYNAMIC MARKET

Mexican sales are projected to grow from $6 billion to $11 billion in the 2000–2005 period; by that time, it would account for 37% of total Latin American sales and overtake Brazil as the region's top market.[21] The financial crisis caused by the peso devaluation depressed demand in the late 1990s, and its rebound is expected to drive sales—assuming, however, a relatively mild and brief recession in the United States, given the dependence of Mexico on the U.S. economy. This forecast is also heavily dependent on continued double-digit price growth. On a per capita basis, IMS projections are for a jump of $60 in annual sales in 2000 to $103 in 2005 in Mexico, versus $39 to $47 in Brazil and $102 to $116 in Argentina. This represents a compound annual growth rate of over 11% for Mexico, versus only 3 to 4% for the two other markets.[22] This may be affected by government actions in other countries, especially Brazil. In 2001, Merck agreed to cut the price of its antiretrovirals (Crixivan and Stocrin) by 80% in Mexico. This is likely to set a precedent for further cuts in the future. A counterbalancing factor will be an income increase for the large younger population segment—also applicable to Brazil. In addition, the planned removal of the last remaining trade barriers in the NAFTA bloc by 2005 should boost trade further and have a positive impact on the economy. Generics are also meeting more resistance than in Brazil. A 1997 Health Ministry effort to introduce compulsory generic prescribing was defeated by joint action by physicians and research-based companies.[23]

OTC (over-the-counter) drug sales, which had slowed recently due to lower patient purchasing power, are expected to grow to a 25% market share by 2005. This would slow overall price growth, since OTCs have lower margins than ethical drugs, but it would allow companies to maintain brand equity by switching their prescription products (especially in areas such as respiratory and dermatologicals) to OTC status. The bulk of drug sales is through retail pharmacies, which accounted for 81% of the market in 2000 and are projected to hold steady in the next five years. Consolidation is likely to continue in this sector, as independent pharmacies face competition from chains and nonpharmacy outlets.[24]

BRAZIL: TRANSITIONAL STAGE

Brazil is a transitional market in several ways: Its demographics are between Argentina's Europe-like profile and Mexico's younger population, and its patent situation and market growth are also intermediary. It registered three straight years of decline in dollar sales in 1998–2000, due to its economic difficulties in the period. The government has a highly conflicted approach to pricing. The Health Ministry's commitment to price cuts for HIV drugs is offset by its trade counterpart. In March 2001, Secex, the foreign trade secretariat, imposed a 76% antidumping duty on Novo Nordisk for importing low-price insulin from Denmark. Concurrently, local producer Biobrás brought a case against Lilly and obliged it to agree to a minimum price on its Humalog insulin, which would result in a $3 million cost increase for free insulin distribution by the Health Ministry. The 1996 patent law did result in an additional $2 billion in foreign investment, including Glaxo's $200 million plant in Rio de Janeiro, in operation since 1998, but investment flows may shift toward Mexico if government threats persist.[25]

In addition to a probable strong growth in generics, OTC products are projected to grow, partly due to pan-regional coordination. In March 2001, the Latin American self-medication industry (ILAR) was set up with a charter to harmonize registration, switching, labeling, and advertising and to promote self-medication.

ARGENTINA: ECONOMIC CONSTRAINTS

IMS projections for the Argentinean market are for a growth of $3.7 billion to $4.5 billion in the 2000–2005 period; this is related to projected price increases, since volume growth is expected to be negative in this period. Given the deep economic turmoil, later forecasts will trend sharply downward. Argentina is unique among the top markets in several ways, from the availability of drug reimbursement to the commanding presence of copy companies and a manufacturer-controlled distribution system. Firms have countered wholesalers and cut distribution costs by about 20% by setting up their own channels, which now process an estimated 65% of pharmaceuticals. Leading distributors include such companies as Rofina (owned by local producer Roemmers but not linked to it exclusively), Disprofarma (partly owned by local firm Bagó), and Farmanet (linked to Aventis, Novartis, and Boehringer Ingelheim).

Company Strategies. In this difficult environment, multinationals have to balance pan-regional efficiencies and local responsiveness. They are now consolidating around two manufacturing and sales platforms: Brazil and Mexico. Foreign companies are strongest by far in Mexico, where they account for nearly 90% of production. Unlike the trend in the rest of the region, multinationals stayed in Mexico through the 1970s and 1980s, despite import restrictions and price controls. Brazil, by contrast, has strong local producers, and the largest, Aché, is the only local company among the top 10 in the region by sales. In total, however, local producers hold only about one-fifth of the market. In Argentina, the situation is reversed, with a dominance of local producers—all grew historically by manufacturing copies of foreign original brands. The same pattern applies to Chile and Uruguay. The Argentina market is fragmented; the lead player is local producer Roemmers, but it had only an 8% market share in 2000. Weak local innovation greatly limits strategic options. Specialists such as Incyte and other technology companies, and shapers such as Celera Genomics, creating and dominating a value chain segment (in this case, genomics research), do not have Latin American equivalents. Multinationals such as Bristol-Myers Squibb and Novartis are dominant as global integrators and have built or rebuilt their presence with acquisitions of local companies. Some of the locals are attempting to become regional players through alliances, but they are all facing increasing pressure.

TRANSFORMATION OF LOCAL FIRMS

All local producers, especially copy companies losing government protection, face a need to transform themselves. They are accomplishing this in different country-specific ways. The Argentinean companies have strong sales forces and physician relationships and some, like Gador, are well focused on a few therapeutic areas. They are therefore attractive as alliance partners, and Bagó has recently entered with Pfizer into a co-marketing agreement for Viagra and other drugs which includes a commitment not to produce copy products in this area.[26]

Although copy products are expected to retain a strong market share for several years, all producers are attempting to diversify. Consolidation has also started with Roemmers acquiring a 45% stake in Gador in 1999, after two smaller equity deals with other local producers.[27] In Brazil, the top-tier local producers have gone further toward true discovery. The four top locals, Aché, Eurofarma, Biosintética, and Farmasa, have a combined estimated market share of only 9%, one-fourth of which is in the low-margin public sector. Major transformation paths include more original R&D, expansion into generics, and exports. EMS and Teuto are taking advantage of the generics law to develop a generic portfolio of over 200 products. In research, Biosintética is sourcing R&D from local universities, and Extracta has entered into a research partnership funded by $3 million from GlaxoSmithKline to develop a compound database.

Product acquisition may also be promising, as multinationals may want to divest mature off-patent brands.[28]

In Mexico, local players are led by Sanfer, Senosian, and Laboratorios Columbia. Some of these have already developed export sales; Fermic, a producer of bulk antibiotics, now exports 85% of its products, versus only 5% before 1990. Similarly, Liomont plans to export OTC products to the United States and Europe, to increase its export revenues from 2% to 20% of total within three years. As in Brazil, some locals are developing original research as well as expanding exports. Columbia has purchased companies in Argentina and Spain, and has grown its sales from less than $5 million in 1987 to nearly $200 million in 2000, with about half of its revenues from outside Mexico. It has also formed research partnerships, including an agreement with Romark in the United States; Columbia bought a 5% stake in Romark against marketing rights in the European Union and the Americas for its antibacterial nitazoxanide (NTZ) in the peptic ulcer category. Given competitive pressures on local producers in all markets, acquisitions and alliances are expected to continue.

MULTINATIONAL FIRMS: COMPETITIVE POSITIONS

New linkages have been equally attractive to local companies and to multinationals in recent years, as foreign companies are regaining the ground lost when many left the region in the 1980s. Because, unlike many U.S. firms, Europeans tended to stay during this "lost decade," they still dominate the market. Aventis, Roche, and Novartis hold the top three positions, and Boehringer Ingelheim and Glaxo are also ranked among the top 10. Like the domestic industry, the multinational sector is fragmented, with the top player, Aventis, holding only a 5% share of the top seven markets. The best and steadiest growth in the 1995–2000 period, however, is Pfizer's, with a 9.2% compound growth rate. As in the rest of the world, growth is driven by launches of breakthrough products, and Pfizer's strong performance in 2000–2001 was due partly to Viagra (with 2001 estimated regional sales of $100 million) and to its co-marketing of Pharmacia's cox-2 inhibitor, Celebrex. On the other hand, Roche suffered from the volatility of its antiobesity drug, Xenical (orlistat). Regional sales of Xenical fell sharply in 2000—demonstrating the unpredictability of lifestyle drugs in difficult economic times.[29] Table 7.9 illustrates the leading companies' current rankings.

ACQUISITIONS AND ALLIANCES

Major companies are combining direct investment and alliances. Pfizer recently made a significant investment in its São Paulo plant which supplies Viagra to the region, but also entered into a co-marketing alliance in Argentina. Acquisitions took off in the 1990s in all three major markets, and involve European as well as U.S. players. In Argentina, Bristol-Myers Squibb purchased Argentia for $150 million in the mid-1990s and Searle bought Sintyal; Sanofi also bought Gramon, but Roemmers rejected approaches by Roche and others.

Some multinationals are banking on the incipient generics market with acquisitions in this area. Novartis, through its generic arm, purchased Argentinean firm Labinca in early 2001 and will add some of its products to Labinca's $50 million line. U.S.-based Ivax has also made several generic acquisitions, including Mexico's Laboratorios Fustery in 2001, thus acquiring a $90 million line and manufacturing facilities. Ivax also bought Laboratorio Chile in 2001 for $395 million in cash. It is Chile's largest producer of branded and generic drugs in the respiratory, cardiovascular, neurological, and gynecological areas. It had 2000 sales of over $173 million and also holds a significant market share in Argentina and Peru. With subsidiaries in Argentina, Uruguay, Peru, and Venezuela as well as Chile and Mexico, Ivax is seeking a dominant presence in the region.

Biotech companies are also starting to expand in the region. In Brazil, Genzyme acquired in June 2001 the privately held Lisfarma

TABLE 7.9 Leading Pharmaceutical Companies in Latin America

CORPORATION	SALES[a] ($ MILLIONS)	MARKET SHARE (%)	% CHANGE, 1999–2000
Aventis	865	5.4	2.8
Roche	857	5.3	3.2
Novartis	779	4.8	5.0
Bristol-Myers Squibb	667	4.1	−2.8
Pfizer	635	3.9	6.2
American Home Products	557	3.5	3.9
Aché Labs	550	3.4	−4.1
Boehringer Ingelheim	550	3.4	5.3
Pharmacia Corp.	503	3.1	14.3
Glaxo Wellcome	430	2.7	6.2

Source: IMS Health, Pharma Prognosis Latin America, 2001, p. 23; sales in top seven markets: Mexico, Brazil, Argentina, Venezuela, Colombia, Chile, Peru; MAT, Sept. 2000.
[a]Retail market sales at ex-manufacturer prices.

for $1.1 million, thus gaining all of Lisfarma's licenses to sell, import, and register drugs. This was expected to reduce approval time by two years for Renagel, a phosphate binder for patients on dialysis for end-state renal disease; Brazil is the world's fourth-largest market for the drug.[30]

Spanish acquisitions in Latin America have not been as prevalent as in other sectors, such as financial services, but this is due to the fact that pharmaceuticals are not a key industry in Spain. However, some activity is starting. Esteve (via its Mexican subsidiary Sintenovo) bought GlaxoSmithKline plant in Mexico for $2.6 million as part of a rationalization following the merger of Glaxo and SmithKline. Esteve plans to invest an additional $2 to $3 million to modernize the plant, which already meets FDA standards.[31]

PAN-REGIONAL VERSUS LOCALIZED APPROACHES

In manufacturing as well as marketing, a key decision for all multinationals operating in Latin America is where to stand on the centralization–localization spectrum. Manufacturing has been significantly consolidated after the onset of NAFTA and Mercosur, and most firms are prioritizing production capacity in Brazil, Mexico, or in both. Several companies are also supplying a product category from a single regional platform; for instance, Roche sources its effervescent products from Argentina and vitamins from Mexico. Although most companies have their regional headquarters in Mexico, as does Bristol-Myers Squibb, or Brazil, as is the case for Novartis, some firms run their Latin American operations from Miami (AstraZeneca) or another U.S. location (Merck and Pfizer).

Merck only recently bought back licenses to distribute its own products in Brazil, Argentina, and Colombia, and centralizes much of worldwide production outside the region in Puerto Rico. Some manufacturing takes place in Mexico, Brazil, and other countries, but many products remain imported. AstraZeneca's regional headquarters, by contrast, is in Miami; its production facilities in Brazil, Mexico, and Argentina are largely limited to packaging imports, but AstraZeneca is planning broader local production in Mexico and one Mercosur country, which would lead to closure of other sites. It also intends to develop its clinical trials activity in the region, since patient recruitment is faster than in Europe, populations are large, and practitioner quality reaches OECD levels.[32]

In marketing, multinationals tend to retain hybrid strategies due to the region's diversity. New megabrands such as Lipitor and Viagra are launched on a pan-regional basis, which fits within an overall objective of global positioning consistency. These, however, still have to coexist with strong local franchises built over decades in formerly closed markets. In 2000, the top 10 products still differed considerably in key markets. In Argentina, five of the top 10 products were local copies, and only two (Lipitor and Bayer Aspirin) were global brands. Brazil's top 10 also included brands specific to the region, such as Aventis's Novalgina, whose active ingredient is actually banned in Europe and the United States; global brands were more dominant than in Argentina (Viagra, Keflex, Tylenol, Capoten), but the third-largest product was Novartis's Voltaren, a very mature brand that demonstrates the conservative nature of both physicians and patients in the region. In Mexico, all top 10 products were those of multinational companies, but also with a coexistence of new products (Xenical, Viagra) and very mature brands (SmithKline's Amoxil).

An almost complete lack of overlap demonstrates the region's diverse product preferences: Only two products (Viagra and Voltaren) were in the top 10 in two markets, and none appeared in all three. Although these variances are expected to decrease in the future, particularly with the harmonizing role played by the Internet, companies will continue to face a difficult choice between centralization (at the risk of killing lucrative local "cash cows") and localization (with related duplication and other costs). Table 7.10 illustrates this mixed pattern.

INTERNET STRATEGIES

In health care, Internet strategies include additional categories versus those of other sectors. In addition to the familiar B2C (business-to-consumer) and B2B (business-to-business) subsectors, manufacturers, payers, and providers also engage in B2P (business-to-physician). This includes e-detailing, e-prescribing, and e-sampling (electronic drug sales, prescriptions, and product samples) and payer–provider connectivity (claims processing and other transactions). An increasingly important additional subsector is C2C (consumer-to-consumer), as patients form their own advocacy networks. In critical therapeutic areas, these are highly influential, both online and off-line. The approval of HIV drugs was accelerated by the lobbying of advocacy groups not only in the United States and Europe but also in Brazil. The same pattern applies in oncology, as drugs such as Herceptin (for metastatic breast cancer) and Gleevec (for chronic myeloid leukemia) target highly defined genotype

TABLE 7.10 Company and Product Variance, 2000

	LEADING COMPANIES				LEADING PRODUCTS			
COUNTRY	CORPORATION	SALES[a] ($ MILLIONS)	% MARKET SHARE	PRODUCT	MANUFACTURER	SALES[a] ($ MILLIONS)	% MARKET SHARE
Argentina	Bagó	253.3	7.4	Lotrial	Roemmers	46.0	1.4
	Roemmers	248.8	7.3	Amoxidal	Roemmers	35.2	1.0
	Roche	180.9	5.3	Ibupirac	Pharmacia	31.3	0.9
	Novartis	132.9	3.9	Taural	Roemmers	22.4	0.7
	Pfizer	125.0	3.7	Sertal Cpto	Roemmers	21.7	0.6
	Pharmacia Corp.	123.0	3.6	Rivotril	Roche	20.0	0.6
	Aventis	113.0	3.3	Alplax	Gador	19.6	0.6
	Gador	100.6	3.0	Voltaren	Novartis	17.0	0.5
	Phoenix	95.6	2.8	Lipitor	Parke-Davis	16.8	0.5
	Chile	91.3	2.7	Bayaspirina	Bayer	16.3	0.5
Brazil	Aché Labs	549.7	10.7	Cataflam	Novartis	70.0	1.4
	Aventis	342.9	6.7	Tylenol	Janssen Cilag	44.4	0.9
	Novartis	337.8	6.6	Voltaren	Novartis	40.2	0.8
	Bristol-Myers Squibb	205.5	4.0	Keflex	Lilly	38.2	0.8

	Company			Product	Manufacturer		
	Roche	191.9	3.7	Lexotan	Roche	36.5	0.7
	American Home	181.3	3.5	Viagra	Pfizer	36.0	0.7
	Johnson & Johnson	170.6	3.3	Dorflex	Aventis	34.7	0.7
	Pfizer	161.4	3.2	Novalgina	Aventis	32.1	0.6
	Boehringer Ingelheim	154.5	3.0	Capoten	BMS	30.9	0.6
	Schering AG	129.8	2.5	Neosaldina	Knoll	30.1	0.6
Mexico	Roche	386.5	8.2	Pentrexyl	BMS	47.4	1.0
	Aventis	290.4	6.2	Neo-Melubrina	Aventis	36.7	0.8
	Bristol-Myers Squibb	287.9	6.1	Dolac	Roche	34.6	0.7
	Schering Plough	241.7	5.2	Tempra	Mead Johnson	31.6	0.7
	American Home	221.6	4.7	Dolo-Neurobion	Merck	27.8	0.6
	Boehringer Ingelheim	221.3	4.7	Amoxil	SKB	26.1	0.6
	Novartis	200.7	4.3	Xenical	Roche	25.6	0.6
	Pharmacia Corp.	187.9	4.0	Viagra	Pfizer	25.2	0.5
	Johnson & Johnson	179.3	3.8	Pharmaton	Boehringer Ingelheim	24.9	0.5
	Pfizer	175.2	3.7	Flanax	Roche	24.6	0.5

Source: IMS Health, Pharma Prognosis Latin America, 2001, p. 56.
*Retail sales at ex-manufacturer prices.

groups, which have global networks and were instrumental in speeding up approval. Gleevec's record FDA approval time of less than three months was in great part due to the influence of patient groups.

In Latin America, the trends prevalent across industry sectors also generally apply in health care: Bricks-and-clicks models are dominant and will probably prevail over "pure play" companies, startups are consolidating and being acquired, and the growth of e-commerce is hampered by an inadequate legal framework. As in other industries, B2B appears the most solid and promising area. Several vertical portals for trading hospital and medical equipment and supplies have been formed, including Brazilian-based Genexis and Connectmed (the latter also involved in payer–provider connectivity). As in the United States, consolidation is accelerating. Major companies are also using B2B and will probably overtake the independent portals in the coming years.[33] Pfizer deals with its key distributors in part via the Internet and also has three initiatives that target physicians. Promedicum.org, a medical reference portal covering 17 therapeutic areas in Spanish, Portuguese, and English, includes full text articles, databases, and links to clinical tools; its endorsement by 15 medical societies in Mexico and Central America supports Pfizer's commitment to medical education.

A pilot e-detailing program to promote Celebrex also allows better reach of nonurban physicians and offers round-the-clock information. Another Pfizer initiative is Sinpmp.com.br (Pfizer's Physician/Patient Integrated System), an online compliance tool for patients on chronic medications. It supports five products and ranges from reminders for drug refills and medical appointments to toll-free customer service, purchase discounts in affiliated pharmacies, and educational materials. It is meant to enhance physician–patient communications and improve compliance of chronic drugs.[34]

As in the United States, B2C portals have consolidated rapidly. Salud was acquired in August 2000 by U.S.-based Millennium Health, and Salutia merged with its competitor, Medicouno, in February 2000. Salutia, founded in 1999, has so far survived, in great part because it shifted its focus from B2C to payer–provider connectivity and because 90% of its current business is in Brazil, versus only 10% in Argentina. Salutia has the first multichannel platform linking 12 HMOs and over 500 providers in Brazil; it aims to streamline areas such as eligibility, authorization, medical auditing, and claims processing. The HMO sector is high fragmented (over 2,000 players in Brazil) and starting to consolidate. It has very few foreign players (Aetna, AIG, and Cigna from the United States and Euromedica and AGF from Europe) and still lacks management technology.

Whereas electronic medical transactions reach 66% of the total in the United States, they are still less than 4% in Argentina and Brazil. The South Cone market for health care connectivity was estimated at $11 million in 2001 but projected by Salutia to grow to $115 million by 2005, with a 46% automation rate. This may be overoptimistic given current constraints. Internet penetration is still less than 10% for physician offices and 35% for institutional providers. As in Europe, future diffusion may rely more on mobile phones than on computers. In addition, major HMOs are now looking at electronic systems as a significant way to reduce costs. A good HMO has a profit margin of only about 3%, but it can increase it significantly with even partial automation. Salutia estimates that 15 to 20% of medical practices have undetected authorization problems, for instance. Salutia expects to break even by 2003, and its current revenue base is still very limited (less than $1 million in 2001), but it received second-round and follow-on funding in March 2001 and January 2002, and may be a good test case for the future outlook of connectivity startups in Latin America.[35]

A major barrier to the growth of all three forms of e-commerce (B2C, B2B, and B2P) remains the lack of a regulatory framework in the region. As in the patent area, Mexico appears to have the most advanced set of regulations. The Law of Intellectual Property and its 1998 amendments recognize rights to electronic databases and computer programs; recent changes in the Consumer Protection Law require marketers to guarantee data confidentiality, and the National Securities and Banking Commission passed regulations in 2000 that address electronic share purchases.

By contrast, e-commerce regulations are nearly nonexistent in Brazil and Argentina. A proposed bill in Brazil addresses privacy, security, and consumer rights but ignores taxation (i.e., a proposal for a flat tax rate on e-transactions). Although 1998 legislation set heavy penalties for infringement, software privacy remains a massive problem, resulting in over $1 billion in lost sales in 1999 and reaching rates of 56% in Mexico, 58% in Brazil, and 62% in Argentina. The later lags most in regulation; the Ministry of Justice is to develop consumer protection schemes for e-transactions, and the Subsecretary of Commerce is to adapt consumer protections laws to the Internet, but implementation is still distant, particularly given the current turbulent political environment.[36]

CONCLUSION

In conclusion, the Latin American health care market is the fourth largest in the world and has a three-pronged appeal for multinationals in both services and manufacturing: a large population with attractive demographics (a rapidly aging segment and a young group with a rising income as it enters the workforce), a regional base of physicians and scientists on a par with those of OECD countries, and a group of local producers and institutions eager to enter into research and marketing alliances. However, these positive market and private-sector forces are countered by political and macroeconomic problems; the most critical of these are a still-inadequate patent protection and insufficient health care coverage as well as corruption and inefficiency at the local and federal levels in most markets. These will need to be addressed aggressively, possibly through public–private partnerships, for the region to regain its innovative capacity and competitiveness vis-à-vis other emerging markets, especially those in Southeast Asia.

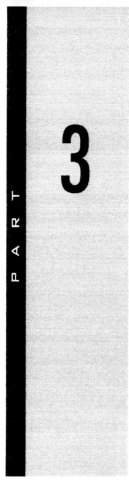

CONCLUSION

CHAPTER 8

WINDOWS OF OPPORTUNITY AND WINNING STRATEGIES FOR LATIN MARKETS

The last decade of the twentieth century was a time of profound economic transformation in Latin America. We began this book with an identification of key drivers of such transformation: global financial systems, regulatory reforms, regional integration, market transformation, and technology (see Figure 1.1). With different levels of intensity and at different times, these drivers have had a profound impact on all Latin American countries, without exception. The impact has transformed industry and business strategy. In Chapters 3 to 7, we analyzed the impact of these drivers on the infrastructure, consumer markets, banking, and health sectors. In this chapter we revisit our initial framework, assess the strategy of adapters and shapers introduced in Chapter 1, and provide recommendations on how firms may continue to operate in Latin markets.

Any strategy for Latin markets must recognize the importance of the U.S. Latin market. The 34 million people of Latin American descent in the United States represent the fourth largest Latin

American nation and the third largest in buying power. The future of any large multinational firm in Latin America will be decided by its ability to lead in the Brazilian, Mexican, and U.S. Latin markets. This golden triangle represents about 67% of the $1.6 trillion market power (see Table 2.1) and total number of households. A strategy that focuses on market dominance in only one or two of these three large Latin markets will not be enough to achieve regional market predominance.

The make up of the markets in the golden triangle could not be more different. Because of geographic distance and the fact that about 60% of the Latin population in the United States is of Mexican origin, the U.S. Latin and Mexican markets are relatively closer than they are to Brazil. The challenge for any firm is to formulate strategies that are effective for all three market cultures. The key to starting such a formulation is to gain a grasp of the Latin market identity.

THE NEW LATIN MARKET:
LATIN AMERICAN OR AMERICAN LATIN?

In his comprehensive analysis of the people and culture of the Americas, Peter Wynn once referred to Latin America as an invention devised in the nineteenth century by a French geographer to describe the nations colonized by Latin Europe. The resulting outcome of migration has shaped a region of diverse races, ethnicities, cultures, and languages sharing a common historical experience.[1] Based on racial mixing alone, a variety of Latin identities emerge: European-Latin, Afro-Latin, Asian-Latin, and Indo-Latin. The diversity of the Latin market has challenged the popular vision shared by many firms of a single Pan-American market. Advertising agencies in particular have attempted to develop regionwide campaigns only to find substantial cultural, demographic, literacy, and language dialect differences even in countries that speak the same language. According to the advertising industry's most representative information source, *Ad Age*, "the so-called Latin market is a lazy description for a complex region of consumers."[2]

Is there a single Latin market? In a strict sense, there are as many Latin markets as nations created out of the Latin European colonization. Argentines are different from Brazilians, and Chileans are different from Mexicans. Furthermore, within large markets like Brazil and Mexico, there are several ethnic markets. Thus, what characterizes the Latin market? At the risk of generalization,

Latin markets may be grouped either by their demographic transformation (see Figure 2.1) or by the subregional corridors mentioned in Chapter 5 (Andean, Southern Cone, Mexican-Central American, Caribbean, and Brazilian). Additionally, about 34 million Latin consumers are part of the large U.S. market.

The key to understanding Latin markets is to define the core of the Latin identity. The Latin identity is only an issue from the perspective of another culture. When the Latin consumer is in his or her cultural milieu, identity is unambiguously national in character. When the Latin consumer is outside his or her cultural context, in the United States, for instance, the Latin identity is ambiguous. Thus, the answer to identifying the Latin core can be found by examining Latin consumers in the United States.

When Latin Americans travel or emigrate to the United States, they are grouped under the single label of Latin. Individually, the Latin person perceives himself or herself as a member of one of the Latin American nations with little in common with other Latin Americans. The immersion in the large American culture results in two adaptation processes. The first is the assimilation to the large dominant American culture. The second one, which is less understood, is the exposure to many other Latin American national cultures, a process that may be referred to as the Latinization or cross-fertilization of the Latin American cultures. This second process holds the key to the Latin core, as it is only in the United States that a true melting pot of diverse Latin American cultures takes place. As these Latin American emigrants socialize, work, or intermarry with others from the same group, the fusion of their cultures produces a new synthetic Latino identity and syncretic popular culture.[3] In this process of discovery of a new Latin identity, it is not clear what aspect of the new Latin identity replaces the national culture and how much of the new American way is assimilated. The level of fusion of these three cultural identities (national, Latin, and American) depends on the level of education, socioeconomic level in the native country, and other traits.

A related process that also influences the Latin core identity is the reverse process of Latinization of the larger American culture. As Americans look for more diversity and new experiences, especially in food and music, they may embrace Latin expressions or gestures and explore Latin products. This process of Latinization of the large U.S. market is of great interest to U.S. firms targeting this ethnic market segment. The potential ethnic crossover of Latin products and culture to the general market is five to ten times more attractive than just targeting the Latin market alone. For instance, the crossover of the traditional Latin flavor dulce de leche in food products such as ice creams and candies has a much greater impact than positioning this flavor only as an ethnic concept. The dulce de leche flavor is now part of Häagen-Daz's global ice cream product line. Mars has tested the dulce de leche flavor in its popular M&Ms. The firm tested the flavor first in the U.S. Latin market, but the expectation is to introduce it into the large U.S. consumer market.[4] Mars could eventually introduce the new flavor to the rest of Latin America and perhaps the world. The change in flavors or colors in the M&M product offering is not a trivial decision for this company.

As a result of assimilation and cross-fertilization of Latin Americans in the United States, three groups emerge. The first group consists of the unassimilated immigrant that retains a strong national culture. This group exhibits little of Latinization or assimilation to the American way. A second group consists of foreign-born assimilated and Latinized persons. This group is fully bilingual and bicultural. The degree of Latinization and assimilation may range from bicultural (American-national culture dominant with little Latinization) to tricultural (all three levels of culture are equally dominant). The third group consists of fully assimilated foreign-born Latin Americans and first- or second-generation U.S.-born Latins. In terms of consumer culture, this group is indistinguishable from the mainstream U.S. culture.

The third group of fully assimilated or U.S.-born Latins operates well in all three cultures. For the U.S.-born, the Latin culture is important because this is what makes them different from the general population. Encouraged by the recent process of Latinization of the U.S. market, Latin youth have rediscovered their heritage as a source of pride.[5]

In reaching the Latin market, firms need to understand that Latin-ness is a continuum that ranges from the purely national to the fusion of two or three similar or different cultures (national, Latin, and non-Latin). The degree and relevance of the three cultural components depend on the geographic location of the consumer. For Latin Americans in their own country, the relevant culture, and perhaps the only aspect to appeal to, is the national culture. In itself, the national culture may be a blend of many local cultures resulting from the complex processes of colonization of native populations and waves of immigration. For Latin Americans outside their own cultural milieu, the approach depends on degrees of assimilation and cross-fertilization mentioned before.

In reaching the complex Latin market, the following market-based strategies may be considered:

1. *Local national strategy.* Ideally, the best strategy is to develop a differentiated approach for each Latin American nation. This strategy is too costly to implement. The compromise is to develop national strategies for large markets where the national culture is distinctive (Mexico, Brazil, and Argentina) and to group the other Latin American markets by regional corridors (Andean, Caribbean, and Central American). In the U.S. Latin market, firms may segment the market by the country of origin of the Latin population.

2. *Latin localization strategy.* This strategy is based on finding the common ground or essential commonalities that are shared by all Latinos in a given consumer category. Clues for such common ground may be found in the new Latin identity created by the process of cross-fertilization of Latin American cultures in the United States. The grasp of these commonalities is still at the early stages of development. Crude generalizations and abstractions can be observed in the approach used in marketing strategies for U.S. Latin markets that describe this group as warm, affectionate, family oriented, traditional, conservative, and religious. To grasp the concept of Latin-ness, more research is needed on Latin consumer inner traits such as aspirations, beliefs, and motivations that may cross national cultures in Latin America as well as Latin consumers in the United States. In the future, U.S. companies may integrate marketing approaches to Latin markets by merging their U.S. Latin operations with those of their subsidiaries in Latin America. P&G, for instance, has established an office in Puerto Rico to coordinate the firm's Latino market effort.[6] Even if such common cultural icons can be found, national localization is important to connect with the different national groups. An example of this approach is the MTV network. In competing for the attention of Latin youth, the MTV network mixes the genres of global, regional (Latin), and local music. Since the preference for regional and local music varies by country, MTV has established separate Latin business units. MTV-Brazil tailors the mix for this country only. MTV-Latin does the same for Spanish-speaking Latin America and customizes the programming for local content. In the United States, MTV targets Latin viewers in the English language but makes itself relevant to this group by sponsoring such events as Latin festivals in cities with large concentrations of Latinos, such as Miami and New York.

3. *American Latinization strategy.* This strategy should be used primarily for the Latin markets in the United States. This approach is to blend the three levels of cultural reference: American, Latin, national. The appropriate blend varies with each one of the groups based on partial to complete assimilation. For instance, if the consumer is fully assimilated but bicultural Latin, the approach should either provide options or channels of communication in either culture. Banks have certainly implemented this strategy by multiple language access to their ATMs and customer service call centers. Furthermore, given the diversity of consumer cultures in Latin America, the American Latinization strategy could just be the answer to reaching the regional market with an approach that is markedly Latin but cannot be ascribed to a particular country. We are not aware of any firm that has instituted this reverse ethnic crossover marketing that in principle seems valid.

4. *Global localization strategy.* The strategies above apply to consumption categories where culture plays a significant part—for example, food, personal care, and entertainment. However, for marketing computers, financial services, or cars, for example, the approach to Latin markets is essentially global with localization of the customer relations and delivery aspects. One example is the strategy used by online portal Terra-Lycos. Terra-Lycos uses a two-prong strategy to reach Latino online users in the United States and Latin America. In the United States, Terra joined forces with Microsoft and Mexican Telmex to acquire the leading Latin portal Yupi and renamed it YupiMSN, which is promoted through Microsoft's own portal MSN.com.[7] For English-speaking audiences in the United States, Terra-Lycos offers the Lycos portal. In Latin America, the firm uses the Terra site, which is offered in every country where the parent company Telefónica operates, whether in Spanish or Portuguese.

STRATEGY IN UNCERTAIN AND VOLATILE MARKETS

Figure 8.1 shows our understanding of how strategy is influenced by major drivers in the region. In this revised framework, we identify four major blocks intimately related to strategy in Latin

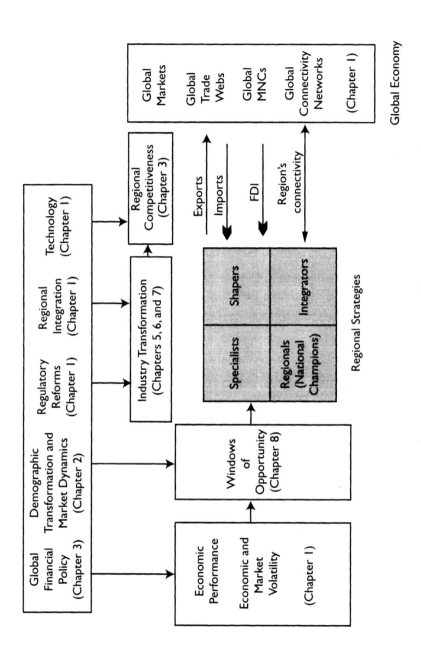

FIGURE 8.1
Network Strategies in Latin Markets

305

America. The first block includes the five drivers identified in Chapter 1: market dynamics, regulatory reforms, regional integration, global financial policy, and new technology. The second block describes the immersion and links of the region with the global economy through the trade and investment flows. The third block captures the impact of drivers and links to the global economy on the region's macroeconomic performance and the volatility of adjustment. The final block is the strategy of firms as they react to industry adjustments and opportunities and challenges they face in this region. We discuss each of these blocks below.

DRIVERS OF OPPORTUNITIES

Dynamic demographic and urbanization changes, analyzed in Chapter 2, indicate that some countries in the region have reached an advanced stage of transformation, whereas others are at early stages. The key markets of Mexico and Brazil are in the middle of this transformation and will slow down rather quickly and reach an advanced stage. Clearly, these changes create great opportunities to serve the needs of masses of young people, but in the long run, firms may look at countries such as Chile and Uruguay for ideas as to how the rest of Latin markets may evolve.

The processes of privatizations, market liberalization, and other structural reforms have changed the economic and business landscape of the region. A major transfer of public assets to the private sector has altered the industry structure in telecommunications, energy, banking, and other sectors analyzed in Chapters 3, 4, and 6. This major transfer was responsible for the major foreign direct investment inflows in the 1990s. Market reforms have opened widely most Latin American economies to the global economy through lowering of trade restrictions. These reform processes may have reached the end of their life cycle either because there is little left to privatize or because structural reforms are already in place. Another reason for the slowdown of reform drivers is increasing political and societal opposition, which questions whether these programs have had any impact at all on the welfare of Latin American society. Politicians may not have the resolve to continue on the path of more market reforms, due to the worsening of income distribution in the region and vulnerability of large masses of disenfranchised poor to economic contractions in the region.

Global financial drivers have also battered the fragile economies of Latin America in recent times. Take, for instance, the impact of global financial shocks. In less than a decade the region has adjusted to the financial shocks caused by the peso devaluation in Mexico in 1994, the Asian crisis in 1997, the Russian default in 1998, and most recently, the Brazilian Real devaluation of 1999. The international and Latin American financial sector has learned from these experiences and will not be caught by surprise by the next crisis. For example, most of the impact of Argentina's default and moratorium of her external debt at the end of 2001 has been localized to Argentina and to a lesser extent, to Brazil and Chile. Unlike the other global financial crises mentioned above, most Latin American countries have already adjusted their economies in anticipation of such an event through currency adjustments and monetary policies. Similarly, the international financial sector has already discounted Argentina by lowering the price of Argentinean floating-rate bonds to junk status, heavily discounting the futures exchange rate for the peso, and cutting further access to capital markets.[8] As a result, Argentinean society will suffer the brunt of the adjustment.

One driver that has been put on hold is regional integration. After the fever of regional market integration in the early 1990s, this has been put on hold after the collapse of Mercosur progress and lack of interest in the discussion on the proposed Free-Trade Area of the Americas (FTAA). The recent approval of trade-promotion authority by the U.S. president may revitalize the initiative of expansion of NAFTA to other countries, but progress on FTAA will depend on the resolve of the United States and Brazil to address the major differences in reaching such a monumental agreement.

Technological transformation is the only driver that is still unfolding in the region. Internet penetration continues to grow at a fast pace. Wireless networks also continue to expand and gain more subscribers. Enterprise technology will continue to be adopted as firms invest in more enterprise integration technologies. In sum, we see a slowdown of the intensity of the main drivers on the region's economy and markets. As these drivers slow down, the region's economies will become less volatile.

WINDOWS OF OPPORTUNITIES

Latin American economic growth in 2001 was a mere 0.6% and the forecast for 2002 is 1.1%.[9] The slowdown of the world's economy in 2001 reduced demand and depressed prices for the region's key commodities, such as copper, oil, and coffee. In addition, declining consumer confidence depressed local demand in many key markets in the region. Although interest rates have decreased in international financial markets, Latin American governments and firms have seen their costs of borrowing increase due to a higher risk premium stemming from a perception of problems ahead for the region. As a result, Latin America went from a good growth performance in 2000 of 4.1% to rapid deterioration in 2001 in reaction to global economic malaise and local problems. The important factor to note here is the rapid change from a positive to a negative scenario in a matter of a few quarters.

We looked at the long-term economic performance of the region since 1990 and found that the region underwent three major cycles of recession and recovery (see Figure 8.2). The first cycle lasted from 1990 to 1994 and ended abruptly as the region adjusted to the devaluation of the Mexican peso in December 1994. This first cycle had a period of four years of continuing growth. The second cycle started in 1996, peaked in 1998, and ended in 1999 with a major devaluation of the Brazilian Real. This cycle lasted three years. The third cycle had a good start in 2000 and ended abruptly in 2001 with

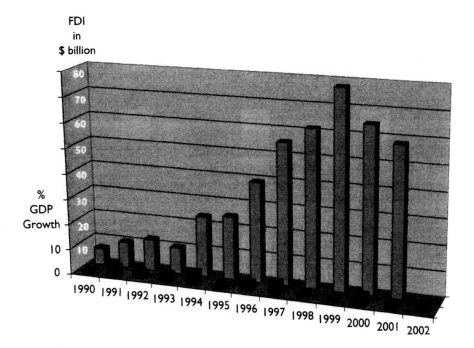

FIGURE 8.2
Cycles of Growth and Foreign Direct Investment in Latin America

the slowdown in the world economy and the impact of the tragic events of September 11. This cycle had a duration of one year. The main point here is that the world and Latin America in particular are adjusting more rapidly to major events in a very short time span.

The upturn of the economic cycles in Latin America present windows of opportunity to invest in the region. The first window of opportunity lasted over a long period. The long cycle of economic growth in the region was mostly fueled by market reforms and privatization programs in Argentina and Mexico. First movers in this window of opportunity not only had time to build their strategies but were insulated from competition, as the Telecom Argentina case discussed in Chapter 4 illustrates. The second window of opportunity came about when countries like Argentina quickly recouped from the impact of the Mexican peso devaluation in 1995 and Brazil launched the plan Cruzado in 1994. A second wave of investors descended on Latin America, but this time the main target was Brazil's privatization and economic reforms. These investors had two years of economic growth (1996–1997). New investors had a shorter time to set up their strategies before facing a generalized slowdown that began as early as 1998 in certain countries (e.g., Brazil). New investors faced first-movers who had become the incumbents and local firms that were in the process of transforming their businesses. The third window of opportunity is very short. In contrast to the first two windows of opportunity, the major driver in this cycle is technology. Latin America's strong growth of Internet, wireless, and other information technology attracted many specialist firms that were riding the high-tech bandwagon before its collapse.

If the first two years of the twenty-first century are an indication of what lies ahead, Latin America's economic roller coaster will be more intense and its cycles of recovery and recession will be rather short. Under this scenario, firms contemplating investing in Latin America have to prepare an entry plan and be quick to adapt to changing circumstances. Under another scenario, Latin America may be entering into a cycle of low but stable growth. Argentina may once more provide a glimpse of how the latter scenario may evolve. The social unrest in Argentina at the end of 2001 that brought down a weak president and a powerful economic minister may be an indication that the political and social problems will be at the forefront of the problems that Latin American governments may have to confront in the next decade.

If the twentieth century brought economic transformation of the region, the next decade will be a time of political and social innovation. The challenges for many Latin American countries rests in resolving the fundamental trade-offs between erratic economic growth and stability, maintaining a free market system and protecting local industry in the context of a global economy, and promoting an active role of the state without interfering in the economy. Resolving these issues will require formidable coalitions and consensus in many countries, as no one political leader has the fortitude to dissemble a decade of reforms and changes. These coalitions will not be able to reverse past reforms, but they will limit and shape them to smooth the intensity of their impacts on society.[10] In this respect, the ability of future Latin American governments will rest on generating innovative economic and social policies and garnering enough political support to gain their acceptance.

The most vulnerable countries that may confront the dilemma of volatile growth or stability are those that face large external financing gaps and presidential elections. Brazil is such a country where these trade-offs have to be resolved soon. With external financing requirements estimated at $80 billion in 2002, 310% of international reserves, Brazil is experiencing a quick reduction of foreign investment inflows, and the Real lost 40% of its value in 2001. Other countries where the electoral vote may decide whether to continue with the status quo or revert to a more protectionist stand are Argentina, Colombia, Costa Rica, and Ecuador.[11]

Thus in the future, investment volatility may have a source more in the political system than in the economic system. In contrast to previous windows of opportunity where the volatility stemmed mostly from the vulnerability of Latin American economies to global financial shocks, future volatility may be based on a change of economic policies or even government intervention in the economy to support more socially responsive measures.

LINKS TO THE GLOBAL ECONOMY

Trade, investment flows, and connectivity link Latin America with the world economy. The patterns of flows of these three channels determine the movement of goods, money, and information within the region and with the rest of the world. The greater the flows, the greater the region's immersion in the global economy. Investment flows have followed the windows of opportunity described above. Because of the long-term nature of investment, the flows do not adjust as quickly to the ups and downs of the region's economy (see Figure 8.3). Instead of three economic cycles, two waves of foreign direct investment can be identified in the period 1990–2001.[12] The first wave of investment

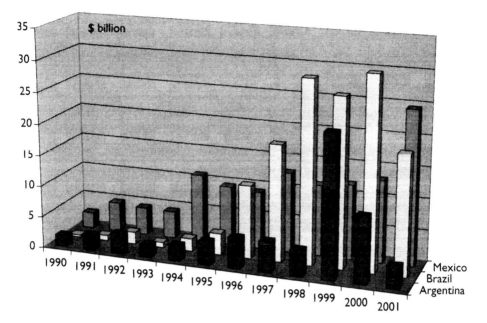

FIGURE 8.3
Waves of FDI in Argentina, Brazil, and Mexico

flows occurred in the period 1990–1994. Early investors focused mostly on privatization of infrastructure assets in Argentina, Mexico, and Chile. This first wave of investors was mostly from European companies in the Southern Cone and U.S. investors in Mexico. The second wave of investments took off in 1995 and peaked in 2000. Investment flows in the second wave were three times the value of the first wave. In contrast to the $20 billion flows of the first wave, foreign direct investments increased to close to $80 billion in 1999. Investors in the second wave were U.S. firms poised to become new global players in new markets, such as wireless telecommunications and energy. Although the major destination was Brazil, foreign direct investment in the second wave was regional. Investors continue to invest in Mexico and Argentina but also in such countries as Colombia, Peru, and Venezuela.

The third wave of investment is characterized by a downward trend in foreign direct investment flows, which started in 2000. Despite good economic growth in 2000, foreign direct investment fell by 22% in 2000 compared to the year before, and by 19% in 2001. With economic slowdown in the region and the world, some observers predict that the downward trend will continue until 2004, followed by a slow recovery.[13] One reason for the decline is the end of major privatization programs in the region that brought one-time investments. Another reason is weakened investor confidence due to the economic problems in Argentina and the uncertainty of the outcome of elections in Brazil. The third reason is the slowdown in the U.S. economy, which has a major impact on Mexico. Very recent inflows reflect long-planned acquisitions, such as Citibank's purchase of Mexico's Banamex, but not major long-term investments.[14]

As reviewed in Chapter 1, Latin America's trade flows are more intense with the rest of the world than within the region. Although the rhetoric of forming a regional trade agreement of the Americas has dominated the debate in public forums, the reality is that Latin American economies are highly embedded in worldwide trade. Despite more than a decade of efforts to pursue regional integration, the extent of intraregional trade has not reached more than 20% at any time and is recently at 17%.

The region's largest economies, Brazil and Mexico, are in a race to increase their participation in the world economy. As Chapter 1 indicated, Mexico is making an effort to become more globally involved and has developed the most complex web of trade agreements of any country in the world. Brazil, on the other hand, has been preoccupied in becoming a global leader in the export of commodities and building a global competitive industrial platform in a few industries, such as automobiles, light aircraft, and consumer electronics. In fact, Brazil and Mexico, together with the Asian emerging power economies of China and India, may become the emerging-country equivalent of the advanced economies triad of the United States, Europe, and Japan. Figure 8.4 illustrates the links of the United States–Europe–Japan economic triad with the three leading emerging economies, which include Brazil and Mexico. Trade flows between the two triad systems are already quite substantial. U.S.–Mexican trade has become very strong with NAFTA. U.S.–China trade, already growing fast, will become even larger with China's entry into the WTO. European trade with China and Brazil is also very strong.

Mexico and Brazil are already part of the global value chain of major multinationals in medium-tech electronics, automobiles, and other consumer durables. In Chapter 3 we saw how the degree of integration of the automobile industry in North and South America leads to increasing trade flows of parts and cars. The U.S. and Mexico industrial networks are already highly integrated through NAFTA. European trade and investment have been historically important in Brazil. Most major European multinationals have

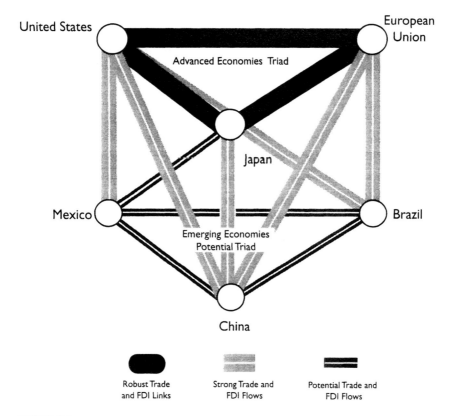

FIGURE 8.4
Extended Triads: Trade and FDI Flows

presence in Brazil and/or Argentina. U.S. multinationals also hold an important presence in the Brazilian car industry, but their subsidiaries have greater links with the European subsidiaries than with the North American production hub. Japan's trade and investment flows in Latin America are more limited to assembly plants in Mexico and the Caribbean, but one can expect a greater participation of Japanese investment in Brazil.

All triad players—the United States, Europe, and Japan—have major investments and trade flows with China. In the future, Mexico and Brazil will attract investment destined to build export platforms for global markets rather than for domestic market opportunities. The extent to which this new investment would flow to Latin America as opposed to Asia will be determined by the competitiveness of its two major economies, Brazil and Mexico. With large adjustments of the Brazilian currency in 2001, this country has become more likely to attract this type of investment than Mexico, which experienced an appreciation of the peso. Both Latin American countries are in a race with China to attract this level of investment. As reviewed in Chapter 3, the race will be difficult for Latin America, which lags in terms of productivity and quality vis-à-vis other world economies. In recent years, Mexico has been able to move quickly to close the gap in electronics and the automobile sectors. In the future, the trade flows that may emerge under a scenario of a greater integration of the two triads are the Mexico–Brazil–China trade.

The losers of a greater integration of Brazil and Mexico with the global economy are Argentina and Chile. In the case of Argentina, several negative factors could deter this country's long-term prospects to participate in one global web trade scenario. Argentina's exports are destined to remain in the region, and the overvalued peso destroyed the competitiveness of Argentinean industry. Furthermore, its recent external debt default will increase the cost of external borrowing for Argentinean firms planning to improve their productivity in the future. In the case of Chile, a model country of the first wave of reforms and investments, its economy is mostly geared toward exporting and exploiting natural resources. Chile has not been able to attract the type of investment for a manufacturing platform that Mexico and Brazil have been able to achieve. Chile is banking on becoming a high-tech platform for the Americas.

With respect to connectivity links, the region is still in the early stages of building regional infrastructure networks. As analyzed in Chapter 4, the effort of the past 10 years has been in building modern telecommunications networks at the national level. Several projects are under way to build subregional city-to-city networks. Major telecommunications firms such as Telefónica and Telecom Italia are behind these major regional projects. Broadband regional networks are also available at the regional level with funding from private investor groups. Internet technology is to a great extent localized. As Chapter 1 indicated, Internet connectivity is mostly local. Major attempts to develop a regional platform for Internet portals have not been successful, and ISP providers are mostly local. Past efforts to develop a regional ISP network by companies such as PSI Net have been halted by the collapse of the global telecommunications and Internet sectors.

Future connectivity flows in Latin America may not only change but may shape new business strategies in the region. Intraregional information, voice, and data flows will surge to unprecedented levels. As discussed in Chapters 1 and 6, global and national bank leaders are focusing their strategies on advantages provided by information technology. The alliance of BBVA and Terra Networks to offer Internet banking may create a new regional electronic banking market. Brazilian bank champions Bradesco and Itaú have built similar core capacity at the national level. Greater use of information technology and the Internet requires increased network capacity to support traffic. The potential for Mexico and Brazil to build such capacity will make these two countries the hubs of connectivity for regional traffic as well as global traffic. Having such capacity will help these two countries integrate further with the global economy triad architecture by providing world-class connectivity with the telecommunications hubs of multinationals. A few other countries, such as Uruguay and Argentina, with very efficient telecommunications networks are also vying to become information hubs for the region.

STRATEGIES FOR LATIN MARKETS

The framework so far has described the dynamics of drivers and adjustment of the region's economies to external shocks and internal market conditions. We also explained the increasing link of the region with the global economy through trade, investment, and connectivity flows. The region's competitiveness, although lagging, is improving in certain sectors and making it possible for Brazil and Mexico to be part of the global supply chain in important sectors such as the automobile industry. In earlier chapters we reviewed the industry transformation in consumer markets, banking, infrastructure, and health. In those chapters we observed the massive transfer of government-owned assets to private ownership. In other sectors, such as consumer goods, the transformation has been characterized by industry consolidation and integration through mergers and acquisitions. The strategy of global players in the retail industry shows their intent to build regional strategies. In Chapter 1 we identified the two broad global strategies of shapers and adapters. Shapers, in turn, were said to be either specialists or integrators. Latin American-owned companies were identified as regionals. In Chapter 4 we refined this framework in terms of the degree of business integration and market aggregation. Based on these two dimensions, we identified the subcategories of strategy as broad regional integrators, narrow regional integrators, broad regional specialists, and narrow regional specialists.

The analysis has identified that a few Latin American firms have become formidable national champions. These strong national firms could emerge as regional integrators or as global specialists.

The next generation of Latin stars will follow the examples of Cemex or Embraer at the global level or Bimbo and Gruma at the regional level. In Chapters 4 and 5 we analyzed the performance of strategies in the infrastructure and consumer markets and retail sectors. Our analysis of the infrastructure sector found that specialists tend to have high returns on sales (ROS) and net worth (RONW); integrators had low returns. In terms of assets, by their nature of business, specialists have small asset and revenue bases, whereas integrators have large asset size and revenues. National champions in infrastructure were mostly state-owned utilities with poor returns and medium-sized assets and revenues. The largest national champion, Telmex, is the largest Latin American firm in terms of revenues, market capitalization, and revenues and also delivered the best returns of all firms in the infrastructure sector. In the consumer sector, we found similar results. Specialists achieved better returns than integrators and national champions. In this case, however, broad regional specialists were as large in size as integrators. National champions in consumer goods were also large in size, but their returns on sales and net worth were average. We did not identify any shapers in the consumer goods sector. In the banking industry (see Chapter 6) we found that the top 50 Latin American banks had large asset bases. Most of the banks follow a broad regional integration strategy, and very few, such as Santander, are able to act as shapers. Given that the nature of the banking business is different from the two other sectors, it is difficult to compare the performance results of banks and that of the other sectors we analyzed. The strategies of pharmaceuticals companies reviewed in Chapter 7 revealed that the dominant players are dominant global integrators that have built their presence in Latin American through acquisitions. One or two national champions claim some market share in their local markets, notably Aché in Brazil and Roemmers in Argentina, but have very weak prospects to expand regionally due to weak innovation and poor patent protection.

Our analysis of the regional strategies in the infrastructure and consumer goods sectors provides a broader perspective of strategy in Latin America. The strategy profile of 113 firms is shown in Table 8.1. The results in this table reveal that 44 firms used a broad regional integration strategy and 24 firms used a narrow regional integration strategy. Among the specialists, seven were broad regional specialists, and only one firm was a narrow regional specialist. Among the national firms, 26 were privately owned national champions and 11 were state-owned enterprises. In terms of size, broad regional specialists are very large in terms of employment, market

TABLE 8.1 Performance of Alternative Strategies in Latin Markets[a]

Strategy	Number of Firms	Total Assets ($ millions)	Employment	Market Capitalization, 12/31/00 ($ millions)	Net Worth ($ millions)	Revenues ($ millions)	Revenue Change 2000/1999 (%)	Net Profit ($ millions)	Net Profit/Revenue (%)	Net Profit/Net Worth (%)
Broad regional integrator (BRI)	44	3,847	6,979	3,115	1,549	1,795	14.4	73	1.63	7.6
Broad regional specialist (BRS)	7	3,201	33,211	5,236	1,793	2,963	25.5	111	3.3	2.4
Narrow regional integrator (NRI)	24	2,504	11,686	4,773	973	2,597	16.1	79.6	5.8	9.2
Narrow regional specialist (NRS)	1	2,112	676	1,247	1,088	480	11.6	126	11.6	26.3
National champion (NC)	26	3,102	22,845	3,102	1,201	2,354	23.1	170	3.5	7.5
State-owned enterprises (SOE)	11	8,148	5,014	3,905	5,333	1,465	2.6	160.6	2.1	2.3
All firms	113	7,582	12,618	4,217	1,792	2,123	16.3	112.7	3.2	7.1

Source: Compiled from Tables 4.7 and 5.2.
[a]Financial sector and health sector firms not included.

capitalization, and revenues. These specialists were found mostly in distribution-intensive mass consumption businesses, such as the beverage sector. Broad regional integrators are asset intensive, as indicated by their large average asset value. These broad regional integrators are mostly in infrastructure business. In terms of revenues, broad regional specialists and national champions have experienced the largest increases in revenues in 2000. Firms using the latter two strategies also report the largest average profit of all firms in our analysis. The worst performers in terms of change of revenues were state-owned enterprises. In terms of returns, the best performer is the single national specialist, with returns on sales of 11.6% and a 26.3% return on net worth. The next-best performer strategy is the narrow regional integrator, with an average return on sales of 5.8%, almost twice the average return for all firms, and a 9.2% return on net worth.

We did not find shaper strategies in infrastructure and consumer goods. In Chapter 1 we pointed out that Mexico's Cemex and Spain's BBVA were examples of shaper strategies. These two companies were not included in our database, because of the limitation on the comparability of firms in the banking business with the other sectors in our analysis. In the case of Cemex, our focus on the infrastructure sectors was on the operations and not on the companies providing inputs to the sector. As mentioned in Chapter 1, Cemex can be described as a shaper in the construction industry. Cemex is also a global player, one of the top three largest firms in the cement industry. Cemex's intensive use of informational technology has helped this firm to become the top performer in the building-materials industry in 2001. Cemex's profit margin of 15.6% was much better than that of its two largest global competitors, Lafarge and Holderbank, and five times the industry average of 2.8%.[15]

A strategic control map provides a visualization of our analysis of types of strategy and performance. The examination of several combinations of performance (return on sales and return on net worth) and size (value of total assets, employment, market capitalization, and revenues) was consistent in providing the same conclusion: that specialists are positioned in the upper-left quadrant and integrators are clearly positioned in the lower-right-hand quadrant. For illustration purposes, we include the chart that shows the relation of total revenues and return on net worth (see Figure 8.5 and the supporting information in Table 8.2). Figure 8.5 suggests that in between these two extremes, one finds a spread of firms with a combination of broad regional specialists, national champions, narrow regional integrators, and state-owned enterprises. Shapers could be

TABLE 8.2 Performance of Firms of Different Revenue Size in Latin Markets

Revenue Cluster	Number of Firms	Average Revenue ($ billions)	Average Total Assets ($ billions)	Average Number of Employees	Average Market Capitalization ($ billions)	Average Net Worth ($ billions)	Average Change in Revenue (%)	Average Profits ($ millions)	Average Return on Revenues (%)	Average Return on Net Worth (RONW) (%)	Best in Revenue Group (Strategy)[a]
Greater than $10 billion	1	10.7	16.4	74,911	40	5.1	19.5	2,756	26	53	Telmex (NC)
Between $5 and $10 billion	7	7.4	9.7	18,495	7.0	6.4	67.6	443	6.8	8.6	Sanborns–Mexico RNW = 12.2 Wal-Mart Mexico (BRI) RONW = 12.2
Between $3 and $5 billion	15	3.7	7.4	25,845	4.0	2.8	12.9	217	3.8	5.8	FEMSA–Mexico (BRS) RONW = 14.5
Between $1 and $3 billion	55	1.8	2.8	12,159	3.7	1.3	12.9	53	3.1	10.1	Nestlé-Brazil (BRI) RONW = 23.3
Less than $1 billion	35	0.6	1.9	2,590	1.3	0.9	12.6	23	1.8	2.8	Alestra–Mexico (NRI) RONW = 27.7

[a]NC, national champion; BRI, broad regional integrator; BRS, broad regional specialist; NRI, narrow regional integrator.

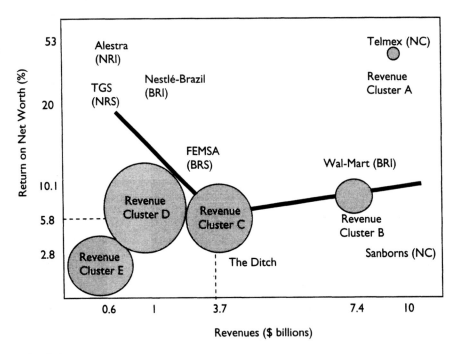

FIGURE 8.5
Latin American Strategic Control Map

identified in the upper-right-hand quadrant of large size and high performance. Besides the examples of Cemex and BBVA in banking, the only other firm that falls in such a quadrant is Telmex. In a strict sense, Telmex is not a shaper since this company has not altered the industry strategy in the same way as Cemex and BBVA have, with their emphasis on technology. Telmex is a very large incumbent in the telecommunications sector that up until now has enjoyed market protection. In the future, as competition intensifies in this sector and Telmex expands regionally, the company's position in the chart will move closer to that of the broad regional integrators.

The strategic map in Figure 8.5 clearly shows the pull of the two possible extremes of strategy in Latin America: integration and specialization. In our snapshot of strategy in 2000, the majority of companies are clustered in the lower-left-hand quadrant. The position of firms as small or average-size companies with average to low returns is not sustainable in the future. In contrast, a handful of firms have achieved large size and generate greater returns than those of their smaller rivals. A handful of small firms have pulled out of the pack and have been able to deliver superior returns. These small champions are a mix of specialists, narrow regional integrators, and broad regional integrators. The majority of firms in Latin markets have to decide whether they want to become specialists or integrators. The threshold for such a decision is indicated in Figure 8.5 as the ditch, the change in slope between the small exemplars and the large integrators. The threshold for the ditch appears to be at annual revenues between $3 to $5 billion and $7.4 billion in total assets.

A shift to specialization may require shedding assets and concentrating on core businesses where above-average returns can be generated. A shift to an integrator position is more troublesome. Firms in this group do not seem to have any incremental advantage over smaller competitors, as indicated by similar average increases in revenues and returns on sales with the disadvantage of a larger employment base. As firms succeed in crossing the threshold size, the average increase in revenues is multiplied by a factor of 5 and returns increase by a factor of 1.5 or more. As not all firms will succeed in crossing the ditch, many will become casualties of increased competition from larger competitors or will pursue consolidation with other firms facing the same dilemma.

A shift toward increased size and integration may lead the industry to consolidate.[16] The effort here is to increase the scale and size of business. To do so, firms may increase their size through acquisitions. For foreign multinationals, this approach may be the only way to continue delivering profits and revenue growth in stagnant markets. For Latin American multinationals, increasing scale through acquisitions or organic growth will be extremely difficult, given the high costs in international capital markets for Latin American investments. In either case we anticipate substantial industry consolidation as firms in the lower quadrant are either integrated into other consolidators or exit the market. Narrow regional integrators seem to have broken out of the pack of vulnerable firms as they have achieved a relatively large size and are delivering good returns. Broad regional integrators of relatively smaller size have achieved scale in other ways, through asset size. As physical assets are local by nature, improvement in long-term returns may rest on the ability to connect dispersed assets to provide regional services in new sectors, such as the Internet and data transmission.

WINNING STRATEGIES

Having analyzed the opportunities and challenges of Latin markets in four different sectors, it is useful to differentiate the key factors for each type of strategy.

Integrators
- Use global scope and diversity as a buffer against downturns. Example to follow: Cemex.
- Rationalize manufacturing using Mexico and Brazil as the Latin American platforms and leveraging similar production assets in China and India. Example to follow: GM—leverage of Mexico's and Brazil's operations with European and U.S. operations.
- Optimize supply chain and leverage presence in regional business-to-business (B2B) exchanges. Example to follow: Latinexus—B2B marketplace, a consortium of Latin American largest industrial firms.
- Leverage global or regional brand and converge to the middle mass market. Examples to follow: Wal-Mart and Nestlé.

Specialists
- Broad regional specialists
  - Focus on expertise at one sliver of regional and global value chains, where best-in-class advantage commands above-industry returns. Example to follow: Embraer.
  - Focus on the right consumer value for uncertain times; do not compete on price. Examples to follow: FEMSA and Bimbo.
- Narrow regional specialists
  - Focus on one or two top regional markets where geographic synergies and shared assets can be leveraged. Examples to follow: Alestra and Telecom Italia.
  - Quickly capture growth opportunities in a single market corridor and develop dominant market position through, superior quality and brand resonance. Examples to follow: Mexico's Gruma and Brazil's Natura.

Shapers
- Rapid integration of acquired firms. Example to follow: Santander.
- Leverage financial, infrastructure, and marketing support of collaborators or parent firm. Example to follow: Terra Networks.

- Shape fragmented regional markets and turn them into global markets. Example to follow: Unilever's ice cream market.

Regionals and National Champions

- Rapid transformation into a global competitor. Example to follow: Brazil's Sadia.
- Leverage incumbent's advantages and achieve large scale. Examples to follow: Mexico's Telmex and Sanborns.
- Collaborate with global or regional integrators, shapers, or specialists. Examples to follow: Disco and Banco Itaú.
- National brand leadership offering best consumer value possible. Examples to follow: Brazil's Pão de Açúcar and Chile's Falabella.

BRAND RELEVANCE: KEY TO IMPLEMENTING WINNING STRATEGIES

For all strategies, the greater challenge in Latin America is to build a brand strategy. The cycles of economic expansion and contraction in the region have clearly changed the consumer market landscape. In their search for value, Latin American consumers are scrutinizing every decision made in the marketplace. The shortening and intensity of economic cycles in recent years have created greater uncertainty.

As reviewed in Chapter 5, firms have to invest in offering consumer value that is relevant to the Latin consumer situation. Consumer relevance in these markets, however, is a challenging task. The region is a mosaic of cultures and languages, and its population is at different stages of transformation. In large countries such as Brazil and Mexico, different parts of the country are markets on their own. The rich and emerging Latin market in the United States can be tapped in many different ways. For some Mexican companies, such as Mexico's Gruma, the U.S. Latino market is an extension of its home base. For others, such as Telecom Argentina, the strategy may be one of capturing the telecommunications flows between the United States and the Southern Cone.

Building a brand architecture for Latin markets requires meeting the economic, trust, belonging, and comfort values that consumers demand. The brand strategy for integrators also requires breaking out of the vicious cycle of commoditization and continuous price discounts through migration to the middle market and aiming at the largest market segment. Specialists by nature will aim at either the high or low end of the market. Given that the fundamental architecture is effective, the brand strategy can be localized to the mosaic of market situations that characterizes Latin markets. In some categories, such as telecommunication or energy services, the localization will be minimum. In other categories, such as consumer goods, high localization across the region and within the country will be necessary.

CONCLUSION

The Latin world is a challenging region in which to do business, but it offers many rewards. First-movers had time to adjust to different conditions and changing regulations. Newcomers to the region will not have that luxury. The cycles of economic upturns and downturns have intensified. Multiple drivers affect Latin markets in many different ways and different time frames. The essence of strategy in the new Latin markets is to identify the windows of opportunity and timing of entry. Early movers have built different business architectures based on their geographic and business scope. National champions have emerged to contest the challenge of integrators and specialists. In this struggle, success will be decided in the two largest markets of Brazil and Mexico. These two countries offer different platforms for success, and some firms may have to choose the focus of their Latin American success. For global firms, Brazil and Mexico are essential components of their global value chain. The future of the region may not be decided in the marketplace but in the political arena. The pressure to minimize the vulnerability of the region to global shocks and the market driven economies is increasing. This certainly creates an additional source of uncertainty for investors. In the long term, the Latin markets leverage global strategies and create powerful networks in a vast region of common cultural and historical experiences.

ENDNOTES

CHAPTER 1

1. Luis Andrade, Jose Barra, and Heinz-Peter Elstrodt, "All in the *Familia*," *McKinsey Quarterly,* 2001, no. 4, Emerging Markets, pp. 83–84.

2. Ronald Grover, "Media Giants Are Glued to Latino TV," *Business Week,* Sept. 24, 2001, pp. 105–106.

3. Tom Lowry and Diane Brady, "At GE, New Pride in the Peacock," *Business Week,* Nov. 19, 2001, pp. 79–80; Dana James, "Hola, Telemundo," *Marketing News,* Nov. 5, 2001, p. 16.

4. Media survey, *Marketing News,* July 2, 2001, pp. 11–18.

5. Bob Rouse, "Latin High Tech Forum," industry presentation, Nov. 6, 2001.

6. Morgan Stanley Dean Witter and United Nations Development Program; cited in Lynda Applegate, "Submarino.com: The Challenges of B2C E-Commerce in Latin America," Harvard Business School Case 9-801-350, June 2001.

7. Paul Coombes and Mark Watson, "Corporate Reform in the Developing World," *McKinsey Quarterly,* 2001, no. 2, p. 91.

8. Emerging-Market Indicators, *Economist*, Sept. 22, 2001, p. 90.

9. *Tendencias*, Latin American Market Report of InfoAmericas, Sept. 2001, pp. 1, 4.

10. Clifford Kraus, "Economic Pain Spreads from US Across Latin America," *New York Times*, Oct. 14, 2001, p. A3.

11. Jane Eddy and David Beers, "Recent Terrorist Attacks on U.S. Will Put Latin American Economies Under Additional Pressure," *Standard and Poor's Sovereigns Analysis*, Oct. 2, 2001, p. 1.

12. "The Fallout in Europe," *Business Week Special Report*, Oct. 28, 2001, p. 52.

13. Economist Intelligence Unit, *Latin America at a Glance*, 2001, pp. 9, 13.

14. "Mexico Overtakes Brazil," *Economist*, Sept. 8, 2001, p. 38.

15. Geri Smith, "Mexico's Wagon Is Hitched to a Falling Star," *Business Week*, Oct. 1, 2001.

16. *Latin America at a Glance*, p. 55.

17. ECLAC, *Foreign Investment in Latin America and the Caribbean*, 2000, pp. 25–26, 41.

18. *Latin America Monitor*, Nov. 2001, p. 6.

19. *Latin America Monitor*, Oct. 2001, pp. 5–6, and Nov. 2001, pp. 5–6.

20. Manual Pastor and Carol Wise, "From Poster Child to Basket Case," *Foreign Affairs*, Nov.– Dec. 2001, pp. 59–72.

21. Joshua Goodman, "Thinking the Unthinkable," *Business Week*, Nov. 19, 2001, p. 58.

22. "No Good Options" and "Fingers Crossed," *Economist*, Jan. 5, 2002, pp. 30–31.

23. *Latin America at a Glance*, p. 41.

24. "All in the *Familia*," *Economist*, Apr. 21, 2001, pp. 19–22.

25. Felipe de la Balze, "Finding Allies in the Back Yard: NAFTA and the Southern Cone," *Foreign Affairs*, July–Aug. 2001, p. 8.

26. Charles Whalen, "NAFTA's Scorecard: So Far, So Good," *Business Week*, July 9, 2001, pp. 54–56.

27. Geri Smith, "Is the Magic Starting to Fade?" *Business Week*, Aug. 6, 2001, pp. 42–43.

28. Felipe de la Balze, "Finding Allies in the Back Yard: NAFTA and the Southern Cone," *Foreign Affairs*, July–Aug. 2001, pp. 11–12.

29. "Mexico Moves for More FTAs," *Latin America Monitor*, Nov. 2001, p. 6.

30. *Integration and Trade in the Americas*, IDB Periodic Note, Dec. 2000, pp. 68–69.

31. Geri Smith, "Mexico Pulls Off Another Trade Coup," *Business Week*, Feb. 7, 2000, p. 56.

32. "A Stronger Performance," *Business Latin America*, July 2, 2001, p. 5.

33. "Another Blow to Mercosur," *Economist*, Mar. 31, 2001, p. 33.

34. Ian Katz, "Adios Argentina—Hello, Brazil," *Business Week*, Jan. 17, 2000, p. 56.

35. William Landers, *Latin America Technology Industry Update*, Credit Suisse First Boston, Jan. 17, 2001, pp. 44–48.

36. "PC Penetration Continues to Grow," Roper Starch Worldwide Presentation, 2001.

37. Strategy Research Corporation, *2001 Latin America Market Planning Report*, p. 24.

38. *Latin America at a Glance*, p. 36.

39. *Latin America at a Glance*, p. 34.

40. eMarketer, *The eLatin America Report*, 2001, pp. 20–26.

41. Landers, op.cit., pp. 7–8.

42. Ibid., p. 9.

43. Lynda Applegate, "E-Commerce in Latin America," Harvard Business School Case 9-801-388, June 2001, p. 12.

44. Landers, op. cit., pp. 52–53.

45. Applegate, "E-Commerce in Latin America," pp. 13–17.

46. eMarketer, *The eLatin America Report*, 2001, p. 64.

47. Ibid., pp. 54–56.

48. Ibid., p. 48.

49. *E-Business in Latin America*, Todito.com Case Study, Economist Intelligence Unit, 2000, p. 67.

50. Boston Consulting Group/Visa, *Online Retailing In Latin America*, Oct. 2000, pp. 20–21.

51. Ibid., p. 17.

52. *Online Retailing in Latin America*, p. 12.

53. Ibid., pp. 28–34.

54. Andy Robinson, "Terra Lycos: Mano a Mano with Yahoo?" *Business Week*, Jan. 8, 2001, p. 54.

55. Christina Hoag, "Empire Building: The Slow Track," *Business Week*, Sept. 11, 2000, pp. 126E3–4.

56. Lourdes Casanova and Gonzalo Jimenez, "AOL Latin America and Cisneros Group: A Successful Story?" INSEAD Case 301-143-1, 2001, pp. 8–12.

57. Simon Romero, "Starmedia Will Restate Its Financial Results," *New York Times*, Nov. 20, 2001.

58. *E-Business in Latin America*, pp. 153–160; Octavio Pereira Lopes, "B2B in Latin America," GP Investimentos presentation, Americas Society, June 19, 2001.

59. William Landers, *Will's Wired World*, Credit Suisse First Boston, Sept. 27, 2000.

60. Lopes, op. cit.

61. *Foreign Investment in Latin America and the Caribbean*, pp. 37, 39–40.

62. Hugh Courtney, "Making the Most of Uncertainty," *McKinsey Quarterly,* vol. 4, 2001, pp. 40–47; the following section applies some of the concepts in the article to the Latin American environment.

63. Lowell Bryan, Jane Fraser, Jeremy Oppenheim, and Wilhelm Rall, *Race for the World,* Harvard Business School Press, Boston, 1999, pp. 91–93. This section adapts this book's typology to the Latin American business situation.

64. Mauro Guillén and Adrian Tschoegl, "The New Conquistadors: Spanish Banks and the Liberalization of Latin America Financial Markets," Wharton School Case 300-133-1, 2000, p. 19; the following section draws from information in the case as well as from company interviews.

65. Peter Williamson and Charlotte Butler, "Cemex in Asia," INSEAD Case 301-078-1, 2001, pp. 1–2. The following section draws from case information and from company interviews.

66. *E-Business in Latin America,* p. 158.

67. Lourdes Casanova, "AmBev, The Dream Project," INSEAD Case 301-044-1, 2001, pp. 1–2; the following section draws from case information and from company interviews.

68. Lopes, op. cit.

CHAPTER 2

1. Economist Intelligence Unit, *Country Monitor,* Dec. 25, 2000.

2. Strategy Research Corporation, *2001 Latin American Market Planning Report.*

3. Some observers of market trends suggest that the middle class of Latin America lives in the United States. See Economist Intelligence Unit, *Consumer Marketing in Latin America,* 1999.

4. New Strategist Publications, *American Incomes: Demographics of Who Has Money,* Ithaca, N.Y., 2000.

5. Strategy Research Corporation, *2000 U.S. Hispanic Market.*

6. See E. Stroudsburg, "Latin Lure: Demographic Attracts Marketing Dollars and Focus," *Beverage World,* Jan. 31–Feb. 28, 1999. Also, *Dallas Morning News,* "Minorities' Power to Purchase to Reach $56 Billion in Texas," Sept. 8, 2000.

7. *2000 U.S. Hispanic Market.*

8. Lora et al., *Dealing with Economic Insecurity in Latin America,* World Bank, 2000.

9. ECLAC, *Social Panorama of Latin America 1999–2000,* S.00.II.G.18, Santiago, Chile, 2000.

10. A common estimate of variability is the standard deviation of the series.

11. *Social Panorama of Latin America 1999–2000,* Chap. 2.

12. "Demographic Flux," *Business Latin America,* June 23, 1997.

13. http://www.census.gov/populations/so...hispanic/cps98/98gifsshow/sld009.htm

14. See John Holcombe, "Understanding Regional Income Estimates," *Business Latin America*, Sept. 5, 1994, for a discussion on estimating Latin American household buying power in Latin America.

15. "The Challenges of an Aging Population," *ECLAC News*, vol. 20, no. 10, Oct., 2000.

16. "The New Face of Urbanization in the Cities of Latin America and the Caribbean," *CEPAL News*, vol. 20, no. 11, Nov., 2000.

17. *2000 U.S. Hispanic Market.*

18. "Radiografía del Consumo en la Argentina," *Mercado*, Editorial Coyuntura, 1999.

19. Holcombe, op. cit., p. 3.

20. "Employment: Aquilles' Heel of Reforms," *CEPAL News*, vol. 20, no. 8, Aug. 2000.

21. Ibid.

22. TGI Latina Survey quoted in http://www.zonalatina.com/Zldata161.htm

23. Quentin T. Wodon, *Poverty and Policy in Latin America and the Caribbean*, World Bank Paper 457, 2000.

24. CEPAL, *La Brecha de la Equidad en America Latina y el Caribe: Una Segunda Evaluacion*, Santiago, Chile, 2000.

25. E. Klein and V. Tokman, "La Estratificación Social Bajo la Tensión en la Era de Globalización," *Revista de la Cepal*, no. 72, Dec. 2000.

26. We based this statement on the Gini coefficients in Table 2.3. The Gini index measures the extent to which the distribution of income among households or individuals within an economy deviates from a perfectly equal distribution. A Gini index of zero represents perfect equality. The higher the number, the larger the inequality. An index of 1.0 represents perfect inequality or one person owning all income. World Bank, *Entering the 21st Century: World Development Report*, 2000.

27. Miguel Szekely and Marianne Hilgert, *The 1990s in Latin America: Another Decade of Persistent Inequality*, Luxembourg Income Study, Working Paper 235, Dec. 1999.

28. Economist Intelligence Unit, *Consumer Marketing in Latin America*, 1999.

29. Since a breakdown of consumption expenditures of U.S. Latin households was not available, in this section we referred mainly to Latin American countries.

30. Proximity to the United States may have a greater influence on Mexican households breakfast food preferences.

31. Euromonitor, *Consumer International 1999/2000*, p. 137.

32. *InfoAmericas-Tendencias*, "Latin America 2001."

33. Audit & Surveys Worldwide, *Pan Latin American Kids Study*, 1998.

34. *Business Week*, June 15, 1992.

35. *Wall Street Journal*, Jan. 11, 1995, p. 2.

36. *Business Week*, Feb. 9, 1998.

37. John Holcombe, "Austerity Hits Brazil in the Pocketbook," http://www. strategyresearch.com/IS_Latin_america_marketing.htm

38. "Radiografia del Consumo," *Mercado,* Nov. 2000.

39. For instance, in Argentina it accounts for about 35% market share of all categories. In the food categories, the share is 50%. *Mercado,* "Revolucion en el universo de marcas," Jan. 2, 2001.

40. Ronald Soong, *Shopper Typology in Colombia.* A study based on data from the Colombia Consumer Survey, part of a Panamerican consumer survey conducted by TGI in 1999.

41. Ronald Soong, "Buying Name Brands in Argentina," based on TGI's Argentina Survey, 1999.

42. Ibid.

43. Chip Walker, "The Global Middle Class," *American Demographics,* Sept. 1995.

44. Gabriel Molina, "Latin American Consumers Beyond Borders," presentation by the Gallup Organization.

45. The top 10 metro markets in terms of buying power are based on total buying power of the urban market. Some small Latin American cities exhibit larger household income, but their total buying power is not significant.

46. "La Nueva Clasificacion Socio-economica para el Consumidor en Chile," *La Tercera,* Sept. 9, 1999.

47. Audits & Surveys Worldwide, *Los Medios y Mercados de Latinoamerica,* 1996.

48. IBOPE-Latin Panel, *Ciclo de Vida do Consumidor,* 2000.

49. Rolando Arellano, *Los Estilos de Vida en el Perú: Consumidores & Mercados,* Consumidores y Mercados, Lima, 2000.

50. *2000 U.S. Hispanic Market.*

51. *Mercurio,* Mar. 24, 2001; also, *InfoAmericas,* Jan. 2001.

52. "Telenovelas and Soap in Latin America," http://www.zonalatina.com/ z1data131.htm

53. Ronald Soong and Donato Verdin, "Is There a Latin American Audience for Regional Media?" http://www.zonalatina.com/Z1data05.htm; see also Kotzrinker, "Viaja Bien el Contenido?" http://www.baquia.com/com/legacy/ 13301.html

54. Audits & Surveys, *Telecommunications in Latin America,* 1999.

55. Ibid.

56. Although we discuss the developments of this new medium in detail later in this section, it should be noted that the statistics used when referring to this medium are for reference because of the rapid change in the adoption and use of this new medium. Estimates vary with the source, and the industry has not developed a uniform measuring standard. At this point of our discussion, we refer to the early developments of the Internet in Latin America. Also, to compare the Internet with other platforms of connectivity, in this part of our discussion we focus on household, not individual, penetration.

57. This section is based on Carrie Hatten and Daliah Korsun, *Latin American Internet Penetration, Uses and Trends,* George Washington University, Aug. 2000.

58. IDG Now.

59. http://www.hispanicbusiness.com/news/news_print.asp?id=2898

60. William Landers, *Latin American Internet Industry Update,* Credit Suisse First Boston, Feb. 3, 2000, p. 4.

61. Quoted in *Mercurio,* Apr. 4, 2001.

62. William Landers, "The Impact of Internet and Information Technology in Latin America," presentation at the Americas Society, New York, May 1, 2001.

63. http://idgnow.uol.com.br/idgnow/internet/2001/03/0060

64. Mary Meeker et al., *The Latin America Internet Report,* Morgan Stanley Dean Witter, Feb. 2000, p. 46.

65. Roland Soong, "Latin American Internet Activities," http://www.zonalatina.com, Dec. 18, 1999, p. 2.

66. Ibid.

67. Meeker, p. 58.

68. Pyramid Research, *Latin America: Survey Reveals Internet User Behaviour,* http://www.ebusinessforum.com, Apr. 5, 2000, p. 1.

69. Landers, *Latin American Internet Industry Update,* p. 7.

70. Michael Pastore, *Latin American E-Commerce Showing Signs of Growth,* Internet News, http://www.internetnews.com, Apr. 26, 2000, p. 1.

71. "Beyond Banking," *Business Latin America,* Economist Intelligence Unit, July 17, 2000, p. 3.

72. Landers, *Latin American Internet Industry Update,* p. 15.

CHAPTER 3

1. Ernesto J. Poza, "Global Competition and the Family-Owned Business in Latin America," *Family Business Review,* vol. 8, no. 4, Winter 1995, pp. 301–312. Ray Fisman and Tarun Khanna, *Facilitating Development: The Role of Business Groups,* Harvard Business School Working Paper 98-076.

2. "Corporate Titans: Most Powerful Latin CEOs," *Latin CEO,* Oct. 2000, pp. 51–64.

3. Wilson Peres, ed., *Grandes Empresas y Grupos Industriales Latinoamericanos,* Siglo Ventiuno Editores, Mexico City, 1998; Mark Granovetter, "Coase Revisited: Business Groups in the Modern Economy," *Industrial and Corporate Change,* vol. 4, no. 1, 1995; Mark Granovetter, "Business Groups," in Neil J. Smelser and Richard Swedberg, eds., *The Handbook of Economic Sociology,* Princeton University Press, Princeton, NJ, 1994.

4. Celso Garrido and Wilson Peres, "Las Grandes Empresas y Grupos Industriales Latinoamericanos en los Años Noventa," in Wilson Peres, ed., *Grandes Empresas y Grupos Industriales Latinoamericanos,* Siglo Ventiuno Editores, Mexico City, 1998, pp. 30–31.

5. "En la Mira de Slim," *América Economía,* June 29, 2000.

6. Ivan Lansberg and Edith Perrow, "Understanding and Working with Leading Family Businesses in Latin America," *Family Business* Review, vol. 4, no. 2, Summer 1991, pp. 127–147; Luís F. Andrade, José M. Barra, and Heinz-Peter Elstrodt, "All in the *Familia,*" *McKinsey Quarterly,* vol. 4, 2001.

7. Timothy Habbershon, "Improving the Long-Run Survival of Family Firms," Family-Controlled Corporation Program, Wharton School, University of Pennsylvania, 2000; Joseph Ganitsky and Jeffrey A. Barach, "Successful Succession in Family Business," *Family Business Review,* Summer, vol. 8, no. 2, 1995, pp. 131–155.

8. In 1996 the 100 largest industrial enterprises registered total sales of $164 billion compared with GDP in the same region that year of $1.7 billion.

9. Tarun Khanna and Krishna Palepu, "The Future of Business Groups in Emerging Markets: Long Run Evidence from Chile," *Academy of Management Journal,* vol. 43, no. 3, June 2000, pp. 268–286.

10. Daniel J. McCosh, "Concrete Results," *Latin CEO,* Oct. 2000, pp. 39–48.

11. James A. Tompkins, "The Next Buzzword: Deverticalization," *Food Logistics,* May 1998.

12. Khanna and Palepu, op. cit.

13. Profiles on a number of GGEs and their owners may be found at http://www. lanota.com/perfiles; and in various issues of *Latin CEO* and *América Economía.*

14. Andrea Mandel-Campbell, "Profile: Carlos Slim, Telmex: A Mexican with the Midas Touch," *Financial Times,* July 10, 2000.

15. Pankaj Ghemawat et al., *Strategic Response from Argentine Economic Groups to the Competitive Shock of the 90s,* IAE, Escuela de Dirección y Negocios, Universidad Austral, Working Paper, Dec. 2000.

16. "La Hora de las Vacas Sagradas," *América Economía,* Feb. 7, 2001; *The Impact of Privatization in the Americas.*

17. Jonas Prager, "Is Privatization a Panacea for LDCs? Market Failure versus Public Sector Failure," *Journal of Developing Areas,* vol. 16, Apr. 1992, pp. 302–303.

18. Paul Starr, "The Meaning of Privatization," *Yale Law and Policy Review,* vol. 6, 1988, pp. 6–41; John Moore, "British Privatization: Taking Capitalism to the People," *Harvard Business Review,* Jan.–Feb. 1992, pp. 115–124; Ralph Bradburd, "Privatization of Natural Monopoly Public Enterprises: The Regulation Issue," *IFC Discussion Papers,* No. 14, International Finance Corporation, World Bank Group, Feb. 1992.

19. Narendar V. Rao, C. Bhaktavatsala Rao, and Steve Dunphy, "International Perspectives on Privatization of State-Owned Enterprises," Proceedings of the Annual Conference of the Southwest Small Business Association, Dallas, TX, Mar. 1994.

20. Yair Aharoni, *The Evolution and Management of State-Owned Enterprises,* Ballinger, Cambridge, MA, 1986.

21. OECD, *Corporate Governance, State-Owned Enterprises and Privatization*, Organization for Economic Cooperation and Development, Paris, 1992, p. 26.

22. Mehdi Haririan, *State-Owned Enterprises in a Mixed Economy: Micro Versus Macro Economic Objectives*, Westview Press, Boulder, CO, 1989; Antonio Martín del Campo and Donald Winkler, "State-Owned Enterprise Reform in Latin America," World Bank, *Occasional Paper Series 2*, 1991.

23. Gabriel Roth, *The Private Provision of Public Services in Developing Countries*, Oxford University Press, Oxford, 1987; World Bank, *Bureaucrats in Business: The Economics and Politics of Government Ownership*, World Bank, Washington, DC, 1995; OECD, "Best Practice Guidelines for Contracting Out Government Services," Public Management Service, *PUMA Policy Brief 2*, Feb. 1997.

24. *The Evolution and Management of State-Owned Enterprises*, p. 341.

25. R. Joseph Monsen and Kenneth D. Walters, *Nationalized Companies: A Threat to American Business*, McGraw-Hill, New York, 1983.

26. *América Economía*, "Las Intocables," July 27, 2000.

27. Ibid.

28. Ibid.

29. "Company Profile: Petróleos Mexicanos," *Hoover's Online*, http:/www.hoovers.com

30. Henry Tricks, "Pemex in Modernization Drive," *Financial Times*, Feb. 13, 2001.

31. Geri Smith, "Pemex Still in the Dark Ages," *Business Week*, Mar. 26, 2001.

32. "Las Intocables."

33. Petróleos de Venezuela S.A., home page, http://www.pdv.com

34. "Venezuelan President Chávez Leads Conoco/PDVSA Joint Project Dedication Ceremony," http://www.hoovers.com, Feb. 13, 2001.

35. Nelson Rios and Allan Cohen, "Babson College and Petróleos de Venezuela Find Value in Global Executive Education Alliance," *Corporate University Review*, vol. 5, May–June 1997.

36. "PDVSA Announces 10-Year Business Plan," *OilOnline*, Apr. 11, 2000.

37. "Company Profile: Petrobrás," http://www.hoovers.com; see also http://www.Petrobrás.com.br

38. Jonathan Wheatley, "Pumping Up Petrobrás: Can Philippe Reichstul Ready the Giant for Competition?" *Business Week*, intern. ed., Dec. 18, 2000.

39. "PetroCosm and Petrobrás Agree to Create a Digital Marketplace in Brazil for the Oil and Gas Industry," *Business Wire*, Feb. 22, 2001.

40. "Petrobrás," *Financial News*, Mar. 19, 2001.

41. "Brazil Petrobrás Lowers 2001 Output Target," *Reuters Company News*, Apr. 20, 2001.

42. "A New Sense of Purpose," an interview with Henri Philippe Reichstul, president of Petrobrás, *First Magazine*, vol. 14, no. 2, 2000.

43. "Petrobrás Selects Citibank for NYSE-Listed ADR Program Representing Preferred Shares," *Business Wire*, Feb. 22, 2001.
44. "Repsol YPF, Petrobrás Close to Final Accord on Asset Swap," *AFX News—Asia*, Apr. 8, 2001.
45. We use the definition of the United Nations Economic Commission on Latin America and the Caribbean, applied to Mercosur, in classifying small businesses as those with up to 100 employees; medium businesses; up to 300; and microenterprises up to 20.
46. Francisco Gatto, "Mercosur: Its Challenges to Small and Medium-Sized Industrial Enterprises in Terms of Competition" *CEPAL Review*, vol. 68, Aug. 1999, pp. 61–77.
47. Ibid.
48. Wilson Peres and Giovanni Stumpo, "Small and Medium-Sized Manufacturing Enterprises in Latin America and the Caribbean Under the New Economic Model," *World Development*, vol. 28, no. 9, 2000, pp. 1643–1655.
49. Ibid.
50. Banco Interamericano de Desarrollo, *Promoviendo Crecimiento con Equidad*, Washington, DC, 1998.
51. Ibid., p. 20.
52. "Canción Triste," *América Economía*, Mar. 25, 2000, pp. 36–37.
53. U.S. Agency for International Development, *Commercial Bank Downscalers in Latin America*, Microenterprise Development Brief, No. 37, Oct. 1998.
54. "Chile Banking Chilean Government, BBVA to Finance Employee Training," *EFE News Service*, Jan. 16, 2001; "Bank BBVA Offers Credit to Small, Mid-Sized Firms in México, *EFE News Service*, Mar. 31, 2001.
55. Romina Nicaretta, "Bank Woos Brazil's Poor with Post-Office Branches," *Miami Herald*, Apr. 30, 2001.
56. Enrique Ghersi, "The Informal Economy in Latin America," *Cato Journal*, vol. 17, no. 1, Spring–Summer 1997.
57. Hernando de Soto, *The Other Path*, Harper & Row, New York, 1989, p. xii; see also, Victor E. Tokman, ed., *Beyond Regulation: The Informal Economy in Latin America*, Lynne Rienner, Boulder, CO, 1992.
58. "The Informal Economy in Latin America."
59. Albert Berry and Maria Teresa Mendez, *Policies to Promote Adequate Employment in Latin America and the Caribbean*, Employment and Training Papers 46, International Labor Organization, 1999.
60. Inter-American Development Bank, *Facing Up to Inequality in Latin America*, Inter-American Development Bank, Washington, DC, 1999. The report cites labor laws designed to protect workers (e.g., restrictions on hiring temporary workers, extra hours, high costs of firing) but that have a negative impact on other groups, such as women and labor market entrants who are not prime-age urban formal male workers.
61. "Latin America Economy: Relying on the Black Economy," *Financial Times*, Aug. 23, 1999.

62. Eduardo Lora and Mauricio Olivera, *Macro Policy and Employment,* report prepared for the 1998 IDB/IIC annual meeting.

63. Fundación Invertir, "Underground Economy," Web-based article, May 5, 2000.

64. Mexico's Jan. Unemployment 2.31% vs 2.28% Yr. Ago," *Dow Jones Newswires,* Feb. 19, 2001.

65. "México Tem Mais Trabalho Informal," *Gazeta Mercantil,* Aug. 23, 2000.

66. Albert Berry, "Small and Medium Enterprise (SME) Under Trade and Foreign Exchange Liberalization: Latin American and Canadian Experiences and Concerns," *Canadian Journal of Development Studies,* vol. 17, no. 1, 1996, pp. 53–74.

67. Statistics derived from ECLAC, Unit on Investment and Corporate Strategies, Division of Production, Productivity and Management, 2000.

68. This section draws heavily upon Michael Mortimore, "Corporate Strategies for FDI in the Context of Latin America's New Economic Model," *World Development,* vol. 28, no. 9, pp. 1611–1626.

69. There were sectoral restrictions in natural resources, the petroleum sector, and services. In manufacturing, governments pushed for mixed companies and joint ventures while reserving specific sectors, such as auto parts and petrochemicals, for locally owned firms. Restrictions on operations were common and included performance requirements and compulsory licensing of technology to local firms. Financial restrictions included limits on the repatriation of capital, profit remittances, and royalties, and the exclusion of foreign firms from access to the national financial market.

70. Stephen Blank and Jerry Haar, *Making NAFTA Work: U.S. Firms and the New North American Business Environment,* North-South Center, University of Miami, and Lynne Rienner, Coral Gables, FL, 1998. For analysis of the earlier phase of government policy changes and MNC responses, see Robert Grosse, *Multinationals in Latin America,* Routledge, London, 1989.

71. Additionally, Fundación Chile, a nonprofit technology incubator, founded in 1976, promotes technology transfer and new company formation. It is a showcase example for melding scientific and technological activities with business. Derek Hill, *Latin America: R&D Spending Jumps in Brazil, Mexico, and Costa Rica,* National Science Foundation, Division of Science Resources Studies NSF 00-316, 2000.

72. John P. Tuman and John T. Morris, eds., *Tranforming the Latin American Automobile Industry,* M.E. Sharpe, Armonk, NY, 1998.

73. Dale B. Truett and Lila J. Truett, "Government Policy and the Export Performance of the Mexican Automobile Industry," *Growth and Change,* Summer 1994, vol. 25, no. 3, p. 301; Michael Mortimore, "Transforming Sitting Ducks into Flying Geese: The Example of the Mexican Automobile Industry," *Desarrollo Productivo,* CEPAL, United Nations, vol. 36, 1995; Clement Ruíz Durán, Enrique Dussel Peters, and Taeko Taniura, *Changes in Industrial Organization: The Mexican Automobile Industry and Economic Liberalization,* Institute of Developing Economies, JRP Series 120, 1997.

74. Michael Mortimore, "Mexico's TNC-centric Industrialization Process," in Richard Kozul-Wright and Robert Rowthorn, eds., *Transnational Corporations and the Global Economy,* Macmillan, London, 1998.

75. Thomas A. O'Keefe and Jerry Haar, "The Impact of Mercosur on the Automobile Industry," *North-South Agenda Paper,* North-South Center, University of Miami, 2001.

76. Inflows of FDI of $27,164 million accounted for 41% of the total privatization program from 1991 through July 1998, while 59% came from Brazilian investors.

77. Michael E. Porter et al., *The Global Competitiveness Report 2000,* Oxford University Press, New York, 2000.

78. Heinz-Peter Elstsrodt, William W. Lewis, and Gustavo Lopetegui, "Latin American Productivity," *McKinsey Quarterly,* vol. 3, 1994, pp. 21–35.

79. Joseph Ramos, *Política Industrial y Competitividad en Economías Abiertas,* CEPAL, Santiago, 1996.

80. Martin N. Baily et al., "Will Brazil Seize Its Future?," *McKinsey Quarterly,* vol. 3, 1998, pp. 75–91.

81. Jorge H. Forteza and Gary L. Neilson, *Towards the Next Generation Multinational in Latin America,* Booz Allen & Hamilton, McLean, VA, 1999.

CHAPTER 4

1. Alejandro Jadresic, "Investment in Natural Gas Pipelines in the Southern Cone of Latin America," World Bank, 2000; "Brazil's Natural Gas Systems: Sources, Markets, Regulations, and Business," *Oil & Gas Journal,* Aug. 9, 1999; ISI Emerging Markets, *The Electricity Industry in Mexico, 1994–2000,* Mar. 27, 2001.

2. Marianne Fay, "Financing the Future: Infrastructure Needs in Latin America, 2000–2005," World Bank, 2000.

3. Fay, op. cit.

4. Fay, op. cit.

5. Paul Hennemeyer, "Energy Reform and Privatization: Distilling the Signal from the Noise," in F. Basañes, E. Uribe, and R. Willig, eds., *Can Privatization Deliver? Infrastructure for Latin America,* John Hopkins University Press, Baltimore, MD, 1999.

6. International Telecommunication Union, *Americas Telecommunications Indicators 2000,* Executive Summary.

7. International Telecommunication Union, *World Telecommunication Indicators 2000/2001.*

8. International Telecommunication Union, *Americas Telecommunications Indicators 2000,* Executive Summary.

9. Ibid.

10. "Infrastructure Brazil: Telecommunications," http://www.infrastruturabrasil.gov.br/perfis/tele.asp

11. Enersis Annual Report, Enersis divested of the transmission company Transelec in 2000.

12. Hennemeyer, op. cit.

13. Hennemeyer, op. cit.

14. Armando Piñeiro, Após a Privatizacao, BNDES presentation, Rio de Janeiro, Brazil, Dec. 4, 2000.

15. *EnergyOnline Daily News,* Apr. 14, 1998.

16. Gaspetro is the majority owner of the Brazilian side of the pipeline. The other partners are two other consortia (Enron–Royal Dutch/Shell and BHP Petroleum–El Paso Energy). Gaspetro also has minority participation on the Bolivian side of the pipeline. See J-P. Prates, "Brazil's Three Natural Gas Systems: Sources, Markets, Regulations, and Business Perspectives," *Oil & Gas Journal,* Aug. 9, 1999.

17. Similar projects to connect the Argentinean and Brazilian electric systems are also in place. Spain Endesa's transmission subsidiary, Cien, expects to complete a transmission line by Dec. 2001. See http://www. infrastruturabrasil.gov.br/noticia

18. *OECD Economic Surveys: Mexico,* 1999.

19. http://www.eia.doe.gov/emeu/cabs/mexico2.html

20. Jaun Rosellon and Jonathan Halperin, Regulatory Reform in Mexico's Natural Gas Industry, World Bank Report 2000.

21. Pablo Spiller and William Savedoff, "Commitment and Governance in Infrastructure" in F. Basañes et al.

22. Humberto Campodonico, Las Reformas Estructurales del Sector Eléctrico Peruano y las Características de la Inversión 1999–2000, ECLA, Serie de Reformas Económicas 25, 2000.

23. Carlos Diaz and Raimundo Soto, *Open-Acess in the Chilean Telecommunications and Electricity Sectors,* Inter-American Development Bank, Aug. 1999.

24. For more information, see Fjestad and K. Haannæs, "Strategy Trade-offs in the Knowledge and Network Economy," *Business Strategy Review,* vol. 12, no. 1, 2001. Also P. H. Longstaff, *Networked Industries: Patterns in Development, Operation, and Regulation,* Center for Information Policy Research, Harvard University.

25. These strategies are identified in Chapter 1 based on the work of Lowell Bryan et al., *Race for the World,* Harvard Business School Press, Boston, MA, 1999.

26. CIT, *The Yearbook of Latin American Telecommunications,* 2001.

27. The migration to global networks is documented in T. Malnight, "The Transition from Decentralized to Network-Based MNC Structures: An Evolutionary Perspective," *Journal of International Business Studies,* 1996.

28. See C. Cranges and A. Estache, *Regulatory Trade-offs in the Design of Concession Contracts,* World Bank. Also A. R. Parker, "Strategic Choices in a

Dynamically Changing Regulatory Environment," *Journal of Business Research*, vol. 51, 2001.

29. For a full account on this case, see F. Robles and A. Garrastuzi, *Telecom Argentina: Competing in Unrestricted Markets,* George Washington University, 2001.

30. Devaluation of Argentina's peso in early 2002 shifted the exchange risk to the operator as tariffs were set in local currency.

31. *Business Latin America,* Mar. 23, 1998, p. 4.

32. "Telecom Italia Looks to Latin America," *Global News Wire,* Sept. 28, 2000.

33. "Telecom Argentina USA," EmpresasNews.com, Apr. 24, 2001.

34. *Wall Street Journal,* Dec. 16, 2001, p. 17.

35. Telecom Argentina had to pay two points over LIBOR for a syndicated $150 million loan used to finance a PCS network in southern Argentina: *Business News Americas,* Jan. 5, 2001.

36. "Preliminary Overview of the Economies of Latin America and the Caribbean," *CEPAL News,* Jan. 2002.

37. Telecom Argentina, Consolidated Third Quarter Report, 2001. The situation in 2001 was as bad for Telefónica Spain, which reported a decline of 65% in profits in the first quarter of 2001. See *Global News Wire,* May 15, 2001.

38. "Argentina Told of Conditions for Aid," *Washington Post,* Jan. 10, 2002.

39. Incumbents such as Mexico's Telmex have a great advantage, as they control access to the network.

40. "For AES, Phones Are Its Business, Too," *Washington Post,* Sept. 4, 2001.

41. Other indicators, such as return on assets or return on capital employed (ROCE), could have been used. We used the mentioned indicators because of complete information for all firms on these two aspects.

42. "The Largest World Companies," *Financial Times,* 2001.

CHAPTER 5

1. Emerging-market indicators, *Economist,* Sept. 8, 2001, p. 113.

2. Brazil is the only country in the region where inflation is on the increase, due to depreciation of the Real in 1998.

3. Patterns of broad consumption changes were reported in Chapter 2. A number of single-country reports indicate greater detail of specific changes within a given consumer category. For more details about these micro changes, refer to the following sources. Changes in consumption preferences in Chile, *Qué Pasa,* June 1999. Also, "Ten Key Consumption Trends in Argentina, 2000," "Argentinean Youth in 21st Century," and "Consumption Patterns Among Peruvian Youth," http://www.adlatina.com. Also, "Materialism in Latin America," *TGI Latina,* and "Buying Clothes in Brazil," *TGI Brazil,* http://www.zonalatina.com

4. The soft-beverage market has experienced low demand in 2000 despite a reduction of prices in this category.

5. "El Perfil del Consumidor—Alimentos y Bebidas," *Mercado*, Oct. 9, 2001.

6. Definition and classification of socioeconomic levels in Latin America vary in each country. In an effort to come up with a pan-regional definition and classification that could be comparable across countries, Media and Markets in Latin America, a consumer research organization, identified four groups: A, B, C, and D. The classification includes several socioeconomic variables, including household income, education, and possession of household goods. Socioeconomic class A includes upper-socioeconomic households with more spending power, college education, and high penetration of household goods. The other classes are the middle-to-upper class (B), middle class (C), and working class and subsistence (D). For market segmentation purposes, families in extreme poverty levels are not included in the classification. Within each class, a further breakdown of two or three subgroups represents refinements of the larger segment. A study by the Strategy Research Corporation found the following breakdown of households for the region: 2% in the upper class, 12% in the emerging high middle class, 30% in the middle class, and 56% in the working class. The breakdown varies from country to country. See the following for information on socioeconomic segments in Latin America: "Socioeconomic Levels in Latin America," http://www.zonalatina. com/Z1data07.htm and *2001 Latin American Market Planning Report*, Strategy Research Corporation.

7. *Meio & Messagem,* Mar. 14, 2001, p. 36, and May 7, 2001, p. 40.

8. McCann-Erickson, "New Young Consumers Around the World," *Pulse*, Aug. 2000. http://www.adlatina.com/pages/investigaciones/invest.php3?id=183; "Consumption in Young Venezuelan Consumers," Insotev, Apr., 2000; "Generation Y in Argentina," *Clarín*, July 7, 1999; Young & Rubicam, *Young Peruvian Consumers.*

9. GM Latin America is targeting the midsize market with its European-made car Astra. The Astra is available in Brazil, Mexico, Argentina, and Chile. GM is adding Venezuela in its attempt to dislodge Toyota's market leadership in the middle-class market. Toyota's midpriced Corolla has been the standard of global class quality in Latin America. Venezuela's midsize market represents about 16% of total car sales in that country. Initially, GM's German subsidiary will export Astras to Venezuela until an assembly plan comes on line in 2002. *La República,* Nov. 15, 2001.

10. The reader should recall from Chapter 4 that Mexico planned to liberalize the telecommunications sector fully in 1998.

11. Prodigy is the second-largest national ISP in Latin America. Brazil's UOL with about 1 million subscribers is number 1. Regionally, Spain's Terra is the largest because of the aggregation of all its national customer bases but is number 2 in Brazil and Mexico.

12. Banco Itaú, *Annual Report 1999.*

13. *Meio & Mensagem,* Mar. 14, 2001.

14. *Exáme,* May 4, 2000.
15. Interview with Natura's integrated marketing manager by one of the authors, May 16, 2001. Natura's sales productivity is greater than close competitor Avon, which uses 500,000 sales representatives in Brazil. *Global Cosmetics,* Mar. 2000.
16. Natura, *Annual Report, 2000.*
17. Interview with Natura, ibid.
18. In a more recent study, Landor surveyed hi-tech brands worldwide. The results of the study for Brazil showed that only three of the top 20 brands were Brazilian (Brastemps, Embratel, and Globo). Not surprisingly, the rest of the top 20 were well-known global brands such as Microsoft, Intel, and Yahoo!. Landor found a similar situation in Mexico. Only three Mexican brands ranked among the top 20. These Mexican brands were Telmex, TV Azteca, and Televisa. *Landor Global Image Power,* June 2001.
19. "Itaú e a Marca Mais Valiosa do Brasil," *Meio & Mensagem,* Mar. 14, 2001.
20. Nielsen, *Consumer Habits and Attitudes in Argentina,* 2000.
21. Several brand-building strategy models predicated the use of building blocks. See Kevin L. Keller, *Strategic Brand Management: Building, Measuring, and Managing Brand Equity,* 2nd ed., Prentice Hall, Upper Saddle River, NJ, 2003; and David Aaker and Erich Joachimsthaler, *Brand Leadership,* Free Press, New York, 2000.
22. Adlatina, "El Mercado de las Telecomunicaciones en la Argentina." http://www.adlatina.com/pages/invest.php
23. The average number of hours watching TV does not vary much among different countries in Latin America.
24. Audits & Surveys, *Telecommunications in Latin America,* 1998.
25. Bombril, Icono de la Cultura Brasileña, http://www.adlatina.com/pages/investigaciones/invest.php
26. ECLAC, *Foreign Investment in Latin America and the Caribbean,* 2001.
27. An analysis by the EIU showed that the foreign direct investment country ratings for Brazil and Mexico had been converging in the period of 1998–2000. Projections for these ratings based on a number of factors that determine foreign direct investment flows indicate that Mexico will overtake Brazil as the preferred destination by 2005. *Infoamericas,* Mar. 2001. Further analysis of the use of Brazil and Mexico as the regional base can be found in "Clash of the Titans: Brazil vs. Mexico," *Tendencias,* Nov. 2001.
28. Strategic Research Corporation, *2000 U.S. Hispanic Market,* 2001.
29. Gruma, *Annual Report 2000.*
30. Gruma holds 80% control of corn flour production.
31. Gruma S.A., U.S. Securities and Exchange Commission, Form 20-F, File 1-14852.
32. In 2001, Gruma sold out its industrial bread business to Mexico's Bimbo. Telephone interview with Gruma's U.S. office.
33. Gruma, *Annual Report.*

34. Two examples serve to illustrate this point. Sadia markets minisized lasagnas that appeal either to individuals or small families. In another example, Sadia's frankfurters are fractioned in several parts. Consumers can use as many parts per meal as they wish and save the rest.

35. Interview with Sadia's Chairman Luiz Fernando Furlan, São Paulo, May 14, 2001.

36. Latin American markets are not a priority for this company. Sadia has some distribution facilities in Argentina, Uruguay, and Chile and representative offices in Bolivia and Paraguay.

37. "Sintonía No Paladar," *Forbes Brazil*, Mar. 9, 2001.

38. Sadia, *Annual Report 2000*. According to one report, Sadia managed to create economic value to its shareholders in the order of $614 million. See Exáme, Mehores, and Mairores, As 500 Maiores Empresas do Brasil, July 2001.

39. *Gestión*, May 2001.

40. Falabella acquired the failing transformation of a Sears' department store by a Colombian group. Sears divested from a number of international stores in the late 1980s and early 1990s to concentrate its effort to the U.S. market. A Colombian group of investors took control of Sears' assets in Peru but failed to materialize any significant business in Peru.

41. The giant U.S. big-box specialty retailer targeted Canada, Chile, and Argentina as the first markets to expand.

42. This section is based on the case Terra Networks in Latin America, developed by one of the authors in collaboration with Anjali Mahadevan, M.B.A. student at George Washington University. We should also note that the fusion of Terra with the U.S. portal Lycos has catapulted the company to global portal status with presence in the United States, Europe, and Asia.

43. StarMedia Network, a pure-play ISP, with no multinational parent company, is the exception. StarMedia was the first pan-regional portal in Latin America. When launched, StarMedia offered its services in Argentina, Brazil, Chile, Colombia, Mexico, Puerto Rico, Uruguay, and Venezuela.

44. The consolidated revenues include Unilever's acquisition of BestFoods in 2000, a multinational company on its own with strong presence in Latin America. Unilever Financial Report, http://www.unilever.com

45. "500 Largest Latin American Firms," *América Economia*, Aug. 2001. Unilever's third largest Latin American subsidiary, Mexico, generated revenues of $524 million in 1999; see Table 5.1.

46. We acknowledge the contribution of Luiz Kawal, Seema Patel, and Julie Walton, all students at George Washington University, in the preparation of this section.

47. *Consumer International 1996, 1999/2000*, Euromonitor.

48. *Consumer International and European Marketing Data Statistics*, Euromonitor, 1999.

49. Unilever, News Release: "Twin Acquisitions Reinforce Unilever's Mexican Business," Dec. 2, 1998.

50. Electronic interview with Unilever business development manager for Latin America, July 21, 1999.

51. "Adiós a las Marcas," *América Economia,* July 2, 1998, p. 32.

52. *Consumer International 1999/2000,* ibid.

53. "Unilever Enters Argentinean Ice Cream Market," *Ice Cream Reporter,* July 20, 1999, p. 29; "Ice Cream Fixation," *Latin Trade,* Mar. 24, 1999, p. 14.

54. Under precarious financial situation, Exxel sold Freddo to its original owners, Grupo Galicia. *Clarin,* Oct. 26, 2001.

55. Häagen-Daz has introduced the dulce de leche dessert worldwide with great success.

56. "Crescimento Vigoroso," *Gazeta Mercantil,* Mar. 2, 1998, p. 26, and "Yopa e Kibon Perdem Mercado," *Gazeta Mercantil,* Aug. 12, 1998, p. C-3. Also, "Latin Heat," *Dairy Fields,* vol. 182, no. 4, 1999, p. 96, and "Last Licks; More Häagen-Dazs News," *Ice Cream Reporter,* Dec. 20, 1999, p. 29.

57. *Ice Cream Reporter,* 1997.

58. Self-service retail formats include supermarkets, large-scale hypermarkets, department stores, and convenience stores.

59. Carrefour's first investment in Brazil was in 1974. The global retailer's second investment in Latin America was in Argentina in 1982. See Brenda Sternquist, *International Retailing,* Fairchild Publications, New York, 1997, for an account of Carrefour's international expansion.

60. According to the Nielsen survey, op. cit., 46% were less than 34 years old and 85% were women.

61. According to consumer satisfaction experts, these are hygiene factors.

62. Rosenburg, ibid.

63. PriceWaterhouseCoopers, *U.S. Retail Perspectives,* 2001.

64. *La Republica,* Nov. 11, 2001.

65. "Nestlé y CCU se Lanzan a la Venta Directa del Público," *Mercado,* Nov. 21, 2000.

66. Firms included in the table had annual revenues of $1 billion in 2000 in a given country. There is no attempt to consolidate the results of subsidiaries of major multinationals in Table 5.2.

67. Ambev's brands include Brahma beer and Guarana soft drink. The company has established a strategic alliance with Pepsi to market Guarana worldwide. FEMSA's brands include Dos Equis, Sol, and Tecate. FEMSA's main national rival is Grupo Modelo, which produces Corona, the premier Mexican global beer brand. Modelo revenues are not large enough to be included in Table 5.2.

CHAPTER 6

1. Ernesto Aguirre, "Basic Reforms of the Banking Systems in Latin America," *Asian Banking Law Forum,* Bangkok, Thailand, Aug. 17, 2000.

2. Ibid; see also Carl-Johan Lindgren, Gillian Garcia, and Matthew Saal, *Bank Soundness and Macroeconomic Policy,* International Monetary Fund, Washington, DC, 1996.

3. This section draws heavily from market analyses from Standard & Poors, Moody's, and the Bank for International Settlements in Basle.

4. Organization for Economic Cooperation and Development, *Economic Survey of Brazil,* 2001, Policy Brief, June 2001.

5. Eliana Maria Filippossi, "Foreign Capital in the Brazilian Financial System," *International Financial Law Review,* Jan. 2001. The Spanish bank had already acquired three other Brazilian banks: Banco Geral do Comércio ($130 million), Banco Noroeste ($260 million), and Grupo Meridional ($650 million), which includes the Banco Bozano, Simonsen. The 10 largest banks in Brazil are (1) Banco do Brasil, (2) Caixa Econômica Federal, (3) Bradesco, (4) Banco Itaú, (5) Banco Santander, (6) Unibanco, (7) ABN Amro Bank, (8) Banco Safra, (9) HSBC Bank Brasil, and (10) Nossa Caixa Nosso Banco.

6. Luciana del Caro, "Bancos Têm Baixa Produtividade," *Gazeta Mercantil,* Apr. 22, 1998.

7. Ricardo Queiroz, "Lucros e Ineficiência," Ricardo Queiroz Advocacia, http://www.ricardoqueiroz.adv.br

8. "Um Banqueiro Contra o Crime," interview with Ernst Welteke, presidente of Banco Central da Alemanha, *Dinheiro,* Aug. 13, 2001.

9. Organization for Economic Cooperation and Development, *Economic Survey of Brazil,* 2001, Policy Brief, June 2001.

10. Jerry Haar and Krishnan Dadapani, eds., *Banking in North America: NAFTA and Beyond,* Pergamon, New York, 1999.

11. Elizabeth McGuerry, "The Banking Sector Rescue in Mexico," *Economic Review,* Federal Reserve Bank of Atlanta, Third Quarter, 1999, pp. 14–29.

12. U.S. government, *Mexico: FY2001 Country Commercial Guide,* U.S. Department of State, Washington, DC, 2001.

13. Government of Mexico, "The Mexican Banking System: Towards Consolidation," *Mexico's Bimonthly Economic News,* no. 9, Ministry of Finance and Public Credit of Mexico, Mar. 6, 2000.

14. Standard & Poor, *Trends in Latin American Financial Institutions, 2000–2001,* Standard & Poor, New York, Mar. 2001.

15. Economist Intelligence Unit, "Bank Mergers and Sales Set to Continue," *Economist Intelligence Unit Briefs,* Apr. 25, 2001; Economist Intelligence Unit, "BBVA Beats Banacci in Bidding War for Bancomer," *Economist Intelligence Unit Briefs,* June 19, 2000.

16. Francis MacDermot, "Electronic Banking: Financial Fertiliser," *Business Latin America,* Nov. 27, 2000.

17. Noah Elkin, "Online Banking: When Time Is Money," *eMarketer,* Apr. 19, 2001.

18. Mauricio I. Cepeda, Marcos Fernandes, and Andrea C. Waslander, "Brazil's Head Start in Online Banking," *McKinsey Quarterly,* no. 2, 2001.

19. Ibid.

20. Ibid.

21. Elkin.

22. InfoAmericas, "Internet 1: Brick and Mortar 0," *Industry Report,* Apr.–May 2000.

23. Mauricio I. Cepeda, Marcos Fernandes, and Andrea C. Waslander.

24. MacDermot.

25. "The Virtual Threat," *Economist,* May 18, 2000.

26. InfoAmericas, "AT&T Secures Colombian Contract," *Latin Finance,* July 2001.

27. Jessica Toonkel, "Citi Plans Web Site for All Latin America," *American Banker,* Oct. 2, 2000.

28. James Swenson, "An Online Launching Pad," *Latin Finance,* June 2001.

29. Ibid.

30. For a comprehensive survey of Latin American consumers and the Internet, see Boston Consulting Group, *Online Retailing in Latin America: Beyond the Storefront,* Boston Consulting Group and Visa International, Latin America and Caribbean Region, Oct. 2000.

31. Tom Dobis and Philip D. Peters, "Regionalizing Payments in Latin America," *Global Treasury News,* Dec. 11, 2000.

32. Ibid.

33. Jonathan Bell, "Spurring Electronic Trading," *Latin Finance,* Aug. 2001.

34. Ibid.

35. James Swenson, "Shifting Interest Off-Line," *Latin Finance,* July 2001.

36. InfoAmericas, "Internet 1: Brick and Mortar 0," *Industry Report,* Apr.–May, 2000.

37. Michael Contreras, "Risk Levels Down, Opportunities Up," *Latin Finance,* Aug. 2001.

38. The other two are Banco Serfin and Bancomer, owned by BSCH and BBVA, respectively.

39. "The Super Banks of Spain," *Business Week,* Apr. 23, 2001; see also Mauro F. Guillén and Adrian E. Tschoegl, "The New Conquistadors: Spanish Banks and the Liberalization of Latin American Financial Markets," Wharton School, University of Pennsylvania, case study, 2000.

40. Jonathan Wheatley, "A Bad Case of Indigestion," *Latin Finance,* Feb. 2001.

41. "New Market Conditions Boost Credibility of Banking Sector," *Washington Times,* July 15, 1999.

42. Emilio Botín, "Merger Is Not the Only Route," speech presented at a Les Echos conference, Paris, Feb. 24, 2001.

43. "Citigroup to Buy Mexican Bank," *Miami Herald,* May 18, 2001; "Mexico's Banacci Chairmen Cash in with Citigroup Sale," *Bloomberg Latin America,* May 19, 2001; "Sandy Weill's Big Bet," *Latin Finance,* July 2001.

44. Ludger Kübel-Sorger, Svilen Ivanov, and Giles Brennand, *Restoring Good Returns: Investment Banking's Challenge,* Boston Consulting Group, Boston, 2001.

45. Maria O'Brien, "A Shrinking Universe," *Latin Finance*, July 2001.

46. P.J. Kallf, *International Consumer Banking*, ABN Amro, 1998, p. 1.

47. Kumagae Hinki-Junior, "Analysis, Integration and Review," *Latin Finance*, Aug. 2001.

48. Ibid.

49. Greenwich Associates, *Greenwich CFO Survey*, Greenwich, CT, 2000.

50. Jonathan Bell, "Meeting in the Middle," *Latin Finance*, Aug. 2001.

51. Patrick McGeehan, "Showdown on Wall Street," *New York Times*, June 15, 2001.

52. Randall Smith and Suzanne McGee, "Banks' Lending Clout Stings Securities Firms," *Wall Street Journal*, June 15, 2001.

53. *Restoring Good Returns: Investment Banking's Challenge*.

54. Joshua Chaffin, "Fund Drought Still a Problem: Venture Capital," *Financial Times*, Survey of Latin American Finance, Mar. 10, 2001.

55. Douglas A. Beck, Jane N. Fraser, A.C. Reuter-Domenech, and Peter Sidebottom, "Personal Services Goes Financial," *McKinsey Quarterly*, vol. 2, 1999, pp. 38–47.

56. Ibid.

57. "The Super Banks of Spain," *Business Week*, Apr. 23, 2001.

58. In Oct. 1999, in anticipation of the aforementioned developments in the European Union, BBV announced its merger with Argentaria, another Spanish bank.

59. "Latin America: Banco Bilbao Vizcaya Becomes a Powerhouse," *Country Monitor*, Economist Intelligence Unit, Feb. 16, 2000.

60. Mike Zellner, "The Spanish Acquisition: The Final Adventure," *Latin Trade*, Apr. 1, 2001.

61. *Country Monitor*.

62. Eduardo Garcia, "Spain's BBVA Plans to Boost Stake in BBVA-Bancomer," *Bloomberg Latin America*, Sept. 13, 2001.

63. "BBVA Voted 'Best Mexican Bank' by Banking Magazine," *Agencia Efe*, Sept. 3, 2001.

64. "Online Extra: Q&A with BBVA's Ybarra and Gonzalez," *Business Week*, Apr. 23, 2001.

65. Interview with Ricardo Espírito Santo, board member, Banco Espírito Santo, Sept. 28, 2001.

66. For an excellent review of Banco Itaú's evolution, see "The Big Bank Theory," *Latin CEO*, May 2001; see also "Banco Itaú," http://www.securities.com, Internet Securities, Inc., 2001, and http://www.itau.com.br

67. Romina Nicaretta, "Banco Itaú Buys Lloyd's Unit," *Bloomberg News*, Oct. 4, 2001.

68. In a move to further upgrade the bank's communications and Internet infrastructure, Banco Itaú and Telefónica Data Corp., a subsidiary of Madrid-based Telefónica, formalized an agreement in which the Spanish telecommunications firm will operate Itaú's corporate networks. Telefónica plans to invest $93 million directly and indirectly in Itaú subsidiaries that operate the bank's communications operations. Telefónica has an option to increase its investments by an additional $93 million. Itaú estimates that the telecommunications network will reduce its overhead costs by 24%. "Itaú and Telefónica Form Alliance," *Latin Finance,* July 2001.

69. Brian Caplen and Michael Peterson, "Latin America Awards," *Euromoney,* July 2000.

70. "Financial Services: Latin America," *Business Latin America,* July 9, 2001.

71. *ABN Amro Annual Report 2000,* ABN Amro Holding, N.V., Amsterdam, The Netherlands, 2001.

72. Interviews with Bruce Kelley, group vice president, Miami Agency, ABN Amro Bank, Aug. 22, 2001; and Sept. 27, 2001.

73. Ibid.

74. "Merrill Lynch to Close Argentine Stock Brokerage, Cronista Says," *Bloomberg Latin America,* July 20, 2001.

75. Interview with Jeff Hughes, managing director and chairman, Latin America and Canada, Corporate and Institutional Client Group, Merrill Lynch, Aug. 20, 2001.

76. "Shaking up Merrill," *Business Week,* Nov. 12, 2001.

77. Robert Preston and Jeffrey Schwartz, "Merrill Lynch Institutionalizes E-Biz," InternetWeek.com, Mar. 2, 2001.

78. "Emerging Markets Opportunity," presentation by Victor Menezes, chairman and CEO Citibank, N.A., Apr. 10, 2001.

79. "Getting to Know the New Emerging Markets Organization," *Emerging Markets on the Record,* Citigroup, vol. 1, no. 1, July 2001.

80. "Citigroup in Latin America," corporate presentation, Latin America Global and Corporate Bank, Citigroup, 2001.

81. "B2B Boom," *Latin CEO Magazine,* Sept. 2001.

82. Interview with Victor Menezes, chairman and CEO of Citibank, N.A., Aug. 23, 2001.

83. "Sandy Weill's Big Bet," *Latin Finance,* July 2001.

84. A full array of financial services includes corporate banking, treasury services, trade finance and trade services, cash management, custody services, e-business, investment banking, private equity, and trust and fiduciary.

85. Interview with Michael Contreras, executive vice president, Latin America Corporate and Investment Bank, Citigroup, Sept. 21, 2001.

86. Ibid.

87. Philip L. Zweig, "Mexico will Reap Dividends from Citigroup," *Wall Street Journal,* May 23, 2001.

88. Lowell L. Bryan, Timothy G. Lyons, and James Rosenthal, "Corporate Strategy in a Globalizing World," *McKinsey Quarterly,* no. 3, 1998, pp. 6–19.

CHAPTER 7

1. World Bank, *World Development Indicators*, 2000; cited in *Latin America at a Glance*, Economist Intelligence Unit, 2001, p. 25.

2. *Social Panorama of Latin America 2000–1*, ECLAC (Economic Commission for Latin America and the Caribbean), Sept. 2001, pp. 1–9; also *Social Panorama 1999–2000*, Nov. 2000, p. 281.

3. Ibid., pp. 4–5, 8.

4. *Latin America at a Glance*, pp. 21–23.

5. *Social Panorama 1999–2000*, p. 112.

6. A. F. Amoset et al., "Rising Global Burden of Diabetes," *Diabetic Medicine*, 1997:4, Supplement 5: 81–85, cited in Daniel Whitaker, *The Pharmaceutical Marketplace in Latin America, Spectrum Life Sciences*, Decision Resources, June 28, 2001, p. 8-4.

7. This section draws from *Pocket Prognosis Latin America 2001–5*, IMS Health, 2001, pp. 63–83, 167–177.

8. IMS Health, *Pharma Prognosis Latin America*, p. 40.

9. Hamilton Almeida, "La Fuerza de los Medicamentos Genéricos," *Gazeta Mercantil Latinoamericana*, July 8, 2001, p. 5N.

10. Daniel Whitaker, *The Pharmaceutical Marketplace in Latin America*, p. 8-8.

11. "Seeds Sown for Future Growth," *Economist*, Nov. 17, 2001, pp. 65–66.

12. PhRMA, Submission Under "Special 301" Section of Trade Act of 1974 to Assistant U.S. Trade Representative, Feb. 16, 2001

13. Jillian Clare Cohen, "Public Policies in the Pharmaceutical Sector: A Case Study of Brazil," World Bank, LatinAmerica/Caribbean Regional Office, Human Development Department, LCSHD Paper Series no. 54, Jan. 2000.

14. Daniel Whitaker, op. cit., pp. 8-5 to 8-7.

15. Peg Willingham, "An Incomplete Picture of Public Health Issues and Intellectual Property Rights in Brazil," *Revista Panamericana de Salud Pública*, 9(6), 2001, pp. 420–422.

16. Michael Porter and Scott Stern, "Innovation: Location Matters," *Sloan Management Review*, Summer 2001, pp. 28–36.

17. "R&D Spending," *Economist*, Oct. 27, 2001, p. 100

18. The Cuba section draws from Daniel Whitaker, "Cuba's Biotech and Health Care Sectors: Potential Market Opportunities for International Investors," *Spectrum Life Sciences*, July 11, 2000, as well as from industry interviews conducted by Françoise Simon.

19. IMS Health, *Pocket Prognosis Latin America*, 2001, pp. 74–80.

20. *Pharma Prognosis Latin America*, pp. 20–21.

21. "IMS Health Forecasts 7–8% Annual Growth in Key Latin American Markets through 2005," News Release, IMS Health, Apr. 5, 2001.

22. *Pharma Prognosis Latin America*, pp. 14–17.

23. Daniel Whitaker, *Pharmaceutical Marketplace in Latin America*, p. 8-9.

24. *Pharma Prognosis,* p. 2.

25. Whitaker, op. cit., pp. 8-7, 8-8.

26. Interviews by Françoise Simon with Olivier Brandicourt, regional president for Latin America, Pfizer, Dec. 7, 2001 and Feb. 5 and 14, 2002; this section draws from several other industry interviews conducted by F. Simon in 2001.

27. *Pharma Prognosis,* pp. 4, 44.

28. *Pocket Prognosis,* pp. 76–78.

29. *Pharma Prognosis,* pp. 22–24, 52.

30. "Deal Making," *In Vivo,* Windhover Information, May 2001, p. 89 and June 2001, p. 86.

31. *Pharma Prognosis,* pp. 4, 43–44; Whitaker, op. cit., pp. 8-3, 8-10.

32. Whitaker, op. cit., pp. 8-11, 8-12.

33. "E-Business in Latin America," Economist Intelligence Unit, 2000, p. 155.

34. Olivier Brandicourt, "The Win–Win Opportunities of e-Health in Latin America," presentation at the Americas Society, New York, Jan. 24, 2002.

35. Sebastian Popik, CEO, Salutia, "The Connectivity Opportunity in Brazil and Argentina," presentation at the Americas Society, New York, Jan. 24, 2002.

36. *Latin America at a Glance,* 2001, pp. 94–97.

CHAPTER 8

1. Peter Wynn, *Americas: The Changing Face of Latin America and the Caribbean,* Pantheon Books, New York, 1992.

2. "Latin American Report: The Golden Triangle?" *Ad-Age,* Feb. 11, 2002.

3. Arlene Davila explores the dynamics of assimilation and cross-fertilization in her outstanding ethnography work of the Latino market in the U.S. See *Latinos Inc.: The Marketing and Making of a People,* University of California Press, 2001.

4. "Food Appeals to 2 Palates," *Ad Age,* Nov. 19, 2001.

5. It is not surprising that major companies have signed Latin pop stars to endorse their products to the general market and connect better with the Latin youth. For instance, Pepsi signed the Colombian pop rock star Shakira for advertisements and concerts for U.S. audiences.

6. "Minorities: An Almost-invisible $1 Trillion Market," *Business Week,* June 11, 2001.

7. "Seeking Entrée to Hispanic Doorways," *Advertising Age,* Feb. 11, 2002.

8. *Financial Times,* "Market Sees Argentina as Localized Disaster," Dec. 22, 2001; also Standard & Poor, *Latin American Roundup: Argentina and the Region,* Dec. 7, 2001.

9. ECLA, *Early Economic Assessment of Latin America.*

10. Opinion polls in Latin America showed a concerning trend of declining support to democracy, which fell 12 points, to 48% in 2001 but showed strong support for trade deals. Latinobarometro, *Latin Trade,* Nov. 2001.

11. Standard & Poor, Recent terrorists' attacks on U.S. will put Latin American economies under additional pressure, Oct. 2, 2001.

12. ECLA, *Foreign Direct Investment in Latin America and the Caribbean 2000.*

13. Tendencias, *Foreign Direct Investment in Latin America: What to Do After the Family Jewels Are Sold,* Mar. 2001.

14. Tendencias, *Are the Good Times Over? Foreign Direct Investment Declines in Latin America,* Sept. 2001.

15. Forrester, "Thriving in the Recession: Cemex," Dec. 15, 2001.

16. In a recent study of the dynamics of competition, Seth and Sisodia argue that every market will be dominated by three major players (integrators), with small specialty players filling the niche markets. In their analysis, the authors use market share instead of revenue size and argue that the ditch starts at 5%. They also contend that the dominant position for the three largest players occurs in the range 10 to 40% market share. They argued that any company caught in the middle faces the threat of being acquired or destroyed. For more information, see their book *Rule of Three: Surviving and Thriving in Competitive Markets*, Free Press, New York, 2002.

INDEX

drivers of opportunities, 306–7
global economy, links to, 310–15
strategies for, 315–21
uncertain/volatile markets, strategy in, 304–6
windows of opportunities, 307–10
Nicaragua:
inequality in income distribution, 55
population profile, 261
telecommunication reform, 139–40
North American market platform, 190–92
Norvasc, 263
Nossa Caixa Nosso Banco, 232
Novartis, 270, 281, 286, 288, 289
Novo Nordisk, 286
Núcleo, 161

○

OECD (Organization for Economic Co-operation and Development), 116
O'Globo, 160
Oxfam, 276–77

P

P&G, 4, 183, 209
Pan-regional expansion strategies, 208
Pan-regional Latin market strategy, 195–97
Pan-regional strategy, 190
Panama, telecommunication reform, 139
Panamco (Mexico), 210
Pão de Açúcar (Brazil), 31, 205–6, 212, 323
Paraguay:
and Mercosur, 19–20
population profile, 261
telecommunication reform, 139
Parsa, Tim, 26
Patagon, 229
Patent protection, 273–74
Paxil, 263
PDVSA (Venezuela), 99–102
Pemex (Mexico), 98–99, 141, 143
PepsiCo, 92, 209
Perdigao, 193
Peres, Wilson, 84
Perez Companc (Argentina), 91

Peru:
inequality in income distribution, 55
population growth rate, 48
telecommunication reform, 139
Petrobrás (Brazil), 94, 102–4, 141
Pfizer, 281, 288–89, 290, 294
Pharmaceutical markets, 281–95
acquisitions and alliances, 289–90
Argentina, 286–87
Brazil, 285–86
Mexico, 285
multinational firms, 288
regional trends, 281–84
transformation of local firms, 287–88
Polar beer (Venezuela), 92, 184, 212
Poor mass market, 66–67
Porter, Michael, 277
Portugal, and technology, 20
Portugal Telecom, 29
Positioning to meet consumer value, 173–78
conventional approach, 173–75
convergence to the center, 175–77
Natura (Brazil), 177–78
PPG (Policosanol), 280
Prepagas, 269
Prevacid, 263
Pricing, drugs/health services, 271–73
Primary care promotion, 266
Procter & Gamble, 4, 183, 209
Prodigy/Telmex, 27
Promedicum.org, 294
Proxima (Mexico), 128
Prozac, 263
PT Multimedia, 29
Puerto Rico:
advanced demographic transition, 48
buying power, 56–57

Q

Quilmes (Argentina), 180, 184

R

Ranbaxy, 272
Rede Globo, 180
Reforms:
energy reforms, 136–37, 141–43
state monopolies, unbundling of, 133–38
telecommunication reforms, 138–40